CW01095572

Cultural Worlds of the Jesuits in Colonial Latin America

edited by Linda A. Newson

**INSTITUTE OF
LATIN AMERICAN
STUDIES**

SCHOOL OF
ADVANCED STUDY
UNIVERSITY
OF LONDON

University of London Press
Institute of Latin American Studies, School of Advanced Study,
University of London, 2020

British Library Cataloguing-in-Publication Data
A catalogue record for this book is available from the British Library

This book is published under a Creative Commons Attribution-
NonCommercial-NoDerivatives 4.0 International (CC BY-NC-ND 4.0)
license. More information regarding CC licenses is available at https://
creativecommons.org/licenses/.

This book is also available online at http://humanities-digital-library.org.

ISBN:
978-1-908857-62-0 (paperback edition)
978-1-908857-74-3 (.epub edition)
978-1-908857-73-6 (.mobi edition)
978-1-908857-75-0 (PDF edition)

DOI: 10.14296/520.9781908857750 (PDF edition)

Institute of Latin American Studies
School of Advanced Study
University of London
Senate House
London WC1E 7HU

Telephone: 020 7862 8844

Email: ilas@sas.ac.uk
Web: http://ilas.sas.ac.uk

Cover image: *Mappa Geographica exhibens Provincias, Oppida, Sacella &c
quae Mensibus Novembri ac Decembri anni 1751 et ... anni 1752 peragravit
ad Indorum Chilensium terras...* Hieronymus Strübel, 1777. Courtesy of John
Carter Brown Library.

Contents

List of figures

Notes on contributors

Oriol Ambrogio is a PhD candidate in history at the King's College London, where he is preparing a thesis on missionary administration and native responses to the sacraments on the peripheries of Spanish America in the colonial period, under the supervision of Professor Francisco Bethencourt. He is interested in Jesuit missionary efforts among semi-sedentary and non-sedentary populations, focusing on how Christian rituals were perceived and reinterpreted according to the indigenous cultural traditions. He has given papers at the Institute of Latin American Studies, King's College and Chapel Hill University seminars and at the conference of the Renaissance Society of America.

Gauvin Alexander Bailey is professor and Alfred and Isabel Bader Chair in southern baroque art at Queen's University, Kingston, Ontario. He has held fellowships with the John Simon Guggenheim Foundation and Villa I Tatti, among others and was the 2017 Panofsky professor at the Zentralinstitut für Kunstgeschichte in Munich. He is also *correspondent* étranger of the Académie des Inscriptions et Belles Lettres at the Institut de France and a fellow of the Royal Society of Canada. His latest book is *Architecture and Urbanism in the French Atlantic Empire: State, Church, and Society, 1604–1830* (2018).

Capucine Boidin is professor in Latin American anthropology at Sorbonne Nouvelle in the Institute of Advanced Studies in Latin America (IHEAL) and teaches Guarani language at INALCO (Langues'O). She is currently the director of IHEAL. From 2011 until 2016 she coordinated a project funded by ANR and called LANGAS (General languages from South America) (Quechua, aimara, guarani, tupi, XIX–XVI). With an open access database, this project is a pioneer in digital humanities applied to non-western languages in order to sustain anthropological history based on Amerindian manuscripts. She is writing a book called *Words within History: Contribution to Guaraní Political Anthropology (XVI–XIX)*.

Samir Boumediene is a researcher at the Institut d'Histoire des Représentations et des Idées dans les Modernités (Lyon). Trained in history and epistemology, he published his PhD on the history of New World medicinal plants in 2016 under the title *La colonisation du savoir*. He has published several articles on the history of drugs, medicine and plants. His current research deals with the notion of discovery in early modern times and with the history of questionnaires.

William Gervase Clarence-Smith was until the end of July 2019 professor of the economic history of Asia and Africa at SOAS, University of London, and editor of the *Journal of Global History* (Cambridge University Press). He has published on the history of various animals around the world and is currently undertaking research for a global history of mules. He has also written about the history of different missionary orders, including the Jesuits in the Philippines.

Caroline Egan is a lecturer in colonial literary and cultural studies in the Spanish and Portuguese Section at the University of Cambridge. She researches and publishes on the literatures and cultures of colonial Latin America, particularly 16th- and early 17th-century works in and about Amerindian languages and their circulation in a transatlantic context. She is currently developing a comparative project on the idea of orality in this period, including studies of the Nahuatl-language compositions collected in the *Cantares Mexicanos*, the lyric production of the Jesuit missionary José de Anchieta and the historiographical *Comentarios reales* by the Inca Garcilaso de la Vega.

Kate Ford trained as a theatre designer. Her first visit to the mission to the Chiquitos in Bolivia in 2007 was prompted by a talk by the late Jesuit musicologist, T. Frank Kennedy. She did an MA in Latin American art and architecture at the University of Essex before returning to the theatre for a year. In 2009 she began a PhD at Essex, completing it in 2014 and returning once more to theatre design. She is currently co-chair of the Anglo-Bolivian Society in London and works as a costume designer.

Barbara Ganson is professor of history and director of Caribbean and Latin American studies at Florida Atlantic University in Boca Raton, Florida. She completed her PhD in history at the University of Texas at Austin. With Clinia M. Saffi she translated and edited the memoirs of Antonio Ruiz de Montoya (1639), *The Spiritual Conquest: Early Years of the Jesuit Missions in Paraguay* (2017). She is also the author of an award-winning book, *The Guaraní under Spanish Rule in the Rio de la Plata* (2003).

Virginia Ghelarducci received her BA in philosophy and MA in philosophy and forms of knowledge from the University of Pisa, Italy. She is currently pursuing a PhD in Latin American Studies at the School of Advanced Study, University of London, investigating the influence of astrology on early modern medicine, with a particular focus on colonial medicine in the Americas. Her project aims to show how the Spanish encounter with a New World, including a new natural environment and a new constellation, stimulated the observation and collection of new medicinal plants which changed the perspective on astrological medicine.

Vivien Kogut Lessa de Sá is teaching associate in Portuguese studies at the University of Cambridge. She has lectured and published on early modern travel writing, especially in connection to Brazil, and on comparative studies of Brazilian, Portuguese and English literatures. Her book *The Admirable Adventures and Strange Fortunes of Anthony Knivet: An English Pirate in Brazil* (2015) offers a critical edition of one of the earliest English descriptions of Brazil.

Linda A. Newson is director of the Institute of Latin American Studies, School of Advanced Study, University of London and emeritus professor of geography at King's College London. She has published extensively on the demographic and cultural impact of Spanish colonial rule in the Americas and the Philippines and on the Portuguese African slave trade to Peru. Her most recent book is *Making Medicines in Early Colonial Lima, Peru: Apothecaries, Science and Society* (2017). She has received awards for distinguished scholarship from the Conference of Latin Americanist Geographers and the Royal Geographical Society and is a fellow of the British Academy.

Eduardo L. Ortiz is emeritus professor of mathematics and of the history of mathematics at Imperial College London; visiting professor at the Massachusetts Institute of Technology; the Université d'Orleans; the Université de Rouen; a Guggenheim fellow at Harvard University; fellow of the Institute of Mathematics and its Applications (Great Britain); the Royal Academy of Science (Spain); the National Academy of Science (Argentina). In 1990 he received the José Babini History of Science prize (Ministry of Science and Technology/CONICET, Argentina).

Clarissa Sanfelice Rahmeier is lecturer in humanities at the Escola Superior de Propaganda e Marketing, São Paulo, Brazil. She has researched the links between material culture and identity in several contexts, such as the South American missions, prehistoric and modern England and contemporary São Paulo. Publications include 'Materiality, Social Roles and the Senses' (*Journal of Material Culture*); 'Sociedade, Corpo e Cultura' (*Opsis*); 'Land, Power and Status in Material Culture Studies' (in *An Archaeology of Land Ownership*); and contributions to *Landscape in the Long Durée* (with Christopher Tilley and others) and *Existir na Cidade* (co-edited with Pedro de Santi).

Leonardo J. Waisman retired recently as a research fellow at Argentina's CONICET. He has published on the Italian madrigal, American colonial music, performance practice, popular music of Argentina and the social significance of musical styles. He has worked extensively on the music of Jesuit missions in South America and on the operas of Vicente Martín y Soler, including a comprehensive biography. As a conductor specialising in Baroque music, he has toured America, Europe and the Far East and recorded two CDs for the Melopea label. His most recent book is *Una historia de la música colonial hispanoamericana* (2019).

Introduction

Linda A. Newson

The Jesuits had a profound effect on cultural and intellectual life in Latin America. In 2017 the Institute of Latin American Studies, University of London, held an international conference to mark the 250-year anniversary of the expulsion of the Jesuits from Spanish territories in 1767. At that time they were administering over 250,000 Indians in over two hundred missions. However, Jesuit activities went far beyond the conversion of native peoples to Christianity. The Jesuits pioneered interest in indigenous languages and cultures, compiling dictionaries and writing some of the earliest ethnographies of the region. They also explored the region's natural history and made significant contributions to the development of science and medicine. On their estates and in their missions the Jesuits introduced new plants, livestock and agricultural techniques, while they left a lasting legacy on the region's architecture, art and music.

It was the desire of the conference to capture the diversity of Jesuit contributions to Latin American culture. This volume of 12 essays includes papers from scholars of history, linguistics, religion, art, architecture, music, medicine and science. No volume could cover all the fields in which the Jesuits had an influence, but following the conference two scholars were invited to contribute papers on the role of the Jesuits in medicine and music. The essays presented in this volume are not overviews of Jesuit contributions to particular fields, each of which could be a book on its own, but are either studies based on original unpublished research which are representative of new scholarship in these domains or are reviews of research on specific topics which have not been examined previously. Scholarly books on the culture of the Jesuits often focus on one theme or region and approach it from a particular disciplinary standpoint. An exception is the monumental two-volume work *The Jesuits: Cultures, Sciences, and the Arts 1540–1773* (Toronto, 1999 and 2006), edited by John O'Malley, Gauvin Alexander Bailey, Steven Harris and Frank Kennedy, which is both multidisciplinary and global in scope. This edited book shares the aim of this work in considering the wide range of fields in which the Jesuits were active, but has a narrower geographical focus on Latin America. The contributors to this volume include a range of scholars, from well-established

L.A. Newson, 'Introduction', in L.A. Newson (ed.), *Cultural Worlds of the Jesuits in Colonial Latin America* (London: Institute of Latin American Studies, 2020), pp. 1–7. License: CC-BY-NC-ND 2.0.

authors to those just embarking on their academic careers; they are from
Argentina, Brazil, Canada, France, the USA and the UK. The book consists
of four main sections, though there is considerable overlap between them and
several essays could be placed under other section headings.

Art, architecture and material culture

The first section of the book focuses on different aspects of the art, architecture
and material culture of the Jesuits in Latin America. While in most cases the
Jesuits themselves were not involved in material production, they did exert an
influence on the styles and images which were used, a practice which reflected
their belief in the importance of the visual arts to evangelisation. Yet from the
beginning of the 20th century, some scholars began to argue that there was
no uniform 'Jesuit style'.[1] What the Jesuits had was a common approach or
strategy – a *noster modus procedendi* [our way of proceeding] – which favoured
the adaptation of art styles to local circumstance. Thus, the styles took account
of indigenous cultures and landscapes, while reflecting the experience of
individual Jesuits and the practical issues they faced. Their approach was what
Gauvin Bailey has summarised as 'accommodating and assimilating'.[2] All three
chapters in this section exemplify this understanding.

First, new scholarship on Jesuit art sees it as developing in a global context,
while at the same time recognising the role which individual knowledge and
experience might play in promoting a distinct style in particular places. In
his richly illustrated contribution, Gauvin Bailey shows how Jesuit global
connections were manifest in the introduction to Brazil of an *ecclesiastical*
Chinese style from Beijing by the French Jesuit brother sculptor Charles de
Belleville around 1707. He notes that this Chinese style differed from that
in Spanish America, where Asian artwork was associated with *secular* objects,
which were introduced by traders rather than missionaries. He argues that
this style depicted Jesuit missionary victory in Asia with the aim of inspiring
missionary work in the Americas.

Another focus of recent scholarship on Jesuit artistic production is the way it
was influenced by the encounter with indigenous cultures. This is most evident
in Kate Ford's chapter on the Jesuit mission to the province of Chiquitos in
the eastern lowlands of present-day Bolivia. Ford shows how the decoration
on Chiquito churches echo local indigenous practices of body-painting and
incorporate motifs made on rock and clay vessels which had traditionally
been used to protect them from harm. She also shows how, at the same time,

---

1   For a bibliographical summary of the subject and new approaches to scholarship see: G.A.
     Bailey, 'Le style jesuite n'existe pas: Jesuit corporate culture and the visual arts', in J.W.
     O'Malley et al. (eds.), *The Jesuits: Cultures, Sciences and the Arts 1540–1773* (Toronto:
     University of Toronto Press, 1999), pp. 38–89.

2   Bailey, 'Le style jesuite n'existe pas', p. 73.

the Jesuits, wishing to conform to European standards of construction in a region which lacked stone and marble, improvised by ordering the painting of decorative and architectural features common in baroque stone-built churches onto the adobe they were forced to use in their construction. Hence, her chapter concludes that the painted churches of the mission to the Chiquitos reflect both Jesuit attempts to disguise the churches' perceived deficiencies and indigenous attempts to protect them from supernatural harm.

Another strand of recent research on Jesuit art in Latin America concerns the physical production of art objects in workshops, especially those in the missions. In her study of the 30 Guaraní missions in the Jesuit province of Paraguay, Clarissa Rahmeier examines the different methods employed in pottery-making by the Guaraní and the Jesuits. Through examining the materiality of pottery and pottery-making, she shows how it reflected a degree of assimilation, exchange, accommodation and the persistence of traces of both cultures; and that the cultural encounter can therefore be better described as transculturation.

Jesuit mission life

As research on colonial Latin America in general has moved away from institutional history towards understanding the social, cultural and political lives of the popular classes, so also has research on the social life of the missions adopted a more critical approach. The early historiography often romanticised life in the missions, portraying native people as innocent children and passive recipients of European culture.[3] In reality, the process was more complex, as native peoples resisted, adapted to and accommodated Spanish mission life. Barbara Ganson, well-known for her book *The Guaraní under Spanish Rule in the Río de la Plata* (2003), follows this argument here in her study of gender relations. Using new sources, including a Guaraní text, she analyses the cases of the punishment of two women involved in adultery in the former Jesuit mission of Jesús de Tavarangue in 1782. She shows how the patriarchal society the Jesuits had established in the missions continued in one town under the post-expulsion Franciscan administration.[4] However, she also argues that women did not always accept their subordinate position, but resisted in different ways, although often at considerable personal cost.

One of the romantic images of life in the Jesuit missions derives from their musical performances. The practice of music was promoted by the Jesuits, since

3   E.g., R.B. Cunninghame Graham, *A Vanished Arcadia; Being Some Account of the Jesuits in Paraguay, 1607 to 1767* (London: Heinemann, 1901); and P. Caraman, *The Lost Paradise: The Jesuit Republic in South America* (New York: Seabury, 1975).

4   Following the expulsion, secular administrators and Franciscan, Mercedarian and Dominican missionaries took over the administration of the Paraguayan missions (B. Ganson, *The Guaraní under Spanish Rule in the Río de la Plata* (Stanford: Stanford University Press, 2003), p. 118.

it was seen as integral to the process of Christian conversion and worship. In his overview of studies of musical practice in colonial Spanish America, Leonardo Waisman shows how research on Jesuit music has centred on the Jesuit provinces of Paraguay (including Chiquitos) and Moxos, where archival sources in the form of musical scores are most abundant. He then aims to fill a gap in the literature by studying musical practices in the province of Mainas in the Upper Amazon. Using missionary accounts, particularly those by German Jesuits who laboured in the region in the 18th century, Waisman shows how knowledge of musical practices can be gleaned from other sources. He concludes that despite several attempts by the Jesuits to introduce more advanced musical instruments and polyphony to the province of Mainas, musical practice there did not reach the sophistication of that in the province of Paraguay.

Stationed in the missions, many Jesuits learned native languages in order to facilitate evangelisation, often compiling dictionaries, grammars, catechisms and confessionals. This proved more difficult in areas where there was no written language and the oral language had to be structured and systematised before it could be included in dictionaries and grammars. Capucine Boidin exemplifies this process of 'translation' from an oral to written language in her analysis of an extensive corpus of Tupi-Guaraní documents written between 1628 and 1832, showing how the 'translation' might lead to the transformation of the language itself.[5] She demonstrates how the Jesuits, confronted by a multiplicity of languages on the coast of Brazil and in Paraguay, developed different *linguas francas* to aid evangelisation and create literate native elites that are still used today. The process of creating a Brazilian *lingua franca* is also examined by Vivien Kogut Lessa de Sá and Caroline Egan in a later chapter.

Jesuit evangelisation

Jesuit methods of evangelisation differed widely, not least because of the different cultural and political contexts in which priests worked. The significance of local circumstances is evident in Oriol Ambrogio's comparative study of the perceptions and acceptance of baptism by native societies on the colonial fringes of Spanish America, in north-west Mexico, southern Chile and the Chaco. He argues that native people were often fearful of missionaries as powerful *curanderos-hechiceros* capable of healing the sick but also of causing

5   For a classic study of the issue of translation and evangelisation see V.L. Rafael, *Contracting Colonialism: Translation and Christian Conversion in Tagalog Society Under Early Spanish Rule* (Ithaca, NY: Cornell University Press, 1988). For a study of the Jesuits' approach to systematising Quechua see: S. MacCormack, 'Grammar and virtue: the formulation of a cultural and missionary program by the Jesuits in Early Colonial Peru', in J.W. O'Malley et al. (eds.), *The Jesuits II: Cultures, Sciences and the Arts 1540–1773* (Toronto: University of Toronto Press, 2006), pp. 576–601; and A. Durstan, *Pastoral Quechua: The History of Christian Translation in Colonial Peru, 1550–1650* (Notre Dame, IN: University of Notre Dame Press, 2007).

death. However, in other cases they might see the acceptance of Christianity and baptism as providing an opportunity for socio-political advancement. This divergence in the approach to the adoption of Christianity is attributed by him to differing economic, social and political conditions. He argues that economic stability and regular food supplies in north-west Mexico and among the non-sedentary Guaycuruas encouraged them to perceive the missions as a means of promoting their material interests, whereas the lack of a sustained Jesuit presence and the piecemeal acceptance of baptism among the Mapuche in Chile served to perpetuate intertribal conflict.

How indigenous people should be brought to the Catholic faith was a persistent topic of debate among the Jesuits. Exemplifying how views on the process of evangelisation might diverge, Virginia Ghelarducci explores the writings of a Jesuit missionary, Giovanni Anello Oliva, who worked in colonial Peru and Bolivia in the early 17th century. At that time, frustration with the slow progress of the Christianisation of Andean peoples led to official campaigns to eradicate idolatrous practices. However, Anello Oliva, with a deep knowledge of Andean culture, argues that true conversion could only be achieved by having a well-organised education system based on a combination of quality teaching, persuasive argumentation and knowledge of indigenous cultures and language.

The importance of indigenous language in evangelisation is the focus of a study by Vivien Kogut Lessa de Sá and Caroline Egan. They examine a document written by a Jesuit in 16th-century Brazil, entitled 'Doutrina Christã na Linguoa Brasilica', which is currently housed in the Bodleian Library in Oxford. The authors show how the Jesuits, in seeking to find terms which were understandable to potential converts, used Tupi words for doctrinally significant concepts, such as 'God' or 'father', but rendered others in Portuguese or in a combination of both. They argue that the Jesuits were concerned with imposing a stable, permanent alphabetic framework on the Tupi language and believed that through enunciating the words the native Tupi would ultimately be converted to Christianity, an approach they characterise as 'proleptic'.

Jesuit agriculture, medicine and science

Jesuit scientific activities in Latin America were more intimately linked to their missionary goal than they were in Europe.[6] The Jesuits' spiritual quest to reveal the magnificence of God's work in nature was combined with the search for knowledge about places, peoples and plants. This knowledge was not only essential for their work in unfamiliar natural and cultural environments, but,

6   For an overview of Jesuit scientific activities in Spanish America see A.I. Prieto, *Missionary Scientists: Jesuit Science in Spanish South America, 1570–1810* (Nashville, TN: Vanderbilt University Press, 2011); and L. Millones Figueroa and D. Ledezma (eds.), *El saber de los jesuitas, historias naturales y el Nuevo Mundo* (Madrid: Iberoamericana; Frankfurt am Main: Vervuert, 2005).

through the commercialisation of certain activities, could generate a revenue which could further their missionary enterprise. This last theme is taken up in the essays on Jesuit involvement in mule breeding and the medicine trade.

Much has been written about the biological consequences of European arrival in the Americas in 1492 and some attention paid to the role of the Jesuits in the process. A particular focus has been on the agricultural estates they established, but also on the introduction of new foods, agricultural equipment and techniques more broadly.[7] Despite the fact that mules were essential to the transport system, as well as vital in agriculture and mining, they have not been subject to scholarly study for Latin America as a whole. Approaching the question from the perspective of debates over how innovative and profitable Jesuit agricultural enterprises were, William Clarence-Smith provides a comprehensive overview of mule breeding on Jesuit estates in Latin America which fills this obvious gap. Samir Boumediene also considers the commercial activities of the Jesuits in the context of their large-scale trade in new medicines to urban centres in Europe. He shows how this trade was facilitated by their network of colleges, convents and missions which enabled books, texts, people, drugs and curiosities to circulate. He exemplifies this process by focussing on the commodification of drugs and using the example of cinchona, which came to be known as Jesuit's bark.

The importance of the Jesuits' global network of missions and colleges in enabling scientific developments is also evident in Eduardo Ortiz's account of the development of the physical sciences. While some attention has been paid to the contribution of the Jesuits to knowledge of the natural world, much less has been written about their role in this field. Eduardo Ortiz shows that even though scientific developments sometimes conflicted with religious beliefs, the Jesuits made internationally recognised advances, especially in mathematics and astronomy, even constructing their own instruments. At the same time, the global reach of the Jesuit order and its colleges, combined with their rigorous training and an emphasis on accuracy, meant they formed the basis of an international network of observatories, which enabled significant progress in cosmic physics in the 20th century.

There are many areas, thematic and geographical, which it has not been possible to cover in this volume. However, it demonstrates that Jesuit activities continue to attract scholarly interest and generate exciting new research which is representative of the best scholarship currently being conducted on colonial Latin America.

---

7   See N. Cushner's trilogy: *Lords of the Land: Sugar, Wine and Jesuit Estates of Coastal Peru* (Albany, NY: SUNY Press, 1980); *Farm and Factory: The Jesuits and the Development of Agrarian Capitalism in Colonial Quito, 1600–1767* (Albany, NY: SUNY Press, 1982); and *Jesuit Ranches and the Agrarian Development of Colonial Argentina 1650–1767* (Albany, NY: SUNY Press, 1983).

Bibliography

Bailey, G.A. (1999) 'Le style jesuite n'existe pas: Jesuit corporate culture and the visual arts', in J.W. O'Malley, G.A. Bailey, S.J. Harris and T.F. Kennedy (eds.), *The Jesuits: Cultures, Sciences and the Arts 1540–1773* (Toronto: University of Toronto Press), pp. 38–89.

Caraman, P. (1975) *The Lost Paradise: The Jesuit Republic in South America* (New York: Seabury).

Cunninghame Graham, R.B. (1901) *A Vanished Arcadia; Being Some Account of the Jesuits in Paraguay, 1607 to 1767* (London: Heinemann).

Cushner, N. (1980) *Lords of the Land: Sugar, Wine and Jesuit Estates of Coastal Peru* (Albany, NY: SUNY Press).

— (1982) *Farm and Factory: The Jesuits and the Development of Agrarian Capitalism in Colonial Quito, 1600–1767* (Albany, NY: SUNY Press).

— (1983) *Jesuit Ranches and the Agrarian Development of Colonial Argentina 1650–1767* (Albany, NY: SUNY Press).

Durstan, A. (2007) *Pastoral Quechua: The History of Christian Translation in Colonial Peru, 1550–1650* (Notre Dame, IN: University of Notre Dame Press).

Ganson, B. (2003) *The Guaraní under Spanish Rule in the Río de la Plata* (Stanford, CA: Stanford University Press).

MacCormack, S. (2006) 'Grammar and virtue: the formulation of a cultural and missionary program by the Jesuits in early colonial Peru', in J.W. O'Malley, G.A. Bailey, S.J. Harris and T.F. Kennedy (eds.), *The Jesuits II: Cultures, Sciences and the Arts 1540–1773* (Toronto: University of Toronto Press), pp. 576–601.

Millones Figueroa, L. and D. Ledezma (eds.) (2005) *El saber de los jesuitas, historias naturales y el Nuevo Mundo* (Madrid: Iberoamericana; Frankfurt am Main: Vervuert).

O'Malley, J.W, G.A. Bailey, S.J. Harris and T.F. Kennedy (eds.) (1999 and 2006) *The Jesuits: Cultures, Sciences, and the Arts 1540–1773*, 2 vols. (Toronto: University of Toronto Press).

Prieto, A.I. (2011) *Missionary Scientists: Jesuit Science in Spanish South America, 1570–1810* (Nashville, TN: Vanderbilt University Press).

Rafael, V.L. (1988) *Contracting Colonialism: Translation and Christian Conversion in Tagalog Society Under Early Spanish Rule* (Ithaca, NY: Cornell University Press).

I. Jesuit art, architecture and material culture

1. The Jesuits and Chinese style in the arts of colonial Brazil (1719–79)

Gauvin Alexander Bailey

The Jesuit mission to China, founded outside Guangzhou in 1583 by the Italian polymath Matteo Ricci (1552–1610), rapidly became the Society's most celebrated global enterprise, owing principally to the Jesuits' own prodigious publication campaign; and was hailed around the world as a harbinger of Christian victory from Manila to Lima.[1] Its cultural dimensions were particularly lauded, notably Ricci's and his successors' contributions to Chinese literature, mnemonics and science, as well as the mission's promotion of the fine arts, which began in Ricci's lifetime but reached its apex under the 17th- and 18th-century Qing Dynasty, especially under the Kangxi (r. 1661–1722) and Qianlong (r. 1735–96) emperors. During this time about 25 missionary painters worked at court or for the four main Catholic foundations in Beijing, alongside colleagues who specialised in clock making, cartography, mathematics and hydraulics.[2] This international corps of painters, sculptors and architects included several Italians, Frenchmen and Germans and operated under the auspices of both the Portuguese and French Jesuit missions in Beijing, as well as for other Catholic orders such as the Augustinians or Lazarists. Jesuit artists such as the Neapolitan Giuseppe Castiglione (1688–1766) generated an acculturative style of painting which

---

1   On Ricci see: R. Po-chia Hsia, *A Jesuit in the Forbidden City: Matteo Ricci 1552–1610* (Oxford: Oxford University Press, 2012); M. Fontana, *Matteo Ricci: A Jesuit in the Ming Court* (Plymouth, MA: Rowman & Littlefield, 2011); J. Sebes, 'Ricci, Matteo', in C.E. O'Neill and J.M. Domínguez (eds.), *Diccionario histórico de la Compañía de Jesús* (Rome: Institutum Historicum S.I. and Madrid: Universidad Pontificia Comillas, 2001), pp. 51–3; F. D'Arelli (ed.), *Le marche e l'oriente* (Rome: Instituto Italiano per l'Africa e l'oriente, 1998); J. Spence, *The Memory Palace of Matteo Ricci* (New York: Penguin, 1985).

2   M. Musillo, *The Shining Inheritance: Italian Painters at the Qing Court, 1699–1812* (Los Angeles, CA: University of California Press, 2016); E. Corsi, *La fábrica de las ilusiones: los jesuitas y la difusión de la perspectiva lineal en China, 1698–1766* (Mexico City: El Colegio de México, 2004); D. Fu, 'Western missionary painters and Imperial architectural paintings of the Qing dynasty', in H.S. Chan (ed.), *The Golden Exile: Pictorial Expressions of the School of Western Missionaries' Artworks of the Qing Dynasty Court* (Macau: Macau Museum of Art, 2002), pp. 261–4; C. Beurdeley and M. Beurdeley, *Giuseppe Castiglione: a Jesuit Painter at the Court of the Chinese Emperors* (London: Lund Humphries, 1972).

G.A. Bailey, 'The Jesuits and Chinese style in the arts of colonial Brazil (1719–79)', in L.A. Newson (ed.), *Cultural Worlds of the Jesuits in Colonial Latin America* (London: Institute of Latin American Studies, 2020), pp. 11–40. License: CC-BY-NC-ND 2.0.

Figure 1.1. Dashuifa (Great Fountain) Xiyanglou, Yuanming Yuan, China (completed 1759) (Photo: author).

combined Chinese aesthetics and compositions with baroque perspective and shading, especially depictions of the emperor's horses, battles and treasures – a style favoured by the emperor for its illusionistic effects and known at court simply as *xianfa* or 'line method'. Jesuit artists also oversaw the construction of fantasy European fountain pavilions for Qianlong at the imperial summer palace gardens at Yuanming Yuan, or 'Garden of Perfect Clarity', north-east of Beijing (1747–83) (fig. 1.1).

Known as the Xiyanglou (literally 'Western Multi-storeyed Buildings'), they were built in a combination of Italian baroque, Franco-German rococo and traditional Chinese styles.[3] The pavilions were the talk of Europe thanks to

3   G.A. Bailey, 'Rococo in eighteenth-century Beijing: ornament prints and the design of the European palaces of the Yuanming Yuan', *The Burlington Magazine*, 159 (Oct. 2017): 778–88; P. Luengo, 'Yuánmíng Yuán en el siglo XVIII: arte entre la diplomacia y la filosofía; entre Europa y Pekín', *Araucaria*, 18 (Jan.–June 2016): 193–216; K. Kleutghen, *Imperial Illusions: Crossing Pictorial Boundaries in the Qing Palaces* (Seattle and London: University of Washington Press, 2015); G.M. Thomas, 'Yuanming Yuan/Versailles: intercultural interactions between Chinese and European palace cultures', *Art History*, 32 (2009): 115–43; C.Y. Liu, 'Architects and builders of the Qing Dynasty Yuanming Yuan Imperial Garden Palace', *University of Hong Kong Museum Journal*, 1 (2002): 38–59, 151–61; H. Zou, 'The jing of a Perspective Garden', *Studies in the History of Gardens and Designed Landscapes*, 22 (2002): 293–326; R. Thiriez, *Barbarian Lens: Western Photographers of the Qianlong Emperor's European Palaces* (Amsterdam: Gordon and Breach, 1998); V. Droguet, 'Les Palais européens de l'empereur Qianlong et leurs sources italiennes', *Histoire de l'art* 25/26 (1994): 15–28; M. Pirazzoli-t'Serstevens (ed.), *Le*

Figure 1.2. Southern Cathedral (Nan Tang) in Beijing. Photo by Adolf Erazmovich Boiarskii, 1874. (Courtesy of the National Library of Brazil).

published Jesuit descriptions and a series of luxury engravings commissioned by the emperor in 1783 – the first appearance of this European technique in China. Although the Western features of the pavilions encouraged Jesuit commentators to refer to the Xiyanglou as the 'Versailles of Beijing', they were in fact little more than a veneer of columns, pilasters and entablatures of grey stone and white marble over a Chinese-style wooden post-and-lintel frame with hip roofs. They also included grey brick walls covered in a red plaster similar to those in the Forbidden City and decorative polychrome tile revetments in low relief.

The four churches in the capital surrounding the Forbidden City – three of them Jesuit and one Lazarist – were built in styles which also combined European modes with Chinese techniques and forms such as the hip-and-gable roof and complex wooden bracketing systems. Such was the case with the oldest, the Nantang (Southern Hall) (fig. 1.2), built in 1650 by Jesuits under Portuguese auspices and rebuilt in 1703–33 by Fernando Buonaventura Moggi (it was later restored after an earthquake in 1775).[4]

Yuanmingyuan: jeux d'eau et palais européens de XVIIIe siècle à la cour de Chine (Paris: Editions Recherches sur les Civilisations, 1987).

4   P. Luengo, 'Identidad y globalización en las fachadas jesuitas de Pekín en el siglo XVIII', in A. Zamora and J. Ibáñez Fernández (eds.), *La Compañía de Jesús y las artes. Nuevas perspectivas de investigación* (Zaragoza: Universidad Zaragoza, 2014), pp. 279–99; E. Corsi, 'Pozzo's Treatise as a workshop for the construction of a sacred Catholic space in Beijing', in R. Bösel

The Chinese-style gate and pavilions in the courtyard make the approach to the church resemble that of a Daoist or Buddhist temple; and it even boasted two carved guardian temple lions on either side of the gate to the inner courtyard. In fact, as with all the Catholic churches in Beijing, the Nantang complex quite intentionally used such courtyards and pavilions to fit into the cityscape despite the obviously foreign style of its church – this can still be seen in the outbuildings of the site today, although the baroque-style church there now was only built in 1904.[5]

However, one of the most immediate yet least familiar consequences of the Jesuits' artistic activities in Beijing took place in distant Brazil, in the churches of Bahia, Minas Gerais and the backcountry of São Paulo over a sixty-year period from around 1719, but probably a decade earlier. Unlike the rest of Latin America, where Asian-inspired decorative styles appeared in strictly secular settings, architects and designers incorporated imitation Chinese artworks and styles into the decoration of their churches, chapels and oratories.[6] Artworks such as Japanese-inspired folding screens (*biombos*) or imitation blue-and-white porcelain had been manufactured in Spanish America (primarily New Spain) from as early as the mid 17th century, although arguably the most sophisticated product of this cultural exchange was a kind of tapestry made by Andean weavers in southern Peru in the 17th century in imitation of a Ming dynasty Chinese imperial costume accessory known as a rank badge or Mandarin square.[7] Brazil was unique in using such ornamentation in an *ecclesiastical* setting: there churches included imitation-lacquer painted panels – featuring both landscapes and floral designs – on sacristy and chancel ceilings, choirstalls, organ cases and often quite extravagant private oratories, as well as

and L. Salviucci Insolera (eds.), *Artifizi della matafora: diciotto saggi su Andrea Pozzo* (Rome: Artemide, 2012), pp. 233–43; L. Wang, 'Church, a "sacred event" and the visual perspective of an "etic viewer": an 18th century western-style Chinese painting held in the Bibliothèque Nationale de France', in R. Oliveira Lopes (ed.), *Face to Face: the Transcendence of the Arts in China and Beyond – Historical Perspectives* (Lisbon: CEIBA, 2014), pp. 370–99.

5   S. Naquin comments that 'Christian churches also enclosed their differences within a Chinese-style compound. The layout of the North Church (Beitang) … followed Chinese principles for the gate and exterior wall, but inside, the tall façade of a single, massive Western-style church rose above the surrounding buildings. Within the courtyards, formal European plantings created a distinctly foreign garden' (S. Naquin, *Peking: Temples and City Life, 1400–1900* (Berkeley and Los Angeles, CA: University of California Press, 2000), pp. 34–5).

6   M.Á. Fernández (ed.), *Return Voyage: the China Galleon and the Baroque in Mexico, 1565–1815* (Puebla and Mexico City: Gobierno de Estado de Puebla, 2016); D. Carr (ed.), *Made in the Americas: the New World Discovers Asia* (Boston, MA: MFA Publications, 2015); G.A. Bailey, 'Asia in the Arts of Colonial Latin America', in J.J. Rishel (ed.), *The Arts in Latin America, 1492–1820* (Philadelphia, PA and New Haven, CT: Philadelphia Museum of Art and Yale University Press, 2006), pp. 57–69.

7   E. Phipps, J. Hecht and C. Esteras Martín (eds.), *The Colonial Andes: Tapestries and Silverwork, 1530–1830* (New York: Metropolitan Museum of Art, 2004), pp. 250–4; S. Cammann, 'Chinese influence in colonial Peruvian tapestries', *Textile Museum Journal*, 1 (Dec. 1964): 21–34.

stone, wooden and ceramic sculptures forming part of the interior and exterior decoration of churches.[8] The fashion enjoyed an extraordinarily long lifespan across a remarkable geographic range, lasting until the end of the 1770s, when it began to be ushered out by French neoclassicism. However, unlike in Spanish America, where Asian styles arrived via trade goods, this Brazilian vogue for ecclesiastical Chinese style was inspired at first directly from Beijing around 1708 and by one man: the little-known French Jesuit brother sculptor Charles de Belleville (1657–1730), known in China as Wei Jialu.[9]

Although Chinese style in Brazilian churches occurred first in a pair of Jesuit complexes, one a combination novitiate and mission in Bahia and the other a mission in Tupi-Guaraní territory south-west of São Paulo, it was quickly adopted by non-Jesuits, including Franciscans, regular and secular clergy, lay confraternities (*irmandades*) and a cathedral chapter. Frustratingly, almost no documentation survives which might shed light on the commissioning, chronology or ideologies behind these works and the majority of such interiors may, in fact, have been lost to the vagaries of time. We can rely on only a few scraps of information from Jesuit archival sources and – as will be explored below – a single book printed by the Jesuits around the time these works were being executed. The book supports the idea that Asiatic imagery served as a reminder of what was perceived as Christian victory over paganism, publicising in Brazil the Jesuits' missionary exploits in China and elsewhere in Asia. The Franciscans, who had been working in China for centuries longer than the Jesuits, used Chinese forms for the same reason – and not without a hint of rivalry with their co-religionists – and, indeed, the implicit triumphalism of Asian ornament made it attractive to colonial Catholics in general in locations occupied by Amerindians and with a growing population of African slaves. Unlike the cultural hybridisation of Spanish America, the artistic exchange represented by Asian-style décor in Brazil left these marginalised people out of the equation, even if in a single case a native plant was incorporated into the design and in others Brazilian-style churches and bell towers appear in the Chinese landscapes.

Belleville in China

Belleville hailed from Rouen and joined the Jesuit novitiate in Bordeaux in 1680 at the age of 23.[10] As a professionally trained sculptor (probably

8   See, in particular, J.R. Teixeira Leite, *A China no Brasil: influências, marcas, ecos e sobrevivências chinesas na sociedade e na arte brasileiras* (Campinas: Unicamp, 1999).

9   J.W. Witek, 'Belleville, Charles de', in C.E. O'Neill and J.M. Domínguez (eds.), *Diccionario histórico de la Compañía de Jesús* (Rome: Institutum Historicum S.I. and Madrid: Universidad Pontificia Comillas, 2001), p. 404.

10 Witek, 'Belleville', p. 404; J.P. Duteil, *Le mandat du ciel: Le role des jésuites en Chine* (Paris: AP editions - Arguments, 1994), p. 42; D.E. Mungello, *The Great Encounter of China and the West, 1500–1800* (Lanham MD: Rowman & Littlefield, 1999), p. 67; J. Dehergne,

*Figure 1.3. Charles de Belleville, altar of the Assumption, before 1688. Oak.
Cathédrale Saint-Front, Périgueux, France. (Photo: author).*

specialising in architectural sculpture such as retables, or altarpieces), Belleville
would first have undergone a three-year education as a young boy followed by
a three-year apprenticeship in a master's workshop, after which he would have

Répertoire des jésuites de Chine de 1552 à 1800 (Rome and Paris : Institutum Historicum S.I.,
1973), p. 30; Beurdeley and Beurdeley, *Giuseppe Castiglione*, p. 194; S. Leite, *Artes e ofícios
dos jesuítas no Brasil 1549–1760* (Lisbon and Rio de Janeiro: Broteria, 1953), pp. 129–30; L.
Pfister, *Notices biographiques et bibliographiques sur les Jésuites de l'ancienne Mission de Chine:
1552–1773* (Shanghai: Chang-Hai, Mission Catholique, 1932–34), pp. 536–7.

achieved the rank of journeyman (*compagnon*).[11] Throughout Europe Jesuits typically sought out promising young boy artists and artisans to join the society as brothers (temporal coadjutors) and often sent them to the overseas missions to build and decorate their churches.[12] After he entered the novitiate Belleville served the Society in France for the better part of two decades, sculpting and building statues and retables for Jesuit churches in places like La Rochelle (*c.* 1680–83) and Poitiers (1683–88 or 1689); his personnel records identified him as a 'carpenter' (*faber lignarius*) and 'sculptor' (*sculptor*).[13] He even carved a bust of Louis XIV for a manufactory in Périgueux in July 1686 which drew enough attention for it to be discussed in the newspaper *Mercure Galant* and to be processed through town to the accompaniment of fireworks and theatrical performances.[14] Two of his works in France are known, both of them massive structures of oak. In 1698 he sculpted and built the monumental unpainted altarpiece of the *Assumption* for the Jesuit church in Périgueux (Dordogne), now moved to the Cathédrale Saint-Front (fig. 1.3); and around the same time he constructed the giant gilded-oak tabernacle at the chapel of the Collège Henri IV at Poitiers (*c.*1690–97) with gilt-bronze appendages and fine marquetry work.[15]

These bulky, high-relief constructions gave no hint that the sculptor would be capable of the kind of intricate Chinese-style painting he undertook in China and Brazil – in fact, there is no evidence that he trained as a painter in France, although he certainly would have had knowledge of draughtsmanship and a possible relative with the same name worked as a *peintre ordinaire du Roi* in Paris at the time.[16] The triptych is framed by bulky Solomonic columns, a decorative entablature and balustrade, crowded figural panels of the *Assumption of the Virgin* and *God the Father in Glory* and freestanding sculptures of the Angel Gabriel and the Virgin forming an *Annunciation* on the wings. Jesuit

11 P. Maffre, *Construire Bordeaux au XVIIIe siècle: les frères Laclotte, architectes en société* (Bordeaux: Société Archéologique de Bordeaux, 2013), pp. 55–71.

12 For an example in 18th-century Central Europe, where an unusually large number of young painters, architects and sculptors were recruited, see G.A. Bailey, *The Spiritual Rococo: Décor and Divinity from the Salons of Paris to the Missions of Patagonia* (Farnham: Ashgate, 2014), pp. 242–50.

13 Leite, *Artes e ofícios*, p. 129.

14 P. Clauer, *L'Intermédiaire des chercheurs et curieux: questions et réponses, communications diverses à l'usage de tous, littérateurs et gens du monde* III, 30 (1894): 161–2; *Mercure galant* (Aug. 1686): 282–7. Unfortunately, the article does not provide the material of the sculpture.

15 M. Burgues, 'Aspects techniques du tabernacle de la chapelle du collège Henri IV de Poitiers', *Bulletin de la Société des antiquaires de l'Ouest et des musées de Poitiers*, 5th ser., 3 (Oct. 1989), p. 324.

16 As was traditional with artists in early modern France, Belleville probably came from an artistic family. He may have been related to a painter also called Charles Belleville (1651–1716), who died in Paris in the Faubourg Saint-Jacques and was a *peintre ordinaire du Roi* (H. Herluison, *Actes d'état-civil d'artistes français, peintres, graveurs, architectes, etc.* (Paris: Baur, 1873), pp. 34–5).

personnel records from the time he was in France also describe Belleville as an 'eminent sculptor' (*sculptor egregius*),[17] suggesting that the Jesuits were already eyeing him out as a potential mission artist because of his exceptional talent; in the end he was chosen as one of only a pair of artists (along with the Italian painter Giovanni Gherardini) to accompany the first French maritime mission to China on the ship *Amphitrite* – the first ship ever to sail directly from France to China – from the Atlantic port of La Rochelle in 1698.[18] Directly sponsored by Louis XIV, this high-profile mission – it was an embassy in all but name – was led by Joachim Bouvet (1656–1730) and also included Jesuit scholars from the French Academy of Sciences and trunk-loads of luxury goods, from mirrors to firearms.

The *Amphitrite* reached Guangzhou in November 1698, where Belleville started work with extraordinary speed. As the only European architect or artist in the city he must have built and decorated the 'beautiful' and 'exalted' new Jesuit church (*c.* 1699–before 1701) commissioned by Carlo Giovanni Turcotti (1643–1706), the Jesuit visitor to the province of Japan and vice-province of China, which one Jesuit went so far as to call the 'most beautiful building that there is' in the whole city.[19] Belleville proceeded rapidly to Beijing to oversee the construction of the first church for the French Jesuit mission, officially the Church of the Saviour but popularly known as the Beitang (or Northern Hall). Belleville, described as 'one of our brothers' and 'a very capable architect', is directly credited as its architect by Père de Tartre in a 1701 letter to his father which describes it as already being complete and 'in the European style'.[20] The Beitang was built on land donated in 1693 by the Kangxi Emperor in gratitude after the Jesuits cured him of malaria with quinine extracted from the Peruvian cinchona plant, known as 'Jesuit's bark' – another outcome of the Society's worldwide mission network (see chapter 11). Built partly of marble,

---

17   Leite, *Artes e oficios*, p. 129.

18   M. Keevak, *Embassies to China: Diplomacy and Cultural Encounters Before the Opium Wars* (Singapore: Springer, 2017), pp. 151–2; Teixeira Leite, *A China no Brasil*, p. 172.

19   Witek states categorically that Belleville built the Guangzhou complex (Witek, 'Belleville', p. 404). On Turcotti, see L. Brockley, *Journey to the East: the Jesuit Mission to China, 1579–1724* (Cambridge MA: MIT Press, 2007), pp. 178–9; J.W. Witek, 'Turcotti, Carlo Giovanni', in C.E. O'Neill and J.M. Domínguez (eds.), *Diccionario histórico de la Compañía de Jesús* (Rome: Institutum Historicum S.I. and Madrid: Universidad Pontificia Comillas, 2001), pp. 46–7. The descriptions 'beautiful' (*schöne*), from the 1703 Jesuit Annual Letter, and 'exalted' (*exhaussée*) from a 1704 letter by Père de Fontaney to Père de la Chaise, are typical of the frustrating lack of detail lavished upon Jesuit architectural projects by commentators (J. Stöcklein, *Allerhand so Lehr- als Geist-reiche Brief, Schrifften und Reis-Beschreibungen* (Augsburg and Graz: Philipp, Martin and heirs of Johann Veith, 1726), p. 17; *Lettres édifiantes et curieuses, écrites des missions étrangeres* XVII (Paris, 1781), p. 357). Père de Tartre's remark that the church was 'le plus superbe edifice qu'il y ait' is from a 1701 letter to his father (*Lettres édifiantes*, p. 74).

20   His exact words are: 'L'édifice est à l'Européen. Un de nos Freres qui est très-habile architecte, a conduit tout l'ouvrage'. Père de Tartre identifies him as 'Le Frere de Belleville' in a footnote (*Lettres édifiantes*, p. 75).

Figure 1.4. Anonymous Chinese painter. Façade of the Beitang church of the French Jesuit mission, c. 1701–3 (detail). Gouache on canvas. Bibliothèque Nationale de France (Photo: author).

it contained illusionistic mural paintings in the style of Andrea Pozzo executed by Gherardini, including a false dome, as at the Roman church of Sant'Ignazio (1685), and a ceiling painting showing St Michael and the angels descending through a cloudburst. Belleville also contributed to the decorations, as was noted in a personnel record from 1704 which states that he 'made beautiful paintings for our churches'.[21] The Beitang also housed the Beijing Jesuits' formidable library, in an adjacent building which was the former residence of a demoted member of the imperial court. Housing around 5,000 volumes, this collection boasted numerous books on architecture, perspective, hydraulics, fortification, fountain design and gardens, including two editions of Vitruvius,

21 Teixeira Leite, *A China no Brasil*, p. 173.

Italian and German books on fountains and three books of views of Versailles and its gardens and other French palaces.[22]

The appearance of the Beitang façade is preserved in a scroll painting of the period, which shows it to be a partial simulacrum of the façade of the Jesuit church of Saint-Louis (now Saint-Louis-Saint-Paul) in Paris, built by Jesuit architect Étienne Martellange (1627–41) (fig. 1.4).[23] The church's nationalist flavour is not surprising, given that it was paid for by Louis XIV and that the original idea of a French Jesuit mission in China had been the brainchild of the King's ultra-nationalist minister Jean-Baptiste Colbert (1619–83). Especially noteworthy is the façade's oculus window with its sunrays, the paired columns and pilasters and the division into three bays with a high arch in the centre. By contrast, the Portuguese-run Nantang, rebuilt at precisely the same time and completed in 1733, was constructed in an emphatically Portuguese style, although with the adjustments to Chinese taste in the forecourt already noted above (Fig. 1.2). These facades show that patriotic feelings ran high even among rival groups of Jesuits: indeed, few mission episodes better illustrate this sentiment than that of 18th-century Beijing. It is, therefore, somewhat ironic that Belleville ended up spending the rest of his life decorating churches for the Portuguese Jesuits in Brazil.

Although many scholars have maintained that Belleville served the Kangxi Emperor at court in the Forbidden City, as did so many of his colleagues, and even that he trained eunuch artists there, I have yet to find definite proof that he contributed to anything outside the Jesuit compound.[24] If he did train Chinese painters he would have done so either in the *xianfa* mode of perspective painting or in the naturalistic depictions of birds and flowers so beloved at court. At any rate, Kangxi treated Belleville with courtesy and even had him sent to the Qing imperial summer mountain resort in Chengde to recover from the illness, no doubt brought on by sheer exhaustion, which led to his removal from China in 1707 or 1708.[25] En route to France Belleville left the ship at Salvador de Bahia for what was to be a short medical leave but which ended up lasting the rest of his life.

22 Pirazzoli, *Le Yuanmingyuan*, p. 8. For a list of the works in the Jesuit library in Beijing, which include French and Italian architectural treatises, see H. Zou, 'Appendix: Books on architecture and gardens in the Jesuit libraries in Beijing', *Studies in the History of Gardens and Designed Landscapes*, 22 (2002): 317–20; G.A. Bailey, *Art on the Jesuit Missions in Asia and Latin America* (Toronto: University of Toronto Press, 1999), p. 93. On diplomatic gifts of French engravings to Qianlong see M. Reed, 'Imperial impressions: the Qianlong Emperor's print suites,' in P. ten-Doesschate Chu and N. Ding (eds.), *Qing Encounters: Artistic Exchanges between China and the West* (Los Angeles, CA: Getty Research Institute Los Angeles, 2015), pp. 124–39.

23 Luengo, 'Identidad y globalización', pp. 284–6.

24 Mungello, *The Great Encounter*, pp. 174–5; Teixeira Leite, *A China no Brasil*, p. 173.

25 The Jesuit personnel records are unclear about the exact dates as the 1709 edition lists him as being en route from China to France and only in 1710 is he listed among those living in Bahia. It is most likely that he reached Bahia sometime in 1708 (Dehergne, *Répertoire*, p. 30).

Belleville in Brazil and his legacy

In contrast to his relatively well-documented sojourn in China, we know almost nothing about Belleville's 22 years in Brazil except for what can be gleaned from the Jesuit triennial reports, which are frustratingly unspecific about artists and architects. Among the four surviving personnel catalogues from Bahia during his lifetime – those for the first and last eight years of his stay are missing – most just call him an *associator*, which means a person who accompanies a priest when he goes on a journey. Nevertheless in 1719 he is specifically called a 'painter and sculptor' (*pintor e estatuário*); and the catalogues of 1720 and 1722 call him a 'painter' (*pintor*).[26] He lived at the Jesuits' headquarters in Salvador, of which the church (begun 1657) is now the cathedral. Its celebrated sacristy ceiling – it was finished in 1694 and therefore Belleville would have known it well – served as motivational propaganda for Jesuits working in the mission field, as it was adorned with portraits of Jesuit saints and martyrs around the world, including Asia. Belleville must have recovered quickly from his illness as he was already reviewing and correcting the plan of the new Jesuit Novitiate at Jiquitaia (Bahia) and was on hand to witness the laying of the foundation stone there on 9 March 1709.[27] Belleville is also thought to have contributed to the ornamental paintings in the Salvador church, but nothing survives there which can be attributed to him with any certitude – there is certainly no Chinese-style ornament of any kind. Referring to his death, on 29 September 1730, the Jesuit Annual Letter notes that he was well known for his architecture and was a paragon of humility in deflecting praise for his architectural work.

Although it, too, lacks documentation, only one surviving artwork has convincingly been attributed to the French Jesuit because of its extraordinarily accurate Chinese ornamentation and because it was executed just over a decade after his arrival in Bahia.[28] This work is the sacristy ceiling at the novitiate and college church of Nossa Senhora in Belém da Cachoeira, an Amerindian village about 130 kilometres to the north-west of Salvador, built between 1687 and 1701 (fig. 1.5).[29]

The church, the last remaining building in the complex, originally occupied the middle of one of the smaller sides of a rectangular cloister. It has a single nave, *Capela–Mor* (chancel) and sacristy flanked by lateral corridors and clerestories with balconies opening onto the chancel. As was traditional in the region, the

26 Leite, *Artes e ofícios*, p. 130.

27 Leite, *Artes e ofícios*, p. 130.

28 The first scholar to make the attribution was G. Bazin, in *L'Architecture religieuse baroque au Brésil* (São Paulo and Paris: Librairie Plon, 1958), vol. 2, p. 12. See also Teixeira Leite, *A China no Brasil*, pp. 171–8, 125–250; S.M. Fonseca, 'Orientalismos no Barroco em Minas Gerais e a circularidade cultural entre o Oriente e o Ocidente', *Revista de Cultura*, 22 (1995): 109–16; E.M. Brajniko, 'Traces de l'art oriental sur l'art brésilien du début du XVIIIème siecle', *Revista da Universidade Federal de Minas Gerais*, 9 (1951): 56–79; Leite, *Artes e ofícios*, p. 130.

29 Bazin, *Architecture religieuse*, vol. 2, pp. 11–12.

Figure 1.5. Charles de Belleville, Ceiling in the sacristy of the Jesuit church of Nossa Senhora de Belén de Cachoeira, Bahia, Brazil (c.1719) (Photo courtesy of Dennis Carr).

bell tower is covered with blue-and-white tiles and broken crockery. As these ceramics were inspired by Chinese porcelain – some may, in fact, be Chinese – the tower serves as another reflection of the taste for Chinese decorative arts. The church underwent three major renovations during Belleville's time in Brazil: one in 1707 involving the ornamentation of the church and sacristy – very probably too early for him to have been there; and then in 1719, when two pulpits were installed; and finally in 1726, when humidity had so damaged the church that its façade and towers were rebuilt in stone.[30] The most probable date for Belleville's ceiling is 1719, since the renovations that year involved the interior of the building and there are traces of Chinese-style floral ornament on the underside of the pulpit.

The wooden ceiling takes the form of six sunken panels, organised into two rows of three and bordered with a grid of raised frames and with gilded lotus-blossom bosses at the junctures. The entire ceiling is painted on a black background in imitation of Chinese lacquers. The most colourful part is the floral wreath around the central medallions, containing luxurious, three-dimensional flowers, including peonies, roses and morning glory executed in pink, red, white and green oil pigments. The central medallion, painted in gold, centres on a foliate arabesque within a bold outline and the boundaries of

30   Bazin, *Architecture religieuse*, vol. 2, p 11.

Figure 1.6. Detail of a ceiling from the Chang Ling tomb of Ming emperor Yongle, 1424 (Photo: author).

the panel are delineated in a golden border and bear another abstracted floral and foliate band in white with pink roses at the corners. The raised grid of frames is painted with gilded foliate motifs and outlined in seal red and blue. The only departure from Chinese iconography is the addition of passionflower blossoms with their distinctive pinwheel shape and radial filaments. Although, as their name indicates, they were considered a symbol of Christ's Passion, they are also native to Brazil and demonstrate that the French painter was keen to integrate his local surroundings. The same flower, incidentally, appears in the carved decoration of the churches of the Jesuit reductions in Paraguay around the same period.[31]

The most interesting thing about this ceiling is that it is neither an example of Chinoiserie – European fantasy Asian ornament – nor does it imitate Chinese luxury goods made exclusively for export trade. As can be seen here in a detail of the ceiling in the Chang Ling Tomb of Ming Emperor Yongle from 1424, coffer-like wooden ceilings with floral wreaths surrounding medallions and with painted bosses at the junctures of the grid have long been typical of Chinese imperial palaces, halls and temples (fig. 1.6). This kind of ceiling can also be found throughout the halls and pavilions of the Imperial Palace in Beijing, including an 18th-century example in the northern sector gardens.

31 Bailey, *Art on the Jesuit Missions*, p. 181.

Since Belleville would have been familiar with this form from his probable visits to the Forbidden City and the Chengde villa, it is perfectly conceivable that he based his ceiling on those structures. Belleville's frames with arabesques in gold and white also recall imperial lacquered screen panels. The richness and realism in the flower wreath in Belleville's panels also resemble the kind of so-called 'bird and flower paintings' produced by his Jesuit colleagues and their Chinese apprentices at court. In addition to his sacristy ceiling, Belleville also painted a frieze of painted peonies, roses and possibly tulips in oil on plaster around the upper part of the wall of the *Capela–Mor* and under the choir – these were rediscovered during the recent renovation. This is significant as Chinese-style decoration in later Brazilian churches also tended to be concentrated in the sacristy and chancel. By contrast, the illusionistic painted wooden vault of the *Capela–Mor* is executed in the traditional Luso-Italian manner with false cornices, plinths and cartouches, as well as putti (cherubs) and floral garlands.

Belleville's example was followed within a decade in two ceilings in a Jesuit missionary church 2,000 kilometres to the south, in a Tupi-Guaraní *aldea* called Embu, now a crafts community on the outskirts of São Paulo known as Embu das Artes. The mission church of Nossa Senhora do Rosário in Embu, a strikingly plain structure with opulent altarpieces, was built by local Amerindians on a former cattle ranch under the leadership of father Belchior Pontes around 1694–1700.[32] At the time it was a remote location, since the present state of São Paulo was sparsely settled by whites and black slaves in comparison with the cities of the north-east. His successor Domingos Machado (in office 1720–51) built the adjacent residence and rebuilt the *Capela-Mor* (inscribed 1735), the side altars (which Germain Bazin dates to 1720) and the sacristy, which, given its stylistic similarity to the *Capela-Mor*, must also date from the 1735 campaign.[33] The ceiling of the *Capela-Mor* is divided into nine rectangular panels with large acanthus leaf grotesques framed by a Chinese-style interior band of stylised chrysanthemums and foliage painted in white against a field of seal red. Wider bands in a similar style surround each panel, now red-on-white with flowering branches like magnolias. Both types of band reappear along the frieze at the top of the chancel walls, the wider one above and the narrower one below. Unlike the designs at Belém da Cachoeira these patterns are quite generic and only vaguely Chinese in style, as if recalling a half-remembered pattern from an imported silk.

The sacristy features a similar, although flat, roof with nine large rectangular panels adorned with acanthus grotesques around symbols of Christ's Passion (Fig. 1.7). Here the wider band is painted with prunus and rose scrolls in green, pink, red and blue on a white ground and the interior ones with Chinese landscapes featuring pagodas, hills, trees and birds, but also tiny churches in

---

32 P. Tirapeli, *Igrejas paulistas: barroco e rococó* (São Paulo: UNESP, 2003), pp. 230–37; Bazin, *Architecture religieuse*, vol. 2, p. 159.

33 Tirapeli, *Igregas*, p. 232; Bazin, *Architecture religieuse*, vol. 2, p.159.

Figure 1.7. Anonymous, ceiling of the sacristy, Jesuit Church of Nossa Senhora do Rosário in Embu, São Paulo, Brazil (c. 1735–40) (Photo: author).

white on red. Unlike the floral scrolls, which are again somewhat generically reminiscent of Chinese textiles or perhaps wallpaper, the landscapes are characteristic enough to be traced to specific models. However, with the death about five years earlier of the only Jesuit painter with direct knowledge of the arts of imperial China, this new painter turned to something more familiar and readily available in colonial Brazil: the Chinoiserie false-lacquered furnishings painted in a technique known in English as 'japanning'. As D. Carr has shown, japanned furniture was very popular in western Europe in the first decades of the 18th century and spread throughout the colonial world – including to the Thirteen Colonies, Jamaica, New Spain and the viceroyalty of Peru – thanks to itinerant artisans as well as printed manuals. One of these manuals was by a Jesuit: Filippo Buonanni's *Trattato sopra la vernice detta comunemente cinese* (Rome, 1720), to which this chapter will return in due course.[34] Although the Embu painter paints his scenes in white instead of gold, the designs are very similar to those of European japanned desks and cabinets of the same period, such as a bureau made *c.* 1735 either in England or Germany, with discreet little scenes with pavilions, fences, pagodas and small human figures and birds alternating with floral motifs, all against a red background, although human figures are less prominent in the Embu ceiling (Fig. 1.8). Also unlike European japanned furniture is the inclusion of churches in the Embu ceiling,

34   D. Carr, 'In search of japanning in the Colonial Americas', *Antiques & Fine Art*, 15 (Spring 2015): 204–11 (p. 205).

Figure 1.8. Bureau cabinet, German or English, c.1735. Wood, japanned, with engraved brass mounts. (Courtesy of the Victoria & Albert Museum).

little buildings crowned with crosses and high, pitched roofs, porches at the front and on the sides of the *Capela-Mor* and twin bell towers.

Embu is the last known Jesuit foundation in Brazil to include Chinese-inspired motifs in its chancel and sacristy. Paradoxically, the region with the highest concentration of surviving Chinoiserie church interiors was a place where religious orders had been forbidden entry by royal decree since 1711: the gold and diamond mining region of Minas Gerais, considered to be one of the cradles of Brazilian baroque and rococo.[35] As has been the case with the Embu paintings, scholars have traditionally attributed these Chinoiserie decorations to either Belleville or Chinese immigrant artists, but they are clearly made by Portuguese or Brazilian-born painters as they are no more authentically Chinese than the japanned furniture of Europe. The earliest and most famous example – in fact it predates Embu by ten years – is a series of seven false-lacquer landscape panels in gold on blue surrounding the traditionally baroque high altarpiece in the tiny wayside church of Nossa Senhora do Ó in Sabará

---

35   O.E. González and J.L. González, *Christianity in Latin America: A History* (Cambridge: Cambridge University Press, 2008), p. 113. For an excellent study of the architecture of the region, see M. Andrade Ribeiro de Oliveira, *O rococó religioso no Brasil* (São Paulo: Cosac Naify, 2003), pp. 213–93.

(dedicated to the pregnant Virgin). This was begun sometime after 1717 but only decorated around 1725, after Belleville's ceiling had been completed.[36] This tiny chapel even takes on a pseudo-Chinèse appearance on the exterior, its pagoda-like tower and curving eaves resembling one of the spindly pagodas on the Embu friezes. Such towers became commonplace in Minas Gerais.

At Sabará the nine Chinoiserie panels are not on the ceiling but surround the entrance to the *Capela-Mor*, with its vigorous baroque gilded altarpiece, in the part of the church known since early Christian times as the 'triumphal arch' since it separates the mortal world of the congregation from the heavenly Jerusalem represented by the chancel and celebrates the triumph of Christianity over paganism.[37] Therefore, by placing these panels around this opening the designer of the church has conceivably made a quite explicit statement of Christian conquest, using the Asian style as a metaphor for paganism. The panels, painted in gold on blue backgrounds, include one or two small architectural motifs, notably pagodas and multi-storeyed temples, as well as phoenixes and other birds, craggy rocks, hillocks, prunus trees, Confucian scholars, boats and fishermen. Unlike at Embu, however, none of them depict churches – in fact, lofty pagoda towers like the one at Kew Botanic Gardens in England are the most prominent motifs on the panels. The blue colour on the main panels is unusual as a background for Brazilian examples, but certain European japanned pieces were executed in blue or green. It is clear when comparing the Sabará panels to those on contemporary furniture that the latter are the most likely models. Indeed, Sabará and the rest of Minas Gerais were inundated with such luxury furnishings since its mines made it one of the richest places on earth at the time. Thus, at Sabará the motivation behind such Asiatic imagery was not merely spiritual but had a decidedly profane resonance: these churches, like the people who commissioned them, were concerned with being stylish.

The church with the largest concentration of Chinoiserie décor is the cathedral of Nossa Senhora da Assunção in Mariana (1714–35), also in Minas Gerais, constructed by Jacinto Barbara Lopes and António Coelho da Fonseca and elevated to a cathedral in 1745.[38] Like the Sabará chapel it also has pagoda-like belfries, as does the nearby Capela do dos Anjos de Nossa Senhora (*c.* 1784), thereby turning the townscape itself into a kind of fantasy Chinese village. The chinoiseries, commissioned by the first bishop, Don Frei Manuel da Cruz (d. 1764), date from around 1748 to 1751 – a full three decades after those at

---

36 Bazin, *Architecture religieuse*, vol. 2, pp. 102–3. Bazin was unable to find a single document relating to the construction of this church – 'on ne possède malheureusement aucun document sur ce joyau de l'art baroque' – and the date of 1725 is based on stylistic analysis. See also P. Tirapeli, *Igrejas barrocas do Brasil* (São Paulo: Metalivros, 2008), pp. 218–21.

37 L.H. Zirpolo, *Historical Dictionary of Baroque Art and Architecture* (Lanham: Scarecrow Press, 2010), p. 515.

38 Bazin, *Architecture religieuse*, vol. 1, pp. 77–8; Tirapeli, *Igrejas barrocas*, pp. 232–5.

Figure 1.9. Chinoiserie panels, choirstall of the Cathedral of Nossa Senhora da Assunção, Mariana, Minas Gerais, Brazil (c.1753). (Photo author).

Belém da Cachoiera. In this church the Chinese motifs appear on wooden panels adorning not the ceiling or the triumphal arch but exclusively places associated with music. The largest are a set of panels along the back of both the choirstalls (fig. 1.9). Painted in gold and black against a background of seal red, the panels are adorned with five layers of landscapes, including flowers, blossoming prunus trees, willows, birds, fountains and garden pavilions with trelliswork, but also churches. The human figures – some are promenading under the shade of a parasol while others hunt with rifles or are on horseback – are Europeans instead of Chinese. Camels, elephants and panthers, exotic animals from beyond China, round out the motifs and demonstrate that the imagery has become a pan-Asian fantasy. Another series of Chinoiserie panels form the front of the choir stall, this time painted with floral posies on a black background framed in red. In the main panels the black pigment is used for the landscapes which also serve to separate the scenes, while the silver is used for details such as faces and the putto atop the very European-looking fountains. The layout of the panels recalls folding screens, a popular format both for European japanned furniture and Chinese export screens of a sort known in

Europe as a 'Coromandel screen' because they were shipped to western markets via European entrepots on the Coromandel Coast of south-east India such as Madras or Pondicherry.[39] Coromandel screens or European japanned screens made in imitation of them were often mounted on walls in Europe or colonial America.

The most unusual location for chinoiseries in the church is on the base of the monumental pipe organ, constructed by the German organ-maker Arp Schnitger (1701) and originally in the Franciscan church in Lisbon. The organ was moved to Mariana in 1752 as a gift from Dom João V of Portugal; and the *chinesices* were probably painted over the original panels of the organ at this time, which would make them contemporary with those of the choir stalls and probably by the same painters.[40] When its doors are shut the whole exterior is painted with gilded decoration on a red background: in the two main panels above the keyboard with landscape scenes similar to those on the choirstalls; and on the sides with lighter floral and bird motifs. By contrast, the insides of the doors are painted in gold on black with a red frame, again with small architectural and landscape scenes. As at Belém da Cachoeira, Embu and Sabará, these Chinese-style motifs are limited to marginal regions of the church's interior, which otherwise remains resolutely Luso-Brazilian in style, with bulky Solomonic retables and Italianate, illusionistic ceiling paintings in the *Capela-Mor*. It is as if these exotic elements needed to be kept to a minimum so as not to make the interior appear like a pagan temple. They would also have been seen primarily by insiders: canons of the cathedral, choristers, the bishop and the organist.

The association between Chinoiserie and religion went beyond public places of worship and into the home. Particularly in Bahia and Minas Gerais, Asian fantasy cabinets were manufactured expressly to be used as household shrines, such as an elaborate wooden oratory made in Minas Gerais sometime in the mid or later 18th century and now in the Museu de Arte Sacra in São Paulo.[41] Two of its four doors are painted with landscapes in blue and white, in imitation of Chinese porcelain, against a seal-red background; the inside of the statue niche is painted to resemble Chinese silks with multicoloured posies and blue foliate motifs on a bluish ground, and – most extraordinarily – the crown of the cabinet takes the form of a fantasy pagoda roof with turned-up eaves, the sort of building which appears in Chinoiserie landscapes. Sometimes even saints are dressed à la chinoise, as in the case of an 18th-century sculpture of St Cecilia playing her harp in the sacristy at Mariana cathedral but dressed in Chinese imperial robes and with a Mandarin-style topknot.[42]

39 C. Frank, *Objectifying China, Imagining America: Chinese Commodities in Early America* (Chicago, IL: University of Chicago Press, 2011), p. 80.

40 L.A. Esteves Pereira, 'Two More Arp Schnitgers in Portugal?', *Organ Yearbook*, 14 (1983): 17.

41 The inventory number for this remarkable piece in the Museu de Arte is: 135mas.

42 Teixeira Leite, *A China no Brasil*, p. 294.

Figure 1.10. Anonymous, wooden temple lion, Jesuit residence of Nossa Senhora do Rosário in Embu, São Paulo, Brazil (early 18th century). (Photo author).

An important Chinese-inspired form of probably Jesuit origin to be found in Brazilian churches is the temple lion, made either of wood, stone or fired clay. In this case, as with Belleville's ceiling, they are modelled after authentic Chinese examples rather than Chinoiserie forms. In China such lions served as symbolic guardians at the entrances to temples, palaces, imperial tombs, government offices and the larger homes. They are generally squat and muscular with pug-like noses and a mane formed of scrolls or topknots; and their mouths open up into wide snarls baring fangs. They were produced in pairs, the female shown playing with a cub and the male holding a sphere under his paw. We know from ships' manifests that Chinese temple lions, probably ceramic ones, were shipped to Brazil from Macau in this period. By this time Chinese imports had become quite common in Brazil: so common, in fact, that most great houses had impressive collections of polychrome porcelain from the Jingdezhen kilns, many from the Kangxi and Qianlong periods. The Museu de Arte in Bahia even preserves a fine pair of 18th-century temple lions, painted under the glaze in archaic yellow and green, which would originally have come from a private residence or perhaps a church foundation.[43]

Temple lions appear in three known churches in Brazil: in Embu and in two Franciscan foundations in the far north-east, a monastery in João Pessoa and a Third Order chapel in Recife.[44] The wooden Embu lions, probably from around the same period as the sacristy ceiling, form a quartet meant to support a wooden bier for a statue of the Dead Christ (fig. 1.10).

The ensemble was brought out into the streets to feature in Holy Week processions and then rested in the church until Easter morning. Seated on their haunches, the lions look skyward with wide grins and almond eyes and their manes are formed of tight scrolls. They are traditionally thought to be Chinese but they are unlikely to have been made in China as they do not have the typical twisting torso or snarling lips of Chinese lions, nor do they have the orb or lion cub under their paws. While it might seem odd at first that Daoist lions would have been employed to carry the bier of Christ during a religious procession, their supportive role might have served as a metaphor for the support Chinese converts brought to the Catholic church – or even for that hoped-for end goal of a Christian China ruled from the Forbidden City by a benevolent Catholic monarch. They could also simply represent Christ's victory over paganism. I. Zupanov has recently suggested that a similar message lay behind the tradition in Portuguese Goa of carving Hindu *naga* snake deities on the pedestals supporting church pulpits, in which the position of the priestly orator on top of the *nagas* demonstrates Christianity's triumph over Hinduism and also the support given to Christianity by the Brahmin converts who formed the Christian upper class in the colony.[45]

As it happens, the tradition of incorporating Chinese lions into church decoration did not begin in Brazil – as we have already seen – but in Catholic Asia, where they appeared in front of church forecourts, flanking doors, or on their facades. This practice most probably began with the Jesuits, as with the two lions flanking the entrance to the Beitang in Beijing. The oldest set is probably the suite of six lions clambering atop the massive granite façade of the church of Our Lady, better known as Saint Paul's, in Macau, carved between the 1620s and 1644.[46] These lions look authentic because they were carved by Chinese sculptors who were probably accustomed to carving them for temples. Especially noteworthy in this case are the way the lips are pulled back in a scowl and the stylised curvature of the manes, which recall the way clouds are carved in Chinese sculpture. Two other pairs – females with a cub and males with an

43 *O Museu de Arte da Bahia* (São Paulo: Banco Safra, 1997), p. 259.

44 Teixeira Leite, *A China no Brasil*, pp. 165–6.

45 I.G. Zupanov, 'The pulpit trap: possession and personhood in colonial Goa', *Res*, 65/66 (2014/2015): 229–315.

46 C. Guillén Nuñez, *Macao's Church of Saint Paul: a Glimmer of the Baroque in China* (Hong Kong: Hong Kong University Press, 2009), pp. 98–9, 116–37.

orb – guard the main entry and flank the patio of the Augustinian church of San Agustín in Manila (completed 1607) and are believed by scholars to date at least from the 18th century; and others can be found in the Philippines at the shrine of Our Lady of Caysasay in Taal (Batangas) and in churches in Vigan (Ilocos Sur), Morong (Rizal) and the cathedral of the Santo Niño in Cebu.[47] The San Agustín quartet, too, were clearly carved by Chinese sculptors, of whom there was a large community just north of the Pasig River from Spanish Manila: the piece has the typical lips pulled back into a scowl, the four canine teeth, the stylised scrolling mane, and – above all – the cub.

The other two surviving Brazilian examples are Franciscan. The Friars Minor had their own reasons for touting Christian victory in Asia. Although the Franciscan missions in Qing China were lower-profile than those of the Jesuits, concentrating on ordinary people rather than the elites, they more than made up for it with their antiquity. In fact, the Franciscans sent the first Catholic missionaries to Mongolia and Yuan Dynasty China centuries before the European era of overseas exploration. This mission began with Giovanni di Piano Carpini, who walked barefoot from Umbria to the Mongol court in Karakorum in 1245, initiating a sporadic mission that lasted until about 1370 and involved some 240 friar missionaries.[48] One of them, Giovanni da Montecorvino, established an active mission in Khanbaliq, present-day Beijing and the Yuan capital; and he acquired the lofty title of Archbishop of Khanbaliq and Patriarch of the East in 1307 and translated the Psalms and New Testament into the Mongol language, Uighur. Very few visual remains survive of this mission today: only a handful of tombstones of Italian Christians living in China, such as those of Andrea di Perugia, Franciscan bishop of Quanzhou from 1332, and Caterina Vilioni, daughter of an Italian merchant living in Yangzhou in 1342.[49] Whatever jealousy the Franciscans may have felt toward the Jesuits in contemporary China – not to mention in 16th- and 17th-century Japan, where the two orders were constantly at loggerheads – they made up for with their history. Less than 20 years after the death of Francis of Assisi, in the fervent era of the crusades, the Friars Minor had claimed China for their own.

Both these pairs of Brazilian Franciscan lions date from the 1770s, which happen to be the decade of the worldwide suppression of the Jesuit Order. Is it not possible that these symbols of Christian victory might also be intended as a celebration of the Franciscans' recent triumph over their bitterest rival in the missionary field? One is a ceramic pair of recumbent lions flanking the side entrance at the Third Order Franciscan church of São Francisco in

47 P.G. Galende and R.T. José, *San Agustín: Art & History 1571–2000* (Manila: San Agustin Museum, 2000), pp. 147–9.

48 C. Dawson, *Mission to Asia* (Toronto: University of Toronto Press, 1980), pp. 3–72, 224–31; L. Arnold, *Princely Gifts and Papal Treasures: The Franciscan Mission to China and its Influence on the Art of the West 1250–1350* (San Francisco CA,: Desiderata, 1999).

49 J.R.S. Phillips, *The Medieval Expansion of Europe* (Oxford: Clarendon 1988), pp. 104–5.

Figure 1.11. Stone temple lion, forecourt of the Franciscan church of Santo António (popularly known as São Francisco), João Pessoa (c.1734 or 1779). (Photo author).

Recife, made around 1770 and now in very poor condition – indeed, they are almost unrecognisable as lions.[50] The other is a pair of stone rampant lions at the Franciscan monastery of Santo António (popularly known as São Francisco) in João Pessoa further to the north-east, carved around 1779 (fig. 1.11).

In both cases the pair of lions guard the entry to the forecourt; in the case of Santo António they are perched on the outer extremities of the perimeter walls, welcoming visitors into the monastery enclosure, just as their counterparts did at the Jesuit Beitang in Beijing. These two lions are the most striking in Brazil, with their pushed-in nose, menacingly raised eyebrows, fierce grin with prominent canine teeth, luxuriously scrolling mane and volute-like tail. They were probably carved by the same people who executed the upper part of the façade in 1779, which is known precisely for the bulkiness and three-dimensional quality of its stonework, with two of the most prominent volutes in Brazilian architecture. The lions look very Brazilian: they are more rigid and frontal than Chinese examples, lacking the latter's sinuous line and taut musculature but possessing a blunt power and creative treatment of line which make them unique in Latin America. Despite these differences, the closeness

50 Tirapeli, *Igrejas barrocas*, pp. 104–7; L.D. Silva, *Pernambuco Preservado: histórico dos bens tombados no Estado de Pernambuco* (Recife, 2002), pp. 172–7; Teixeira Leite, *A China no Brasil*, pp. 207–8; Bazin, *Architecture religieuse*, vol. 1, pp. 126–7; vol. 2, pp. 122–3, 144–5.

to Chinese prototypes in their stance, the position of the tail and shape of the nose indicates that the João Pessoa carver had access to an original.

The artists who painted and carved these Chinese-inspired artworks in Brazilian churches have left us no record of their motivation. As a temporal coadjutor Belleville was unlikely to have been a literary man and no writings of any kind by him survive. As for the artists who executed the *chinesices* in Embu, Sabará and Mariana, we do not even know their names. The same goes for the sculptors of the churches at João Pessoa and Recife. It would be quite reasonable to dismiss these Chinese-style church decorations as merely decorative, since they participate in a worldwide fashion for things Asian, whether it be actual export-ware ceramics and lacquers or imitation ones such as the japanned furniture of England or the porcelain of Meissen or Spode. Some, as in Minas Gerais, echoed the stylish interiors of the great houses of the region and spoke as much about the church patrons' material wealth as they did about the Heavenly Jerusalem. However, as noted throughout this chapter, one of the main motivations seems to have been a desire to use Asiatic styles to communicate messages of Christian, specifically missionary, triumph. While this theory must remain conjectural in the case of the Brazilian works discussed above, there is, fortunately, at least one source which makes this association quite explicit: Filippo Buonanni and his deceptively humble little book on varnishing (first published in 1720), which is one of the earliest and most influential treatises on the subject, translated immediately into multiple languages.

Buonanni's book is a curious blend. A practical guide to japanning furniture, with illustrations of the tools of the trade (but, curiously, no decorative motifs), this book, published one year after Belleville's ceiling, is a religious tract disguised as a DIY manual. Buonanni (1638–1723) was no mere furniture maker: a professor of mathematics at the Collegio Romano, he was also well-known for his experimental work with microscope lenses and, after 1698, was the curator of Athanasius Kircher's famed curiosity cabinet or museum at the college, for which he published the first catalogue in 1709.[51] The patriotic dedication in Buonanni's book to the Marquis of Abrantes, Portuguese ambassador to the Holy See – and by extension to João V of Portugal – explicitly associates japanning with Portuguese military conquest and Catholic (specifically Jesuit) spiritual victory in the Americas and Asia, using a kind of ostentatious language which seems out of place in a modest guide to making furniture. It opens:

> After many vast reigns of America and of the Oriental Indies were made
> tributaries to the Crown of Portugal by its indomitable heroes, any
> smallest fruit plucked there is usually appreciated by the participants in the
> conquest; and thus, the memory of the palms is renewed, with which were

---

51 F. Perugini, 'Filippo Buonanni and the Treatise', in F. Buonanni, *Techniques of Chinese Lacquer: the Classic Eighteenth-century Treatise on Asian Varnish*, ed. and trans. by F. Perugini (Los Angeles, CA: J. Paul Getty Museum, 2009), p. ix.

woven the crowns in honor of their bravery. For such reason, I persuaded myself that this little volume would be received with benign hand by Your Excellence, since the subject stated in it has origin from that land, to where the Royal Liberality, after having introduced there the Catholic Faith, continuously sends and there supports operators to cultivate it; and because it can reawaken the memory of the triumphs obtained with armed hand in similar ventures by the ancestors of the very noble lineage of Your Excellence whose merits make it shine.[52]

Buonanni reminds the monarch of Portugal's support of the Jesuits' campaign to introduce the Catholic Faith into those regions and hopes his book could help to commemorate this Christian victory. He then cites the first two books to introduce the art of varnishing into Europe, both, of course, by Jesuits: Martino Martini's 1655 *Novus Atlas Sinesis* [*New Atlas of China*] and Kircher's 1667 *China Illustrata*.[53] In Buonanni's generous rewriting of history, by bringing Chinese lacquer-work to the world's attention the Jesuits, therefore, not only invented Chinoiserie, but also employed the style as a symbol and reminder of Christian, and specifically Jesuit, missionary victory in Asia. For a religious order long credited with devious methods of using culture for propagandistic purposes, this was very devious indeed.

It is clear from the Jesuits' 17th-century publication campaign and from Jesuit churches in Asia and Brazil that the Society of Jesus felt proprietary about China; and that for them its arts – even decorative arts such as furniture – could be employed as a visual reminder of Jesuit victory in what was considered the most ancient and formidable non-Christian power in the world. As such, these decorative schemes, like the sacristy ceiling in Salvador, also served as motivational art to inspire missionaries towards similar work in the Americas. The Jesuits were the first to introduce Chinese or Chinese-inspired styles into the churches and private oratories of Brazil, ensuring a lasting association between this secular style and sacred space which was not just unique in Latin America but also unknown in Europe. Certainly, individual churchmen in Europe were enthusiastic about Chinese goods –as C. Johns has recently noted, Pope Benedict XIII (r. 1724–30) even built a gallery at Castelgandolfo to house his collection of Chinese paintings of beautiful women – but even the pope did not decorate churches with them.[54] Paradoxically, the Brazilian association between China and the Church outlasted the Jesuits themselves, perpetuated by their Franciscan rivals as a symbol of their own Asian exploits and perhaps even their victory over the Society. However, for most colonial Brazilians and patrons such as secular clergy, lay confraternities and private citizens, ecclesiastical Chinoiserie had simply become a tradition, one which

---

52 Buonanni, *Techniques of Chinese Lacquer*, p. 2.

53 Buonanni, *Techniques of Chinese Lacquer*, pp. 10–11.

54 C.M.S. Johns, *China and the Church: Chinoiserie in Global Context* (Oakland, CA: University of California Press, 2016), pp. 70–71.

was encouraged in no small way by what people considered to be its stylishness and avant-garde quality, like the latest Paris fashions which also took elite Brazil by storm at the end of the century.[55]

Bibliography

Andrade Ribeiro de Oliveira, M. (2003) *O rococó religioso no Brasil* (São Paulo: Cosac Naify).

Arnold, L. (1999) *Princely Gifts and Papal Treasures: The Franciscan Mission to China and its Influence on the Art of the West 1250–1350* (San Francisco, CA: Desiderata).

Bailey, G.A. (1999) *Art on the Jesuit Missions in Asia and Latin America* (Toronto: University of Toronto Press).

— (2006) 'Asia in the arts of Colonial Latin America', in J.J. Rishel (ed.), *The Arts in Latin America, 1492–1820*, 57–69 (Philadelphia, PA and New Haven, CT: Philadelphia Museum of Art and Yale University Press).

— (2014) *The Spiritual Rococo: Décor and Divinity from the Salons of Paris to the Missions of Patagonia* (Farnham: Ashgate).

— (2017) 'Rococo in eighteenth-century Beijing: ornament prints and the design of the European palaces of the Yuanming Yuan', *The Burlington Magazine*, 159 (Oct): 778–88.

Bazin, G. (1958) *L'Architecture religieuse baroque au Brésil*, 2 vols. (São Paulo and Paris: Libraire Plon).

Beurdeley, C. and M. Beurdeley (1972) *Giuseppe Castiglione: A Jesuit Painter at the Court of the Chinese Emperors* (London: Lund Humphries, 1972).

Brajniko, E.M. (1951) 'Traces de l'art oriental sur l'art brésilien du début du XVIIIème siècle', *Revista da Universidade Federal de Minas Gerais*, 9: 56–79.

Brockley, L. (2007) *Journey to the East: The Jesuit Mission to China, 1579–1724* (Cambridge, MA: MIT Press).

Buonanni, F. (2009 [1720]) *Techniques of Chinese Lacquer: The Classic Eighteenth-century Treatise on Asian Varnish*, trans. and ed. by F. Perugini (Los Angeles, CA: J. Paul Getty Museum).

Burgues, M. 'Aspects techniques du tabernacle de la chapelle du collège Henri IV de Poitiers', *Bulletin de la Société des antiquaires de l'Ouest et des musées de Poitiers*, 5th ser., 3 (1989): 324.

Cammann, S. (1964) 'Chinese influence in colonial Peruvian tapestries', *Textile Museum Journal* 1 (3): 21–34.

---

55 On the susceptibility of colonial Brazilians to French fashion see Bailey, *The Spiritual Rococo*, p. 305.

Carr, D. (ed.) (2015) *Made in the Americas: The New World Discovers Asia* (Boston, MA: MFA Publications).

— 'In search of japanning in the Colonial Americas', *Antiques & Fine Art*, 15 (Spring 2015): 204–11.

Clauer, P. (1894) *L'Intermédiaire des chercheurs et curieux: questions et réponses, communications diverses à l'usage de tous, littérateurs et gens du monde* III, 30: 161–2.

Corsi, E. (2004) *La fábrica de las ilusiones: los jesuitas y la difusión de la perspectiva lineal en China, 1698–1766* (Mexico City: El Colegio de México).

— (2012) 'Pozzo's treatise as a workshop for the construction of a sacred Catholic space in Beijing', in R. Bösel and L. Salviucci Insolera (eds.), *Artifizi della matafora: diciotto saggi su Andrea Pozzo* (Rome: Artemide), pp. 233–43.

D'Arelli, F. (ed.) (1988) *Le marche e l'oriente* (Rome: Instituto Italiano per l'Africa e l'oriente).

Dawson, C. (1980) *Mission to Asia* (Toronto: University of Toronto Press).

Dehergne, J. (1973) *Répertoire des jésuites de Chine de 1552 à 1800* (Rome and Paris: Institutum Historicum S.I.).

Droguet, V. (1994) 'Les Palais européens de l'empereur Qianlong et leurs sources italiennes', *Histoire de l'art* 25/26: 15–28.

Duteil, J.P. (1994) *Le mandat du ciel: Le role des jésuites en Chine* (Paris: AP editions – Arguments).

Esteves Pereira, L.A. (1983) 'Two more arp schnitgers in Portugal?', *Organ Yearbook*, 14: 17.

Fernández M.Á. (ed.) (2016) *Return Voyage: The China Galleon and the Baroque in Mexico, 1565–1815* (Puebla and Mexico City: Gobierno de Estado de Puebla).

Fonseca, S.M. (1995) 'Orientalismos no Barroco em Minas Gerais e a circularidade cultural entre o Oriente e o Ocidente', *Revista de Cultura*, 22: 109–16.

Fontana, M. (2011) *Matteo Ricci: A Jesuit in the Ming Court* (Plymouth, MA: Rowman & Littlefield).

Frank, C. (2011) *Objectifying China, Imagining America: Chinese Commodities in Early America* (Chicago, IL: University of Chicago Press).

Fu, D. (2002) 'Western missionary painters and imperial architectural paintings of the Qing dynasty,' in H.S. Chan (ed.), *The Golden Exile: Pictorial Expressions of the School of Western Missionaries' Artworks of the Qing Dynasty Court* (Macau: Macau Museum of Art), pp. 261–4.

Galende P.G. and R.T. José (2000) *San Agustín: Art & History 1571–2000* (Manila: San Agustin Museum).

González, O.E. and J.L. González (2008) *Christianity in Latin America: A History* (Cambridge: Cambridge University Press).

Guillén Nuñez, C. (2009) *Macao's Church of Saint Paul: A Glimmer of the Baroque in China* (Hong Kong: Hong Kong University Press).

Herluison, H. (1873) *Actes d'état-civil d'artistes français, peintres, graveurs, architectes, etc.* (Paris: Baur).

Hsia, R. Po-chia (2012) *A Jesuit in the Forbidden City: Matteo Ricci 1552–1610* (Oxford: Oxford University Press).

Johns, C.M.S. (2016) *China and the Church: Chinoiserie in Global Context* (Oakland, CA: University of California Press).

Keevak, M. (2017) *Embassies to China: Diplomacy and Cultural Encounters before the Opium Wars* (Singapore: Springer).

Kleutghen, K. (2015) *Imperial Illusions: Crossing Pictorial Boundaries in the Qing Palaces* (Seattle, WA and London: University of Washington Press).

Leite, J. R. Teixeira (1999) *A China no Brasil: influências, marcas, ecos e sobrevivências chinesas na sociedade e na arte brasileiras* (Campinas: Unicamp).

Leite, S. (1953) *Artes e ofícios dos jesuítas no Brasil 1549–1760* (Lisbon and Rio de Janeiro: Broteria).

Lettres édifiantes et curieuses, écrites des missions étrangeres XVII (Paris, 1781).

Liu, C.Y. (2002) 'Architects and builders of the Qing Dynasty Yuanming Yuan Imperial Garden Palace', *University of Hong Kong Museum Journal*, 1: 38–59, 151–61.

Luengo, P. (2014) 'Identidad y globalización en las fachadas jesuitas de Pekín en el siglo XVIII', in A. Zamora and J. Ibáñez Fernández (eds.), *La Compañía de Jesús y las artes. Nuevas perspectivas de investigación* (Zaragoza: Universidad Zaragoza), pp. 279–99.

— (2016) 'Yuánmíng Yuán en el siglo XVIII: arte entre la diplomacia y la filosofía; entre Europa y Pekin', *Araucaria*, 18: 193–216.

Maffre, P. (2013) *Construire Bordeaux au XVIIIe siècle: les frères Laclotte, architectes en société.* (Bordeaux: Société Archéologique de Bordeaux).

Mercure galant (August 1686): 282–7.

Mungello, D.E. (1999) *The Great Encounter of China and the West, 1500–1800* (Lanham, MD: Rowman & Littlefield).

Musillo, M. (2016) *The Shining Inheritance: Italian Painters at the Qing Court, 1699–1812* (Los Angeles, CA: University of California Press).

Naquin, S. (2000) *Peking: Temples and City Life, 1400–1900* (Berkeley, CA and Los Angeles, CA: University of California Press).

O Museu de Arte da Bahia (São Paulo: Banco Safra, 1997).

Pfister, L. (1932–34) *Notices biographiques et bibliographiques sur les Jésuites de l'ancienne Mission de Chine: 1552–1773* (Shanghai: Chang-Hai, Mission Catholique).

Phillips, J.R.S. (1988) *The Medieval Expansion of Europe* (Oxford: Clarendon).

Phipps, E., J. Hecht and C. Esteras Martín (eds.) (2004) *The Colonial Andes: Tapestries and Silverwork, 1530–1830* (New York: Metropolitan Museum of Art).

Pirazzoli-t'Serstevens, M. (ed.) (1987) *Le Yuanmingyuan: jeux d'eau et palais européens de XVIIIe siècle à la cour de Chine* (Paris: Editions Recherches sur les Civilisations).

Reed, M. (2015) 'Imperial impressions: the Qianlong emperor's print suites', in P. ten-Doesschate Chu and N. Ding (eds.), *Qing Encounters: Artistic Exchanges between China and the West* (Los Angeles, CA: Getty Research Institute Los Angeles), pp. 124–39.

Sebes, J. (2001) 'Ricci, Matteo', in C.E. O'Neill and J.M. Domínguez (eds.), *Diccionario histórico de la Compañía de Jesús* (Rome: Institutum Historicum S.I. and Madrid: Universidad Pontificia Comillas), pp. 3351–3.

Silva, L.D. (2002) *Pernambuco preservado: histórico dos bens tombados no Estado de Pernambuco* (Recife [no pub.]).

Spence, J. (1985) *The Memory Palace of Matteo Ricci* (New York: Penguin).

Stöcklein, J. (1726) *Allerhand so Lehr- als Geist-reiche Brief / Schrifften und Reis-Beschreibungen* (Augsburg and Graz: Philipp, Martin and Heirs of Johann Veith).

Thiriez, R. (1998) *Barbarian Lens: Western Photographers of the Qianlong Emperor's European Palaces* (Amsterdam: Gordon and Breach).

Thomas, G.M. (2009) 'Yuanming Yuan/Versailles: intercultural interactions between Chinese and European palace cultures', *Art History*, 32: 115–43.

Tirapeli, P. (2003) *Igrejas paulistas: barroco e rococó* (São Paulo: UNESP).

— (2008) *Igrejas barrocas do Brasil* (São Paulo: Metalivros).

Wang, L. (2014) 'Church, a "sacred event" and the visual perspective of an "etic viewer": an 18th century Western-style Chinese painting held in the Bibliothèque Nationale de France', in R. Oliveira Lopes (ed.), *Face to Face: The Transcendence of the Arts in China and Beyond (Historical Perspectives)* (Lisbon: CEIBA), pp. 370–99.

Witek, J.W. (2001) 'Belleville, Charles de', in C.E. O'Neill and J.M. Domínguez (eds.), *Diccionario histórico de la Compañía de Jesús*, (Rome: Institutum Historicum S.I. and Madrid: Universidad Pontificia Comillas), p. 404.

— (2001) 'Turcotti, Carlo Giovanni', in C.E. O'Neill and J.M. Domínguez (eds.), *Diccionario histórico de la Compañía de Jesús* (Rome: Institutum Historicum S.I. and Madrid: Universidad Pontificia Comillas), pp. 3846–7.

Zirpolo, L.H. (2010) *Historical Dictionary of Baroque Art and Architecture* (Lanham, MD: Scarecrow.)

Zou, H. (2002) 'Appendix: books on architecture and gardens in the Jesuit libraries in Beijing', *Studies in the History of Gardens and Designed Landscapes*, 22: 317–20.

— (2002) 'The jing of a perspective garden', *Studies in the History of Gardens and Designed Landscapes*, 22: 293–326.

Zupanov, I.G. (2014/15) 'The pulpit trap: possession and personhood in colonial Goa', *Res*, 65/66: 229–315.

2. Two 'ways of proceeding': damage limitation in the Mission to the Chiquitos

Kate Ford

The churches of the Mission to the Chiquitos in the eastern part, the Oriente, of what is now Bolivia are essentially theatrical (fig. 2.1); and on first seeing them ten years ago I wondered why – until I began research.

Figure 2.1. A nocturnal procession during Holy Week arriving at the door of the restored church of La Inmaculada, Concepción. (Source: A.E. Bösl (1988), Una joya en la selva boliviana *(Zarautz: Banco Nacional de Bolivia), photograph between pp. 162 and 163).*

It then became apparent that their 18th-century Jesuit missionary architects were acutely aware of the lowly nature of the adobe from which the new churches were built and, accustomed from their seminary days to beginning-of-year theatre presentations with spectacular scenic effects, took the obvious steps to disguise this. To the indigenous artisan painters, whose forebears had

K. Ford, 'Two 'ways of proceeding': damage limitation in the Mission to the Chiquitos', in L.A. Newson (ed.), *Cultural Worlds of the Jesuits in Colonial Latin America* (London: Institute of Latin American Studies, 2020), pp. 41–68. License: CC-BY-NC-ND 2.0.

covered numinous sites all over the region evangelised by the mission with drawings and carved images and who were part of a culture in which body modification was thought to protect the human from the supernatural, this protective inscription would have seemed a sensible precaution.

This chapter begins by looking at marked rock sites in this region, at archaeological finds and at the practice of tattooing and painting the body; and it notes the persistence of belief to this day in the potency of both the image and its site. It then looks briefly at the growth of the Chiquitos mission from its unpromising beginnings and at the construction of the churches, comparing the colours and iconography of rock markings with what was to be painted on the church walls. The similarity of the role of indigenous shaman with that of a mission priest is observed: both individuals, in indigenous eyes, were seen to receive supernatural succour from the consumption of mysterious liquids. It concludes that the churches of the mission to the Chiquitos represent an artistically fortuitous encounter between two equally valid cultural practices and should not be read as a narrative of 'clever' Jesuits and 'child-like' indigenous people. The 76 years of the mission to the Chiquitos were the blink of an eye in the history of the Oriente, across which a mobile, flexible, pragmatic indigenous society with widespread links in trade, language and beliefs had moved for at least 20,000 years in pre-European times.[1] This society believed itself to be at the mercy of supernatural beings, whether those beings were the deities of the Manasica people or the *jichis* of Chiquito belief. The former were mocked by the missionary Lucas Caballero in 1706 in an ode written to his patron, Juan José Fernández Campero de Herrera, the first Marqués de Tojo, entitled 'Sátyra contra los Dioses de los Manasicas'.[2] It should be remembered that, certainly at the beginning of the mission, the indigenous deities lambasted by Caballero in the 'Sátyra' were as real to the missionaries as the 'Devil' of Christian theology,[3] while the *jichis*, the shape-shifting spirits of the Chiquitos, subsequently documented by 20th-century ethnologists, were regarded by the Chiquitos as capable of inflicting devastating harm if enraged.

Marked rock sites

The constant and creative flux of the largely nomadic indigenous past – underwritten, like the classical or biblical past well known to the Spanish invaders, by the universal imperatives of 'man's need to eat; and the authority

1   D.E. Ibarra Grasso and R. Querejazu Lewis, *30,000 años de prehistoria en Bolivia* (La Paz and Cochabamba: Los Amigos del Libro, 1986), p.14.

2   L. Caballero, S.J., *Relación de las costumbres y religión de los indios manasicas*, edited by M. Serrano y Sanz (Madrid: Librería General de Victoriano Suárez, 1933 [1706]), pp. 38–43.

3   L. Caballero, S.J., 'Diario de la cuarta misión a los manasicas y paunacas, 1707', in J. Matienzo et al. (eds.), *Chiquitos en las Anuas de la Compañía de Jesús (1691–1767)* (La Paz: Instituto Latinoamericano de Misionología de la Universidad Católica Boliviana, 2011), pp. 46–83 (p. 64).

of such professionals as the warrior, the healer, and the poet or scribe', as Brotherston puts it[4] – was endlessly recalled in song and story and existed iconographically in the markings drawn on or carved into rock. The 2014 register of the Sociedad de Investigación del Arte Rupestre de Bolivia includes 50 sites of rock paintings or carvings in the Oriente, many with evidence of later overdrawing, indicating that the site retained its ideological significance over centuries.[5] Indeed, German researchers in the 1960s and 1970s were led to remote sites by eager indigenous guides, who could not explain the marks but sensed a link to their ancestors.[6] Bolivian rock marking tends to be either in places with an amphitheatre-like quality or hidden away and 'secret'.[7] In an article published in 2007 on the drawings in the cave of Juan Miserandino near Santiago de Chiquitos, S. Calla Maldonado notes that although the 'shamanic model' of interpretation of rock markings is criticised by some as too general, the diverse nature of the marks and the numerous ways in which they can be read make it impossible to discredit.[8] Given the geographical location of this region between the Amazon and the Chaco, it is probable that any ceremonies involved in the process of rock marking would have incorporated the consumption of hallucinogens, smoked or drunk, by a priestly elite. In 1706 the missionary Lucas Caballero noted the use of a 'foul-smelling' black liquid in the process of initiation of a new *mapono* [shaman][9] by the Manasica people whom he was intent on converting and ridiculed the claim by his interpreters that this dark liquid enabled the *mapono* to 'fly',[10] as, of course, a psychotropic drug would have done ('fly' retaining its inverted commas here).

In 1981 the anthropologist Jürgen Riester published a monograph, *Arqueología y arte rupestre en el oriente boliviano*, as an offshoot of anthropological

---

4   G. Brotherston, *Image of the New World: The American Continent Portrayed in Native Texts* (London: Thames and Hudson, 1979), p. 18.

5   Matthias Strecker of the Sociedad de Investigación del Arte Rupestre de Bolivia (SIARB) defines a sacred site as one where it can be assumed rites were performed by specialists (conversation 1 Feb. 2011).

6   The *rupestre* expert Karl Kaifler recalled his period in San José de Chiquitos in the 1970s when, once his interest in rock markings became known among Chiquitanos and Ayoréodes, he was told by them of more and more sites. His escorts to each site were pleased the sites were there; they told him that they did not understand the marks but that they were 'to do with their ancestors' (conversation with Karl Kaifler, 7 March 2014); Riester writes: 'While I was in Santiago I learnt from an old Chiquitano man that there were rock drawings to the southwest. Thanks to the help of this man I was able to visit this site' (J. Riester, *Arqueología y arte rupestre en el oriente boliviano* (Cochabamba and La Paz: Los Amigos del Libro, 1981), p. 167).

7   Conversation with Matthias Strecker of SIARB, 1 Feb. 2011.

8   S. Calla Maldonado, 'Documentación de las pinturas de la Cueva de Juan Miserandino, Reserva Municipal del Valle de Tucuvaca, Depto. de Santa Cruz', *Boletín*, 21 (2007): 17–37 (23).

9   The use of the word 'shaman' is controversial. It is used here in the sense of a figure from a professional elite charged with mediating encounters with the supernatural.

10 Caballero, *Relación*, pp. 26, 29–30.

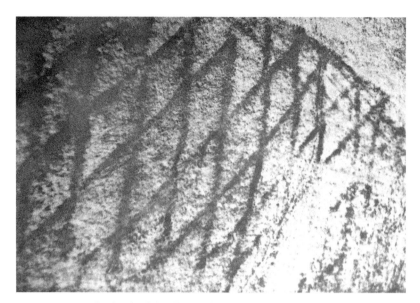

Figure 2.2. Part of a rhomboidal grid marked in reddish pigment on a rock face in the Serranía de Santiago. (Source: J. Riester, Arqueología y arte rupestre en el oriente boliviano *(Cochabamba and La Paz: Los Amigos del Libro, 1981), p. 176).*

fieldwork in the 1960s and 1970s.[11] The sites Riester investigated – most of them extremely remote and only accessible after several days' journey on horseback and foot – are in the Serranía de San Simón and at Piso Firme,[12] both in the north of the 18th-century mission's vast catchment area; in the north-west, he explored a site beside the river San Julián, 20 kilometres from Yotaú. In the east, his study covered the area around Roboré, Santiago and Yororobá;[13] he also visited Piedra Marcada, south of Concepción.

In his survey of the area around Roboré, Riester found rock drawings of 'single, double and triple wavy lines transformed into a great variety of zigzags' and 'motifs in the form of a grid and of rhomboids that partly cover an area 5m x 2.50m'[14] (fig. 2.2) and a variety of what he interpreted as zoomorphic and anthropomorphic drawings, together with circular motifs, comb-like short vertical lines linked horizontally in a row and smaller lozenge grids made with red ochre pigment.[15]

11 The book's psychedelic cover font and publication in a series called 'Bolivia mágica' have not stopped it from being quoted in subsequent, more specialised work, an indication of its pioneering importance.

12 Piso Firme was investigated by SIARB in 1999.

13 SIARB investigations in these areas took place from 1989 to 1993.

14 Riester, *Arqueología*, p. 175.

15 Riester, *Arqueología*, pp. 163–203.

Four hundred kilometres to the west, drawings in the River Mizque area documented by Roy Querejazu Lewis in 2001 show a startling similarity of motifs, perhaps indicating a common sacred sensibility across the pre-Spanish Oriente, not just in the practice of marking rock but also in the character of the marks.[16] In the course of his research, Querejazu Lewis discovered that certain sites retained associative significance: on his second visit to Lakatambo during a period of drought in the late 1980s he found offerings of coca leaves and pebbles in small man-made dimples in the rock which had not been there on his first visit.[17] Calla Maldonado notes that a folk tale current in 2004 around Roboré described *brujos*, witches, meeting in the cave of Juan Miserandino, where there were two walls of rock drawings.[18] The meaning of the marks might have been lost but their presence continued and continues to lend significance to particular sites.

Their meaning might not have been entirely lost, however: a modern example indicates continuity of belief allied to the mark rather than the site. At a site between Santiago de Chiquitos and Roboré, Riester described his elderly Chiquitano[19] guide's analysis of one drawing: 'It seems important here to give the interpretation of an *indígena*. Pedro Masiaré's point of view is of limited value but it is founded in a religious world closer to that of the authors of the rock drawings than an anthropologist's is'.[20] The image that most affected Pedro Masiaré was one of a lozenge grid in which he saw Hichi-tuúrsch, the water *jichi* of Chiquito/Chiquitano belief, in the form of a serpent. This drawing has some lozenge shapes filled in with a smaller lozenge, what might or might not

Figure 2.3. Rock drawing given an ancient interpretation by a 20th-century Chiquitano. (Source: J. Riester, Arqueología y arte rupestre en el oriente boliviano *(Cochabamba and La Paz: Los Amigos del Libro, 1981), p. 177).*

16 R. Querejazu Lewis, *El Arte Rupestre de la Cuenca del Rio Mizque* (Cochabamba: Sociedad de Investigación del Arte Rupestre Boliviano, 2001).

17 Querejazu Lewis, *El Arte Rupestre*, pp. 97–8.

18 Calla Maldonado, 'Cueva', 19.

19 Chiquitanos is the modern name of the Chiquitos, in use since the mid 20th century.

20 Riester, *Arqueología*, p. 184.

be figures with linked arms and a horizontal motif made of much smaller linked diamond shapes (fig. 2.3). [21] Hichi-tuúrsch was 'Ysituu', the water spirit of the Manasicas, documented by Caballero in his *Relación* of 1706. [22] If Masiaré's exegesis did indeed explain the drawing, belief in Hichi-tuúrsch would appear to date from considerably further back in history than the 18th century when Caballero noted it, as well as continuing in the modern day.

Archaeological finds

Riester also carried out small-scale archaeological digs in the 1960s in both the north and south of the territory which became the mission's hunting ground for new members from the 1690s to the expulsion of the Jesuits from South America in 1767. In the far north of the area, at Piso Firme at the junction of the rivers Paraguá and Iténez, and at El Abasto, he found undecorated urns containing fragments of bone with lids in the shape of a bowl, [23] the size of the urns – between 32cm and 65cm tall and between 40cm and 95cm in diameter – indicating that what they were made to contain was just the bones or ashes of the dead rather than an entire body. Cremation was still carried out in the 18th century in this region. In his *Relación historial* of 1726 the missionary Juan Patricio Fernández recorded a ritual surrounding the burning of a body and the putting of ashes into a clay urn by an unnamed, non-evangelised people in the north-west of the Mission area, a sight, he wrote, that so terrified the earlier missionary Lucas Caballero's indigenous escort on an evangelising expedition in the early 1700s that the party fled: 'When night fell the body was carried to the centre of the plaza and after the deceased's friends and relations had embraced the body for the last time it was placed on a pyre. The fire was lit and the corpse was reduced to ash which, with tremendous ceremony and weeping, was gathered and put into a clay urn'. [24] Riester's 20th-century finds were buried between 4cm and 90cm deep and protected by a similar fear on the part of the inhabitants of the area: if an urn was discovered when sinking the uprights for a new house in the 20th century, it was left in place and the house was re-sited. [25]

Inside the urns and nearby, Riester found (as well as fragments of bone) small bowls and jars, plain and decorated. Although the urns were plain, the bowls and jars were in many cases incised with stylised depictions of what

21   Riester, *Arqueología*, p. 183, drawing 48 on p. 178.

22   Caballero, *Relación*, pp. 27–8. Transcription of the Chiquito language (now known as Besɨro) varies according to whether the author was Spanish- or German-speaking.

23   Riester, *Arqueología*, p. 13.

24   J.P. Fernández S.J., *Relación historial de las misiones de indios chiquitos que en el Paraguay tienen los padres de la Compañía de Jesús*, ed. and intro. by D.J. Santamaría (San Salvador de Jujuy: CEIC, Facultad de Humanidades y Ciencias Sociales, Universidad Nacional de Jujuy, 1994 [1726]), p. 160.

25   Riester, *Arqueología*, p. 32.

Figure 2.4. Schematic drawings of incised decoration on three bowls disinterred at Campo Grande (top), El Abasto (middle) and Puerto Rico (bottom). (Source: J. Riester, Arqueología y arte rupestre en el oriente boliviano *(Cochabamba and La Paz: Los Amigos del Libro, 1981), pp. 73 (Campo Grande), 50 (El Abasto), 91 (Puerto Rico)).*

seems to be a face, or two faces, one each side,[26] enclosed by bent arms, hands resting on a putative belly. The faces' mouths are rectangular with stepped zigzag lines radiating from each of the four corners and some pieces show lines which could be tattooed or painted marks on the cheeks.[27] The designs are set into a band encircling the outside of the bowl or jar with the patterning fitting into a space delineated by bands of closely parallel lines or alternating dots which make a zigzag pattern. The patterned areas and the faces they frame have equal importance in the design and both are given space to breathe. They give the impression of a maker sufficiently confident with technology and imagery to change and adapt the model. The patterns on the decorative bands vary: rhomboids in a mesh pattern;[28] curlicues;[29] and upright and slanting

26 Riester, *Arqueología*, p. 43 (Piso Firme).

27 Riester, *Arqueología*, p. 73 (Campo Grande), pp. 50–51 (El Abasto), p. 60 (10 de Abril).

28 Riester, *Arqueología*, p. 73 (Campo Grande, vertical rhomboid mesh); p. 89 (Puerto Rico, horizontal rhomboid mesh).

29 Riester, *Arqueología*, p. 75 (Campo Grande); p. 50 (El Abasto).

variants of the Greek-key pattern (fig. 2.4). [30] The design is incised into the clay, mostly with a solid line, sometimes dotted; sometimes the grooves have been emphasised with white earth or chalk. [31]

During anthropological fieldwork in the same period with the now almost extinct Guarasug'wé people in Campo Grande in the north of the province of Velasco, Riester came across a modern bowl on top of a ten-year-old grave with a roughly incised face-on-decorated-band design similar to his nearby Piso Firme finds and was told by an old Guarasug'wé woman: 'This piece of pottery was to hold food for the dead. We do the face like that because that's the way our ancestors did. Perhaps it's Yanaramai [the supreme being of Guarasug'wé belief] you see on the bowl'.[32] While Riester's Chiquitano guide near Roboré reacted fearfully to what he read as an image of Hichi-tuúrsch, the 20th-century Guarasug'wé maintained a tradition of engraving faces on funerary vessels while acknowledging they might not understand what it meant (that tantalising 'Perhaps' …). Both reports suggest that the image, old or new, understood or not, and however clumsily executed, retained iconographic potency, possibly allied to its site and the material on which it was crafted.

Body marking

Rock and clay were not the only surfaces on which identity was inscribed in the Oriente. As Jesuit chroniclers recorded, before the arrival of missionaries tattooing and body painting were widely practised, not just among the peoples in the mission area but also among those to the north, south, east and west of it. Several of the vessels Riester disinterred in the 1960s were engraved with a 'face' with what could be lines painted or tattooed on the cheeks (Fig. 2.4 shows schematic drawings of three of these).[33] In the pre-Mission period altering the appearance of the body in this area would have identified it with a societal group and have been thought to make it more powerful and lift it into a zone of contact with the supernatural. The modified body was protected against malignant spirits as well as possessing some of their power through the combination of blood-letting, the pigments, the media – spittle, ash and charcoal – used to mix them or to fix the design and the designs themselves.[34] The Chiquitos mission priest Julian Knogler was later to describe

---

30 Riester, *Arqueología*, p. 37 (Piso Firme, bowl); p. 91 (Puerto Rico, bowl); p. 41 (Piso Firme, bipod vessel).

31 Riester, *Arqueología*, pp. 54–5 (El Abasto); p. 91 (Puerto Rico).

32 Riester, *Arqueología*, p. 80.

33 Riester, *Arqueología*, p. 49.

34 R. Karsten, *Civilisation of the South American Indians with Special Reference to Magic and Religion* (London: Dawsons, 1968 [1926]), pp. 188–9.

Figure 2.5. European engraving of Xaraye people in the 16th century. (Source: U. Schmidel, Viaje al Río de la Plata 1534–1554 *(Buenos Aires: Cabaut, 1903 [1567]) and facsimile at http://www.cervantesvirtual.com, Chapter XXXVI [no pag.]).*

the modifications made to the bodies of indigenous peoples in his *Relato*,[35] stating that they were evidence of the 'strange nature' of people of a 'lower level of civilisation'.[36] They were, rather, evidence of the cautious nature of these people, who had, over the course of time, evolved strategies they believed capable of thwarting supernatural caprice.

The only contemporaneous pictorial record of body painting practice in this area following the arrival of the Spanish is an engraving illustrating the Bavarian mercenary Ulrich Schmidl's record of his soldiering in the region in the 16th century. This was not drawn from life by Schmidl but made later by a European artist who gave the two main protagonists a distinctly Teutonic look. It shows extensively painted or tattooed figures in a Xaraye settlement on the upper River Paraguay apparently parleying with European soldiers (fig. 2.5).[37]

---

35 J. Knogler, S.J., *Relato sobre el país y la nación de los chiquitos en las Indias occidentales o América del sud y las misiones en su territorio, redactado para un amigo* [1767–72], in W. Hoffmann, *Las misiones jesuíticas entre los chiquitanos* (Buenos Aires: Fundación para la Educación, la Ciencia y la Cultura, 1979), pp. 121–85.

36 Knogler, *Relato*, pp. 140–41.

37 U. Schmidl, *Viaje al río de la Plata 1534–1554*, trans. by S. Lafone Quevedo (Buenos Aires: Cabaut, 1903 [1567]) and facsimile at: http://www.cervantesvirtual.com, Ch XXXVI (no pag.).

Written accounts of the appearance of ethnic Chiquitos occur in an addendum to the 1689–99 *Carta Anua* of the province of Paraguay[38] and a little later in the Jesuit Francisco Burgés's 1703 *Memorial*.[39] Burgés's words were elaborated on by the aforementioned Fernández in his *Relación historial* 20 years later.[40] Both chroniclers refer to lip and ear piercings but do not mention painting or tattooing. Fifty years later, after the expulsion of the Jesuits, Knogler, however, left another account:

> Some anoint themselves with the earth that is around here, paying particular attention to the head so that it looks as if they are wearing a pointed helmet. Others paint stripes on their bodies using colourants extracted from roots and plants. As the paint is easy to remove, they can adorn themselves with different-coloured designs [subsequently]. The women tattoo themselves on the face with thorns with which they prick a star, a flower, a bird or an animal. They pulverise a little piece of charcoal and rub it into the outline of the design. Once the wounds have healed nothing can rub out the little black marks.[41]

'Around here' was around the mission of Santa Ana de Velasco in the north-east of the Chiquitos mission area, which Knogler founded in 1755 and many of whose inhabitants were ethnically Guaycurú while nominally Chiquito (all members of the Mission were given the identity Chiquito by the Jesuits regardless of their natal ethnicity). The Jesuit missionary-naturalist José Sánchez Labrador, who served among the Guaycurú in a different Mission, left a full description of them in his post-expulsion *El Paraguay Católico*, written in the 1770s. He notes that women were both painted and, from the age of puberty, tattooed – lower-class women with an organ-pipe-like design over the forehead (top image in fig. 2.4) and sometimes from the bottom lip to the chin – while the arms of upper-class women were tattooed from shoulder to wrist with 'squares and triangles'. Fish bones were used to prick the design, which was fixed with ash or plant ink. 'Fortitude during this strange procedure was a sign of bravery', he records.[42] He describes lines drawn over the whole body among Guaycurú men and 'drawings, grid- and lattice-patterns principally on the face'. In earlier times, he notes, men's bodies had been stencilled with

---

38 J. Matienzo, R. Tomichá, I. Combès and C. Page (eds.) (2011) *Chiquitos en las Anuas de la Compañía de Jesús (1691–1767)* (La Paz: Instituto de Misionología, Universidad Católica Boliviana), p. 21.

39 F. Burgés, S.J., *Memorial al rey nuestro señor en su real, y supremo consejo de las Indias sobre las noticias de las misiones de los indios llamados chiquitos* [1703], in R. Tomichá Charupá O.F.M. Conv (ed.), *Francisco Burgés y las Misiones de Chiquitos: El Memorial de 1703 y documentos complementarios* (Cochabamba: Editorial Verbo Divino, 2008), p. 91.

40 Fernández, *Relación historial*, p. 37.

41 Knogler, *Relato*, p. 140.

42 J. Sánchez Labrador, S.J., *El Paraguay Católico*, vol. 1 (Buenos Aires: Coni Hermanos, 1910 [c.1770]), pp. 285–6.

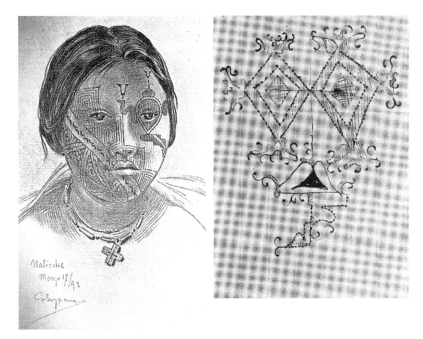

Figure 2.6. Drawing of a painted or tattooed Caduveo (Kadiwéu) woman by Guido Boggiani in 1892 (right); and a drawing on paper made by a Caduveo (Kadiwéu) woman in the 1930s for Claude Lévi-Strauss (left). (Source: C. Lévi-Strauss, Tristes Tropiques, *translated by J. and D. Weightman (London: Jonathan Cape, 1973 [1955]), photograph between pp. 224 and 225).*

'stars' and 'suns' over previous painting in 'colours and black'.[43] These 'stars' and 'suns', like Knogler's 'flower', 'bird' and 'animal', are a European interpretation of motifs which would have carried a different meaning to those on whose skin they were marked.

The missionised Guaycurú 'Chiquitos' were the forebears of the Caduveo [modern spelling: Kadiwéu] on the east side of the upper River Paraguay whose body-marking practice was documented by Claude Lévi-Strauss in the 1930s, when tattooing had been replaced by painting. He noted that old women equipped with a bamboo spatula dipped in the 'juice of the *genipapo*'[44] improvised freehand scrolls and arabesques, spirals, Ss, crosses and Greek-key patterns on the faces of young women, which were halved and sometimes quartered by vertical and horizontal lines.[45] To avoid the expense of 1930s photography, Lévi-Strauss asked the painters to draw on sheets of paper the designs they would normally put on a face, the success of this exercise

43   Sánchez Labrador, *Paraguay*, p. 285.

44   C. Lévi-Strauss, *Tristes Tropiques*, trans. by J. and D. Weightman (London: Jonathan Cape, 1973 [1955]), p. 187. The ink was made from the fruit of Genipa americana, family Rubiaceae.

45   Lévi-Strauss, *Tristes Tropiques*, pp. 193–5.

indicating to him that the marks were not dependent on 'the natural contours of the human face'[46] (fig. 2.6, right).

Far to the south of the mission to the Chiquitos Martín Dobrizhoeffer, in the Jesuit mission to the Abipones in the (now Argentinian) southern Chaco in the mid 18th century, recorded elaborate tattooing practice among the Abipones:

> They mark their faces in various ways, some of which are common to both sexes, others peculiar to women. They prick the skin with a sharp thorn and scatter fresh ashes on the wound. They all wear the form of a cross, impressed on their foreheads and two small lines at the corner of each eye extending towards the ears, besides four transverse lines at the root of the nose between the eyebrows as a national mark.[47]

To the south-east of the mission's catchment area were the people now known as the Ayoréode, the Zamucos of the 18th century, condemned in the *Anuas* for their resistance to evangelisation, but persisting until the 20th century in marking the body with soot and with pigment from a red rock called *kuredé*, scraping the stone with another to grind off grit, which was moistened with saliva.[48]

Arrival of the Jesuits and foundation of the Mission

By the 1690s the colonised Oriente had become a rich hunting ground for both Portuguese and Spanish slavers. Its inhabitants were captured and sold to Brazilian sugar plantation owners or local Spanish *encomenderos*, or were sent to certain death in Potosí. In 1690 Campero de Herrera, patron of the missionary Lucas Caballero, founded a Jesuit college in Tarija to develop a mission to the Chiriguanos to the north of Tarija, a project which was strategically important as the Chiriguano people were resisting the authority of the viceroy in Lima. Campero petitioned successfully for the college to be under the jurisdiction of the Jesuit province of Paraguay rather than that of the province of Peru as attempts to settle the Chiriguanos had begun already from the former's college in Córdoba. The Jesuit priest José de Arce was sent north-east from the newly founded college in 1691 with orders to find a route to the River Paraguay to facilitate the journey from Buenos Aires, where ships from Cádiz carrying new missionaries docked, through Asunción to Santa Cruz de la Sierra and Charcas. However, on his journey, moved by the sight of a group of Chiquito slaves in Santa Cruz, Arce ignored instructions and instead, on the last day of December

---

46 Lévi-Strauss, *Tristes Tropiques*, p. 185.

47 M. Dobrizhoffer, S.J., *An Account of the Abipones: An Equestrian People of Paraguay*, trans. by S. Coleridge, vol. 2 (London: John Murray, 1822), pp. 19–20.

48 M. Bórmida and M. Califano, 'Los Ayoreo del Chaco Boreal', in J. Zanardini (ed.), *Cultura del Pueblo Ayoreo* (Asunción: Centro de Estudios Antropológicos de la Universidad Católica, 2003), pp. 91–3.

1691, founded the mission of San Francisco Xavier de los Piñocas (later San Javier) to the north-east of Santa Cruz.

Over the next 69 years 11 more mission pueblos were established, some abandoned after a couple of years and others merged into the nine pueblos extant at the time of the expulsion in 1767.[49] The province of Peru, which had controlled the three Jesuits sent to Santa Cruz in 1585 to minister to the Spanish and Criollo population and had administered the mission to the Moxos since 1682, claimed that a shortage of missionaries prevented it from taking on responsibility for staffing another mission. Though acknowledged as being part of the Jesuit province of Paraguay in letters from the Jesuit general in Rome, Michele Angelo Tamburini,[50] the mission to the Chiquitos was seen as a means to an end, that is, as a base for investigating the possibility of a river route from Buenos Aires to Charcas – a goal which was not to be achieved until six months before the expulsion of the Jesuits from South America in 1767. It continued to be regarded as less important than the hoped-for mission to the Chiriguanos, as well as being perceived as a kind of poor relation to the earlier, richer mission to the Guaraní to the south, the flagship of the Paraguay missions.

Jesuit prejudice against the Order's missionary wing

'Ministry to the Indians requires little study', Diego Álvarez de Paz, the Jesuit rector of Cuzco, had written in 1601, 'because it is not necessary to tell them about subtle concepts or preach Holy Scripture'.[51] As A. Maldavsky explains, in the 17th century the Jesuit Order in the province of Peru was prejudiced against its missionary wing, a powerful lobby within the Order claiming that ministry to the Spanish was of far greater importance than 'hear[ing] the confessions of four little Indians'.[52] The Treaty of Utrecht (1715) allowed the recruitment of keen young seminarians to the mission to the Chiquitos from the Jesuit

---

49 The foundation of San Javier was followed by that of San Rafael de Velasco in 1695 and San José de Chiquitos in 1697. San Juan Bautista de los Xamarus, which no longer exists, was founded in 1699, as was La Inmaculada Concepción. San Ignacio de los Boococas was founded in 1707 (within two years it had been incorporated into Concepción); San Ignacio de Zamucos in 1719; San Miguel de Velasco in 1722; San Ignacio de Velasco in 1748 after the abandonment of San Ignacio de Zamucos in 1745; Santiago de Chiquitos in 1754; Santa Ana de Velasco in 1755; and Santo Corazón de Jesús de Chiquitos in 1760. Dates vary slightly according to different authors. These dates are taken from G.A.P. Groesbeck, 'Evanescence and Permanence: Toward an Accurate Understanding of the Legacy of the Jesuit Missions of Chiquitos' (2012), viewed in 2013 at www.LaGranChiquitania.com.

50 Matienzo et al. (eds.), *Anuas*, p. 115, n. 157.

51 A. Maldavsky, 'The problematic acquisition of indigenous languages: practices and contentions in missionary specialization in the Jesuit province of Peru (1568–1640)', in J.W. O'Malley et al. (eds.), *The Jesuits II: Cultures, Sciences and the Arts, 1540–1773* (Toronto: University of Toronto Press, 2006), pp. 602–15 (p. 607).

52 Maldavsky, 'Acquisition', p. 608.

provinces of Austria, Bohemia and the Upper and Lower Rhine,[53] which were unaffected by the discrimination between Spanish, Creole and Mestizo Jesuits which had riven the province of Peru a century earlier. However, what still prevailed was what V. Fraser calls the 'hierarchy' of building materials, especially in the case of a building carrying the cultural weight of a church. Marble was regarded as being at the top of a list of ideal building materials and mud and straw were at the bottom.[54] Protecting the souls of the Chiquitos from the devil – and their persons from Spanish and Portuguese slavers, which was what, after all, had inspired Arce – needed to be done in a way which protected this branch of the Order from the intellectual and architectural snobbery of its more urbane members and reinforced its position in the province of Paraguay. How better could this be done than by building dazzling churches?

The construction of the churches which remain today started 50 years after the mission's foundation, once the pueblos were secure from indigenous attacks. The Swiss missionary Martin Schmid, who served in the mission from 1730 to 1767, began the construction of his first church in San Rafael in 1745, together with housing for the priests and the indigenous population of the pueblo. Both stone for building and money were in short supply in the second half of the 18th century; what there was, by then, was plenty of manpower. In addition, among the pre-evangelisation Chiquitos there had existed a practice called *metórr*, whereby a community would rally round to construct a large building, the 'men's house' in a settlement, which was used for the segregation of men and teenage boys and for hospitality. The churches were based on this roof-on-posts local structure, with the addition of walls made of adobe due to the lack of stone; they were roofed at first with *pasto* (dry grass) and later with tiles. Housing – long houses to accommodate ten families – was built in the same way.

Decoration as protection

Fear of criticism by the Order, as much as the desire to beautify the church, led Schmid and his colleagues to attempt to disguise the humble nature of adobe and make the building look as much like a European baroque stone-built church as possible. Architectural features like pilasters and door and window surrounds were moulded and painted, or sometimes just painted on illusionistically, and tiny flakes of mica found in the area around San Rafael, San Miguel and Santa Ana were laid on the interior walls and some furnishings instead of silver or gold leaf. However, as we have seen, the Jesuits were not

53 P. Caraman, *The Lost Paradise: An Account of the Jesuits in Paraguay (1607–1768)* (London: Sidgwick and Jackson, 1975), p. 317.

54 V. Fraser, 'Hierarchies and roles of materials in building and representation', in V. Fraser and G. Brotherston (eds.), *The Other America: Native Artifacts from the New World* (Colchester: University of Essex, 1982), pp. 41–56 (p. 42).

alone in thinking that adornment of a significant site, an important object or a vulnerable entity offered status and protection. Even in the 20th century the church was believed to have a *jichi*, a spirit, lurking behind it, as Fischermann and Quiroaga and Balza Alarcón argue.[55] There is little doubt that by marking the walls of these churches with the ur-patterns of curlicues and lozenges, which recall pre-evangelisation rock drawings and petroglyphs and the incised designs on clay vessels subsequently excavated in the region, the 18th-century members of the missions with a tradition of body marking and modification to the same ends hoped to provide the vulnerable 'body' that was the church building with protection from supernatural damage while continuing their forebears' practice of marking numinous places.

Since UNESCO's recognition of the Chiquitos mission as a World Heritage Site in 1990, the story of the mission has been about wise, kindly Europeans and 'artistic' Chiquitos. This ignores the fact that the Chiquitos had no concept of 'art'. The notion of mark-making on a significant object or site being purely decorative would have been baffling to them. Aesthetics had nothing to do with it:[56] it was a matter of survival – and their part in the process of 'disguising' the churches was fundamental. The building of the churches of Schmid and his colleagues was a collective endeavour. There were rarely more than two priests in a mission and one of them was frequently away on expeditions: searching for the elusive Asunción/Chiquitos/Charcas route which Arce had been charged with forging in 1691; searching for indigenous peoples to evangelise; or chasing groups of them who had decided to leave the mission. In the *Anua* of 1714–20 it is recorded that 'while one group of Fathers runs the temporal and spiritual administration of these pueblos, others are engaged on the apostolic exploration of the vast heathen territory outside it'.[57] Undoubtedly Schmid, the Bohemian Juan José Messner, the Spanish Bartolomé de Mora and whoever designed the other churches rolled up their sleeves, but the bulk of the work of construction and decoration would have been carried out by indigenous members of the mission.

The conservator at the mission to the Chiquitos, María José Diez Gálvez, writes: 'The Chiquitano painters not only decorated the moveable pieces in the

---

55   B. Fischerman and R.M. Quiroaga, 'Viviendo en el bosque', *El Deber*, 21 Sept. 1996, cultural section, pp. 3–5; R. Balza Alarcón, *Tierra, territorio y territorialidad indígena: un estudio antropológico sobre la evolución en las formas de ocupación del espacio del pueblo indígena chiquitano de la ex reducción jesuita de San José* (Santa Cruz: Apoyo para el Campesino-Indígena del Oriente Boliviano, 2001), p. 259.

56   V. Fraser, 'Ixmiquilpan: from European ornament to Mexican pictograph', in S. Diez-Ruiz et al. (eds.), *Altars and Idols: The Life of the Dead in Mexico* (Colchester: University of Essex, 1991), pp. 13–16 (pp. 15–16); E. Wake, *Framing the Sacred: The Indian Churches of Early Colonial Mexico* (Norman, OK: University of Oklahoma Press, 2010), pp. 102, 177. Both make the point about a parallel agenda in relation to early colonial Mexico.

57   Matienzo et al. (eds.), *Anuas*, p. 107.

churches but also the churches themselves'.[58] Their work would undoubtedly have been supervised, perhaps to prevent the risk of the painter 'falling into innocent heterodoxy', as J. Plá notes in relation to indigenous engravers in the Guaraní missions.[59] This was, however, in this author's view never a risk in the Chiquitos mission. A polarised Chiquito cultural history of spirits/humans and a social history of patron/peon has led, as V. Silva points out, to the Other, in the eyes of the modern Chiquitanos she investigates, being an entity which needs to be turned from predator into provider by means of obedience and appeasement.[60] Given a guide sketch drawn directly on the wall by, say, Schmid, or shown an engraving of a cartouche around the depiction of a saint in a book from the priest's library, one must assume the craftsmen would have copied it exactly to the best of their ability.[61] Knogler remarks that 'those who are good at writing copy books we need in a hurry, like catechisms, missals, calendars and pieces of music'.[62] '[T]hose who [were] good at writing' were probably those entrusted with the job of painting the walls – and they would, again, have 'cop[ied]', but the physical and sensory act of painting on a sacred surface was theirs, with all the cultural connotations it carried. As P. Connerton writes, '[t]he world of the percipient, defined in terms of temporal experience, is an organized body of expectations based on recollection'.[63] The artisans would, of course, have been male: the pre-evangelisation women who made decorated clay vessels[64] and pricked freehand designs on the faces of pubertal girls were relegated to the hearth by the missionaries.

No plans of the original Chiquitos churches have been found, nor any sketches of how they were adorned. This reflects what may have been embarrassment at the time about the humble materials involved and that the construction resembled a 'native' building. Martin Schmid was not praised as an architect/builder in the *Cartas Anuas*, only as a musician, which was the

58   M.J. Diez Gálvez, *Los bienes muebles de Chiquitos: Fuentes para el conocimiento de una sociedad* (Madrid: Agencia Española de Cooperación Internacional, 2006), p. 379.

59   J. Plá, 'El grabado en las misiones jesuíticas', *Cuadernos Hispanoamericanos*, 198 (1966): 577–92 (12).

60   V.C. Silva, 'Extracción, dueños y patrones entre los Chiquitanos del Valle del Alto Guaporé, frontera Brasil-Bolivia', in D. Villar and I. Combès (eds.), *Las tierras bajas de Bolivia: miradas históricas y antropológicas* (Santa Cruz de la Sierra: El País Srl., 2012), pp. 297–317 (pp. 316–17).

61   Despite exhaustive research in the mission music archive, not one single piece of music has been found which can categorically be attributed to an indigenous musician. Given the score of a piece of liturgical music to perform, it is difficult to imagine an obedient 18th-century Schmid- or Messner-trained Chiquito musician choosing to improvise a descant or an instrumental part.

62   Knogler, *Relato*, p. 156.

63   P. Connerton, *How Societies Remember* (Cambridge: Cambridge University Press, 1989), p. 6.

64   In the *Relación* Caballero notes fired clay vessels made by Manasica women ringing like metal to the touch (Caballero *Relación*, p. 17).

reason he was sent there. The fact that the churches could not be built of stone or even brick, let alone marble, was glossed over by Schmid in his letters to his family at the time (intended for a sympathetic audience, though no doubt they would have been widely circulated once they reached Switzerland), which note the scene-painting/*trompe l'œil* techniques used to overcome this failing.[65] However, it became apparent in Knogler's *Relato*, written post-expulsion, that it was definitely considered a failing: 'We do what we can to make [the churches] beautiful and respectable', Knogler writes, making the best of what was evidently considered a bad job.[66] The 1762 *Anua local*, which was written for a more general readership than Schmid's letters, mentions 'fine, well-decorated churches'[67] but does not mention they were built of adobe; neither does Esteban Palozzi's *Informe* (1763) to the governor of Santa Cruz, though he writes of 'very good churches, quite well adorned'[68] (Palozzi was then the superior of the mission).

It is arguable that no plan was drawn up because the builders would have found difficulty in understanding it. However, in the mid 18th century, at a time when all educated people were taught to draw, why did Schmid, with his four churches, and those who built churches subsequently during the life of the mission, not, as far as is known, leave a visual record of them – like a little sketch, perhaps, in a letter? A clue lies in an observation by Sánchez Labrador: 'While [the Guaycurú's] female captives collect wood and water . . . and their male captives hunt and fish, the masters are just sitting there drawing lines on their bodies. In this way they spend entire days in total disregard of what needs to be done, amusing themselves with frivolous things while their families suffer'.[69] Sánchez Labrador's judgmental tone is directed as much at the 'idle' Guaycurú as it is at recreational sketching since he also drew, but his work was a record of flora and fauna. It is notable that Sánchez and Florian Paucke (in the mission to the Mocobies in the western Chaco) are the only Jesuit missionaries to this huge region to have left any pictorial record on paper of their time there; and Sánchez's work was not published until about 1770, after the expulsion, while Paucke's frequently comic scenes of mission life did not see the light of day until the 20th century. It is possible that fear of condemnation by Church or political authorities for using humble materials during the period of construction of the mission churches was felt so strongly by Chiquitos mission priests that it was thought safer to commit nothing other than edifying words to paper.

65 Hoffmann, W., *Vida y obra del P. Martin Schmid SJ (1694–1772)* (Buenos Aires: Fundación para la Educación, la Ciencia y la Cultura, 1981), p. 149. This contains Schmid's letters.

66 Knogler, *Relato*, p. 171.

67 Matienzo et al. (eds.), *Anuas*, p. 379.

68 Matienzo et al. (eds.), *Anuas*, p. 407.

69 Sánchez Labrador, *Paraguay*, p. 286.

For the Chiquito church painters, however, 'drawing lines on their bodies' was – culturally and just about within living memory of the painters – very far from a waste of time. Sánchez remarks amusedly on how the Guaycurú expressed concern to him that the Jesuits did not paint their own bodies, thereby laying themselves open to spirit attack.[70] Body painting was frowned upon in the mission to the Chiquitos, though tolerated outside the church building.[71] What can be seen outside and inside the church building is a transmission of the idea of status and protection which transcended cultural differences, or, rather, happened to say the same thing in two mutually incomprehensible languages. Lévi-Strauss's experiments with face-painters and paper in the 1930s showed him that the surface on which considered marks were made did not affect the quality of the mark-making. Extrapolating his conclusion to the mission to the Chiquitos 200 years earlier and 600 kms to the north-west may seem over-imaginative, but I have already drawn parallels between rock markings 400 kms apart and noted the similarity between Dobrizhoeffer's observations on Abipone tattooing practice in the southern Chaco and those of Sánchez Labrador on the eastern side of the upper River Paraguay, 1,000 kms apart. Before the foundation of the mission reductions this was a highly mobile society. Once having thrown in their lot with the Jesuits, the peoples who inhabited the pueblos of the mission to the Chiquitos would surely not have been perplexed by the use of meaningful marks on a flat, white-washed church wall instead of on the contours of the body, an uneven rockface or a curved bowl. Both Fraser and Wake suggest that in an early colonial Mexican context the motifs on church walls would have held a different meaning for the craftsmen who carried out the work from the one they held for the priest who ordered them to be made.[72] The baroque scrolls and geometrics were intended by Schmid and his colleagues to disguise an essentially local style of building and foliate Renaissance adornment was no doubt regarded by them as decorative (fig. 2.7), but in the context of the Chiquitos mission the marks were probably seen by both parties to perform the same function, that of protection.

Colour and iconography

It is easy to compare the colours on the church walls with the similar colours of rock drawing; pigment for the restoration of the churches in the 1970s (and the original work) came from four sites between San Ignacio and Santiago.[73]

70 Sánchez Labrador, *Paraguay*, p. 287.

71 Participants in a 'caza espiritual' painted their faces red for the expedition (Diez Gálvez, *Los buenes muebles*, p. 382, n. 9). Knogler reports that mission members were not allowed to receive communion 'adorned with feathers and painting' (Knogler, *Relato*, pp. 176–7).

72 Fraser, 'Ixmiquilpan', pp. 15–16; Wake, *Framing the Sacred*, pp. 102, 177.

73 C. [K.] Kaifler, 'Tres sitios de pinturas rupestres en la parte occidental de la Serranía San José, Depto. de Santa Cruz, Bolivia', *Boletín*, 7 (1993): 59–95, at p. 59.

Figure 2.7. Wall painting behind a crucifix in the sacristy, San Rafael. (Source: P. Querejazu (ed.) (1995), Las misiones jesuíticas de chiquitos *(La Paz: Fundación BHN, 1995), p. 114, photograph 237 by Plácido Molina).*

The majority of the conserved original motifs on the church walls, as well as the new and restored ones, are in light and dark red, dark grey and yellow-orange, as are the drawings on rock. Comparing the iconography is more challenging. It is difficult for a non-expert to look beyond what appears to be a confusing mass of isolated images on rock randomly placed with no apparent bearing on one another or the site. If, as suggested, these markings were made under the influence of a hallucinogenic drug, their haphazard nature is understandable. It is equally difficult to decipher drawings or petroglyphs on cattle-trodden or overgrown *lajas* [flat rocks]. However, two frequently occurring motifs appear in the churches. One is a circle with radiating spokes. Riester found one on a *laja* at Yororobá near Santiago. 'Here we have a circle 105cm in diameter facing east with lines radiating from the centre', he writes, continuing, 'without doubt we are dealing with a solar symbol'.[74] Perhaps that is so, in which case the thinking behind the painting of the ceiling of the sacristy at San Miguel by the professional artist living illicitly in the mission, Antonio Rojas, with a depiction of a red sunburst bordered with grey clouds with cherubim peeping out would fit with indigenous as well as European graphic practice, as would the florid sunburst-framed windows in the façades of San Rafael, San Javier

74 Riester, *Arqueología*, pp. 194–8.

Figure 2.8 View of San Miguel showing the lozenge-shaped mouldings on the doors. (Source: P. Querejazu (ed.), Las misiones jesuíticas de chiquitos *(La Paz: Fundación BHN, 1995), p. 60, photograph 123 by Plácido Molina).*

and Concepción (and the painting of a shining sun, only visible from the choir loft, above the inside of San Javier's façade window). However, indigenous people did not 'do' art for art's sake – and, as noted above, there is the strong probability that the 'stars' tattooed on the faces chronicled by Knogler and the 'stars' and 'suns' stencilled onto the Guaycurúes recorded by Sánchez Labrador were only described as such because that is what they looked like to a European. The radial rock drawing looks like a sun because that is how Europeans learn to draw the sun as infants. However, it is not what the sun looks like: as we squint at the sun it looks like a ball. On rock, radial lines might have indicated going or coming; many of the inhabitants of this region were nomadic or seasonally nomadic. Alternatively, the image might have some connection with the way hammocks were slung in a Chiquito house and, consequently, represent a period of stasis after seasonal wandering or a long hunting expedition: 'In their houses', Knogler writes, 'they sink a post deep into the earth in the middle of the house and all tie one end of their hammocks to it; when the other end is fastened to the wall the whole forms the shape of a wheel with the hammocks as spokes'.[75]

The other image is a rhomboid shape. Rhomboids, slanting grids and lattices all over Oriente rock sites indicate that repeating geometric motifs may have had cultic meaning at the time they were drawn, the repetition perhaps being as meaningful as the shape. A recurring feature of mission churches are

75 Knogler, *Relato*, p. 144.

the rhomboidal mouldings on doors (fig. 2.8) and the friezes of lozenge shapes along walkways.

Ekhart Kühne, the architect who worked on the restoration with the then Jesuit Hans Roth – who has been semi-sanctified among modern Chiquitano – noted the use of painted geometric motifs stencilled onto walls in the churches of Martin Schmid, the duplication of motifs articulating the purpose of different spaces within the building while maintaining artistic unity.[76] Again, the repetition was as meaningful as the shape.

Performing the numinous – sacraments, souls and shamans

Siting a mission church called for practical considerations to be taken into account – flat land, the proximity of suitable trees to be felled, orientation (though this was flexible and may have had more to do with indigenous than missionary sensibilities) – and the criteria for the site of a mission pueblo were dictated by Jesuit writ. However, once erected, painted and consecrated, well into the lifespan of the mission, I suggest the actual physical building of a church in the mission to the Chiquitos represented the sacred to members of each pueblo in the same way that a marked rock site did. A heightened sense of reality, induced by emotion rather than drugs, was there to be felt by priest and congregation – and it would perhaps not have escaped the attention of a mission priest's acolytes that he partook of a 'dark liquid' as part of the rite, as the *maponos* had in the past. In his *Relación historial* Fernández gives a lurid account of the night-time processions of the Thursday of Holy Week:

> After listening to a fervent homily on the passion of Christ they dress
> themselves in penitential garments and, imitating the trials of the
> Redeemer, some carry heavy crosses on their backs while others wear
> crowns of sharp thorns; some, with hands tied behind the back, are
> dragged along the ground; some stay upright holding out their arms in the
> form of a cross; some flagellate themselves with vicious whips.[77]

Missionary hyperbole in letters and in the *Anuas* impressed a European readership. In a letter to a fellow Jesuit dated 10 October 1744 Martin Schmid wrote dramatically: 'The result of our efforts to govern these souls is astonishing: the mats that cover the floor of the church are soaked with the tears of the penitents and the whole church resounds with their sighs. The homily is interrupted several times by the strenuous bouts of self-flagellation our listeners inflict upon themselves'.[78] Unsurprisingly, given the simplified version of Catholicism vouchsafed to them, the ritual surrounding the sacraments appears to have been at least as important to mission members as

---

76 E. Kühne, *Die Missionskirchen von Chiquitos im Tiefland von Bolivien: Bau und Restaurierung der Kirchen von Martin Schmid (1694–1772)* (doctoral thesis, ETH, Zurich, 2008), p. 148.

77 Fernández, *Relación historial*, p. 75.

78 M. Schmid, S.J., letter, 10 Oct. 1744, in Hoffmann, *Vida y obra del P. Martin Schmid*, p. 141.

the divine grace the latter might bestow. The Eucharist was received between one and four times each year as part of a rigidly choreographed mass policed by indigenous marshals who escorted the barefoot, white-clad communicants to the altar rail.[79] The journey to an invalid made by a priest with the viaticum was especially revered. The unexpected recovery of some of those who received the sacrament could only have added to its reputation as a magical remedy for illness in indigenous eyes. This was an inversion of the experience of early missionaries, who found that, as they were only able to baptise an unshriven adult on the point of death, this sacrament was regarded as so dangerous that infants would be hidden away from an evangelising party to protect them from the same fate. So popular was the viaticum, however, that it was recorded in the *Anua* covering the period from 1735 to 1742 that priests had learnt to check whether a visit to a sick mission member was in fact needed before embarking on an unnecessary journey.[80] An *Epígrafe* attached to the same *Anua*, though possibly exaggerated, records a nocturnal journey to an invalid's house in San José accompanied by 'all the inhabitants of the pueblo' along streets lit by 200 candles and strewn with flowers.[81] It is possible to imagine that the group hysteria Schmid describes, if it really was the case, was induced by the size and splendour of the church, but it might have been aided by an atavistic collective memory of liturgical ritual directed by an authoritarian figure in a site with supernatural associations. As Connerton writes, 'images of the past and recollected knowledge of the past are conveyed and sustained by (more or less) ritual performances'.[82]

The authoritarian figure of the shaman and his role as go-between were fundamental to the process of engagement with the supernatural undergone by the Manasica people, as Caballero reported in 1706. The role of a Jesuit mission priest was identical. J.W. O'Malley writes of the Order's use of the word 'soul': 'By "soul" Jesuits meant the whole person. Thus they could help souls in a number of ways, for instance by providing food for the body or learning for the mind ... They sought to be mediators of an immediate experience of God that would lead to an inner change of heart or a deepening of religious sensibilities already present'.[83] In a passage in his 1706 *Relación* Caballero describes an encounter between *mapono* and deity: '[S]peaking to the illustrious presence, the shamans and witch-doctors say to him "You are welcome, Father Tata" – that is what they call him'. He then adds: 'and they also used to call me by the

---

79 Knogler, *Relato*, p. 174.

80 Matienzo et al. (eds.), *Anuas*, pp. 292–3.

81 Matienzo et al. (eds.), *Anuas*, p. 216.

82 Connerton, *How Societies Remember*, p. 40.

83 J.W. O'Malley, S.J., *The First Jesuits* (Cambridge, MA: Harvard University Press, 1993), quoted in M. Zampelli, '"*Lascivi spettacoli*": Jesuits and theatre (from the underside)', in J.W. O'Malley et al. (eds.), *The Jesuits II: Cultures, Sciences and the Arts, 1540–1773* (Toronto: University of Toronto Press, 2006), pp. 550–71 (p. 553).

same name'.[84] Caballero lists the various duties of the *mapono*: 'the priest, the wizard, the chaplain of the gods, the doctor of law, and the person to whom all the people of the village bring their doubts and problems'.[85] Thirty-eight years later Schmid, in a letter to his brother dated 17 October 1744, consciously or unconsciously referencing Caballero's words, refers to mission priests as 'councillors and judges' before adding a list of practical skills crucial to the material well-being of 'souls':

> Thus [the priests] are councillors and judges, doctors and surgeons;
> they are builders, carpenters and cabinetmakers; they are blacksmiths,
> locksmiths, tailors, cobblers, millers, bakers, cooks, shepherds, gardeners,
> painters, wood-carvers, lathe-operators, coachbuilders, brickmakers,
> potters, weavers, tanners, candlemakers, coppersmiths, tinsmiths and
> whatever else is required of an artisan nature in an ordered community.[86]

How could newly reduced indigenous people fed with rudimentary Catholicism and the children and grandchildren later reared on this Catholicism combined with stories of pre-evangelisation life (even if they were dutifully portrayed as the 'bad old days' rather than the 'good old days') have failed to associate the office of mission priest with that of shaman? If, in the collective memory, sites with supernatural significance were associated with shamans, hallucinogens and drawing, how very natural it must have seemed to mission members that a Jesuit priest-architect empowered by the daily consumption of a 'dark liquid' which only he could drink should either pick up a chalk or a paintbrush himself or order others to do so? This being the case, how equally natural it must have seemed that what should be obediently drawn by indigenous craftsmen on the church walls should be the curves and rhomboids which had delineated supernatural experiences undergone by pre-mission shamans?

The Jesuit way – 'modus noster procedendi'

In 1566 the Society of Jesus had won the consent of Philip II of Spain to send missionaries to the Americas and the first group of seven priests arrived in Lima two years later. By 1591 seven colleges had been founded in Peru with the aim of educating the young, ministering to the Spanish and indigenous populations of the cities in which they had been established and providing a base for relatively local attempts at evangelisation. The Jesuits did not see their function as administering mission pueblos and, indeed, in some circles of the Order, as explained above, the missionary role was regarded as less worthy than that

---

84 Caballero, *Relación*, p. 23.

85 Caballero, *Relación*, p. 31.

86 M. Schmid, S.J., quoted in B. Krekeler, *Historia de los chiquitanos* (Santa Cruz de la Sierra: Apoyo para el Campesino-Indígena del Oriente Boliviano, 1993), p.138. The date of this letter appears to be the same as the date of the letter from Schmid to a fellow Jesuit referred to above. This is not impossible, though it seems unlikely. The origin of the possible error cannot be traced.

of preaching to the Spanish. However, in 1576 the then viceroy, Francisco de Toledo, had given the Order the task of governing the Dominican-established reduction of Juli in Peru. As latecomers to the challenge of converting indigenous peoples in the Americas and with a methodology of conversion based on the acquisition of indigenous languages initiated by Juan de Atienza, the first Jesuit provincial of Peru, and put into practice at Juli, where priests were encouraged to learn Aymara (see chapter 8), the Jesuits saw themselves as different from other orders. 'Modus noster procedendi', the Ignatian 'way of doing things', distinguished 17th- and 18th-century Jesuit missions from those of other orders, as did the Order's self-perceived answerability only to the king of Spain, rather than to the secular Church and local political authority. Jesuit missions, therefore, have more in common with each other than they do with missions of other orders. Priests corresponded with priests in other missions, they had sometimes served in other missions, they had read the same books, they inherited the ethos of Juli and they absorbed the edifying, extravagant eulogies of deceased priests, especially those who had died while attempting to evangelise. In letters home and in the *Cartas Anuas* they praised their charges' quick acquisition of skills useful in mission life – musicianship, the ability to copy and obedience – and denigrated the shocking practices which the imposition of Catholicism had supposedly made obsolete. Principal among these were cannibalism (for which there is no evidence at all but which could be counted on to appall readers of the *Anuas*),[87] polygamy[88] and drunkenness.[89] Priests were part of a gentleman-scholar culture to which indigenous people could never be privy.

87 References to cannibalism abound in the *Cartas anuas*. See Matienzo et al. (eds.), *Anuas*, pp. 45, 50, 133, 167, 217, 343. In some cases the instances referred to are hearsay and could equally well relate to evidence of the practice of endocannibalism, in which a corpse is disinterred and either the whole of what remains is burnt (Karsten, *Civilisation*, p. 434: 'among Amazon tribes'); or the flesh is scraped off the bones and the bones are burnt (Karsten, *Civilisation,* p. 433: 'among the Indians of north-west Brazil'). Fernández mentions the discovery of piles of bones and pieces of fresh meat in a settlement deserted in a hurry by the Cozoca people as an evangelising party from San Javier approached (*Relación historial*, p. 206). This could be evidence of a variant of endocannibalism which involves the flesh being removed from the bones immediately after death, before the bones are painted and covered with feathers before burial (Karsten, *Civilisation*, p. 32: 'among the Bororo'). Other cases in the *Anuas* report information delivered to a mission priest by a member of a tribal group with a grudge against another group, who clearly understood how this information could be used to his advantage against an enemy.

88 Before evangelisation Chiquito *caciques* would have two or three wives, sometimes sisters. Fernández explains this was because one wife was not able to make sufficient *chicha* (fermented maize beer) to satisfy the numbers the *cacique* was obliged to entertain by virtue of his office (Fernández, *Relación historial*, p. 37).

89 Fernández reports that missionary priests did everything they could from the beginning to stamp out drunkenness, provoking the Chiquito to 'reach furiously for their clubs and arrows' (Fernández, *Relación historial*, p. 39), but Knogler, in his much later *Relato*, was still forced to note that 'this wretched drink was a constant worry to us' (Knogler, *Relato*, p. 149).

The quasi-sanctity attributed to individual priests in the early days and after the expulsion, the political imperative, the role of the Jesuit colleges, the simultaneous power and peril of the sacraments as understood by indigenous mission members, the use of a *lengua general*, the relegation of women to the home and the existence of a body of Jesuit poetry which explains Caballero's rarely, if ever, referenced 'Sátyra contra los dioses de los manasicas': all are mentioned in this book – and all are reflected in the mission to the Chiquitos.

'Modus illium procedendi' – the indigenous way

It can look as if there was only one agenda at work in the mission, that of the Jesuit juggernaut. However, once historical, art-historical and ethnological sources are juxtaposed, the churches of the mission to the Chiquitos can be seen to offer visual evidence for a more nuanced story. Before the compilation of a dictionary of the Gorgotoqui language by the Jesuit priest Andrés Ortiz, seconded to Santa Cruz de la Sierra in the 16th century, and the transcription of Chiquito in the 18th century by Mission priests, the spoken languages of the Oriente were unwritten. Marks on rock and clay are difficult for modern eyes to read but they survive as a record that a language of distinction and belief existed and was expressed iconographically in the Oriente. Adorned rock sites can be posited as sacred places, as texts of a supernatural experience and as palimpsests of indigenous identity, due to the over-drawing visible at some sites. After evangelisation, a mission church performed the same function for indigenous mission members. In its architecture, based on an indigenous building, in its cosmetic baroque embellishment employing a fusion of European decorative imagery and indigenous memory, even perhaps in its jutting porch echoing the overhangs which have protected adorned rock from the elements for millennia, a complex cultural multi-layering can be seen. If the Chiquitano of the late 20th century adhered to old beliefs, as modern studies show they did, it is reasonable to assume that, as they were the ones to stencil rhomboids onto the cloister walls of mission church complexes originally, the Chiquitos of the 18th-century mission did so as well. The house of the new God in a mission pueblo, combining the idea of a 'body' in need of protection with being a supernatural site to be marked under the auspices of an authority figure, was embellished in a way which involved significant inscription of narrative and identity by means which simultaneously strengthened and defended it. The Jesuits adopted an explicit programme of disguise while the Chiquitos related an implicit narrative of existence and belief: '*Modus illium procedendi*' – *their* way of doing things.

Bibliography

Balza Alarcón, R. (2001) *Tierra, territorio y territorialidad indígena: un estudio antropólogico sobre la evolución en las formas de ocupación del espacio del pueblo indígena chiquitano de la ex reducción jesuita de San José* (Santa Cruz de la Sierra: Apoyo para el Campesino-Indígena del Oriente Boliviano).

Bórmida, M. and M. Califano (2003) 'Los ayoreo del Chaco boreal', in J. Zanardini (ed.), *Cultura del pueblo ayoreo* (Asunción: Centro de Estudios Antropológicos de la Universidad Católica, Biblioteca paraguaya de antropología), pp. 91–3.

Brotherston, G. (1979) *Image of the New World: The American Continent Portrayed in Native Texts* (London: Thames and Hudson).

Burgés, F., S.J. (2008) *Memorial al Rey Nuestro Señor en su Real, y Supremo Consejo de las Indias sobre las Noticias de las Misiones de los Indios llamados Chiquitos* [1703], in *Francisco Burgés y las Misiones de Chiquitos: El Memorial de 1703 y documentos complementarios*, ed. by T. Tomichá Charupá, O.F.M. Conv. (Cochabamba: Editorial Verbo Divino).

Caballero, L., S.J. (1933 [1706]) *Relación de las costumbres y religión de los indios manasicas*, ed. by M. Serrano y Sanz (Madrid: Librería General de Victoriano Suárez).

— (2011) 'Diario de la cuarta misión a los manasicas y paunacas, 1707', in J. Matienzo, R. Tomichá, I. Combès and C. Page (eds.),*Chiquitos en las Anuas de la Compañía de Jesús (1691–1767)* (La Paz: Instituto de Misionología, Universidad Católica Boliviana), pp. 46–83.

Calla Maldonado, S. (2007) 'Documentación de las pinturas de la Cueva de Juan Miserandino, Reserva Municipal del Valle de Tucuvaca, Depto. de Santa Cruz', *Boletín*, 21: 17–37.

Caraman, P. (1975) *The Lost Paradise: An Account of the Jesuits in Paraguay (1607–1768)* (London: Sidgwick and Jackson).

Connerton, P. (1989) *How Societies Remember* (Cambridge: Cambridge University Press).

Diez Gálvez, M.J. (2006) *Los bienes muebles de chiquitos: Fuentes para el conocimiento de una sociedad* (Madrid: Agencia Española de Cooperación Internacional).

Diez-Ruiz, S. et al. (eds.) (1991) *Altars and Idols: The Life of the Dead in Mexico* (Colchester: University of Essex).

Dobrizhoffer, M., S.J. (1822) *An Account of the Abipones: An Equestrian People of Paraguay*, trans. by Sara Coleridge, vol. 2 (London: John Murray).

Fernández, J.P., S.J. (1994 [1726]) *Relación historial de las misiones de indios chiquitos que en el Paraguay tienen los padres de la Compañía de Jesús*, edited and introduced by D.J. Santamaría (San Salvador de Jujuy: CEIC,

Facultad de Humanidades y Ciencias Sociales, Universidad Nacional de Jujuy).

Fischerman, B. and R.M. Quiroaga (1996) "Viviendo en el bosque', *El Deber*, 21 Sept. (cultural section), pp. 3–5.

Fraser, V. (1982) 'Hierarchies and roles of materials in building and representation', in V. Fraser and G. Brotherston (eds.), *The Other America: Native Artifacts from the New World* (Colchester: University of Essex), pp. 41–56.

— (1991) 'Ixmiquilpan: from European ornament to Mexican pictograph', in S. Diez-Ruiz et al. (eds.), *Altars and Idols: The Life of the Dead in Mexico* (Colchester: University of Essex), pp. 13–16.

Fraser, V. and G. Brotherston (eds.) (1982) *The Other America: Native Artifacts from the New World* (Colchester: University of Essex).

Groesbeck, G.A.P. (2012) 'Evanescence and permanence: toward an accurate understanding of the legacy of the Jesuit missions of Chiquitos', http://www.LaGranChiquitania.com [accessed 2013].

Hoffmann, W. (1979) *Las misiones jesuíticas entre los chiquitanos* (Buenos Aires: Fundación para la Educación, la Ciencia y la Cultura).

— (1981) *Vida y obra del P. Martin Schmid SJ (1694–1772)* (Buenos Aires: Fundación para la Educación, la Ciencia y la Cultura).

Ibarra Grasso, D.E. and R. Querejazu Lewis (1986) *30,000 años de prehistoria en Bolivia* (La Paz and Cochabamba: Los Amigos del Libro).

Kaifler, C. (1993) 'Tres sitios de pinturas rupestres en la parte occidental de la Serranía San José, Depto. de Santa Cruz, Bolivia', *Boletín*, 7: 59–95.

Karsten, R. (1968 [1926]) *Civilisation of the South American Indians with Special Reference to Magic and Religion* (London: Dawsons).

Knogler, J., S.J. (1979) *Relato sobre el país y la nación de los chiquitos en las Indias occidentales o América del sud y las misiones en su territorio, redactado para un amigo* [1767–72], in W. Hoffmann (ed.), *Las misiones jesuíticas entre los chiquitanos* (Buenos Aires: Fundación para la Educación, la Ciencia y la Cultura, 1979), pp. 121–85.

Krekeler, B. (1993) *Historia de los chiquitanos* (Santa Cruz de la Sierra: Apoyo para el Campesino-Indígena del Oriente Boliviano).

Kühne, E. (2008) *Die Missionskirchen von Chiquitos im Tiefland von Bolivien: Bau und Restaurierung der Kirchen von Martin Schmid (1694–1772)* (doctoral thesis, ETH, Zurich).

Lévi-Strauss, C. (1973 [1955]) *Tristes Tropiques*, trans. by J. and D. Weightman (London: Jonathan Cape).

Maldavsky, A. (2006) 'The problematic acquisition of indigenous languages: practices and contentions in missionary specialization in the Jesuit province of Peru (1568–1640)', in J.W. O'Malley, G.A. Bailey, S.J. Harris and T.F. Kennedy (eds.), *The Jesuits II: Cultures, Sciences and the Arts, 1540–1773* (Toronto: University of Toronto Press), pp. 602–15.

Matienzo, J., R. Tomichá, I. Combès and C. Page (eds.) (2011) *Chiquitos en las Anuas de la Compañía de Jesús (1691–1767)* (La Paz: Instituto de Misionología, Universidad Católica Boliviana).

O'Malley, J.W., S.J., G.A. Bailey, S.J. Harris and T.F. Kennedy (eds.) (2006) *The Jesuits II: Cultures, Sciences and the Arts, 1540–1773* (Toronto: University of Toronto Press).

Plá, J. (1966) 'El grabado en las misiones jesuíticas', *Cuadernos Hispanoamericanos*, 198: 577–92.

Querejazu Lewis, R. (2001) *El arte rupestre de la cuenca del río Mizque* (Cochabamba: Sociedad de Investigación del Arte Rupestre Boliviano).

Riester, J. (1981) *Arqueología y arte rupestre en el oriente boliviano* (Cochabamba and La Paz: Editorial Los Amigos del Libro).

Sánchez Labrador, J., S.J. (1910 [c.1770]) *El Paraguay Católico*, vol. 1 (Buenos Aires: Imprenta de Coni Hermanos).

Schmid, M., S.J. (1981) 'Letters', in W. Hoffmann (ed.), *Vida y obra del P. Martin Schmid SJ (1694–1772)* (Buenos Aires: Fundación para la Educación, la Ciencia y la Cultura, 1981).

Schmidl, U. (1903 [1567]) *Viaje al río de la Plata 1534–1554*, trans. by S. Lafone Quevedo (Buenos Aires: Cabaut).

Silva, V.C. (2012) 'Extracción, dueños y patrones entre los chiquitanos del valle del Alto Guaporé, frontera Brasil-Bolivia', in D. Villar and I. Combès (eds.), *Las tierras bajas de Bolivia: Miradas históricas y antropológicas* (Santa Cruz de la Sierra: Editorial El País Srl.), pp. 297–317.

Tomichá Charupá, R. and O.F.M. Conv (ed.) (2008) *Francisco Burgés y las misiones de chiquitos: El Memorial de 1703 y documentos complementarios* (Cochabamba: Editorial Verbo Divino).

Villar, D. and I. Combès (eds.) (2012) *Las tierras bajas de Bolivia: Miradas históricas y antropológicas* (Santa Cruz de la Sierra: Editorial El País Srl.).

Wake, E. (2010) *Framing the Sacred: The Indian Churches of Early Colonial Mexico* (Norman, OK: University of Oklahoma Press).

Zampelli, M. (2006) '"*Lascivi spettacoli*": Jesuits and Theatre (from the Underside)', in J.W. O'Malley, G.A. Bailey, S.J. Harris and T.F. Kennedy (eds.), *The Jesuits II: Cultures, Sciences and the Arts, 1540–1773* (Toronto: University of Toronto Press), pp. 550–71.

Zanardini, J. (ed.) (2003) *Cultura del pueblo ayoreo* (Asunción: Centro de Estudios Antropológicos de la Universidad Católica, Biblioteca paraguaya de antropología).

3. The materiality of cultural encounters in the *Treinta Pueblos de las Misiones*

Clarissa Sanfelice Rahmeier

Cultural encounters occur in our everyday lives at a speed and frequency which are difficult to measure. Such encounters involve contemplation and confrontation. Moreover, they involve negotiation. Responses to cultural encounters vary a great deal and depend upon a number of factors, such as the place where they happen, the social and historical context in which they occur and the material and psychological conditions which they involve. Cultural encounters therefore involve people and things. As cultural beings we come across these kinds of encounter in almost all spheres of our lives, especially in the type of society in which we are immersed today. Although part of our everyday lives, and perhaps because of that, they are usually taken for granted. In colonial situations, however, cultural encounters are more evident. In the colonisation of Latin America they were striking, very visible and tangible. The various responses to these encounters are evident in the written records produced at the time of colonisation and in the material culture which originated from them, as well as in the social and cultural traces which form contemporary Latin America.

This chapter will address the materiality of cultural encounters in the Jesuit missions of South America, where missionaries and the indigenous Guaraní built 'some of the largest and most prosperous missionary complexes in the New World'.[1] Functioning as an arm of the colonial enterprise, the missions represented the crown and the Catholic Church, institutions which intermingled at several points during the course of colonialism. In particular, the chapter will focus on the Jesuit missions established in the 17th and 18th centuries in the River Plate basin, in an area which today is part of Brazil, Paraguay and Argentina. More than thirty missions were founded in this region, forming a belt of settlements, or reductions, known as the *Treinta Pueblos* or thirty pueblos of Paraguay. These missions resulted from the interaction between a handful of priests and thousands of Guaraní. More than 140,000 Indians lived

---

1   B. Ganson, *The Guaraní under Spanish Rule in the Río de la Plata* (Stanford, CA: Stanford University Press, 2013), p. 52.

C. Sanfelice Rahmeier, 'The materiality of cultural encounters in the *Treinta Pueblos de las Misiones*', in L.A. Newson (ed.), *Cultural Worlds of the Jesuits in Colonial Latin America* (London: Institute of Latin American Studies, 2020), pp. 69–87. License: CC-BY-NC-ND 2.0.

in reductions around the Paraná and Uruguay Rivers in 1732, the year the missions' total population reached its highest number.[2] Nearly two hundred years of interaction between the Guaraní and the Jesuits allowed the emergence of a society and culture which are unique in the history of colonialism and possibly in the history of humankind. Instead of producing a narrative of this cultural encounter through its material manifestations, this chapter discusses how the materiality of the missions, particularly the making of pottery, can be interpreted in order to inform us about colonial history, in both empirical and theoretical terms.

The materiality of cultural encounters which contributed to and resulted from the process of introducing civilisation and evangelisation into indigenous communities in Latin America is not uniform, but it is possible to identify some common traces which indicate the level of reception of European practices and values by the Guaraní. In the particular context of the missions, the introduction of new artefacts and techniques, the building of houses, churches and cemeteries combined with the social use of these elements, among many others, contributed to creating choreographies of civilisation which represented as well as reproduced a more comprehensive embodiment of colonialism. The bodies which performed these choreographies objectified some new rules and desired mentalities, reproducing, at different levels and to different degrees, an educated interaction with materiality which helped to communicate the missionary purpose.

Among the many new material forms introduced by the Jesuits in the reductions was the potter's wheel. Designed for producing all sorts of clay objects, this machine, in the context of the missions, helped to reconfigure the relationship between individuals and the products they made and allowed a reassessment of the meaning and reorganisation of labour and time. The production of pottery artefacts through the use of the wheel required a specific set of body movements in accordance with the new structure of thought which was being implemented in the missions. We need to consider, in this context, the importance the body and the senses had for the Guaraní people: for them, the senses and the body constituted the starting point of the process of perceiving, knowing and thinking, an understanding which probably did not conceive of the intellectual and the sensorial dimensions of experience as two contradictory ends.[3]

New techniques associated with the body can be seen, in this sense, as part of the introduction, among the Guaraní, of a civilising project, being at the same time the result of this project as well as a means for its reproduction.[4]

2   Ibid., pp. 52–3.

3   G. Chamorro, 'Historia del Cuerpo Durante la "Conquista Espiritual"', in *Fronteiras*, 10 (2008): 277–99 (297).

4   M. Mauss, 'Techniques of the body', in M. Fraser and M. Greco (eds.), *The Body: A Reader* (London and New York: Routledge, 2005), pp. 73–7.

Putting 'new demands on the bodies and brains of people making, using and appreciating objects',[5] new materials such as the potter's wheel, as well as all the other new artefacts and buildings which structured the missionary context, contributed to shaping the experience of cultural contact in colonial Latin America.

Cultural encounters in the *Treinta Pueblos de las Misiones*

The *Treinta Pueblos* of Paraguay were established in an active frontier region where political delimitations were not clear. The area was part of the Spanish possessions according to the Treaty of Tordesillas (1494), but was claimed by Portugal throughout the 18th century. Circa 1570 the Society of Jesus arrived in Spanish America and, coming later than other religious orders, they worked on frontiers 'where hardly any other Europeans, clerical or lay, would care or dare to go'.[6]

Antonio Ruiz de Montoya, a missionary from Lima who had participated in the establishment of the missions at the beginning of the 17th century, estimated that no fewer than 95,000 natives were baptised in Paraguay between 1612 and 1626.[7] Letters written by the Jesuits to their superiors in Europe describe the success of the conversions, providing a positive view upon which many subsequent interpretations have been based.[8] These letters contributed, for instance, to the construction, in Europe, of the idea of the missions as places where indigenous populations lived in contented poverty, as suggested by the idyllic account of Ludovico Muratori in the first half of the 18th century, *Il Cristianesimo felice nelle missione de padri della Compagnia de Gesù nel Paraguai*.[9]

The positive views of the Jesuit work in the *Treinta Pueblos* conflicts with a more critical literature, which sees the mission as a project through which indigenous populations were alienated from their cultural origins, the latter being annihilated under the rule of the priests and the Spanish crown. We find, however, in the material culture of the missions grounds for a more

---

5   C. Gosden, 'Social ontologies', *Philosophical Transactions of the Royal Society B: Biological Sciences*, 363 (2008): 2003–10.

6   P. Bakewell and J. Holler, *A History of Latin America* (Chichester: Wiley-Blackwell, 2010), pp. 319–20.

7   D. Brading, *The First America: The Spanish Monarchy, Creole Patriots and the Liberal State, 1492–1867F* (Cambridge: Cambridge University Press, 1991), p. 173.

8   In the 18th century the *Lettres édifiantes et curieuses*, an editorial enterprise created by the Jesuits to give an account of their missionary work, constituted, alongside a few travellers' diaries, the main source for information about the life in the missions. Based on these letters, Muratori wrote his own interpretation of the missions, classifying them as an example of happy Christianity. For an interpretation of Muratori's publications on the missions see R. Morais, 'L.A. Muratori e o cristianismo feliz na missão dos padres da Companhia de Jesus no Paraguai' (unpublished master's thesis, Universidade Federal Fluminense, 2006).

9   L. Muratori, *Il Cristianesimo felice nelle missione de padri della Compagnia de Gesù nel Paraguai* (Venice: Giambatista Pasquali, 1743).

complex interpretation of the encounter between the Guaraní and Europeans – one which perceives the phenomenon of the missions in Spanish America as a process of transculturation effected by both the Guaraní and the Jesuits, although not always equally – from which a new cultural complex emerged.

This is not a case of categorising the result of contact as a melting pot, but of acknowledging that colonial situations can easily be (and frequently are) reduced to simplistic and, in the case of the Jesuit experience in Latin America, misleading interpretations. As argued by P. Cornell and F. Fahlander, 'the encounter is seldom a matter of simple processes of local acculturation or assimilation of the way of life in the core areas of an expanding colonial regime. Rather, confrontation with differing social practice, ideologies and differing material worlds often lead to unforeseen results, far beyond the intentions of the involved individuals'.[10]

The term *transculturation*, coined by Fernando Ortiz in the 1940s,[11] evokes the idea of entanglement, simultaneity and coexistence. Although criticised for having covered over racial conflicts in Cuba through a concept which accommodates crucial disparities,[12] Ortiz's contribution helped to stress the idea of cultural integration instead of cultural obliteration in colonial situations. Since its proposition, the term *transculturation* has been re-contextualised and employed in this way: it does not disregard friction and conflict, but stresses the outcomes of a cultural encounter in terms of the contributions each group brings to the new cultural complex which arises from it.

'Transculturation' is a term which has been employed in studies about the Paraguay reductions in recent decades,[13] as it points towards a phenomenon in which both the Guaraní and Europeans contributed to the development of a new sociocultural complex. Because of its stress on coexistence and cultural complementarity, without disregarding power relations, 'transculturation' has been preferred to concepts such as genocide, acculturation and hybridity, which are usually (although with some dispute) applied to evoke the idea of cultural annihilation.

---

10   P. Cornell and F. Fahlander, 'Encounters – materialities – confrontations: an introduction', in P. Cornell and F. Fahlander (eds.), *Encounters, Materialities, Confrontations: Archaeologies of Social Space and Interaction* (Newcastle: Cambridge Scholar Press, 2007), pp. 1–14 (p. 4).

11   F. Ortiz, *Contrapunteo cubano del tabaco y el azúcar* (Barcelona: Ariel, 1973).

12   E. Oliveira, 'Transculturação: Fernando Ortiz, o negro e a identidade nacional cubana, 1906–1940' (unpublished master's thesis, Universidade Federal de Goiás, 2003).

13   Among many other works which base their interpretation of mission culture on the concept of transculturation see A. Kern, 'Das aldeias guaranis às missões jesuíticas: um processo de transformações culturais', *Anais da I Jornada Regional de Cultura Missioneira* (1985): 53–71; and 'Missões: um processo de transculturação no passado, uma possibilidade de integração regional no presente', *Veritas*, 35 (1990): 635–45; Ganson, *The Guaraní under Spanish Rule*; and C. Rahmeier, *Cultura missioneira: interpretações a partir da cerâmica* (Cruz Alta: Unicruz, 2003).

A central Amazonian group in origin, the Guaraní (the name means 'warrior') spread south and established villages along the Paraná, Uruguay and Paraguay rivers and their tributaries 1,500 years before the arrival of the Europeans (2,000 BP).[14] They also occupied subtropical forests, hills and grasslands of Guairá, Tape and the area of Lagoa dos Patos in southern Brazil, as well as the island of Martín García and the area east of the Tigre river delta in the Río de la Plata.[15] During their expansion southwards they came into contact with other indigenous peoples, expelling and assimilating them, in a process called *Guaranisation*.[16]

Horticulturalists with a semi-sedentary organisation in which the *caciques* (male political leaders) and the *pajé* (male spiritual leaders) played a central role, the Guaraní saw their organisation change with the arrival of the Jesuits. In this process, practices which had traditionally accompanied the Guaraní – such as anthropophagy, polytheism, polygamy, rituals involving drunkenness and smoking, burials in decorated ceramic urns, collective habitation in long houses, gender division of labour (with men searching for animal protein and women in charge of horticulture and the production of ceramic utensils for ritual and domestic use) – challenged the idea of civilisation brought by Jesuits and the colonial enterprise.

The Jesuits who organised the missions came from different areas of Europe, or sometimes from other regions of Spanish America. They were part of the Company of Jesus, created in the middle of the Counter-Reformation to secure souls and territories for the Catholic Church in face of the expansion of Protestant religions such as Lutheranism, Calvinism and Anglicanism. They were educated and trained as builders, carpenters, botanists, physicians, craftsmen, painters and farmers,[17] as well as evangelists. In inhospitable territories in the hinterlands of an unknown continent, their secular skills were required more than their knowledge of religion. The Jesuits brought to the hinterlands of Latin America the printing press, new varieties of fruit and vegetables such as lettuce, cabbages, limes, oranges, peaches, pears, rice, coffee, bananas and sugarcane. They also brought cows, sheep and horses; and introduced technical innovations such as iron-mongering, the potter's wheel and gunpowder.

In the missions two or three Jesuit fathers ministered to thousands of Indians – the mission of San Miguel Arcanjo, for example, counted more than four thousand Guaraní. The missions were self-sufficient communities which based their economic activities on agriculture, cattle raising, artisan production and the cultivation of yerba mate. Commercial relations with secular settlers were a

14 A. Kern, *Antecedentes indígenas* (Porto Alegre: Universidade/UFRGS, 1998), p. 104.

15 Ganson, *The Guaraní under the Spanish Rule*, pp. 17–18, referring to A. Métraux, *La religion des Tupinamba et ses rapports avec celle des autres tribus Tupí-Guaraní* (Paris: Leroux, 1928).

16 J. Souza, 'Uma introdução ao sistema técnico-econômico Guarani' (unpublished master's thesis, Universidade Federal do Rio Grande do Sul, 1987).

17 P. Bardi, *Arte da cerâmica no Brasil* (São Paulo: Banco Sudameris do Brasil, 1980), p. 45.

secondary goal, but were necessary to raise capital for the payment of debts and tribute owed to the Spanish crown and for the purchase of church ornaments.[18]

In terms of physical organisation, the missions consisted of a village organised around a central plaza or square. Houses of the *caciques* surrounded this plaza and a church, 'the largest and most imposing structure in every mission',[19] occupied a privileged location. Next to the church were the workshops, the living quarters for the priests, an orchard and a vegetable garden, as well as separate cemeteries for the women and children and for the men. Priests were buried inside the church. Orphans, single women and widows lived in separate quarters known as a *coti guazu*. The Guaraní who were part of a mission but did not belong to the nobility lived in thatched huts outside the main village. To the Guaraní, living in a mission could constitute a guarantee of survival in the face of constant attacks by the *bandeirantes*, who came from São Paulo to hunt Indians and sell them in other areas of Brazil where African slaves were lacking. The Guaraní who lived in the mission were also protected from the European settlers, mainly from Asunción, who were interested in them as a labour force. At the same time, the mission represented a space where limited freedom was granted.

In order to live in a mission the Guaraní had to abandon some of their practices. Rituals involving drunkenness were to be replaced by the ceremony of baptism; anthropophagy[20] was to be translated into the symbolic practice of the Holy Communion; the dead were to be buried in a Catholic cemetery, which was divided according to the gender and age of the deceased;[21] children were to attend the missions' schools; and through them adults were expected to learn the Gospel and the correct behaviour of a vassal of the king. Indian chiefs were expected to lead their people according to the plan for conversion and civilisation. The Guaraní were to pray and sing the Gospel; attend daily masses; cover their bodies; avoid prenuptial sexual relations; learn Spanish; form an army; defend their territory from Portuguese incursions; and work in workshops and the fields. All these norms were introduced into the Indians' life, but to what extent they were followed is a question which cannot be fully answered.[22] We cannot truthfully rely, for instance, on the letters sent annually

18 Ganson, *The Guaraní under Spanish Rule*, p. 62.

19 Ganson, Ibid., p. 71.

20 There are accounts of the persistence of anthropophagy in the context of the Missions. See J.L. Costa Neto, '"Modo de estar" Guarani: Miguel de Artiguaye, política fragmentária e volatilidade do "ser"' (unpublished master's thesis, Pontifícia Universidade Católica do Rio Grande do Sul, 2008).

21 A. Kern, 'Cultura européia e indígena no Rio da Prata nos séculos XVI/XVIII', *Estudos Ibero-americanos*, 19 (2) (1993): 5–18.

22 G. Wilde provides a critical, well-documented account of life in the Paraguayan missions, arguing for the heterogeneity of the missionary contexts on many levels and in many instances; and criticising the spectrum of truth that many written records, lay or official, have incorrectly provided to the historiography when depicting the missions as politically ordered

by the Jesuits to their superiors in Europe, which sought to depict the success of missionary work.[23] In these letters the cultural encounters are described in idyllic terms, portraying an image of the missionary experience in which the possibility or expectation of changing in behaviour – the 'were to' of the sentences above – was presented instead as a real achievement of the Jesuit work.

The Guaraní were infantilised in the narrative, depicted as children who needed to be guided and taught, as innocent creatures to whom the opportunity of becoming complete human beings had been given. This affected other symbolic and practical aspects of missionisation which were part of the colonial project in the Americas: in order to reach the true God the Indians first needed to be educated and civilised, which also implied their subservience to a faraway king. Through the official written record the cultural encounter appears as a work of edification. The material evidence of this encounter, however, points to a more complex and encompassing experience.

The process of transculturation which took place in the missions from the beginning of their formation varied according to the time, the people and the environment in which they were established. The missions had their economic, political and ideological role in the process of the colonisation of Latin America; and the interaction between the players who took part in that process generated events which were marked by different degrees of friction and accommodation which varied over time. The process of transculturation did not imply only peaceful, successful or edifying integration, as narrated by the Jesuits in their official letters, nor was it characterised solely by violence towards, or disease and suffering on the part of, the Guaraní population, the people who were colonised. The material culture which characterised the missionary context is testimony to the fundamental role played by Guaraní traditional culture in shaping the missions of Paraguay in a colonial situation. For instance, the long houses which the *caciques* were allocated in the missions, around the plaza, make it evident that the practice of living with extended families did not disappear under the supervision of the Jesuits.[24] However, while Indians of a high status could keep their multiple households, the Guaraní who did not take part in political decisions were expected to follow the single-family model of organisation as advised by the priests. The coexistence of Guaraní

---

and culturally homogeneous (G. Wilde, *Religión y poder en las misiones de Guaraníes* (Buenos Aires: SB, 2009)).

23 Costa Neto, '"Modo de estar" Guaraní', p. 50.

24 The persistence of the *cacicado*, as well as the maintenance of polygamy among the *caciques* in the missions, are well discussed in many sources and interpreted as one of the many examples of the continuity of Guaraní traditional practices under the rule of the Jesuits. Among many others, both Wilde and Costa Neto provide a well-based account of the practice of polygamy in the missions, discussing its importance for the Guaraní and the way it was negotiated between priests and *caciques* in the missionary context. See Wilde, *Religión y poder*; and Costa Neto, '"Modo de estar" Guaraní', esp. chapter 1.

and European practices and the materiality which accompanied them suggest a world of complementarity. It does not disregard conflict, but acknowledges the persistence of the Guaraní culture in a model of social organisation formally guided by Western thought.

Another example of the inclusive character of the cultural encounter in the missionary experience is the production of carved wooden Catholic images by Indians. The making of statues of saints by the Guaraní, who turned out to be great artisans even by European standards, reveals not simply their acceptance of a new religion, as narrated by the Jesuits, but their own re-reading of the new cultural element: many of the sculptures of saints depicted indigenous faces. Some expressed happiness and contentment, characteristics which were not common in Iberian and South American religious art in the same period.[25] Similarly, the regional flora and the fauna were incorporated into the baroque style brought to the Americas. The diet based on local ingredients coexisted with European foods brought by the Jesuits, such as wheat and domesticated animal protein. The use of native plants to heal the sick also demonstrates the importance of pre-contact practices and expertise in the development of the missions.

These examples of the persistence of Guaraní cultural traces in the material culture of the missions, and therefore in the social dynamics which this materiality evoked, are important in the reconstruction of the narrative of the colonial process. They demonstrate the interdependent character of the cultural encounter, which is often ignored in the traditional colonial literature. It is not the case of epistemologically equalising integration to passive or desired accommodation, but of understanding that, in the missions, although the Catholic religion was an imposition, its acceptance was not complete and did not erase native thoughts, practices and behaviour. The material culture created and utilised in the Jesuit missions of Paraguay points towards this interdependency. However, acknowledging the cultural complementarity and coexistence present in material evidence provides only limited insight into the cultural encounter and the historical production of reality. A concern with the human, embodied experience can, therefore, help to identify the cultural ruptures and persistence experienced in the context of the missions. We can look at how embodiment took place in the missions by looking at the pottery and the techniques involved in its production.

25 Ganson, *The Guaraní under Spanish Rule*, p. 68.

Techniques of pottery production and the embodiment of the Jesuit project

Technical processes are a strategic site for the organisation and reproduction of society.[26] As argued by A. Leroy-Gourhan, techniques can reveal human acts throughout time.[27] Techniques therefore provide insights into the historical production of reality. It is not the case that the use of increasingly complex techniques can necessarily be linked to the acceptance of the new to the detriment of the old, but it can tell us about the level of attainment of a particular skill by a group, as well as the social character of the acceptance or rejection of this skill. Technical variants (in terms of form, decoration, tools, essential operations or whole processes) not only provide evidence for the existence of choices but also reveal them to the observer.[28] Changes in technique also offer insight into social changes as the two live in constant symbiosis.[29]

We can verify, through pottery, the interaction between the technologies of the Guaraní and Europeans in the missions in terms of what changed and what continued to be produced, as well as how objects were produced. More specifically, we can trace a chronology of change in techniques, form, decoration and function of pottery throughout the almost two hundred years of contact between the Guaraní and Europeans, as well as infer the degree of assimilation, exchange, accommodation and persistence of traces of both cultures. The life of this segment of culture, through its production, consumption and discarding, is linked to the life of the mission itself, to the dynamics of colonisation and to the processes of social interaction which developed in that milieu. The introduction of the technology of the potter's wheel by the Jesuits changed the way pottery was made, conceptualised and perceived. These changes also demonstrate variations in culture and social organisation, indicating ruptures and continuities which characterised the cultural encounter.

The introduction of new European techniques into the lives of the Guaraní formed a channel via which a new model of social organisation was taught and reinforced. This new model was associated with new forms of behaviour and, ideally, with new forms of thought. The new concrete sequences of operations (*chaînes opératoires*) involved in the process of pottery-making introduced by the Jesuits to the missions contributed to the embodiment of the values present in the colonial enterprise. Amongst all the techniques introduced by

---

26 M.-C. Mahias, 'Pottery techniques in India: technical variants and social choice', in P. Lemonnier (ed.), *Technological Choices: Transformation in Material Cultures Since the Neolithic* (London and New York: Routledge, 1993), pp. 157–80 (p. 158).

27 A. Leroi-Gourhan, *Evolução e técnicas. I – o homem e a matéria* (Lisboa: Edições 70, 1984).

28 Mahias, 'Pottery techniques in India', p. 158.

29 S. Van der Leeuw, 'Giving the potter a choice: conceptual aspects of pottery techniques', in P. Lemonnier (ed.), *Technological Choices: Transformations in Material Cultures Since the Neolithic*, 2nd edn (New York: Routledge, 2002), pp. 238–88 (p. 240).

Figures 3.1 and 3.2. Woman making a clay pot according to the traditional technique called acordelado (Source: G. Jussara. Artisan: Feliciana Tenazor, Tukúna Indian from Belém village, River Solimão, 1979, from T. Lima, 'Cerâmica indígena brasileira', in B. Ribeiro (ed.) (1986), Suma etnológica brasileira, *vol. 2 (Petrópolis: Vozes), p. 182).*

the Jesuits into South America, the manufacture of pottery has probably the greatest potential for revealing the encounter through embodiment since it has a counterpart in Guaraní culture prior to the arrival of the Jesuits.

The Guaraní technique for pottery making

Like in many other indigenous cultures in which clay objects are hand-crafted by women,[30] in Guaraní culture women and pottery were also intrinsically linked.[31] Men could take part only in the collection and transportation of clay from the river banks, but the ceramics were then prepared by women in a

---

30   As in Côte d'Ivoire, as shown by I. Köhler, 'Movement in making: women working with clay in northern Côte d'Ivoire', in C. Heitz and R. Stapfer (eds.), *Mobility and Pottery Production: Archaeological & Anthropologicval Perspectives* (Leiden: Sidestone, 2017), pp. 189–211; and in the south-eastern United States, as demonstrated by J. Worth, 'Materialized landscapes of practice: exploring Native American ceramic variability in the historic-era Southeastern United States', paper presented at the annual meeting of the Society for American Archaeology, Orlando, FL, 9 April 2016, https://www.researchgate.net/publication/301338915_Materialized_Landscapes_of_PracticeExploring_Native_American_Ceramic_Variability_in_the_Historic-Era_Southeastern_United_States [accessed 1 September 2019].

31   B. Landa, 'A mulher guarani: atividades e cultura material' (unpublished master's thesis, Pontifícia Universidade Católica do Rio Grande do Sul, Porto Alegre, 1995), p. 53.

Figure 3.3. First sequence of clay pot making, before decoration, nearly finished. (Source: J. Gruber. Artisan: Feliciana Tenazor, Tukúna Indian from Belém village, River Solimão, 1979, from T. Lima, 'Cerâmica indígena brasileira', in B. Ribeiro (ed.) (1986) Suma etnológica brasileira, *vol. 2 (Petrópolis: Vozes), p. 183).*

domestic setting mainly according to the *acordelado* technique.[32] Still used in many different contexts around the world, this technique of modelling consists of twisting chunks of soft clay to make coils which are layered from the bottom up until a desired form is reached.[33]

Squatting or sitting on the floor, women engaged directly with the clay throughout the whole process of making a piece, from regulating the earth texture until the decoration, finishing and firing of the object.[34] They put their skills into it; their whole bodies were connected to the actions of making a piece from the beginning to the end. Working the clay with their bare hands against a board or even their thighs in order to make coils, using their fingers to repair gaps and smooth the surface required a corporeal connection which imprinted a very personal mark on the final object. In this way traditional ceramic objects represented not only a tribe or clan but also woman's individuality, deliberately

32 F. La Salvia and J. Brochado, *Cerâmica guarani* (Porto Alegre: Posenato Arte e Cultura, 1989), p. 11; Rahmeier, *Cultura missioneira.*

33 T. Lima, 'Cerâmica indígena brasileira', in B. Ribeiro (ed.), *Suma etnológica brasileira*, vol. 2 (Petrópolis: Vozes, 1986), pp. 173–229.

34 Ibid.

or not. Nail and finger marks on pots illustrate this connection and the artisanal, unique way of working the clay.

The introduction of the potter's wheel by the Jesuits de-personalised the ceramic objects. One could argue that throwing a pot is as much a corporeal technique as is modelling and can thus reveal the artist's presence. However, pats, squeezes, pinches and hand-pressure on the clay objects made according to the *acordelado* technique communicate individuality in a way the potter's wheel does not. The two techniques derived from different cosmologies and served two different purposes in the context of the mission; and these were reproduced on the objects themselves. The use of the wheel required a new physical skill, a re-ordering of time and the reinforcement of the European concept of labour. The articles manufactured through throwing clay on a wheel did not carry the mark of the artisan or the symbol of the ethnic group. They were similar to the pottery produced in other missions or in Europe. The standardisation of production accompanied the civilising project brought to America by the Jesuits, which aimed at eventually turning Indians into Christians through forging a spatial and temporal order which involved objects, practices, concepts and bodies perceived essentially as symbols of Christianity.[35] The potter's wheel, in this context, not only sped up the production of pottery, but ended up being a means through which the embodiment of a new social and moral code took place.

The technique introduced by the Jesuits: the potter's wheel

Under the Jesuits the manufacture of pottery using the wheel was a male task. All male Guarani between the ages of 12 and 50, except those men in charge of agriculture and farming, had to work in the workshops next to the church.[36] Overseen by the priest, the men produced housewares and church ornaments (tiles and bricks were produced in the brickyard). During the harvest the artisans divided their labour between the workshops (for one week) and the fields (two weeks), for which they received rations after attending mass at the end of the day.[37] All tasks carried out in the artisan workshops were overseen by a Jesuit, who guided and controlled their execution. Keeping the Guaraní men busy with work was consistent with the religious view that spare time was a gap which could be filled by temptation, sin or addiction[38] and that in a civilised world it should be filled by the catechism, prayer and labour.[39]

---

35 Wilde, *Religión y poder*, p. 51.

36 F. Tocchetto, 'A cultura material do guarani missioneiro como símbolo de identidade étnica' (unpublished master's thesis, Universidade Federal de Santa Catarina, 1991), p. 32.

37 Ibid., p. 32.

38 M. Flores, *Reduções jesuíticas do guaranis* (Porto Alegre: EDIPUCRS, 1987), p. 80.

39 M. Flores, 'Deus e o Diabo na fronteira com os gentios', *Estudos Ibero-americanos*, 1 (2000): 57–68 (59). In *Religión y poder*, Wilde also points to the guidance that labour and feasting,

The physical contact of the male artisan with the clay was limited almost entirely to his hands. The work was very dependent on the manipulation of instruments, such as shovels, moulds and the potter's wheel, and on the management of the animals used to tread the clay and to carry it from its source to the place of pottery production. The artist engaged with the clay and with the wheel, which directed both his movements and the form of the raw material acquired. The machine had to be understood by the artisan and moulded to his body so that both its spin and speed would be aligned with the artisan's intentions and movements. Despite this connection, the body did not manifest itself in the piece produced. Contrary to the pottery produced by the Guaraní in the traditional, pre-contact way, the personal marks of the artisan were not clearly objectified in an artefact produced using the wheel.

Although the new elements and techniques presented to the Guaraní by the Jesuits had an impact, they were not sufficient to separate them completely from the traditional manner of producing pottery. As previously shown, concessions were made in many aspects of life, such as allowing residence in extended family houses, permitting polygamous relationships and also keeping alive the traditional way of making pottery: by women, individually, in the domestic setting.[40] In other words, even though the ordinary artefacts brought into the Guaraní's life by the Jesuits had a considerable impact in re-ordering their lives and structuring thought, [41] the political, social and economic organisation of the Guaraní was to some extent preserved in order to secure the missions' stability.[42]

Cultural negotiations: material culture and transculturation in the missions

Alone, the production of pottery on the wheel, by male Guaraní, in a delimited territory and controlled by a supervisor during a certain period of time, cannot encompass the whole process of civilisation and conversion to Christianity. However, it can add to other elements which were involved, such as the physical and conceptual transformation of the landscape and the implications for individuals' relationships. Roads, houses, workshops, allotments, communal gardens, a square, a church, cemeteries can all be perceived as 'moments in

---

cyclically celebrated, provided to the rhythm of social life in the missions (p. 70).

40   Tocchetto, 'A cultura material', interprets this permanence as a means of resistance and the preservation of identity in times of change.

41   For a reflection on the relevance of ordinary things in the ordering of people's lives, see D. Miller, 'Artefacts and the meaning of things', in T. Ingold, *Companion Encyclopedia of Anthropology* (London and New York: Routledge, 2002), pp. 396 – 419.

42   Tocchetto, 'A cultura material'; Ganson, *The Guaraní under the Spanish Rule*; Rahmeier, *Cultura missioneira*; Kern, 'Missões: um processo de transculturação'; Kern, *Cultura europeia e indígena*; A. Kern, *Missões: uma utopia política* (Porto Alegre: Mercado Aberto, 1982).

a general technology of localisation'.[43] In this way, the building of a mission involved several instances of the production of locality, all eminently connected to and imbued with ideas of immorality and sin, of private and public property, of heaven and earth, dichotomist concepts which permeated the process of evangelisation and the Western idea of civilisation.

Clothing the people, housing them in a different materiality and within a new spatial organisation, renaming them, reorganising their time, changing burial rituals and the places where they occurred, introducing the sounds of musical instruments and the church bell, organising daily routine according to the ringing of the bell, inaugurating new practices such as ploughing and manufacturing pottery – all this contributed to the production of the locality 'as a structure of feeling'.[44] Through experiencing the locality produced by the Jesuit project, the Guaraní were slowly and systematically embodying colonialism, which allowed the production of a particular *habitus*,[45] one which accommodated the new cultural references and naturalised elements from the civilised world proposed by the Jesuits. In other words, the colonisation associated with the missions allowed the creation of particular routines and, as a consequence, particular somatic spaces.[46] The body and its actions thus became a tool which in different ways incorporated and communicated colonialism. [47]

From a large-scale perspective the missions were indeed part of colonialism. However, we should avoid generalisations when classifying them as such. On a micro-scale, on which the particularities of each cultural encounter are considered, the missions emerge as places where power was not exercised in a uni-directional way. Transformations in daily life were always negotiated between the priests and indigenous populations. These negotiations revealed disputes over power which were transmitted to the material culture of the missions through introductions, obliterations, changes in and continuities of objects and the techniques of their production and consumption.

The Guaraní fashioned a way to remain Guaraní in the changing and challenging circumstances of a mission, behaving in an ambivalent way which

---

43 A. Appadurai, *Modernity at Large: Cultural Dimensions of Globalization* (Minneapolis, MN: University of Minnesota Press, 1996), p. 179.

44 Appadurai, *Modernity at Large*, p. 182.

45 As proposed by Bourdieu in P. Bourdieu, *Outline of a Theory of Practice* (Cambridge: Cambridge University Press, 1977).

46 For a study on the somatic spaces generated in a given materiality see C. Rahmeier, 'Materiality, social roles and the senses: domestic landscape and social identity in the *Estâncias* of Rio Grande do Sul, Brazil', *Journal of Material Culture*, 17 (2012): 153–71.

47 In Merleau-Ponty's sense, which perceives the body as immersed in the world and as a means of communication with it (M. Merleau-Ponty, 'The experience of the body and classical psychology', in M. Fraser and M. Greco (eds.), *The Body; A Reader* (London and New York: Routledge, 2005), pp. 52–4.

revealed more superposition and duplicity than obliteration.[48] The Guaraní did not become Europeans, neither did the Jesuits adopt Indian values and their way of life. Regarding pottery, specifically, its traditional domestic production did not disappear in the missions.[49] Even clay artefacts used in traditional indigenous rituals, such pipes and funerary urns, have been found in archaeological surveys in the mission area,[50] suggesting they were possibly still in use after the arrival of the Jesuits.

The material culture of the reductions reveals a process in which elements of both Guaraní and Jesuit culture coexisted in some aspects, merged in others and, to a great extent, made priests and Indians dependent upon one other. We can, therefore, talk about the emergence of a transcultural form of social and economic organisation in which both Guaraní and European cultural elements coexisted. In order to prosper, the Jesuits had to make concessions. In order to survive, the Guaraní, too, had to make concessions. The Jesuits were entrusted with people to civilise and to whom to teach the catechism. The Guaraní were given guns to protect their people from the *bandeirantes*. The concessions made by each of these groups permeated the whole experience of the missions – from their beginnings in the 17th century until the Guaraní War and the expulsion of the Jesuits from Spanish and Portuguese territories in the 1760s. Regarding the production of ceramics, the choreographies involved in the making of pots, pipes, bricks or church ornaments do not represent the emergence of a community of practice,[51] as sometimes argued for indigenous cultures in similar post-colonial contexts, but indicate the coexistence of two modes of ceramic production: a Guaraní one, conducted by women in the domestic sphere; and a European one, implemented and controlled by priests and relying heavily on male labour. Different cosmologies were present in these two ways of making things and, in the process, of organising people and their time.

The way pottery was produced and consumed throughout the experience of the Jesuit missions is a testimony to the cultural negotiations present in that context. It challenges the dualistic oversimplification of the 'coloniser-colonised' dichotomy, allowing the emergence of multidirectional models of

48 For a comprehensive and pertinent discussion of ambivalence in the context of the missions see Wilde, *Religión y poder*.

49 S. Zuse, 'Permanências e mudanças técnicas na cerâmica de uma redução jesuítico-guarani do início do século XVII na região central do Rio Grande do Sul/Brasil', *Cuadernos del Instituto Nacional de Antropología y Pensamiento Latinoamericano – Series Especiales*, 1 (2013): 160–72.

50 Tocchetto, 'A cultura material', pp. 159–60.

51 M. Pigott, 'Communities of potters: reconsidering colonialism and cultural change through ceramic analysis', paper presented at the 75th annual meeting of the Southeastern Archaeological Conference, Augusta, GA, 14–17 November 2018; Worth, 'Materialized Landscapes of Practice', https://www.academia.edu/38927697/Communities_of_Potters_Reconsidering_Colonialism_and_Culture_Change_through_Ceramic_Analysis [accessed 1 September 2019].

interpretation which acknowledge the so-called 'dominated' populations.[52] In this way, the materiality of the cultural encounters allows the reframing of our understanding of colonialism in accordance with the various empirical conditions it encompasses. The material structure of the missions and the routines they created led to the embodiment of certain Western rules and values and, ultimately, to the formation of a particular *habitus* which contributed to the assimilation of the Jesuit project in colonial Latin America. We cannot forget, however, that the bodies which performed the choreographies of civilisation in this context were the same ones which performed resistance through the very *habitus* which still held some elements of the Guaraní tradition.

Bibliography

Appadurai, A. (1996) *Modernity at Large: Cultural Dimensions of Globalization* (Minneapolis, MN: University of Minnesota Press).

Bakewell, P. and J. Holler (2010) *A History of Latin America.* (Chichester: Wiley-Blackwell).

Bardi, P. (1980) *Arte da cerâmica no Brasil* (São Paulo: Banco Sudameris do Brasil).

Bourdieu, P. (1977) *Outline of a Theory of Practice* (Cambridge: Cambridge University Press).

Brading, D. (1991) *The First America: The Spanish Monarchy, Creole Patriots and the Liberal State, 1492–1867* (Cambridge: Cambridge University Press).

Chamorro, G. (2008) 'Historia del Cuerpo Durante la "Conquista Espiritual"', *Fronteiras*, 10 (18): 277–99.

Cornell, P. and F. Fahlander (2007) 'Encounters – materialities – confrontations: an introduction', in P. Cornell and F. Fahlander (eds.), *Encounters, Materialities, Confrontations: Archaeologies of Social Space and Interaction* (Newcastle: Cambridge Scholar Press), pp. 1–14.

Costa Neto, J.L. (2008) '"Modo de estar" Guarani: Miguel de Artiguaye, política fragmentária e volatilidade do "ser"' (unpublished master's thesis, Pontifícia Universidade Católica do Rio Grande do Sul, Porto Alegre).

Flores, M. (1987) *Reduções jesuíticas do guaranis* (Porto Alegre: EDIPUCRS).

— (2000) 'Deus e o Diabo na fronteira com os gentios', *Estudos Ibero-americanos*, 1: 57–68.

Ganson, B. (2013) *The Guaraní under Spanish Rule in the Río de la Plata* (Stanford, CA: Stanford University Press).

---

52 G. Stein, 'Introduction', in G. Stein (ed.), *The Archaeology of Colonial Encounters: Comparative Perspectives* (Santa Fe, NM: School of American Research Press, 2005), pp. 3–32.

Gosden, C. (2008) 'Social ontologies', *Philosophical Transactions of the Royal Society B: Biological Sciences*, 363: 2003–10.

Kern, A. (1982) *Missões: uma utopia política* (Porto Alegre: Mercado Aberto).

— (1985) 'Das aldeias guaranis às missões jesuíticas: um processo de transformações culturais', *Anais da I Jornada Regional de Cultura Missioneira*: 53–71.

— (1990) 'Missões: um processo de transculturação no passado, uma possibilidade de integração regional no presente', *Veritas*, 35: 635–45.

— (1993) 'Cultura européia e indígena no Rio da Prata nos séculos XVI/XVIII', *Estudos Ibero-americanos*, 19 (2): 5–18.

— (1998) *Antecedentes indígenas* (Porto Alegre: Editora da Universidade/UFRGS).

Köhler, I. (2017) 'Movement in making: women working with clay in northern Côte d'Ivoire', in C. Heitz and R. Stapfer (eds.), *Mobility and Pottery Production: Archaeological & Anthropologicval Perspectives* (Leiden: Sidestone), pp. 189–211.

La Salvia, F. and J. Brochado (1989) *Cerâmica guarani* (Porto Alegre: Posenato Arte e Cultura).

Landa, B. (1995) 'A mulher guarani: atividades e cultura material' (unpublished master's thesis, Pontifícia Universidade Católica do Rio Grande do Sul, Porto Alegre).

Leroi-Gourhan, A. (1984) *Evolução e técnicas. I – o homem e a matéria* (Lisboa: Edições 70).

Lima, T. (1986) 'Cerâmica indígena brasileira brasileira', in B. Ribeiro (ed.), *Suma etnológica brasileira*, vol. 2 (Petrópolis: Vozes, 1986), pp. 173–229.

Mahias, M.-C. (1993) 'Pottery techniques in India: technical variants and social choice', in P. Lemonnier (ed.), *Technological Choices: Transformation in Material Cultures Since the Neolithic* (London and New York: Routledge), pp. 157–80.

Mauss, M. (2005) 'Techniques of the body', in M. Fraser and M. Greco (eds.), *The Body: A Reader* (London and New York: Routledge), pp. 73–7.

Merleau-Ponty, M. (2005) 'The experience of the body and classical psychology', in M. Fraser and M. Greco (eds.), *The Body: A Reader* (London and New York: Routledge), pp. 52–4.

Miller, D. (2002) 'Artefacts and the meaning of things', in T. Ingold (ed.), *Companion Encyclopedia of Anthropology* (London and New York: Routledge), pp. 396–419.

Morais, R. (2006) 'L. A. Muratori e o cristianismo feliz na missão dos padres da Companhia de Jesus no Paraguai' (unpublished master's thesis, Universidade Federal Fluminense, Niterói).

Muratori, L. (1743) *Il Cristianesimo felice nelle missione de padri della Compagnia de Gesú nel Paraguai* (Venice: Giambatista Pasquali).

Oliveira, E. (2003) 'Transculturação: Fernando Ortiz, o negro e a identidade nacional cubana, 1906–1940' (unpublished master's thesis, Universidade Federal de Goiás, Goiânia).

Ortiz, F. (1973) *Contrapunteo Cubano del tabaco y el azúcar* (Barcelona: Ariel).

Pigott, M. (2018) 'Communities of potters: reconsidering colonialism and cultural change through ceramic analysis', paper presented at the 75th annual meeting of the Southeastern Archaeological Conference (Augusta, GA, 14–17 Nov.) https://www.academia.edu/38927697/Communities_of_Potters_Reconsidering_Colonialism_and_Culture_Change_through_Ceramic_Analysis [accessed 1 September 2019].

Rahmeier, C. (2003) *Cultura missioneira: interpretações a partir da cerâmica* (Cruz Alta: Unicruz).

— (2012) 'Materiality, social roles and the senses: domestic landscape and social identity in the *Estâncias* of Rio Grande do Sul, Brazil', *Journal of Material Culture*, 17: 153–71.

Souza, J. (1987) 'Uma introdução ao sistema técnico-econômico guarani' (unpublished master's thesis, Universidade Federal do Rio Grande do Sul, Porto Alegre).

Stein, G. (2005) 'Introduction', in G. Stein (ed.), *The Archaeology of Colonial Encounters: Comparative Perspectives* (Santa Fe: School of American Research Press), pp. 3–32.

Tocchetto, F. (1991) 'A cultura material do guarani missioneiro como símbolo de identidade étnica' (unpublished master's thesis, Universidade Federal de Santa Catarina, Florianópolis).

Van der Leeuw, S. (2002) 'Giving the potters a choice: conceptual aspects of pottery techniques', in P. Lemonnier (ed.), *Technological Choices: Transformations in Material Cultures Since the Neolithic* (2nd edn, New York: Routledge), pp. 238–88.

Wilde, G. (2009) *Religión y poder en las misiones de Guaraníes* (Buenos Aires: SB).

Worth, J. (2016) 'Materialized landscapes of practice: exploring Native American ceramic variability in the historic-era Southeastern United States' (paper presented at the annual meeting of the Society for American Archaeology, Orlando, FL, 9 Apr.), https://www.researchgate.net/publication/301338915_Materialized_Landscapes_of_PracticeExploring_

Native_American_Ceramic_Variability_in_the_Historic-Era_
Southeastern_United_States [accessed 1 September 2019].

Zuse, S. (2013) 'Permanências e mudanças técnicas na cerâmica de uma
redução jesuítico-guarani do início do século XVII na região central
do Rio Grande do Sul/Brasil', *Cuadernos del Instituto Nacional de
Antropologia y Pensamiento Latinoamericano – Series Especiales*, 1: 160–72.

II. Jesuit mission life

4. A patriarchal society in the Rio de la Plata: adultery and the double standard at Mission Jesús de Tavarangue, 1782

Barbara Ganson

On 16 February 1782 administrator Lucas Cano denounced Father Francisco Xavier Dominguez, a Franciscan, for having committed adultery with two married women: Margarita Arandí, a native Guaraní, whose husband had fled from the mission, and Petrona Sánchez, his own wife. Cano also requested the Spanish authorities place his wife in a *casa de ejercicio* (a religious institution which served as a kind of female asylum, workshop or prison) 'among the women who led a bad life and that she remain there until she learned the graveness of her actions'.[1] Cano learned of his wife's infidelity with the Catholic priest from his mulatto slave Pasqual Cano, or possibly second-hand from his slave's mother-in-law. According to the testimony of Pasqual Cano, his master, Lucas Cano, was busy writing something and asked him to bring candles from the living quarters of the priest. His master's wife, Petrona, then offered to accompany her slave. It was around midnight when they arrived at the priest's quarters and Petrona noticed an Indian woman hiding underneath the priest's bed. Pascual testified that he heard some noises coming from the bedroom of the priest, such as furniture being knocked over, along with a guitar. He then saw an Indian woman come out onto the patio and ask for a knife in order to kill the administrator's wife. Since there was none, she went back inside. When no one was willing to assist her, Margarita Arandí then stormed out. Another testimony from a Guaraní using an interpreter stated something different, affirming that his mother-in-law, a Mulata, had heard the two women fighting. Pasqual claimed that Margarita Arandí did not have sexual relations or an affair with the Franciscan priest; only that she washed his clothing and nothing else. Interestingly, the testimony of the slave was taken down during the investigation, even though his legal status could have been discounted. Nevertheless, the interrogators considered his testimony

---

1 'Carta al Gov. Don Francisco Piera', 'Sobre el recurso echo por el Adm. del Pueblo Lucas Cano con el cura del miso Fr. Francisco Xavier Dominguez', Archivo General de la Nación (Buenos Aires) (hereafter AGN), IX 36-9-6, 1782.

B. Ganson, 'A patriarchal society in the Rio de la Plata: adultery and the double standard at Mission Jesús de Tavarangue, 1782', in L.A. Newson (ed.), *Cultural Worlds of the Jesuits in Colonial Latin America* (London: Institute of Latin American Studies, 2020), pp. 91–110. License: CC-BY-NC-ND 2.0.

to be significant enough to include it in their investigation of adultery in this former Jesuit mission town.

This chapter will explore how differences in gender, race, ethnicity and social class were major considerations in how Spanish colonial authorities dealt with cases of adultery in late 18th-century Paraguay. What becomes evident is that the Jesuits, as representatives of the pope and the Catholic Church, had reinforced a patriarchal society in the *reducciones* [settlements] of Paraguay: they shared or reflected the values of the more dominant Spanish culture in the Rio de la Plata. Those authorities who replaced the Jesuits following their expulsion in 1767 practised a double standard by which men of authority, mainly Spanish secular officials, could commit acts of adultery without suffering serious repercussions. Women, on the other hand, whether Guaraní or Spanish, were punished more severely for their infidelity and for having violated the moral values that regulated Spanish colonial society. This practice was contrary to canon law, which viewed adultery as a sin for both men and women. The codes of conduct for men tended to be far more lenient regarding marriage and sexuality, while women who engaged in extramarital affairs received greater condemnation in the town of Jesús de Tavanrangue.

Originally established by the Society of Jesus in 1685 with 150 Guaraní families, the Jesuits moved the mission of Jesús de Tavanrangue to a more favourable site at Mandi-i-soby and Capiibay, north of the Paraná river in what is today south-eastern Paraguay and a UNESCO World Heritage Site.[2] In 1741, 1,850 Guaraní inhabited Jesús de Tavarangue; in 1757 its population was 2,082. Following the Guaraní rebellion against the terms of the Treaty of Madrid in the 1750s, 912 refugees migrated from the eastern Jesuit missions or were relocated there.[3] According to the 1783 census, there were 1,747 *almas* (or souls) in Jesús de Tavarangué, who were divided into 24 *cacicazgos* (an aboriginal polity which assumed the form of a chiefdom).[4] The local economy of Jesús de Tavarangue appeared sustainable. The Guaraní women grew corn, cotton and manioc, while men raised beef cattle, sheep, oxen, horses and mules. In 1783 there were 9,292 head of beef cattle; 549 oxen; 565 horses; 342 mules; 531 sheep; and two burros.[5]

Censuses from the late 18th century indicate a small Spanish or creole presence. Lucas Cano, the 54-year-old Spanish administrator, was relatively advanced beyond middle age for the period. The document does not indicate

2   R. Carbonell de Masy and N. Levinton, *Un pueblo llamado Jesús* (Asunción: Fundación Paracuaria Missionsprokur, 2010), p. 28.

3   R.H. Jackson, 'The population and vital rates of the Jesuit missions of Paraguay, 1700–1767', *Journal of Interdisciplinary History*, 38 (2008): 401–31 (404).

4   Prov. Del Paraguay, Estado del Pueblo de Jesús, AGN 22-8-2; 'Expediente que suspende los tributos y mayor servicio durante diez años a los Indios del Pueblo de Jesús que necesitan para conducir la Iglesia y nuevo Pueblo', AGN 17-3-6, 1782.

5   Ibid.

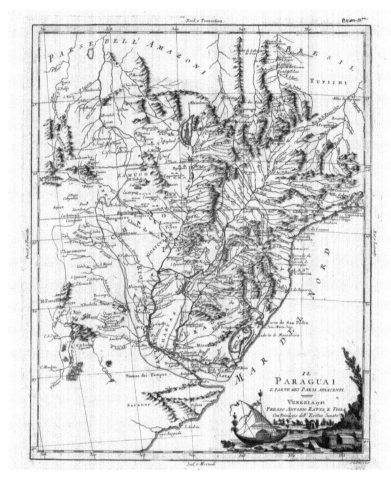

Figure 4.1. Il Paraguai e Paesi Adiacenti. Venezia 1785. Courtesy of Geography and Maps Division, Library of Congress.

the age of his wife, Petrona Sánchez. Lucas Cano and Petrona Sánchez had two sons, who are described as pursuing their studies, but sources do not indicate their level of schooling or type of studies. In all likelihood under the circumstances, the couple had had previous marital disagreements, since Petrona Sánchez had resided in Buenos Aires.

Although this judicial investigation occurred after the Jesuits had left the missions, the patriarchal legacy of the Society of Jesus remained. The Catholic missionaries had established a society in which men played all the significant political, economic and religious roles in the missions. Jesuit missionaries concentrated on the education of male Indian children, especially the sons of caciques who would then teach their parents and play influential roles in the administration of the missions. Boys learned how to read and write, as well as do mathematics. Although Guaraní women provided extensive agricultural labour, girls' education was largely relegated to the performing of domestic chores and the spinning of cotton and wool thread to make clothing for their families. Guaraní men, on the other hand, were trained to serve as militia soldiers, river-boat sailors, blacksmiths, shoemakers, tailors, printers, sculptors, scribes, musicians and pottery-makers, as well as handling livestock, among other tasks.

Gender separation took place not only in the workshops and on the mission ranches, but in the schools and during church services. While Guaraní boys and girls both studied the catechism, the children filed into the church in a separate line with boys entering first; men came next; and then girls, followed by women, all seated according to their gender. Catholic missionaries also enclosed elderly women, single women and orphans in a separate compound or asylum known as the *coty guazú*.[6] These were shelters located next to the church where women's honour and virginity were protected, as well as their physical wellbeing. Usually two or three elderly women raised the orphans and looked after the welfare of the young women. Women left these enclosures to work in the fields and then only in groups. Men exercised authority in the Indian *cabildos* or town councils, as well as in the militias established by the Jesuits to combat Indian slavery, beginning in the 1620s. [7] There were no female members on these councils or constables to patrol the streets of the missions. Nonetheless, women were not without some influence and their voices can be heard in their testimonies.

Petrona Sánchez did not admit she had a fight with the Guaraní laundress, Margarita Arandí, in the bedroom of the priest at midnight. Petrona Sánchez sought out the Franciscan priest but directed her anger towards Margarita Arandí, having discovered her hiding under the priest's bed. Sánchez, however, directly challenged colonial society's dictates for elite women. She refused to adopt the submissive postures of obedience, especially after she had learned that her own husband had had an adulterous affair with a young woman named Thomasa, the daughter of Pedro Pablo Sánchez, a *yerbatero* (trader in yerba mate or Paraguayan tea). Thomasa was the daughter of her *compadre* [godfather; benefactor, influential friend]. Petrona Sánchez struck back at her spouse by committing adultery with the local priest in what became a public scandal known to all in the mission town. Sánchez stood by her by actions and strong sentiments about not loving her husband, having made publicly known his adulterous relationship. She denied having a physical confrontation with a

6   B. Ganson, *The Guaraní under Spanish Rule in the Rio de la Plata* (Stanford, CA: Stanford University Press, 2003), pp. 72–9.

7   A. Ruiz de Montoya, *The Spiritual Conquest: Early Years of the Jesuit Missions in Paraguay* (1639), trans. by B. Ganson and C.M. Saffi (Boston, MA: Institute of Jesuit Sources, 2017), p. 229.

woman of a distinctive social class and ethnicity because she appears to have lost the fight. Contrary to her own testimony, she left the room with facial wounds. It was not only a matter of her sense of honour; she may not have wanted to avoid bringing attention to the nature of their involvement with the priest.

Differential treatment

According to the double standard, men other than those of the cloth could have illicit sexual relationships without facing severe punishment. Under the Code Napoléon in Europe, an adulterous wife could be sent to prison for two years, while a husband who was found guilty went unpunished unless he moved another woman into his house as his concubine; but even under these circumstances he was subject only to a minor fine. In late medieval France, however, the opposite of the double standard was enforced. Men were punished more often than women for having extramarital affairs.[8] People shared the belief that men were responsible for their own behaviour, as well as that of their wives.[9] In certain instances in Europe, however, adulterous women could be put to death. These types of punishment in Europe were harsher than those administered in colonial Spanish America. At Jesús de Tavarangue, Lucas Cano remained in his position as administrator of the town, having retained support from members of the community, despite having been disgraced by his wife and public knowledge of his adultery. What seems to have mattered most was whether he carried out his responsibilities, not his sexual improprieties. Community interests thus prevailed, not misunderstandings, disagreement and the violation of the married couple's marriage vows.

Men exercised considerable power over women in being able to send them away or cloister them both within and outside the missions. Nevertheless, women were not without some recourse in determining their romantic choices. The nature and extent of the native women's sexuality and independence in general are not well understood, but it is clear that Margarita depended on the priest as a source of employment. There is no mention of how she was compensated for her labour. Arandí, however, had to deal with the stigma of her lesser social status of a laundress whose domestic profession made her highly open to the suspicion of being the priest's lover, especially after having been discovered in his living quarters late at night. Margarita Arandí, for her part, explained in her testimony that her husband had fled the mission many years earlier and denied that she had ever had an affair with the priest. She also flatly denied that she had ever fought with the wife of the administrator in

8 S. McDougall, 'The opposite of the double standard: gender, marriage, and adultery prosecution in late medieval France', *Journal of the History of Sexuality*, 23 (2014): 206–25.

9 B.S. Anderson and J.P. Zinsser, *A History of Their Own: Women in Europe from Prehistory to the Present*, 2 vols. (New York: Harper & Row, 1989), vol. 2, p. 150.

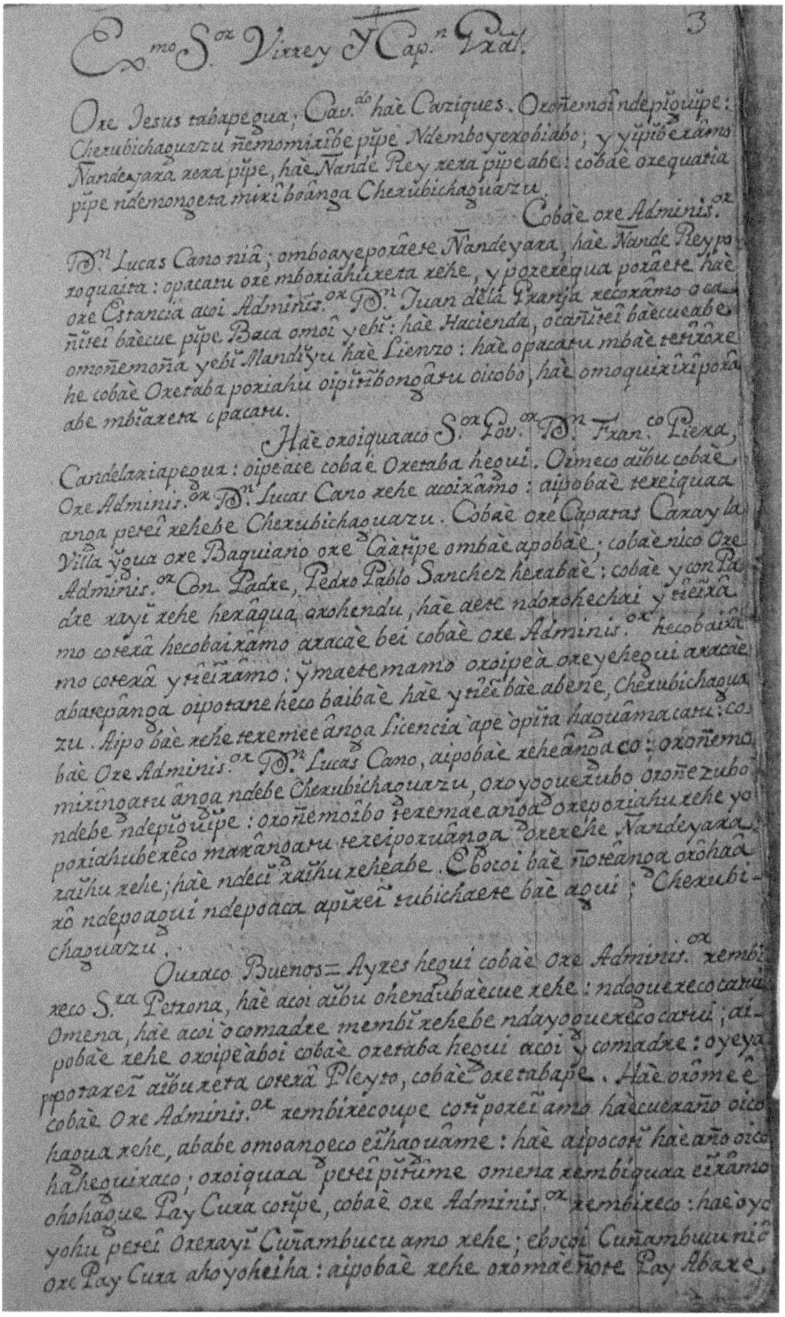

Figure 4.2. Photograph of the first page of the Guarani letter, Mission Jesús de Tavarangue (AGN IX 36-9-6 Misiones, 1782).

the priest's bedroom. It is probable that Margarita Arandí and her 14-year-old brother, Estanislao Arandí, defended her reputation to avoid her being sent to a woman's prison in Buenos Aires or suffering other consequences for having threatened the life of a Spanish woman. Estanislao claimed that the wife of the administrator had never gone into the bedroom of the priest, nor had he ever heard of the priest visiting his sister in her own house. Margarita was spared from being placed in the *coty guazú*, but she was still sent away to reside on a mission ranch on the outskirts of the town. Had the *cabildo* officers and caciques thought more favourably of Petrona Sánchez, this Guaraní woman might have been more severely punished. In this context, the question of the honour of Margarita Arandí, a native woman of lower social class who only washed clothes, did not seem to matter. Margarita Arandí avoided a more severe penalty due to the fact that her spouse had abandoned the mission as a fugitive and she thus did not dishonour him. Her honour was not at stake to the same extent as that of Petrona Sánchez. To be guilty of adultery required one to be married; her spouse had fled some time ago.[10]

Margarita Arandí did not face being consigned to a religious institution apparently due to her lower social class, status, race and ethnicity. Similarly, no one asked or bothered to care whether the young woman Thomasa offered any testimony. She might have confirmed her adulterous relationship with Lucas Cano. The silence in the historical record is quite revealing about the extent of influence exercised by male authorities.

There was no single native response to the news of two women fighting late in the evening in the bedroom of their local Catholic priest. Several Guaraní were reluctant even to admit that their priest had committed adultery with the two married women; some admitted they had no news of the priest having visited other native women. Others had heard rumours of this practice. Nevertheless, some thought the priest should be severely punished with two hundred lashes for having committed such an offence.

Sentiments of oppression and their subordination come through in a letter written by a native in 1782 on the part of the Guaraní from the mission Jesús de Tavarangue (see appendix and fig. 4.2). It is among the approximately one hundred letters the Guaraní wrote in the late colonial period and early 19th century, having learned the value of writing from the Jesuits.[11] Guaraní *cabildo* officers from the Mission Jesús de Tavarangue – Lieutenant Corregidor

---

10 In contrast to Native American women in south-eastern North America, punishment in cases of adultery was far more severe in the 18th century. Cherokee and Choctaw women who were adulteresses, for example, faced sexual humiliation in public, physical mutilation and severe beating (F. Donohue, 'To beget a tame breed of people: sex, marriage, adultery and Indigenous North American women', *Early American Studies*, 10 (2012): 101–31. These primary sources appear, however, to have been analysed through the perspectives of Europeans.

11 See http://www.langas.cnrs.fr/temp/index.htm, a digital archive of Guaraní texts, *Langues Générales d'Amérique du Sud*, prepared by C. Boidin, IHEAL Sorbonne, Paris, 2012–16; Ganson, *The Guaraní under Spanish Rule*, pp. 98–104, appendices 1–5 (pp. 191–203).

Julian Tacurari; Regidor Primero Cacique Principal Miguel Arâendĭ; Cacique Eusebio Guĭrapepo; and the Secretario de Cabildo Ygnacio Aratutĭ – signed the letter on behalf of all those who could not sign their names and addressed it to the viceroy and captain general in Buenos Aires in support of their Spanish administrator, Lucas Cano. These individuals humbled themselves at the viceroy's feet and referred to him as 'their great chief', expressing respect towards the Catholic God and the king.[12] They claimed they had no prior knowledge of the administrator misbehaving or acting in a scandalous manner; otherwise they would have removed him from the town themselves. They requested that he be given permission to remain because their administrator respected God and the laws of their king. 'He treated us poor ones well', they noted. They observed how the former administrator of their ranches and farms, Don Juan del Granja, had not taken care of the ranches, where their cows had wandered off. They said that Cano has helped us 'poor people' and brought peace to the community. They admitted they were aware of rumours that the governor at the mission capital of Candelaria, Don Francisco Perez, wished to replace him; this was the reason the viceroy needed to hear from them. The *cabildo* officers and caciques then asserted that Cano's wife Petrona Sánchez did not treat her husband well, nor did she get along well with the daughter of her *comadre* [godfather's wife].

The indigenous leaders in the town pleaded with the authorities for Doña Petrona Sánchez to 'be sent away to live alone in a place where she will no longer bother anyone', for having been the subject of such a scandal, known by everyone in the town, men, women, children, young and old alike. They explained they learned that the administrator's wife had entered the priest's living quarters without her husband's knowledge, where she had found Margarita, 'one of their own daughters', who worked as the laundress of the priest, and pointed out that it was very late in the day. The administrator's wife and the Guaraní woman began to fight with one another, tossing each other onto the ground. 'We all learned of this, including children, my great chief', the councilmen and caciques explained. They also expressed the sentiment that they could no longer respect the priest when he came to celebrate mass, having had two women fight in his living quarters. They requested that a new priest replace him. They framed their letter using religious terms and humbled themselves before the Spanish authorities, referring to themselves as 'impoverished' and hoping they would not lose their souls because Jesus Christ

---

12 See C. Boidin and A. Otazú Melgarejo, 'Toward Guaraní semantic history: political vocabulary in Guaraní (sixteenth to nineteenth centuries)', in A. Durston and B. Mannheim (eds.), *Authority, Hierarchy, and the Indigenous Languages of Latin America: Historical and Ethnographic Perspectives* (Notre Dame, IN: University of Notre Dame Press, 2018).

had shed His blood. They hoped the viceroy would listen and accept their request; and wished God would grant him a good, long life.[13]

The native letter appears among the judicial records without an original Spanish translation, which suggests that authorities who received the letter knew how to read it in the native language or used translators. Interestingly, the letter was contradictory in that it suggested their administrator had a sexual relationship with the daughter of a yerba mate trader. The members of the *cabildo* and the caciques, however, asked that the priest be sent elsewhere. They expressed no tolerance for a cleric who had violated his vows of celibacy.

During the colonial period in the Rio de la Plata, authorities distinctly dealt with adultery cases according to social class, race, ethnicity and gender. The husband who was married to a woman with a questionable reputation who admitted to having had an illicit sexual relationship was perceived as a victim. He had the power to utilise legal mechanisms and colonial institutions to send his wife to a religious institution. However, when he, as a married man, committed adultery, the act was not even considered a crime or a sin in the Rio de la Plata. It was simply that familiar story of a double standard.

For the Guaraní, however, cases of divorce were unknown in the missions of Paraguay. Flight or abandonment was most probably one solution to any marital disharmony. A Spanish woman was left with little recourse other than to denounce her husband's inappropriate and unacceptable sexual behaviour to the local religious authorities. In this case, Petrona Sánchez, though committing adultery herself, sought revenge for her husband's betrayal and thus created a public scandal and acted against the norms of the Church and colonial society. The administrator's wife stood by her actions in that she claimed she no longer loved her husband, who she asserted had had an affair with the daughter of a *yerbatero*. Even though Margarita Arandí had threatened her life and attacked her, interestingly no one came to Petrona Sánchez's defence. Perhaps Petrona Sánchez's own relatives were deceased or resided far from the mission town. Under other circumstances, an indigenous woman would have faced punishment or imprisonment for assault.

Cacique Don Eusebio Guyrapepo admitted to having seen Margarita Arandí enter the priest's living quarters and knew there was a fight around midnight between Margarita and the wife of the administrator. The priest defended himself by stating that the Guaraní who offered testimonies were not impartial. Don Eusebio Guyrapepo, according to the Franciscan priest, had beat his own wife with a stick and the priest had had to intervene to protect her. This happened to the extent that the Indian *cabildo* had had to punish

13 'Cavildo y Caziques del Pueblo de Jesús, sobre el recurso echo por el Adm. del Pueblo de Jesús, Lucas Cano, con el cura de misiones Fr. Francisco Xavier Dominguez, 1782', AGN IX-36-9-6, Misiones 1783, palaeography translated from Guaraní into modern Spanish by A. Otazu Melgarejo with revisions by C. Boidin, Sorbonne IHEAL, Paris, Oct.-Nov. 2012. See the data base LANGAS, http://langas.cnrs.fr/#/consulter_document/extraits [accessed 15 Sept. 2019].

Don Guyrapepo for mistreating his wife. In turn, several other Guaraní did not
testify that the priest had had any type of relationship or illicit affair with either
of the two married women. They responded that they never heard the priest
leave at night to enter the living quarters of the Indian women. They observed
that he only went to the Indians' houses when they were sick. El Teniente de
Corregidor Julian Tacurari confirmed this.

There are constant twists and turns in the story, according to each testimony.
The Regidor Primero Cacique Principal Don Miguel Arâendî claimed the
Indian Margarita had entered the bedroom of the Franciscan priest and
provided a mattress for her house (obviously implying that the two had
sexual relations), but that he never saw the priest visit other Indian women.
Corregidor Don Enrique Tacurari only mentioned that he had heard the fight
between the wife of the administrator and the Guaraní woman in the priest's
living quarters. Being the *corregidor*, the most important Indian official in
the town, he submitted his testimony even though in reality he had nothing
entirely new to add for the investigators. Either he was posturing or this was an
act of respect or a way of emphasising that his testimony should be included in
the investigation because he was the most important Indian leader in the town.

Aside from some contradictions in the various testimonies, it is evident
that those individuals in colonial Paraguay who suffered the most were the
white Spanish woman, the Guaraní laundress and the Franciscan priest, all
three of whom were expelled from the town. The judicial record made no
mention of the detrimental effects of the allegations of adultery on the Sánchez
children. The exiled Franciscan priest remained in a state of melancholy and
was described as being very sad. He first lived in Mission Candelaria and later
in MissionYapeyú.[14] The final fate of Petrona Sánchez is unknown, but most
probably she was sent away from the town to reside in a religious institution or
with relatives, at least for a time.

Conclusion

Certain individuals, whether a man of the cloth or women from different
social classes, race and ethnicities were apparently unwilling to conform to the
expectations of obedience to male authority or the teachings of the Catholic
Church, or to follow colonial society's rules without objection. Women,
whether they were members of the Spanish colonial elite or Guaraní, however,
were not without some recourse in matters of the heart. Women could exercise
a degree of power through residing in Buenos Aires away from their spouses;
complaining to their local priests; controlling their own body and emotions;
and, on this rare occasion, dishonouring their husbands by committing adultery
with a Catholic priest. Banishment from the town and the use of physical

14 'Sobre el recurso echo por el Adm. del Pueblo de Jesús, Lucas Cano, con el cura del mismo, Fr.
    Francisco Xavier Dominguez', AGN IX-36-9-6, Misiones 1782.

space in confining women to religious institutions, shelters or workhouses were powerful tools, wielded by authorities within the *missions* and by the Catholic Church to deal with individuals who were perceived to have violated colonial society's social norms by committing acts of adultery. Guaraní women could also be subjected to physical domestic abuse without much recourse other than complaint to the local priest. Domestic abuse or physical violence against women was tolerated to a degree in the town, although the Franciscan had intervened on behalf of a *cacique*'s wife. His willingness to assist abused women in this respect was not, however, well received by *cabildo* officers and *caciques*. Ultimately, the community's interests and the strong dislike of a particular Spanish woman by the townsmen largely determined the outcome of these cases of adultery, along with attitudes towards gender, marriage, sexuality, race and ethnicity in this patriarchal society.

Appendix

'Classical' Guaraní paleography	Modern Guaraní	Modern Spanish transliteration
Ex.ᵐᵒ S.ᵒʳ Virrey Y Cap.ⁿ Grâl.	Excᵐᵒ Señor Virrey Y Capitán General	Excᵐᵒ Señor Virrey Y Capitán General
Ore Jesus tabapegua; Cav.ᵈᵒ haè Caziques.	Ore Jesus táva pegua; Cavildo ha'e Caciques.	Nosotros los del pueblo de Jesús; Cabildantes y Caciques.
Oroñemoî ndepĩguĩpe:	Oroñemoî nde py guýpe:	Nos ponemos bajo tus pies:
Cherubichaguazu ñemomirĩbe pype Ndemboyerobiabo;	Che ruvicha guasu ñemomirĩve pýpe Nde mbojeroviávo;	Mi gran Jefe, con mucha humildad y respeto;
yyĩpĩberâmo Ñandeyara rera pĩpe, haè Ñande Rey rera pype abe: cobaè orequatia pype ndemongeta mirĩbo ânga Cherubichaguazu.	ijypyve ramo Ñandejára réra pýpe, ha'e Ñande Rey réra pýpe ave: ko va'e ore kuatia pýpe nde mongeta mirĩvo anga Che ruvicha guasu.	en primer lugar, en nombre de Dios, y en nombre de Nuestro Rey también: a través de esta carta, nos dirigimos brevemente a ti, mi gran Jefe.
D.ⁿ Lucas Cano niâ; omboayeporâete Ñandeyara, haè Ñande Rey poroquaita:	Don Lucas Cano niâ; omboaje porâ ete Ñandejára, ha'e Ñande Rey porokuaita	Don Lucas Cano; que respeta la ley de Dios, y la de Nuestro Rey:
opacatu ore mboriahureta rehe, yporerequa porâete	opakatu ore mboriahu reta rehe, iporerekua porâ ete	que nos cuida bien a todos nosotros los pobres
haè ore Estancia acoi Adminis.ᵒʳ D.ⁿ Juan del Granja recoramo ocañĩrei baecue pype:	ha'e ore Estancia akói Adminis.ᵒʳ D.ⁿ Juan del Granja reko ramo okañy rei va'ekue pype:	y en nuestra Estancia, que se había perdido en tiempos del Administrador Don Juan del Granja :
Baca omoî yebĩ:	Vaka omoî jevy:	él repuso las vacas:
haè Hacienda, ocañĩrei baecue abe omoñemoña yebĩ Mandiyu haè Lienzo:	ha'e Hacienda, okañy rei va'ekue ave omoñemoña jevy Mandyju ha'e Lienzo:	y en la Hacienda, que se había perdido, también él hizo que se produzcan de nuevo algodón y lienzo:
haè opacatu mbaè tetĩrôrehe cobaè Oretaba poriahu oipĩtĩbongâtu oicobo,	ha'e opa katu mba'e tetirõ rehe ko va'e ore táva poriahu oipytyvõ ngatu oikóvo,	y él ha podido ayudar como se debe a nuestro humilde pueblo en todo

'Classical' Guaraní paleography	Modern Guaraní	Modern Spanish transliteration
haè omoquirîrîporâ abe mbĩareta opacatu.	ha'e omokirirĩ porã ave mbya reta opakatu.	y ha podido tranquilizar a todas las personas.
Haè oroiquaaco S.ᵒʳ Gov. D.ⁿ Fran.ᶜᵒ Pieza Candelariapegua:	Ha'e oroikuaa ko S.ᵒʳ Gov. D.ⁿ Fran.ᶜᵒ Pieza Candelaria pegua:	Y sabemos que este Señor Gov. Don Francisco Pieza de Candelaria:
oipeàce cobaè oretaba hegui.	oipe'ase ko va'e ore táva hegui.	quiere sacarle de nuestro pueblo.
Oimeco aĩbu cobaè ore adminis.ᵒʳ D.ⁿ Lucas Cano rehe acoi râmo:	Oiméko ayvu ko va'e ore adminis.ᵒʳ D.ⁿ Lucas Cano rehe akói ramo:	Hay algunos rumores hacia la persona de nuestro Administrador Don Lucas:
Aipo baè tereiquaa ânga peteĩ rehebe cherubichaguazu.	aipo va'e tereikuaa anga peteĩ reheve che ruvicha guasu.	por eso es bueno que sepas de una vez mi gran Jefe.
Cobaè ore Capatas Caray la Villa ỹgua ore Baquiano ore caàtĩpe ombaè apobaè;	ko va'e ore Capatas Carai la Villa ygua ore Baquiano ore ka'atýpe omba'e apo va'e;	Nuestro Capataz (es) un Señor de la Villa, nuestro Baqueano que trabajó en nuestro yerbal.
cobaènico ore Adminis. ᵒʳ con Padre, Pedro Pablo Sanchez herabaè :	ko va'e niko ore Adminis.ᵒʳ kompadre, Pedro Pablo Sánchez héra va'e :	Este es el compadre de nuestro Administrador, que se llama Pedro Pablo Sánchez.
cobaè y con Padre rayĩ rehe herâqua orohendu,	ko va'e ikompadre rajy rehe herakuã orohendu,	Hemos escuchado que este tiene una relación con la hija de su compadre,
haè aete ndorohechai ytĩeîrâmo coterâ hecobairâmo aracaè bei cobaè ore Adminis.ᵒʳ	ha'e aete ndorohechái ytie'ỹ ramo koterã heko vai araka'evéi ko va'e ore Adminis.ᵒʳ	sin embargo, no hemos visto que nuestro administrador sea grosero o de mala conducta jamás,
hecobairâmo coterâ ytĩeîrâmo : ỹmaetemamo oroipeà oreyehegui aracaè	heko vai ramo koterã itie'ỹ ramo : yma ete namo oroipe'a ore jehegui araka'e	si él tuviera mala conducta o fuera grosero hace mucho tiempo que ya le hubiéramos echado nosotros mismos

'Classical' Guaraní paleography	Modern Guaraní	Modern Spanish transliteration
abarepãnga oipotane heco baibaè haè ytĩeĩbaè abene, Cherubichaguazu.	ava tepãnga oipotáne heko vai va'e ha'e itie'ỹ va'e avéne, che rubicha guasu.	quién lo querría a alguien que además de comportarse mal sea escandaloso, mi gran Jefe.
Aipo baè rehe teremee ãnga Licencia àpe opĩta haguãmacatu :	Aipo va'e rehe tereme'ẽ ãnga Licencia ápe opyta haguãma katu:	Por eso te rogamos que des Licencia para que se quede aquí:
cobaè Ore Adminis.ᵒʳ D.ⁿ Lucas Cano, aipobaè reheãnga co :	ko va'e Ore Adminis. ᵒʳ D.ⁿ Lucas Cano, aipo va'e rehe ãnga ko :	nos referimos a nuestro Administrador Don Lucas Cano,
oroñemomirĩngatu ãnga ndebe cherubichaguazu, oroyoguerubo oroñezubo ndebe ndepĩguĩpe :	oroñemomirĩ ngatu ãnga ndéve che ruvicha guasu, orojoguerúvo oroñesũvo ndéve nde pyguýpe :	por esa razón nos humillamos ante ti mi gran Jefe, venimos a ponernos de rodillas a tus pies:
oroñemoĩbo teremae anga oreporiahurehe yoporiahubereco marãngatu tereiporuãnga ore rehe	oroñemoĩvo terema'ẽ anga ore poriahu rehe joporiahuvereko marãngatu tereiporu ãnga ore rehe	para que te fijes en nosotros los pobres y que tengas misericordia con nosotros
Ñandeyara raĩhu rehe ; haè ndecĩ raĩhu reheabe.	Ñandejára rayhu rehe; ha'e nde sy rayhu rehe ave.	por amor de Dios; y por amor de tu madre.
Ebocoi baè ñotêanga orôhaârô ndepo agui ndepoaca apĩreĩ rubichaete baè agui; cherubichaguazu.	Evokói va'e ñote ãnga oroha'ãrõ nde po agui nde po'aka apyre'ỹ ruvicha ete va'e agui; che ruvicha guasu.	Por eso solamente esperamos en tus manos poderosas; mi gran Jefe.
Ouraco Buenos = Ayres hegui cobaè ore Adminis. ᵒʳ rembireco S.ʳᵃ Petrona,	Ou rako Buenos = Ayres hegui ko va'e ore Adminis.ᵒʳ rembireko Sra. Petrona,	Ciertamente, vino de Buenos Aires la esposa de nuestro Administrador, la Sra. Petrona,
haè acoi aĩbu ohendubaècue rehe :	ha'e akói ayvu ohendu va'ekue rehe :	y constantemente escuchaba la murmuración de la gente :

'Classical' Guaraní paleography	Modern Guaraní	Modern Spanish transliteration
ndoguerecocatui Omena, haè acoi òcomadre membĩ rehebe ndayoguereco catui;	ndoguereko katui omena, ha'e akói ocomadre memby reheve ndojoguereko katúi;	no le trataba bien a su marido, ni se llevaba bien con la hija de su comadre;
aipobaè rehe oroipeàboi cobaè oretaba hegui acoi ycomadre:	aipo va'e rehe oroipe'a voi ko va'e ore táva hegui akói icomadre:	por eso la hemos sacado de nuestro pueblo a su comadre :
oyeyapopotareĩ aĩbu reta coterã Pleyto, cobaè oretabape.	ojejapo potare'ỹ ayvu reta koterã Pleyto, ko va'e ore távape.	por murmurar mucho u ocasionar pleito en nuestro pueblo.
Haè orõmeê cobaè ore Adminis.or rembirecoupe cotĩporeĩ amo haècueraño oico hagua rehe, ababe omoangeco eĩhaguâme :	Ha'e orome'ẽ ko va'e ore Adminis.or rembireko upe koty pore'ỹ amo ha'ekueraño oiko haguã rehe, avave omoangekoe'ỹ haguãme :	Y le dimos por eso a la esposa de nuestro Administrador un lugar donde puedan vivir solos, donde nadie les molestará:
haè aipocotĩ haè año oicohaheguiraco; oroiquaa peteĩ pĩtûme omena rembiquaa eĩrâmo oho hague Pay Cura cotĩpe, cobaè ore Adminis.or rembireco:	ha'e aipo koty ha'e año oikoha hegui rako; oroikuaa peteĩ pytũme omena rembikuaae'ỹ ramo oho hague Pa'i Cura kotýpe, ko va'e ore Adminis.or rembireko :	y de donde vivía sola, supimos que una tardecita, al oscurecer sin que supiera su marido, se había ido al cuarto del Pa'i Cura, esta es la esposa de nuestro Administrador:
haè oyoyohu peteĩ orerayĩ Cuñambucu amo rehe; ebocoi cuñambucu niô ore Pay Cura ahoyoheiha :aipobaè rehe oromaèñote Pay Abare mboyerobiahape,	ha'e ojohu peteĩ ore rajy cuña mbusu amo rehe; ebokói cuña mbusu niô ore Pa'i Cura ao joheiha : aipo va'e rehe oroma'ẽ ñote Pa'i Avare mbojeroviahápe,	y encontró a una muchacha, hija nuestra; pues la muchacha es la lavandera de nuestro Pa'i Cura: pues confiábamos en el Pa'i Avare
heta àra ohechañote opabaè Pay Abare rehe yporerequa haba.	heta ára ohecha ñote opa va'e Pa'i Avare rehe iporerekua hába.	Ella veía, sin más, por mucho tiempo todo lo que pasaba, por estar al cuidado de las cosas del Pa'i Avare.
Haè àete acoi peteĩ pĩtume oyapobaiete òyoehe Pay Cura cotĩ oyoyohubo :	Ha'e aete akói peteĩ pytũme ojapo vai ete ojoehe Pa'i Cura kotýpe ojojohúo :	Y precisamente una tardecita se pelearon al encontrarse en el cuarto del Pa'i Cura :

'Classical' Guaraní paleography	Modern Guaraní	Modern Spanish transliteration
oñoîrârô oyoguerecoai guazu oyoitĩbo ỹby rupi;	oñorairõ ojoguerekoai guasu ojoitýbo yvy rupi;	se pelearon fuertemente, maltratándose, tirándose al suelo una a otra;
cobae ore Pay Cura cotĩpe.	ko va'e ore Pa'i Cura kotýpe.	esto ocurrió en el cuarto de nuestro Pa'i Cura.
Cobaè niâ oroiquaa opacatu mitangue rehebe Cherubichaguazu.	Ko va'e niã oroikuaa opakatu mitangue reheve che ruvicha guasu.	Esto lo supimos todos, incluido los niños, mi gran Jefe.
Oreanganiâ oromboyerobia guazutebaè Pay Abare,	Ore anga niã orombojerovia guasute va'e Pa'i Avare,	Nosotros le respetamos al Pa'i Avare,
oroguerecobaè el Vicario de Jesu Christo râmo oroñemomirîngatubo ychupe:	oroguereko va'e el Vicario de Jesu Christo ramo oroñemomirĩ ngatúvo ichupe:	le consideramos el Vicario de Jesu Christo, le obedecemos.
haète ânga noromboyerobiacane bei:	ha'ete ãnga norombojerobiakanevéi:	Pero dejaremos de respetarle:
acoi cuña mocoî ycotĩpe oñoirârô hague rehe	akói kuña mokõi ikotýpe oñorairõ hague rehe	después de haberse peleado dos mujeres en su cuarto,
orômaèhape haè norômopûâî abeco yapura guazu amo Pay Abare rehe oroguenoticatu o Mifsa baèramo hecohape	oroma'ẽ hápe ha'e norõmopu'ãi avéko japúra guasu amo Pa'i Abare rehe oroguenotĩ katu oMisa va'e ramo heko hápe	sin embargo, no le estamos difamando al Pa'i Avare, sino que nos avergonzamos de él cuando celebra la Misa,
aipobaè rehe ndebe año oroiquaa uca Cherubichaguazu,	aipo va'e rehe ndéve año oroikuaa uca che ruvicha guasu,	por eso le comunicamos solamente a ti mi gran Jefe,
oroiquaa râmo Ñande Rey recobia reterâmo nderecohape;	oroikuaa ramo Ñande Rey rekovia rete ramo nde rekohápe;	sabiendo que ocupas el lugar de Nuestro Rey;
haè oroiquaa abe Ñandeyara Justicia, ereyapo porâ haguama orebe.	ha'e oroikuaa ave Ñandejára Justicia, erejapo porã haguãma oréve.	y sabemos también que harás cumplir cabalmente la justicia de Dios para con nosotros.

'Classical' Guaraní paleography	Modern Guaraní	Modern Spanish transliteration
Aipobaè rehe terembou ânga Pay ambuae amo cobaè oretabape ore Pay Cura râmo oromboyerobia yebĩ baèrâma heco marângatu rehe.	Aipo va'e rehe terembou anga Pa'i ambuae amo ko va'e ore távape ore Pa'i Cura ramo orombojerovia jevy va'erãma heko marãngatu rehe.	Por eso envíenos otro Pa'i como nuevo Cura de nuestro pueblo para que volvamos a respetarle por su santidad.
Emaè ânga oreporiahu rehe;	Ema'ẽ anga ore poriahu rehe;	Apiádate de nosotros los pobres;
tocañĩteĩ eme ânga, oreânga poriahu Ñandeyara Jesu Christo ruguĩ marangatu ñemombuca hague,	tokañyteĩ eme anga, ore ánga poriahu Ñandejára Jesu Christo ruguy marangatu ñemombuka hague,	que no se pierda nuestra alma, por la que se ha derramado la sangre de Nuestro Señor Jesu Christo,
haè ymano acĩcatu hague rehe nde maêhape	ha'e ymano asy katu hague rehe nde ma'ẽhápe	y fijándote en el sacrificio de su muerte
terêhendu ânga, haè teremboaye abe ânga cobaè oreyerureha; Cherubichaguazu.	terehendu anga, ha'e teremboaje ave anga ko va'e ore jerureha; che ruvicha guasu.	escuche y cumple nuestro pedido; mi gran Jefe.
Tupâ Ñandeyara tomeê ânga heta roỹ rupi nde recobe marâneỹ haba,	Tupã Ñandejára tome'ẽ ânga heta ro'y rupi nde rekobe marãne'ỹ hába,	Que Dios te dé larga vida buena,
oremboriahu retaupe guarama Cherubichaguazu	ore mboriahu reta upe guarãma che ruvicha guasu	para nosotros los humildes mi gran Jefe.
Theni.te de Corr.or Julian Tacurari	Theni.te de Corr.or Julian Tacurari	Theni.te de Corr.or Julian Tacurari
Regidor Primero Cazique Principal Miguel Arãendĩ	Regidor Primero Cazique Principal Miguel Arãendy	Regidor Primer Cacique Principal Miguel Arãendĩ
Cazique Eusebio Guĩrapepo	Cazique Eusebio Guyrapepo	Cacique Eusebio Guĩrapepo

'Classical' Guaraní paleography	Modern Guaraní	Modern Spanish transliteration
Por los demas del Cav.^{do} y Caziques que nosaben firmar	Por los demás del Cav.^{do} y Caziques que no saben firmar	Por los demás del Cav.^{do} y Caciques que no saben firmar
el Secret.° de Cavildo Ygnacio Aratutî	el Secret.° de Cavildo Ygnacio Aratutî	el Secretario de Cavildo Ygnacio Aratutî

Source: 'Cavildo y Caziques del Pueblo de Jesús, sobre el recurso echo por el Adm. del Pueblo de Jesús, Lucas Cano, con el cura de misiones Fr. Francisco Xavier Dominguez, 1782', Archivo General de la Nacion, Argentina, AGN IX-36-9-6, Misiones 1782; palaeography translated from Guaraní into modern Spanish by A. Otazú Melgarejo with revisions by C. Boidin, Sorbonne IHEAL, Paris, October-November 2012.

Exmo. Sr. Virrey, Captain General.

The community of Jesús, members of the town council and chiefs, kneel down before your feet, our great chief with much humility and respect. In the first place, in the name of God and also in the name of our King, through writing this letter we briefly address you, our great chief. Don Lucas Cano who respects the laws of God and those of our King, who takes care of us poor ones and those who reside on our ranches. Our previous administrator Don Juan of the farm denied us cattle which wandered off on the farms; he also had us produce cotton and cloth, which had been lost. It is he [Cano] who has been able to help us poor people in everything and been able to put everyone at peace. We are aware that the Señor Governor Don Pieza of Candelaria wants to have him removed from this town. There are some rumours about our administrator Don Lucas, with whom we are familiar, so you are now aware of this, my great chief. Our *capataz* [foreman] is from our village and works in the yerba plantation. He is a godfather (or friend) of our administrator who is called Pedro Pablo Sánchez. We heard that the administrator has had a relationship with the daughter of his godfather. Nonetheless, we have never seen our administrator act grotesquely or ever behave badly. If he had behaved badly or was rude, we would have removed him from office a long time ago. We had always wanted someone who never behaved poorly or in a scandalous manner, my great chief. For these reasons, we beg you to give us your permission so that he could remain here. We are referring to our administrator, Don Lucas Cano. For this reason, we kneel before your feet and so that you pay attention to those who are poor and so that you have mercy on us for the love of God and the love of your mother. We are certain that the wife of our administrator, Señora Petrona came from Buenos Aires and have heard the constant local rumours of the people about how she did not treat her husband well. She also did not get along well with her godfather's daughter. For this reason, we have removed her from the town [of her godmother] because there was much talk about the present lawsuit in our town. We say this because the wife of our administrator should reside alone where no one could not bother them. We learned one late afternoon, when it was getting dark and without the knowledge of her spouse, she had gone to the room of the priest; this is, the wife of our administrator. There she found a girl, one of our own who is the laundress for our priest; well we confided in the priest. She knew what had been going on for a long time, nonetheless, with the priest for having looked after him. And precisely one afternoon, the two physically fought with one another in the quarters of the priest. They struggled hard, mistreating one another, throwing each other to the ground. This happened in the bedroom of the priest. Everyone found out about this situation, including the children, my great chief. We had respected our priest and we considered him to be the vicar of Jesus Christ and obeyed him. But we stopped respecting him after the two women fought in his bedroom. Nevertheless, we are not trying to damage his reputation. However, we were ashamed of the priest when he goes to celebrate the mass. And for this reason, we communicate this only to you, my great chief, knowing well that you occupy the position of king. And we know that you will capably do the right thing for God for our benefit. For this reason, you should send another priest whom we could respect, so that we could return to respect your holiness. Please take pity on us poor so that we do not lose our souls for which our saviour Jesus Christ has shed His blood and in light of His sacrifice of His death. May you listen and fulfil our request, my great chief. May God grant you a long life, for we are your humble servants, our great chief.

Lieutenant Corregidor Julian Tacurari first alderman, principal chief Miguel Arãendĩ

Chief Eusebio Guĩrapepo, and for all the remaining members of the *cabildo* and the chiefs who do not know how to sign their names, Secretary of the cabildo, Ygnacio Aratutĩ

Bibliography

Anderson, B.S. and J.P. Zinsser (1989) *A History of Their Own: Women in Europe from Prehistory to the Present* (2 vols., New York: Harper & Row).

Boidin, C. and A.O. Melgarejo (2018) 'Toward Guaraní semantic history: political vocabulary in Guaraní (sixteenth to nineteenth centuries)', in A. Durston and B. Mannheim (eds.), *Authority, Hierarchy, and the Indigenous Languages of Latin America: Historical and Ethnographic Perspectives* (Notre Dame, IN: University of Notre Dame Press).

Boyer, R. and G. Spurling (eds.) (2000) *Colonial Lives: Documents on Latin American History, 1550–1850* (New York and Oxford: Oxford University Press).

Carbonell de Masy, R. and N. Levinton (2010) *Un pueblo llamado Jesús* (Asunción: Fundación Paracuaria Missionsprokur).

Donohue, F. (2012) 'To beget a tame breed of people: sex, marriage, adultery and Indigenous North American women', *Early American Studies*, 10 (1): 101–31.

Durston, A. and B. Mannheim (eds.) (2018) *Indigenous Languages, Politics, and Authority in Latin America: Historical and Ethnographic Perspectives* (Notre Dame, IN: University of Notre Dame Press).

Ganson, B. (2003) *The Guaraní Under Spanish Rule in the Rio de la Plata* (Stanford, CA: Stanford University Press).

Jackson, R.H. (2008) 'The population and vital rates of the Jesuit missions of Paraguay, 1700–1767', *Journal of Interdisciplinary History*, 38: 401–31.

McDougall, S. (2014) 'The opposite of the double standard: gender, marriage, and adultery prosecution in late medieval France', *Journal of the History of Sexuality*, 23: 206–25.

Ruiz de Montoya, A. (2017) *The Spiritual Conquest: Early Years of the Jesuit Missions in Paraguay*, trans. by B. Ganson and C.M. Saffi (Boston, MA: Institute of Jesuit Sources).

5. Music in the Jesuit missions of the Upper Marañón

Leonardo Waisman

The 30 Guaraní pueblos of the province of Paraguay have always been the darlings of music historians of the Jesuit missions. From Muratori's idealising panegyrics in the 18th century to the historiographic and musicological production of the 20th, the expressions of praise and awe at the musical achievements of the Amerindians guided and trained by a handful of priests have formed a continuous and unanimous chain of acclaim.[1] The appearance in the 1980s of the considerable collections of musical partbooks preserved by aboriginal communities in Chiquitos and Moxos has only widened the focus, without displacing it. Chiquitos, of course, belonged to the Jesuit province of Paraguay, although in historiography it had always played second fiddle to the Guaraní region.[2] Moxos, missionised from Lima in the province of Peru and neighbour to Chiquitos, shared the larger part of its musical repertory – although, as this author has remarked elsewhere, it developed some differential traits.[3] In these three networks of towns (usually referred to as *reducciones*, that is, settlements where the natives were 'reduced' or disciplined to European lifestyle and religion) the missionaries succeeded in establishing flourishing musical practices, inspired by and adapted to the requirements of the divine services with their daily, weekly and yearly cycles. Although music-making was widespread in the missions, comprising informal instrumental groups for entertainment and more institutionalised ensembles for feasts and receptions, pride of place belonged to the semi-professional musical chapel of each pueblo, conducted by a chapel master and consisting

---

1 These are mostly contained in short sections on the subject within books and articles with a wider focus. The only book-length treatment is J. Herczog, *Orfeo nelle Indie: I gesuiti e la musica in Paraguay (1609–1767)* (Lecce: Mario Congedo, 2001).

2 For an overview of music in this mission area, see I. Ruiz, G. Huseby and L.J. Waisman, 'Un panorama de la música en Chiquitos', in P. Querejazu (ed.), *Las misiones de Chiquitos* (La Paz: Fundación BHN, 1994), pp. 659–76.

3 L.J. Waisman, 'La música en las misiones de Mojos: algunos caracteres diferenciales', in W. Sánchez (ed.), *La música en Bolivia de la prehistoria a la actualidad* (Cochabamba: Fundación Simón I. Patiño, 2002), pp. 529–46; and 'La contribución indígena a la música misional en Mojos (Bolivia)', *Memoria Americana*, 12 (2004): 11–38.

L. Waisman, 'Music in the Jesuit missions of the Upper Marañón', in L.A. Newson (ed.), *Cultural Worlds of the Jesuits in Colonial Latin America* (London: Institute of Latin American Studies, 2020), pp. 111–26. License: CC-BY-NC-ND 2.0.

of some forty singers and instrumentalists who played European-style music on instruments they had built themselves. Daily mass was accompanied by this chorus and orchestra, whose prowess was celebrated in neighbouring Spanish cities whenever they undertook 'artistic tours', calculated to impress dwellers of centres with much poorer musical forces.[4] A good measure of the accomplishments of these musicians, initially taught by Jesuit musicians but with the practice later sustained by chains of Amerindian teachers and students, is a cycle of so-called *Ofertorios* for insertion into the mass (that is, not belonging to the mass itself, but intended as an enhancement of its rites) preserved in manuscript in the Archivo Musical de Chiquitos.[5] The cycle contains over eighty pieces, ranging from single songs with basso-continuo accompaniment to full Psalms deploying virtuoso solo singers, massive choirs and brilliant orchestral passages.

In recent years musicologists and other scholars have begun to tackle other mission areas in Iberian America: V. Rondón has researched the so-called 'Araucanía' (Southern Chile);[6] M. Holler and P. Castagna the settlements under the Portuguese Crown;[7] E. Bermúdez and D. Farley the missions in the Orinoco Basin;[8] and K. D. Mann those of New Spain (present-day Mexico and the southern USA).[9] The picture which emerges from these studies can explain (though not justify) the discrimination in favour of Paraguay. To start with, the almost complete lack of musical scores preserved in those areas constitutes a signal discouragement to researchers in a discipline traditionally centred on musical works which has often had the objective of restoring music of the past to current musical practice. In addition, and more to the point, it emerges that in none of the regions studied hitherto had the practice of European music reached the richness of media and resources or the level of stability it enjoyed in that frontier area between the Spanish and Portuguese empires, where the Guaraní and later the Chiquito and the Moxo were taught and trained by

4   It must be kept in mind that these were outlying cities (Buenos Aires, Asunción, Santa Fe), not the main musical centres of Spanish settlement such as Lima (Mexico) or La Plata.

5   See the complete edition: L. Waisman (ed.), *Un ciclo musical para la misión jesuítica: Los cuadernos de ofertorios de San Rafael, Chiquitos*, 2 vols. in 3 (Córdoba: Brujas, 2015).

6   V. Rondón, *19 canciones misionales en mapudúngún contenidas en el Chilidúgú (1777) del misionero jesuita en la Araucanía Bernardo de Havestadt (1714–1781)* (Santiago: Revista Musical Chilena y FONDART, 1997).

7   M. Holler, *Os jesuítas e a música no Brasil colonial* (Campinas: UNICAMP, 2010); P. Castagna, 'The Use of Music by the Jesuits in the Conversion of the Indigenous Peoples of Brazil', in J.W. O'Malley et al. (eds.), *The Jesuits: Culture, Science and the Arts, 1540–1773* (Toronto: University of Toronto Press, 1999), pp. 641–58.

8   D.F. Rodríguez, '"Y Dios se hizo música": la conquista musical del Nuevo Reino de Granada. El caso de los pueblos de indios de las provincias de Tunja y Santafé durante el siglo XVII', *Fronteras de la Historia*, 15 (2010): 13–38; E. Bermúdez, 'La música en las misiones Jesuitas en los Llanos orientales colombianos 1725–1810', *Ensayos*, 5 (1998): 143–66.

9   K.D. Mann, *The Power of Song: Music and Dance in the Mission Communities of Northern New Spain, 1590–1810* (Stanford, CA: Stanford University Press, 2010).

the Society of Jesus. Nevertheless, the knowledge gained about these musical cultures, less distinguished from a European point of view, has allowed a comparative perspective which illuminates better the achievements and failures of the Jesuits in the establishment of western musical practices.[10]

The wave of exploration of the Jesuit efforts in different geographical and institutional locations, however, has not included the study of their actions and achievements in the Audiencia de Quito, known as *Misiones del Marañón*, missions of the upper Amazon, or *Misiones de Mainas (Maynas)*, located in present-day territories of Ecuador, Peru and, for a short period, Brazil. In these tropical forest lands, the men of the Society of Jesus endeavoured to 'civilise' and convert to Christianity a variety of ethnic groups, such as the Jíbaro or Shuar, the Cocama, the Omagua, the Encabellado and the Yameo. In successive and somewhat discontinuous waves starting in 1639, they advanced downstream along several tributaries of the Amazon river, establishing villages, some of which survived and flourished for decades; many others were soon abandoned by their inhabitants, decimated by disease, or raided by the neighbouring Portuguese. In fact, the large-scale advance towards the middle course of the Amazon successfully undertaken by the Bohemian Jesuit Samuel Fritz was frustrated in 1710 by a Portuguese fleet which established the limits between the two empires at the juncture of the Yavarí and Amazon rivers – still today the border between Brazil and Peru. The closest Spanish settlements were the small city of San Francisco de Borja on the Marañón river and Lamas on the Mayo river (affluent of the Huallaga); the capital of the missions was established at La Laguna, on the last-mentioned river, a town with 1,000 inhabitants in 1735. Figures 5.1–5.2 represent the central area of the Jesuits' efforts in these lands, in maps drawn by two of the missionaries, Juan Magnin and Samuel Fritz. The later fate of these *reducciones* was not happy: by the time of the expulsion of the Jesuits from Spanish lands (1767) only a few were well established and prosperous and after few decades even these had been deserted.

As usual with mission history, the main sources for study are the writings of the missionaries themselves, mostly in the form of edifying letters sent from their American stations or memories, descriptions and histories written mostly in Europe after their expulsion in 1768.[11] In the case of Mainas, one must

10 It goes without saying that the Jesuit fathers did not conceive of their role as that of promoters of artistic endeavours. Nevertheless, the aesthetic enjoyment of music which transpires from some passages in the writings of Knogler, Schmid or Paucke betrays a joy which seems to indicate that musical practices, in addition to serving as a tool of evangelisation, constituted promoters their own reward.

11 For a basic bibliography of the Mainas *misión* see: F. de Figueroa, 'Informe de las misiones del Marañón' [1661], in F. de Figueroa et al., *Informes de jesuitas en el Amazonas, 1660–1684* (Iquitos: IIAP-CETA, 1986), pp. 143–309; M. Rodríguez, *El Marañón y Amazonas* (Madrid: Antonio Gonçalez de Reyes, 1684); [P. Maroni], 'Noticias auténticas del famoso río Marañón y misión apostólica de la Compañía de Jesús de la provincia de Quito en los dilatados bosques de dicho río, escríbalas por los años de 1738 un misionero de la misma' (MS., Madrid, Academia Nacional de la Historia), http://bibliotecadigital.rah.es/dgbrah/i18n/consulta/

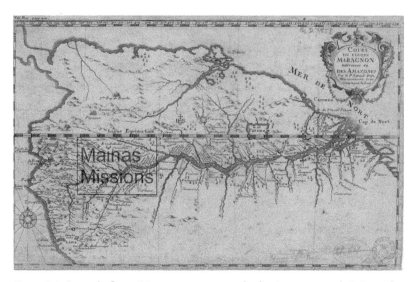

Figure 5.1. Cours du fleuve Maragnon, autrement dit des Amazones par le P. Samuel Fritz, Missionnaire de la Compagnie de Jésus. *Author Samuel Fritz (1656–1725). (Courtesy Bibliothèque nationale de France).*

add the useful and extensive compilation of information from writings of the former missionaries and conversations maintained with the exiles put together in Plasencia by the Jesuit José de Chantre y Herrera in the 1780s; and an ample section on the missions in Juan de Velasco's *History of Quito* (1789).

Reading the accounts of the European protagonists of the missionary adventure one receives images of a harsh history: the project never outgrew the heroic phase, which among the Guaraní, the Moxo and the Chiquito lasted only a few decades. Page after page of these reports describes encounters with previously unknown ethnic groups, the founding of new villages and news about Amerindian groups deemed ripe for evangelisation but not yet Christianised. Mingled with these indicators of Jesuit hopes there are equally abundant stories

registro.cmd?id=6150 [accessed 30 May 2019]; M. Jiménez de la Espada (ed.), *Noticias auténticas del famoso río Marañón y misión apostólica de la Compañía de Jesús de la provincia de Quito en los dilatados bosques de dicho río, escribíalas por los años de 1738 un misionero de la misma* (Madrid: Fortanet, 1889); J. Magnin, *Breve descripción de la Provincia de Quito y de las misiones de Succumbios y de Maynas* [1740] (Quito: Sociedad Ecuatoriana de Investigaciones Históricas y Geográficas, 1989); M.J. Uriarte, *Diario de un misionero de Mainas,* [1774] transcription, introduction and notes by C. Bayle, 2 vols. (Madrid: Bibliotheca Missionalia Hispanica, 1952); J. Chantre y Herrera, *Historia de las misiones de la Compañía de Jesús en el Marañón español* [c. 1780] (Madrid: Avelai, 1901); J. de Velasco, *Historia del reino de Quito* [1789], edited by A. Pareja Diezcanseco (Caracas: Fundación Ayacucho, 1981); F.X. Veigl, 'Gründliche Nachrichten über die Verfassung des Landschaft von Maynas', in Ch.G. von Murr, *Reise einiger Missionarien* (Nuremberg: Johann Eberhard Zeh, 1785); and J. Jouanen, *Historia de la Compañía de Jesús en la antigua Provincia de Quito, 1570–1774* (Quito: Ecuatoriana, 1943).

of violence and destruction: clashes with 'pagan nations' and with Portuguese expeditions; countless rebellions by the aborigines dwelling within their system. Moreover, always hovering around was the menace of epidemics which decimated populations and often meant the complete disappearance of entire ethnic groups.[12] Few passages reveal the degree of stability which in other areas permitted the flourishing of European-style musical practices.

Amidst these unpromising circumstances, nevertheless, music was heard. Early on, the repertoire and resources were meagre. When in 1645 the Spanish Governor of Mainas province, Juan Antonio de Toledo, visited the northern outposts of the Jesuit project on the Napo River in order to formalise the natives' subjection to the crown, he conducted veritable ceremonies of homage, complete with the oath of fealty of medieval tradition. The music for these symbolic rites was mostly provided by a few military drummers and fifers (*cajas y pífanos*), who travelled with the escort of the official and provided a continuous background of sound, only interrupted during the formal, archaic and exotic (for America) speeches in which the governor offered protection and the *caciques* swore loyalty. At the very end of these lengthy ceremonies the missionary led the entire assembly in singing the *Alabado* 'according to their custom, instead of the *Te Deum laudamus*'.[13] A *Te Deum* was prescribed for such a state ceremony in all Catholic countries; if the natives sang the Spanish praise of the Sacrament it was because it was the only liturgical item they knew: it was the earliest and most widespread song in all the Jesuits' American missions.[14]

At the project's very inception, father superior Gaspar Cujía established in the nearby city of Borja a kind of seminary for indigenous children:

> wishing to contribute to the endeavour of civilising the gentiles in a
> most profitable manner, no less efficacious than that of his brethren, he
> conceived, promoted and established in the same city two houses in which
> boys and girls from the friendly nations who would consent in sending
> their children to Borja were assembled. One house was like a seminary for
> youths who learned the general tongue of the Inca [Quechua language],
> Christian doctrine and became acquainted with Spanish customs. From

12 L.A. Newson, *Life and Death in Early Colonial Ecuador* (Norman, OK: University of Oklahoma Press, 1987), pp. 309–14.

13 'poniéndose todos de rodillas, entonó el misionero el Alabado en vez del Te Deum laudamus, que cantaron según costumbre' (Chantre y Herrera, *Historia de las misiones*, p. 386).

14 Among numerous references in contemporary accounts, the seven pages (pp. 93–100) devoted to daily life in the missions in J. Cardiel's *Compendio de la Historia del Paraguay* (Buenos Aires: Fecic, 1984) of 1780 mention no fewer than four different occasions for the performance of this piece. The last one is especially interesting: 'The entire music [chorus and orchestra] sings the *Alabado*, which is then repeated by the whole congregation to the sound of trumpets with a joyful and harmonious blare' (p. 97). In other words, even when the villages had evolved sophisticated, rich musical establishments, the *Alabado* retained its attributes as monophonic communal song. In Mainas the *Alabado* was always sung in Spanish, whereas in most mission areas this was only one possibility among the many local languages or *linguae francae* (Chantre y Herrera, *Historia de las misiones*, p. 632).

Spaniards they [also] acquired abilities [technical training] that could be useful in their villages. The other house was like a boarding house for recently baptised girls who, besides becoming well versed in doctrine and in the Inca tongue, learned from some pious ladies of the town – who volunteered their teaching services – the activities proper to their sex, such as spinning, knitting, embroidery and other such things.

… from these seminaries issued the interpreters for their respective nations, and they were the most useful instruments to introduce into the villages the doctrine, the order and concert necessary for spiritual and political government. If they [also] learned, as became gradually established, singing, music and playing the instruments that are adequate to Church functions, they came to be of great use for the churches and their decorum, and their fellow villagers looked up to them as men of a different class; they respected them and followed their advice in everything … Since these means, invented by Father Gaspar in his Borja parish, proved wonderfully [their efficacy] and provided great assistance to the missionaries, who could avail themselves of good collaborators in their missions, the same fathers began to put it into practice in the villages that were founded subsequently. They kept in their own house several boys whom they raised, keeping them within their eyesight like seminary students; and close to the missionary's quarters, another apartment in the manner of a hospice or children's home, where an old woman, of proven virtue and talents, taught the girls things proper to their age.[15]

In one of the many cases in which Jesuit chroniclers partially contradict each other, Franz Xaver Veigl, a veteran with 15 years in the missions, dismisses the usefulness of the centralised seminary, which he brands as 'only a wish[:] the missionaries had no other resources than to make their own houses function concurrently as seedbeds [or seminaries]', housing some orphans, some of the sons of the *caciques* and some children captured from 'wild' nations for their education and training.[16] Testimonies as to the usefulness of these locally trained children abound. During the 1750s, in the town of Jesús on the Napo river, under the administration of Father Manuel Uriarte:

the children were the missioner's delight. He maintained in his house a school or seminary with several boys whom he supported from the effects that the *mitayeros* brought for him. They first learned the Catechism, then the tongue of the Incas, and some of them a little Spanish. They always were in attendance at Mass, prayed the Rosary, and before going to bed they said other prayers, [after which,] singing the *Alabado* and kissing the Father's hand, went to sleep in the same bedroom as he.[17]

15 Chantre y Herrera, *Historia de las misiones*, p. 139.

16 Veigl, 'Gründliche Nachrichten', pp. 319–20. The centralised facility dismissed by Veigl was to be located in Quito, not Borja.

17 Veigl, 'Gründliche Nachrichten', p. 420: The word *mitayero* clearly derives from *mitayo*, natives who served turns of duty for the Spanish overlords; missionary chronicles from Chantre y Herrera to A. Alemany in the 1880s apply it to native providers of food for the

The villages being, as a rule, less stable, more numerous and smaller than those in other mission areas (averaging fewer than five hundred souls), there were never enough priests to attend to their spiritual and corporeal welfare. The boys who had lived or still lived with the Jesuit served as substitutes when he left to visit other settlements or to recruit more converts. The following passage, which refers to Father Francisco Real, is representative:

> Although Father Real had his hands full with the care of so many rivers and sites, his tasks were redoubled towards the end of that year [1743], because of Father Miguel Bastida's removal from the mission of San José to Quito. He had to take charge both of that town and of his own while awaiting the arrival of Bastida's successor. He did not shy away from such a heavy load: he visited town after town without repose, went from village to village, passed from one river to the next and among all the reduced Indians he promoted with good results the punctual assistance at Catechism sessions, attended daily by children and on certain days by adults. The missionary taught the doctrine himself in the town where he happened to be; in the others, two or three well-instructed boys led the singing of the Catechism, followed by children and grown-ups who repeated the doctrine in this way.[18]

References to musical practices contained in the accounts by the missionaries seem to indicate, beyond their justified pride in the accomplishments of 'their' neophytes, that in the vast majority of cases they were describing monophonic singing, with or without instrumental accompaniment. The genre most often mentioned is that of *coplas* or *coplillas* in Spanish, Quechua, or a local tongue. By way of examples, we may point to Chantre y Herrera's description of daily life, which included evening singing, by the children, of 'several *coplitas* of the Four Last Things, of the Lord's Passion and of the Sorrows of the Blessed Mary, sung by turns [on different days]'; or to Uriarte's laudatory remarks concerning old Andrés Yabaguera, who 'died in my arms … singing all the sacred *coplillas* that he knew and had taught'.[19] In these, the verbal information conveyed seems to have been far more important than the musical expression of devotion.[20] One religious text which shows up repeatedly, often in conjunction with a harp accompaniment, is that of the Litanies of Loreto. Since that prayer is structured as a long series of similar versicles, each answered by a 'choral' response, and

missionaries and for evangelising expeditions (quoted in B. Izaguirre, *Historia de las misiones franciscanas y narraciones de los progresos de la geografía en el oriente del Perú*, vol. 9 [Lima: Talleres tipográficos de la Penitenciaria, 1922], p. 324).

18 Chantre y Herrera, *Historia de las misiones*, p. 390. Father Real was savagely killed by some of his parishioners two years later.

19 Chantre y Herrera, *Historia de las misiones*, p. 641; Uriarte: *Diario*, vol. 1, p. 201. Although Uriarte here calls him Yamaguera, he spells it Yabaguera on p. 148.

20 For an examination of the diverse roles and advocations of music in Amerindian devotion under the Jesuits, see L. Waisman, 'Music for an endless conversion: a cycle of offertories from Jesuit Paraguay', in I. Fenlon and M. Laube (eds.), *Sound in the Early Modern City* (Turnhout: Brepols, forthcoming).

since the use of learned polyphony seems to have been scarce, we can imagine performances based on a slightly variable melodic formula supported by a simple harmonic accompaniment, in the manner of the medieval Spanish *romances* and *chansons de geste*.

The scarcity of resources for European-style music is evident everywhere: for example, in the use of *bobonas* to summon the people to the central square.[21] A key function in the endeavour to 'civilise' the natives, disciplining their sense of temporality and space, entrusted to bells, snare-drums (*cajas*) and shawms (woodwind instruments) throughout the Spanish colonies (and certainly in Jesuit Paraguay), was here assigned to locally developed instruments, built from locally available materials with local know-how. This, of course, is also a strong witness to the continued persistence of indigenous musical practices, less evident (although not totally lacking) in the Guaraní settlements.

A request made by the missionary Johann Baptist Julian in 1724 may reveal a side of music-making of which we know next to nothing in any of the mission areas: 'I await eagerly the Jew's harps promised by Father Jacobus Albelda; if he has forgotten, please send them at the first opportunity, for our Indians are very fond of this music'.[22] It seems evident that these simple instruments were used for private or small-group music-making as a form of leisure; and that the priests used them as gifts or trinkets to endear themselves to the local peoples. The significance of an emerging dependence of the natives on European artefacts even for private recreation seems noteworthy.

The organisation of systems of musical education implemented in Mainas differed somewhat from those in the better-known mission areas and presented some similarities to those employed in the embattled frontier evangelisation of New Spain. The stable music schools which functioned in each Guaraní, Chiquito and Moxo town could not be established in the upper Amazon: it was the priest himself who had to impart musical knowledge and training in the playing of instruments with whatever tools and dexterities he was equipped. In this he might be aided intermittently by temporary visits by laymen from neighbouring cities who came for other reasons but happened also to be musicians. Thus Lieutenant Romero, who in 1756 was sent to Mainas by the ruling *Audiencia* in Quito to preserve order in the face of some skirmishes, 'was very skillful: he made a guitar and a violin from two large gourds with their

---

21   See, e.g., Uriarte, *Diario*, vol. 1, p. 80; and Rodríguez, *El Marañón*, p. 334. It is not easy to identify precisely what a *bobona* was. There is a certain confusion between that vocable and *fututo,* surely related to *pututu,* an Inca trumpet made originally from a conch shell, later from the horn of an ox. It is clear that it involved a hollow body (a gourd, the carcass of an armadillo) and a long tube fashioned from a cane. See V.M. Patiño, *Historia de la cultura material en la América equinoccial,* vol. 4 (Bogotá: Instituto Caro y Cuevo, 1992), p. 341.

22   J.B. Julian, 'Brief aus Süd-Amerika. Numerus 281', in J. Stöcklein (ed.), *Der Neue Welt-Bott mit allerhand Nachrichten deren Missionarien Soc. Iesu,* 40 vols. (Augsburg and Graz: Heirs of Philip, Martin and Johann Veith, 1726–58), vol. 11 (1727), p. 84.

masts and a wooden soundboard, [both of?] which he played gracefully in the evenings, and he was entertaining'.[23]

The missions among the Yurimagua took advantage of the musical abilities of the persons of mixed ethnicity from the neighbouring city of Lamas and of the 'celebrated quality of their voices'. Although they practised their trade by ear, without knowledge of 'solfa' [musical notation], several of these singers were invited to the Jesuit villages and put in charge of the musical education of several children, with optimal results.[24]

Alternatively, indigenous children were sometimes sent to the cities, where they acquired the necessary training from Spanish musicians. In the *reducción* of San Joaquín there was a celebrated harpist who had been sent by the missionaries to Quito in order to acquire his craft.[25] Employing different combinations of these resources, the Jesuits managed to develop, in some of the towns and during brief periods, richer musical practices. The sinuous trajectories of these processes of constructions may be gleaned from the course of events in San Joaquín in the decade of 1750–60:

> Item, there were other four singers for Mass and Office, with their chapel master … and these knew by heart the Masses for the Virgin and others taught them by the missionary, the *Pange lingua*, etc., and another old man, Andrés Yabaguera [had taught them] several devotional *coplas* in the language of the Inca that the children repeated on ordinary days, to several different melodies. After these, Father Iriarte brought with him to La Laguna two skillful *Omagua* boys, Adán and Estanislao, whom he had taught to read and write; they were taught musical notation, harp and violin by two other local musicians that had been sent to Lima by Father Ignacio Falcón when he was procurer [liaison officer and representative of the missionary organisation] for training under competent masters, spending on this endeavor 200 pesos. After returning one year later to the village, already married and trained [in music], they would play at Mass on Sundays, Saturdays and Fridays, as well as for feasts; they in turn taught others, so that we had a decorous Mass service, with two harps and four violins, that could [sound] like the Guaraní. This [practice] gradually passed on to other villages.[26]

The paragraph just quoted also serves to illustrate new developments which took place during the last decades of the mission. Already at the start of the narrative, the level of European musical practices appears higher than that

23   Uriarte, *Diario*, vol. 1, p. 104

24   Chantre y Herrera, *Historia de las misiones*, p. 650

25   Chantre y Herrera, *Historia de las misiones*, p. 652.

26   Uriarte, *Diario*, vol. 1, p. 149; another version on p. 200 and a widely different account in Chantre y Herrera, *Historia de las misiones*, p. 653, who may be confusing fathers Iriarte and Uriarte (who served consecutive terms at the *reducción* of San Joaquín). I have privileged Uriarte's first-hand report and suggest 'lucir como' be translated as 'sound like', although more strictly it should be rendered as 'look like'.

common in the upper Amazon in previous decades: at San Joaquín there was a chapel master, Cosme (the only chapel master I have been able to find in the texts examined). However, his chapel consisted of four singers who could not read music, but rather performed from memory the Latin hymns they had been taught by the missionary and an old Amerindian. Meanwhile, two boys from the missions' capital, La Laguna, had been sent to Lima, the vice-regal capital, to learn from professional (most probably lay) musicians how to read music and to play the harp and violin respectively. When they returned to La Laguna, Father Martín Iriarte of San Joaquín was ready for action: he had taken under his wing two youngsters from the Omagua nation[27] and prepared them by teaching them to read and write. He then sent them to La Laguna, where they stayed for a year as apprentices to the Lima-trained musicians. The circuit was closed when these boys went back to San Joaquín and trained some of their fellow choirboys with their newly acquired skills. The result, wrote the missionary, was fit for comparison with the musical practices of the Guaraní Jesuit missions; thus we confirm that already at that time Paraguay constituted the reference for musical excellence.

The activities of Father Iriarte point to another trait, shared by the Mainas project with the musical establishments in most Jesuit missions: the gradual (though sometimes belated) transformation of practices and repertoires following European tastes and fashions. Trained in music and fond of its practice, this Navarran priest felt a need to 'modernise' the instrumental ensembles accompanying the singing:

> The only thing missing was the accompaniment of good instruments, for the trumpets and cornetts that the Omaguas had already learned did not suit the taste and did not please the delicate ear of the missionary. After he was moved to La Laguna as Superior of the missions, he managed to introduce harp and violins that fitted more suitably with the singing and were sweeter and more agreeable to all those who attended the church services.[28]

Nearing the middle of the 18th century most Spanish sacred musical establishments had made the transition from the previous century's reliance on wind instruments (cornetts, shawms, sackbuts and dulcians) to the Italianate string ensemble. With his musical training, Iriarte seems to have achieved a change similar to that effected in Paraguay by the Tyrolean Anton Sepp 50 years before.[29]

We should not, nonetheless, infer that music at San Joaquín was as rich as that performed in Yapeyú in Guaraníes or San Javier in Chiquitos. Instead of the 40-plus members of the leading chapels of those missions, the San Joaquín chapel numbered six, apparently all of them instrumentalists. Although at least

27 San Joaquín was peopled mostly by two ethnic groups, the Omagua and Yurimagua.

28 Chantre y Herrera, *Historia de las misiones*, pp. 652–3.

29 See, e.g., Herczog, *Orfeo nelle Indie*, p. 186.

some of them could read music, we hear nothing about the scores, copyists or written transmission which were an indispensable part of the establishment among Guaraní, Chiquito and Moxo. To help us to form some idea of the import and complexity of the practices at this late date, we can examine the paragraphs which Chantre y Herrera devotes to music. He begins with a defensive move:

> [O]n this subject of the establishment of music in the missions it is necessary to confess that the neglect of some missionaries, both in its institution and in its furtherance, both with respect to instruments and to what appertains to song, cannot be entirely excused. But neither can the censure be accepted of some who, having never stepped on the threshold of the Mission, and – what is worse – having apparently no knowledge of what has been practised there in this respect, have vented their anger with expressions of little esteem towards the missionaries, going as far as to attribute the little advancement of music at the Mission to the lazy and guilty idleness of the Fathers. [30]

It has not proved possible to find the source of such accusations in Jesuit literature concerning Mainas; perhaps these 'some' were outsiders. Chantre goes on to write on the efforts of Father Bernhard Zurmühlen on behalf of European church music, offering fairly precise information about the decades of the greatest flowering of those practices. This Westphalian Jesuit, whose name is usually given in Spanish as 'Zurmillén', spent the years between 1723 and 1726 among the Omagua and was named father superior of the Mainas missions in the 1720s; he settled in the capital of La Laguna around 1730 and died five years later. Chantre writes:

> Father Bernardo Zurmillén, being a missionary at the town of La Laguna, trained eight or ten boys so that they could sing Mass with songs so harmonious and well-ordered that some fathers accustomed to hearing well-concerted Masses in Europe judged that [the Masses at La Laguna] need not defer in any way to the most harmonious and well put-together concerts of a full musical chapel. That missionary upheld the music [establishment] as long as he was in charge of that town, and he promoted it when he became Superior of the Missions. After his death, with the singers no longer available [dead?] the missionaries who succeeded him either were not able to substitute other singers or let themselves be swayed by the mode of thinking [described in the previous quotation], neglected exceedingly such a praiseworthy practice. In spite of this, at the time of the arrest of the missionaries [1768] La Laguna still had singers who intoned with harmony, order and good taste everything that was included in a three-voiced well-made Mass; one could notice the counterpoint of their voices, exquisite for its sweetness and loftiness. This was sung by two treble boys with very agreeable trebles, [and] given more grace by the tenor and bass of four well-attuned Indians. This same ensemble also sang with sweetness, fluency and consonance the *Salve* and the *Litanies* according to

---

30   Chantre y Herrera, *Historia de las misiones*, p. 649.

Father Zurmillén's method.[31]

The paragraph includes several key points. On the one hand, it highlights the frailty of European musical constructions in Mainas: as soon as the father with a special commitment to music left the village, they went into decay or simply disappeared. On the other, it marks the outer limits of the level of complexity in its practices: three-voiced compositions, praised for their 'sweetness', 'harmony' and 'good taste'. No complex counterpoint, no polychoral effects, no virtuosity – none of the sophisticated or ingenious appeal to the senses which we hear about in the Paraguay missions. Besides, it is clear that, in comparison to 'European concerts', the performing bodies remained far short of constituting a 'full musical chapel', although they could be listened to with equal pleasure.

A contrasting practice was established by a Tyrolean father, Franz Xavier Zephyris (1693/5–1769), first in the *reducción* of Concepción in Xeveros and then in San Regis of the Yameos, both situated in the so-called *misión alta* of the Marañón river (fig. 5.2). Its description suggests more colourful and sonorous performances, based on the polychoral principle: '[H]e introduced a choir of trumpets [clarines], cornetts [cornetines] and flutes and taught 12 boys, chosen for their good voices, to sing the Mass in two choirs; by allocating the instruments to one and the other, he succeeded in establishing a sung Mass that was applauded and celebrated by everyone who heard it, on account of its unexpectedness and of the rare accompaniment and new harmony'.[32]

It is difficult to identify with accuracy the instruments employed by Father Zephyris. Chantre y Herrera does not show particular competence in music; and the arrival of real European trumpets (the standard meaning of 'clarín' in the 18th century) to these inaccessible villages seems rather implausible: although they were part of the *instrumentarium* of most towns in the more prosperous and musically rich mission areas,[33] the limited gamut of sounds produced by natural trumpets would have been of little use for the constitution of choirs to accompany children's voices in a polychoral mode. Perhaps the reference here is to the 'cane trumpets' (*clarín de caña*) with which Father Uriarte celebrated the Resurrection in 1754 in San Joaquín.[34] The term *cornetines* is here translated as 'cornetts', the wooden, horn-like instruments still common in Spanish religious and civic music of the 18th century, but the term *cornetas* was also used by Jesuits as a synonym for *bocinas*, autochthonous trumpets made from a gourd and a mouthpiece of wood or cane. 'Flutes', of course, may refer to any flue wind-instrument, European, American or hybrid. Beyond this lack of precision, however, the text makes it clear that this 'rare

---

31   Ibid.

32   Chantre y Herrera, *Historia de las misiones*, pp. 650–51.

33   Cf. F.C. Lange, 'El extrañamiento de la Compañía de Jesús del Río de la Plata (1767)', *Revista musical chilena*, 165 (1986): 4–58 and 176 (1991): 57–96.

34   Uriarte, *Diario*, vol. 1, p. 153.

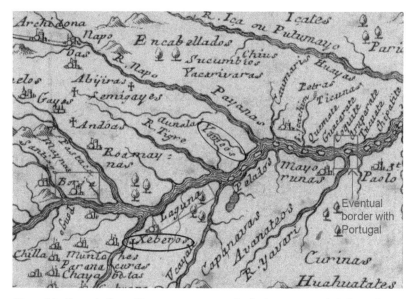

Figure 5.2. Cours du fleuve Maragnon, autrement dit des Amazones par le P. Samuel Fritz, Missionnaire de la Compagnie de Jésus. Author Samuel Fritz (1656–1725).

accompaniment' bespeaks effects of liveliness, bustle and bright colours, rather than the sweetness and gentleness which characterised Zurmühlen's projects.

The Tyrolean Jesuit's achievements perhaps constitute the refinement and complementation of a practice he had found upon arrival at the missions in 1724, which he condemned in no uncertain terms: 'The playing of our Americans comes through as not much better than a brawl of cats and a dog. It consists of wanton lyres, harps, dulcimers, out-of-tune violins and shattered (*bruchhafften*) trumpets, which combine with each other so beautifully that in the middle of this din it is often impossible to make out the genre of the instruments. That is, one cannot tell whether it is a string or wind instrument or whether it is bowed, blown or struck'.[35] This goes beyond the designation of 'colourful'. Zephyris did not, however, neglect the more basic kind of functional music-making which formed the core of the Mainas practices: he composed a long poem in the Quechua language (which most individuals of all ethnic groups would understand) on the central topics of conversion and devotion. Each subject was set in a different poetic metre and to a particular melody; each was sung, accompanied by a distinctive set of instruments, on its appointed day: Sunday, the *coplas* referring to glory; Monday, those of purgatory; the following two days, those of the Four Last Things; Thursday,

---

35 F.X. Zephyris, 'Auszug aus 4. Briefen' [Popayán, 1724 and Latacunga, 1725], in J. Stöcklein (ed.), *Der Neue Welt-Bott*, vol. 11, p. 95. The description of *Trompeten* as *bruchhafften*, although obscure, also suggests cane rather than metal instruments.

the Blessed Sacrament; Friday, the Passion; and Saturday those in praise of the Virgin Mary. Thus, Chantre y Herrera recalls, 'with the sweetness of poetry and the harmony of song, the essential truths of our faith were learned, and its most distinctive devotions instilled'.[36]

Loud and boisterous instruments had also reached the Omagua and Yurimagua areas by that time: the San Joaquín visit of the interim governor of Mainas in 1762 was greeted by 'marches, trumpets (*clarines*), drums and triumphal arches'. As in Xeveros, however, the tradition of communal (monophonic) singing remained central: the parade ended with the 'customary singing of the *Alabado*, with much pleasure and joy'.[37]

The descriptions of masses recounted by Veigl (a missionary much lauded for his musical accomplishments)[38] seem to merge together all the different strands of musical practice we have reported: during the first part of Sunday mass the entire community sang 'the usual prayers in a loud voice'; later, other prayers were accompanied by violin and harp or guitar; the choir then sang the *Alabado*. On Saturdays and high feast days one could hear part-singing by the choir to the accompaniment of trumpets and horns – one assumes in addition to the violins and harps. This would constitute a standard small, festal European orchestra of the mid 18th century minus kettledrums (which perhaps Veigl simply neglected to mention).[39] Since Veigl's description is not localised in a particular village, he may be conflating elements from different performance traditions; or, perhaps, during a few years in a few of the Mainas *reducciones* musical practices could dream of equalling the splendour of Paraguay.

Bibliography

Bermúdez, E. (1998) 'La música en las misiones Jesuitas en los Llanos orientales colombianos 1725–1810', *Ensayos*, 5: 143–66.

Cardiel, J. (1984) *Compendio de la historia del Paraguay* (Buenos Aires: Fecic).

Castagna, P. (1999) 'The use of music by the Jesuits in the conversion of the indigenous peoples of Brazil', in J.W. O'Malley, G.A. Bailey, S. Harris and F.T. Kennedy (eds.), *The Jesuits: Culture, Science and the Arts, 1540–1773* (Toronto: University of Toronto Press), pp. 641–58.

Chantre y Herrera, J. (1901) *Historia de las misiones de la Compañía de Jesús en el Marañón español* [c. 1780] (Madrid: Avelai).

Figueroa, F. de (1986) 'Informe de las misiones del Marañón' [1661], in F. de Figueroa et al., *Informes de Jesuitas en el Amazonas, 1660–1684*, 143–309 (Iquitos: IIAP-CETA).

36   Chantre y Herrera, *Historia de las misiones*, p. 651.
37   Chantre y Herrera, *Historia de las misiones*, pp. 626–7.
38   Chantre y Herrera, *Historia de las misiones*, p. 654.
39   Veigl, 'Gründliche Nachrichten', p. 311.

Herczog, J. (2001) *Orfeo nelle Indie: I gesuiti e la musica in Paraguay (1609–1767)* (Lecce: Mario Congedo).

Holler, M. (2010) *Os jesuítas e a música no Brasil colonial* (Campinas: UNICAMP).

Izaguirre, B. (1922) *Historia de las misiones franciscanas y narraciones de los progresos de la geografía en el oriente del Perú*, vol. 9 (Lima: Talleres tipográficos de la Penitenciaria).

Jouanen, J. (1943) *Historia de la Compañía de Jesús en la antigua Provincia de Quito, 1570–1774* (Quito: Ecuatoriana).

Julian, J.B. (1727) 'Brief aus Süd-Amerika. Numerus 281', in J. Stöcklein (ed.), *Der Neue Welt-Bott mit allerhand Nachrichten deren Missionarien Soc. Iesu*, vol. 11 (40 vols., Augsburg and Graz: Heirs of Philip, Martin and Johann Veith, 1726–58), p. 84.

Lange, F.C. (1986 and 1991) 'El extrañamiento de la Compañía de Jesús del Río de la Plata (1767)', *Revista musical chilena* 165: 4–58 and 176: 57–96.

Magnin, J. (1989) *Breve descripción de la Provincia de Quito y de las misiones de Succumbios y de Maynas* [1740] (Quito: Sociedad Ecuatoriana de Investigaciones Históricas y Geográficas).

Mann, K.D. (2010) *The Power of Song: Music and Dance in the Mission Communities of Northern New Spain, 1590–1810* (Stanford, CA: Stanford University Press).

[Maroni, P.] (1889) *Noticias auténticas del famoso río Marañón y misión apostólica de la Compañía de Jesús de la provincia de Quito en los dilatados bosques de dicho río, escribíalas por los años de 1738 un misionero de la misma*, ed. by M. Jiménez de la Espada (Madrid: Fortanet), http://bibliotecadigital.rah.es/dgbrah/i18n/consulta/registro.cmd?id=6150 (MS., Madrid, Academia Nacional de la Historia) [accessed 30 May 2019.

Newson, L.A. (1987) *Life and Death in Early Colonial Ecuador* (Norman, OK: University of Oklahoma Press).

Patiño, V.M. (1992) *Historia de la cultura material en la América equinoccial*, vol. 4 (Bogotá: Instituto Caro y Cuevo).

Rodríguez, D.F. (2010) '"Y Dios se hizo música": la conquista musical del Nuevo Reino de Granada. El caso de los pueblos de indios de las provincias de Tunja y Santafé durante el siglo XVII', *Fronteras de la Historia*, 151: 13–38.

Rodríguez, M. (1684) *El Marañón y Amazonas* (Madrid: Antonio Gonçalez de Reyes).

Rondón, V. (1997) *19 canciones misionales en mapudúngún contenidas en el Chilidúgú (1777) del misionero jesuita en la Araucanía Bernardo de Havestadt (1714–1781)* (Santiago: Revista Musical Chilena y FONDART).

Ruiz, I., G. Huseby and L.J. Waisman (1994) 'Un panorama de la música en Chiquitos', in P. Querejazu (ed.), *Las Misiones de Chiquitos* (La Paz: Fundación BHN), pp. 659–76.

Uriarte, M.J. (1952 [1774]) *Diario de un misionero de Mainas*, transcription, introduction and notes by C. Bayle (2 vols., Madrid: Bibliotheca Missionalia Hispanica).

Veigl, F.X. (1785) 'Gründliche Nachrichten über die Verfassung des Landschaft von Maynas', in Ch.G. von Murr (ed.), *Reise einiger Missionarien* (Nuremberg: Johann Eberhard Zeh, 1785).

Velasco, J. de (1981 [1789]) *Historia del reino de Quito*, ed. by A.P. Diezcanseco (Caracas: Fundación Ayacucho).

Waisman, L.J. (2002) 'La música en las misiones de Mojos: algunos caracteres diferenciales', in W. Sánchez (ed.), *La música en Bolivia de la prehistoria a la actualidad* (Cochabamba: Fundación Simón I. Patiño), pp. 529–46.

— (2004) 'La contribución indígena a la música misional en Mojos (Bolivia)', *Memoria Americana*, 12: 11–38.

— (ed.) (2015) *Un ciclo musical para la misión jesuítica: Los cuadernos de ofertorios de San Rafael, Chiquitos,* 2 vols. in 3 (Córdoba: Brujas).

— (forthcoming) 'Music for an endless conversion: a cycle of offertories from Jesuit Paraguay', in I. Fenlon and M. Laube (eds.), *Sound in the Early Modern City* (Turnhout: Brepols).

Zephyris, F.X. (1726–58) 'Auszug aus 4. Briefen' [Popayán, 1724 and Latacunga, 1725], in J. Stöcklein (ed.), *Der Neue Welt-Bott mit allerhand Nachrichten deren Missionarien Soc. Iesu*, vol. 11 (1727) (40 vols., Augsburg and Graz: Heirs of Philip, Martin and Johann Veith), pp. 89–95.

6. Beyond linguistic description: territorialisation. Guarani language in the missions of Paraguay (17th–19th centuries)

Capucine Boidin

> *Na kuatia reta mongeta rehe ave rugũãi*
> *aguyjei ereiko ne*
> *imongeta katupyry rehe katu.*
> (1759)[1]

> *No el mucho leer*
> *harta y satisface la vida,*
> *sino más el leer bien.*[2]

> For it is not reading much
> but reading well
> that contents and satisfy the soul

The Jesuits are known for their contribution to the linguistic description of many Amerindian languages, among them the *lingua brasilica* on the coast of Brazil, today known as Tupí, and Guaraní, spoken in the

---

1 J. Insaurralde, *Ara poru aguyjei háva*, 2 vols. (Madrid: Joaquín Ibarra, 1759–60). The quotation is from vol. 1, p. 80 and taken from a digital copy in the Biblioteca Nacional de Madrid. All quotations in Guaraní are transliterated and follow the orthography of the Paraguayan Academy of Guaraní. Palaeographic versions are provided at http://www.langas.cnrs.fr, a site created during the project LANGAS (2011–16), funded by the Agence Nationale de la Recherche and coordinated by this author with the help of C. Itier. Our website and database provide access to palaeography, transliterations and translations of texts in Guaraní, Quechua and Tupí, those Amerindian languages which were considered 'general languages' by the Spanish and Portuguese; and they feature a sophisticated tool for lexical searches.

2 Translation into Spanish by L. Cerno and C. Boidin in 2018. The text in Guaraní reworks the second annotation of the *Spiritual Exercises* of St Ignatius of Loyola: 'For it is not knowing much but realising and relishing things interiorly that contents and satisfy the soul'. *Kuatia mongeta* – literally: 'paper's talk' – is the historical equivalent for 'reading' and *aguyjei ereiko* – 'you live perfectly' – the equivalent for 'holy life'. We use ( ) for literal translation and ' ' for historical translation. A discussion on translation can be found in C. Boidin, 'Mots guarani du pouvoir, pouvoir des mots guarani. Essai d'anthropologie historique et linguistique (XIX–XVI et XVI–XIX siècles)' (Habilitation à diriger des recherches, University of the Sorbonne Nouvelle, Paris 3, 2017).

C. Boidin, 'Beyond linguistic description: territorialisation. Guarani language in the missions of Paraguay (17th–19th centuries)', in L.A. Newson (ed.), *Cultural Worlds of the Jesuits in Colonial Latin America* (London: Institute of Latin American Studies, 2020), pp. 127–45. License: CC-BY-NC-ND 2.0.

province of Paraguay. When José de Anchieta wrote a Tupí grammar (1556) and Antonio Ruiz de Montoya a Guaraní grammar (1640), they shared the same approach (Humanist philology) as their counterparts in Europe to the vulgar languages there.[3] The grammatisation of European and Amerindian languages was carried out at the same time, using similar methodologies and references.[4] In the case of Amerindian languages it was an exo-grammatisation, an analysis from outside. In a European dictionary, the ideal speaker – the one from whom normative examples are derived – is an urban, educated man, just like the authors of the dictionaries themselves. However, in an Amerindian vocabulary, the model, the mouth from which the author constructs his authority, is the 'other', the neophyte Indian.[5] Europeans only gave 'voice' to the Indians at a phonetic and semantic level, not at an epistemological level. Those linguistic descriptions uncovered an Amerindian philosophy of language, yet were based on careful listening to Indian words.[6] The Jesuit grammars which were reprinted at the end of the 19th century in Germany contributed to the development of modern comparative linguistics.[7] Their descriptions are – in the eyes of modern linguists – still accurate in many aspects.[8]

However, those grammars were not only intellectual events, darker or lighter. To print a grammar was, and still is, a political act. For instance, when Antonio Ruiz de Montoya published his Guaraní-Spanish dictionaries, grammars and doctrines in Madrid in 1639 and 1640, he obtained, at the same time, two significant benefits for 'his' Guaraní missions in Paraguay: the right of the Indians to use firearms and to pay tribute directly to the king, thereby escaping the *encomienda*. When the Jesuits signified to the king their linguistic mastery in Guaraní, they thus negotiated direct control over specific Indians and their territories.[9]

3   P. Burke, *Languages and Communities in Early Modern Europe* (Cambridge: Cambridge University Press, 2008). It presents a very useful chronology of first books, grammars and dictionaries printed in European languages (1450–1794), pp. X–XIII.

4   S. Auroux, *La révolution technologique de la grammatisation: introduction à l'histoire des sciences du langage* (Paris: Mardaga, 1994).

5   C. Rodriguez-Alcala, 'L'exemple dans les grammaires jésuitiques du guarani', *Langages*, 166 (2007): 112–26.

6   W. Mignolo, *The Darker Side of the Renaissance: Literacy, Territoriality, & Colonization* (Ann Arbor, MI: University of Michigan Press, 1995).

7   It seems that those Amerindian grammars did not circulate much in Europe before the 19th century (F. Simon, ongoing investigations and personal communication).

8   B. Pottier, 'La gramática del Padre Ioseph de Anchieta', *Suplemento Antropológico*, 32 (1998): 155–76. The grammars produced by the Jesuits were oriented towards the translation of the Christian message and this pragmatic issue helped them to be aware of some specific and effective rules of the language. As they needed to invent neologisms they paid great attention to the logic of agglutination (prefixes and suffixes) (B. Melià, *La lengua Guaraní en el Paraguay colonial que contiene la creación de un lenguaje cristiano en las reducciones de los Guaraníes en el Paraguay* (Asunción: CEPAG, 2003), pp. 187–8).

9   My thanks to J.C. Estenssoro for helping me to take this point into account.

However, grammars and dictionaries were not only imperial policy arguments. Such texts contributed to the expansion of a unified linguistic variant over a vast territory.[10] They were structured and structuring artefacts. They were shaped in local linguistic exchanges and thereby shaped future linguistic communities. This social, semantic and territorial history is complex to relate. In brief, we aim to understand what the Jesuits and their missions did to Tupí-Guaraní languages. How did the missionaries listen, learn, talk and write Guaraní? Who did they listen to, where and when? How did some Jesuits manage to elaborate their catechetical texts in Tupí or Guaraní? What impact did their texts have on oral interactions? On the other hand, how did the Indians listen to these new ideas in their own language? How did they learn to read and write in their newly transformed language?

To answer these questions, we rely on the new perspectives of the Guaraní Corpora. The identified Guaraní corpus amounts to approximately 8,460 original pages, hand-copied or printed between 1628 and 1832, which we can classify as follows:

- 35 per cent constitute metalinguistic works (dictionaries and grammars). These are manuscripts or edited, bilingual volumes, constantly reprinted to this day;
- 50 per cent constitute evangelical works (sermons, catechisms, devotional works). These monolingual manuscripts or printed volumes are usually produced in translation;
- 15 per cent constitute profane documents (narratives, labour dialogues, pharmacopoeia manuals). They are monolingual, only in manuscript form, sometimes produced in translation. H. Thun and his team recently highlighted the importance of these documents and promoted their translation.[11]
- 5 per cent constitute diplomatic correspondence and administrative documents (memorials, testimonies, notes, correspondence) written by traditional and municipal indigenous authorities. In the archives, fewer than half those manuscripts appear with a translation into Spanish. Their historical analysis enabled Eduardo Neumann to demonstrate the existence of a literate, native elite.[12]

Since 2009 it has been easier to gather digital copies from many institutions all over the world. Libraries hold online full digital copies of manuscripts which

---

10 See J.C. Estenssoro and C. Itier, '

11 H. Thun, L. Cerno and F. Obermeier, 'El proyecto Kuatia Ymaguare (PEKY) – "Libros del Pasado"', *Estudios Históricos*, 7 (14) (July 2015): no pag.

12 E. Santos Neumann, 'Práticas letradas Guaranis: produção e usos da escrita indígena – séculos XVII e XVIII. Tese de Doutorado' (unpublished doctoral thesis, Universidade Federal do Rio de Janeiro, 2005), http://objdig.ufrj.br/34/teses/EduardoSantosNeumann.pdf [accessed 4 Sept. 2019].

have only recently been found.[13] It is also easier than ever before to enter the transliterations of them into computer databases and to create an international community of researchers, sharing discoveries day by day. These improvements enhance the identified *corpora* and broaden our knowledge. Even if we are only at the beginning, we know perhaps a little better the extent to and purpose for which Guaraní was written and read within the missions, not only by Jesuits but also by native elites.

Guaraní/Tupí: two languages, two territories

When Jesuits arrived on the coast of Brazil in 1548 the linguistic panorama was complex. They did not find homogeneous, circumscribed languages, or monolingual, monocultural 'groups' of people which they could understand as a whole in order to convert them.[14] More probably they found continuous variations between multiple ways of speaking. They probably were not as surprised as might be expected since linguistic variation and multilingualism also prevailed in Europe at that time.

The Jesuits heard that the Portuguese used a vehicular, autochthonous language with multilingual Indians. This language did not have a glossonym nor was it attached to a specific, unique ethnic group. As the title of Anchieta's grammar indicates, it was 'the most used language on the Brazilian coast'.[15] The encompassing language, called 'lingoa do Brasil' in the first chapter, was linked to many groups located in a vast geographical zone: from the 'Pitiguates do Paraiba' to the 'Tamôyos do Rio de Janeiro' through Tupîs de Sam Vicente. Since it was useful in order to communicate, survive and build missions, the Jesuits learned it, tried to find its internal logic and to fix a more or less standard grammar. They compiled lists of words and started to translate prayers and to write *doctrinas* (see also chapter 9).

13   The use of computers to study the humanities goes back to the Jesuit R. Busa in 1940, but the expression 'digital humanities' and the spread of shared protocols (interoperability) by libraries, publishers and researchers started between 2008 and 2010. In France we prefer to use the expression 'humanités numériques'. The dedicated structure in CNRS, ADONIS, was launched in 2009 and transformed into HUMA-NUM in 2015.

14   The idea that languages are eternal, homogeneous, monads also has a history: S. Auroux (ed.), *Histoire des idées linguistiques*, vol. 1, *La naissance des métalangages en Orient et en Occident* (Liège: Mardaga, 1989); S. Auroux (ed.), *Histoire des idées linguistiques*, vol. 2, *Le développement de la grammaire occidentale* (Liège: Mardaga, 1992); J. Andresen and D. Baggioni, *Histoire des idées linguistiques*, vol. 3, *L'hégémonie du comparatisme*, ed. by S. Auroux (Brussels: Mardaga, 2000). See also the insightful anthropological and historical work of J. Fabian, *Language and Colonial Power: The Appropriation of Swahili in the Former Belgian Congo 1880–1938* (Cambridge: Cambridge University Press, 1986).

15   J. de Anchieta, *Arte de grammatica da lingoa mais vsada na costa do Brasil. Feyta pelo padre Joseph de Anchieta da Côpanhia de IESV. Com licenca do Ordinario & do Preposito geral da Companhia de IESV* (Coimbra: Antonio de Mariz, 1595). Anchieta would have finished his grammar in 1556 but it was only published in 1595 in order to legitimise Jesuits patronage over Indians (C. De Castelnau L'Estoile, "En raison des conquêtes, de la religion et du commerce').

When the Jesuits – and other religious orders – managed to establish settlements, they used this peculiar variant in order to convert Indians coming from remote and different areas. They did not learn as many variants or languages as they heard, nor did they impose Portuguese. They adopted one Amerindian language as the medium for their evangelical labour, the one they had already learned and systematised. Hence they contributed with greater or lesser efficiency to the emergence and consolidation of a supra-ethnic Tupí.[16] However, C. Barros has observed that some missionaries reported that many Indians did not understand this standardised, fixed language.[17] This variant was called *lingua brasilica* during the 17th century, *lingua geral* in the 18th century and Tupí at the very end of the 19th century.[18] Another name, *nheengatu* [the good language] has also been in use since the end of the 19th century to refer to a supra-ethnic variety of Tupí in the Amazonian region and specifically in the Rio Negro region today.[19]

What happened when some Jesuits coming from Brazil arrived in the city of Asunción in 1588 in order to continue their evangelical task? They took their manuscripts in the *lingua geral* with them. They could be useful, as some colonial conquerors stated, because this language was widely understood in the region of Paraguay. In fact, statements about the languages prevalent at the time were contradictory. Some list a great number of distinct languages; others affirm that only one language was spoken. How could they differ so greatly in their observations? It could depend on what type of reality they wanted to portray: diversity (which would underline the difficulties of any mission project) or unity (suggesting hope). In any case, history tells us that these Jesuits lost their manuscripts during their trip from Brazil.[20] They ended up reconstructing the language by building upon the work of the Franciscans, the previous missionaries in the region, namely Fray Luis de Bolaños.[21]

---

16 M.C. Barros Drumond Mendes, 'O intérprete Jesuita na constituição de um Tupi supraétnico', *Papia*, 3 (1994): 18–25.

17 M.C. Barros Drumond Mendes, 'A relaçao entre manuscritos e impressos em tupi como forma de estudo da política lingüística jesuítica do século XVIII na Amazonia', *Revista letras*, 61 (2003): 125–52.

18 M.C. Barros Drumond Mendes, 'Em razão das conquistas, religião, commercio. Notas sobre o conceito de língua geral na colonização portuguesa da Amazônia nos séculos XVII–XVIII', *Mélanges de la Casa de Velázquez*, 45 (1) (2015): 99–112.

19 J. Ribamar Bessa Freire, *Rio babel: a história das línguas na Amazônia* (Rio de Janeiro: Universidade do Estado do Rio de Janeiro; Atlântica Editora, 2004); J. Ribamar Bessa Freire and M.C. Rosa (eds.), *Linguas gerais: politica linguistica e catequese na América do Sul no periodo colonial* (Rio de Janeiro: Universidade do Estado do Rio de Janeiro, 2003).

20 C.A. Page, 'Los primeros misioneros Jesuitas entre Guaraníes y la experiencia de las aldeias de Brasil', *Historia Unisinos*, 20 (2016): 26–38 (32).

21 A. Otazú Melgarejo, *Práctica y semántica en la evangelización de los Guaraníes del Paraguay (S. SVI–XVIII)* (Asunción: Centro de Estudios Paraguayos 'Antonio Guasch', 2006). By comparing the Brazilian and the Paraguayan versions, the authors could provide evidence for the continuities.

In Paraguay the language chosen by the Franciscans already had a specific name: Guaraní. Here the Jesuits adopted and cultivated this glossonym and 'language'. As many observers stated, Guaraní was not very different from the *lingua brasilica*. Nevertheless, with the double colonisation from Spain and Portugal, the colonial frontier divided the territory of the Company of Jesus and the continuum of linguistic variations into two unconnected, differentiated spaces: the Portuguese *aldeias* on the one side and the Spanish *reducciones* on the other. Hence the same religious order operating with the same Amerindian linguistic stratum at the same period (1545–1757 in Brazil and 1588–1767 in Paraguay) built up two different linguistic, orthographic and textual traditions. Indeed, Brazilian Jesuits always refer to Anchieta's grammar; meanwhile, in Paraguay during the same period they refer to the founding fathers, Bolaños and Montoya. Each system became auto-referential and intertextual.

In contemporary history, the Paraguayan war (1864–70) would definitively associate Guaraní with a Paraguayan identity and Tupí with a Brazilian one. Until recently, a specialist in the Tupí corpus and missions usually knew little about the Guaraní corpus and missions and vice versa. The great divide is not easy to deconstruct. Moreover, this colonial and national history explains the origins of the linguistic branches which linguists are accustomed to draw within the 'Tupian languages'. They usually divide the 'Tupian family' into eight branches. Six are located in the state of Rondônia in Brazil. Another, the eighth branch, namely Tupí-Guaraní, covers a huge region from the Amazon river to the Andean foothills. Could this Tupí-Guaraní 'unity' be the outcome of a common mission history and this dichotomy (Tupi/Guaraní) an effect of the colonial frontier? If it is too early to answer these iconoclastic questions,[22] we can affirm that multilingualism existed prior to the Jesuit missions and that Amerindian monolingualism was only achieved or well engaged after their departure in 1767.[23]

Guaraní, a territorialising language

Even if sporadic missions were attempted from 1588, officially the Jesuit province of Paraguay (which included contemporary Uruguay, Argentina and Chile) was created in 1604. Every mission gathered people of various languages

22   W. Dietrich suggests that the Paraguayan war enhanced the divide between Guaraní and Tupí (W. Dietrich, 'La importancia de los diccionarios Guaraníes de Montoya para el estudio comparativo de las lenguas Tupí-Guaraníes de hoy', *Amerindia*, 19–20 (1995): 287–99). We go further and challenge the way historical linguists use an 'empty chronology', that is to say, a timeline out of social history.

23   Letter from father J.S. Labrador to L. Hervás y Panduro, Ravenna, 21 June 1783, in *Comparatio linguarum cognitarum*, "De linguis Paraquariensis", ARSI opp. nn. 342 IV, pp. 174–5. In this letter Sánchez Labrador explains that within the missions some languages are 'capitals' and 'common', such as Guaraní; and others accessories such as Guayaqui or Mbaya. He gives the example of the mission of Concepción, where the neophytes spoke nine different languages.

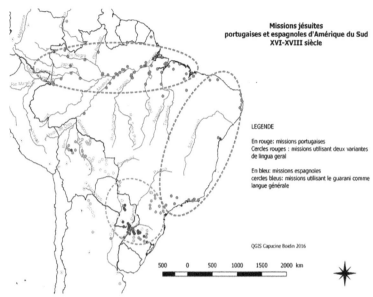

Figure 6.1. Portuguese and Spanish Jesuit missions of South America, 16th–18th centuries. In red: Portuguese missions; red circles where missions use two variants of the lingua geral. In blue: Spanish missions; blue circles where missions use Guaraní as a general language. (Capucine Boidin).

Figure 6.2. Jesuit missions of South America, 16th–18th centuries. Spanish frontier missions in blue; penetration of Portuguese missions in red. (Capucine Boidin).

and cultures. Sometimes they came from the region where the mission was settled, but usually groups of varying sizes came from remote regions.[24] Due to threats from other indigenous groups, Portuguese slave traders or Spanish *encomenderos*, some indigenous leaders decided to negotiate their participation in the Jesuit missions instead of continuing war.[25] In what language did they negotiate? Even if they were not natural Guaraní speakers, this idiom may have been the pivotal language they used in order to establish a translation chain (Spanish into Guaraní, then Guaraní into other indigenous languages). As stated above, the Jesuits learnt Guaraní with the help of previous analytical works and translations done by the Franciscans. On the other hand, Guaraní was already a *lingua franca* in the region of Paraguay for many different indigenous groups. In those complex linguistic interactions, a minimal *colonial vocabulary* in Guaraní could serve to fix the contract between both parties.

A legal document written at the end of the 17th century reports that, years before, the Jesuits proposed, and the Indians accepted, direct vassalage to the king, thus preventing the *encomenderos* from demanding allegiance and providing protection. This document uses Guaraní words, probably in order to reinforce its authenticity, demonstrate the linguistic ability of the Jesuits and indicate the conscious consent of the Indians.[26] However, even if this 'primitive' contract is a retrospective reconstruction, it is highly plausible that this vocabulary was effectively used from the beginning of the missions to define the mutual obligations and rights between the Indians and the king.[27] In the Jesuits' language, the king, *mburuvichavete* [the true superior], proposes to the Indians that they be his 'vassals', that is to say, his *voja* [minor], so as to treat them in the same way as the Spaniards. The king's judge or *oidor*, the *mba'ekuaapára* [el hombre de saber], is meant to protect them with his laws, *kuatia* [paper and graphics]. These four words are the product of a linguistic 'middle ground', a kind of 'third space' of mutual accommodations between

---

24 G. Wilde, 'Relocalisations autochtones et ethnogenèse missionnaire à la frontière sud des empires ibériques (Paracuaria, 1609–1768)', *Recherches Amérindiennes au Quebec*, 41 (2–3) (2011): 13–28.

25 M. Avellaneda, *Guaraníes, criollos y Jesuitas. Luchas de poder en las revoluciones comuneras del Paraguay, siglos XVII y XVIII* (Asunción: Editorial Tiempo de Historia, 2014).

26 AGN, Archivo y colección Andrés Lamas, Leg. 6, *Relacion sumaria de los servicios presentados a la Corona por los indios guaranies de las misiones*, chapter 7, 'Del modo como estos indios de las reduciones pidieron y alcançaron de su mag. A el privilegio dicho de no ser encomendados a los españoles ni servirles sino ser vassalos de su mag.', fols. 7–8. My thanks to M. Avellaneda for sharing with me the copy of the documents in which I could identify those words. See Avellaneda, *Guaraníes, criollos y Jesuitas*, p. 40.

27 Except for *Mba'ekuaapára*, all the words presented in this chapter have been extensively used in our corpus from the 16th to the 19th centuries.

multilingual indigenous and multilingual foreigners (European missionaries and Spanish authorities).[28]

We are witness not only a process of acculturation, westernisation, colonisation and resistance, but possibly a burgeoning double, and mutual, process of re-interpretation. Everybody tries to speak the language of the other and, in order to do so, everyone identifies in the other their own customs or figures. The Jesuits identify the king with the autochthonous chief and vice versa. The Indians identify the judge with their 'verbal art' specialist.[29]. The misunderstandings might be profound at the beginning,[30] but as colonial rule is established a Guaraní vocabulary is indexed to monarchical practices.

In regard to the 'creation of a religious language in Guaraní', the social process and the linguistic result are quite different.[31] It is not a question of diplomacy and negotiation but a story of spiritual conquest and westernization. In the process, the whole of Christian dogma and civilised (that is to say Spanish) way of life had to be translated – and, in fact, after a period of relative tolerance, the Catholic hierarchy controlled the orthodoxy of the outcome. The missionaries had a purpose, to 'reduce' the Indians to *policía Cristiana*, in other words, to reorganise their way of living and believing, reorienting their will and seducing their hearts. It was not only a question of mutual agreement or action, but a question of global and profound transformation.

Nevertheless, missionaries needed native speakers in order to align both languages and create a 'neologos' or 'translanguage'.[32] If they wanted to establish proper correspondences, they had to listen to the way the Indians used each word in different contexts. For instance, Father Montoya registers *iñaká ngorói ita* as they say when the water level falls and the rocks' heads just appear'.[33] We can imagine him sitting on the banks of a river, watching and listening to the Indians or even fishing with them. After gathering those daily observations, the *Lengua* Jesuits (experts in the Guaraní language) could engage in a dialogue

28   A source of inspiration is: R. White, *The Middle Ground: Indians, Empires, and Republics in the Great Lakes Region, 1650–1815* (Cambridge: Cambridge University Press, 2010).

29   Richard Bauman, 'Verbal Art as Performance', *American Anthropologist*, n.s., 77 (1975): 290–311.

30   J. Lockhart, 'Double mistaken identity: some Nahua concepts in postconquest Guise', in J. Lockhart, *Of Things of the Indies: Essays Old and New in Early Latin American History* (Stanford, CA: Stanford University Press, 1999), pp. 98–119.

31   B. Melià, *La lengua Guaraní del Paraguay* and *La lengua Guaraní del Paraguay historia, sociedad y literatura*, Colección lenguas y literaturas Indígenas, 6 (Madrid: Mapfre, 1992). B. Melià coordinated the new edition of the four major works by A. Ruiz de Montoya published in Madrid between 1639 and 1640 (*Tesoro, Arte, Bocabulario, Catecismo*). Hereafter we refer to them with abbreviated forms and in modern editions, indicating the title of the original publication, the date of the modern edition in () and the original ones in [].

32   W.F. Hanks, *Pour qui parle la croix: la colonisation du langage chez les Mayas du Mexique* (Nanterre: Société d'ethnologie, 2009); W.F. Hanks, *Converting Words: Maya in the Age of the Cross* (Berkeley, CA: University of California Press, 2010), chapter 1.

33   Ruiz de Montoya, *Tesoro* (2011) [1639], p. 257.

with *ladino* Indian auxiliaries (skilled in Spanish) and lay interpreters in order gradually to stabilise the translation into words equivalent to those used in Catholic rituals and prayers. Together they established new correspondences to old words (*Tupã*, God; ñemombe'u, 'to tell oneself', i.e., 'confession'); created new ones (*Tupã óga*, 'house of God', 'church'); or introduced Spanish words (*espiritu santo*, the Holy Spirit).

They forged a Catholic register in Guaraní which was to be theologically coherent but also pleasing to Amerindian ears. The result is twofold: descriptive and prescriptive. Today it gives us access to a historical ethnography – Guaraní as it was when the missionaries arrived[34] – and to the prescriptive Catholic language – Guaraní as it had to be used in Catholic contexts.[35] Is the result artificial? Indeed, in some ways this Christian Guaraní is a kind of 'deterritorialised' language, a transformed and transforming tool, a converted language used to convert Indian men and women. It was created in order to be projected or, more accurately, introjected into the new social space of the missions. It helped to build the missions in the uncertain world of the mid 17th century.

Guaraní, a territorialised language

By the end of the 17th century the Jesuit missions had gained economic and political stability. Thirty missions were stabilised between the Paraná and Uruguay rivers at the intersection of Brazil, Paraguay, Argentina and Uruguay, gathering together approximately 100,000 people amongst huge cattle stations and yerba mate plantations. Semi-nomadic hunter-gatherer societies had been transformed into sedentary, agro-pastoral societies. A social division of work took place, not without contradictions and instability. A process of territorialisation effectively took place, producing cultural and linguistic homogenisation among the inhabitants of every missionary town.[36] It transformed Amerindian concepts of space, time and the body – even though these were still expressed in Guaraní.[37] Between 1700 and 1727 a printing press was established in the missions in order to print books in Guaraní.[38] As many monolingual and some

34 G. Chamorro, *Decir el cuerpo historia y etnografía del cuerpo en los pueblos Guaraní: Diccionario etnográfico histórico de la engua Guaraní*, vol. 1 (Asunción: Fondec Tiempo de Historia, 2009); A. Caballos, *Etnografía Guaraní según el 'Tesoro de la lengua Guaraní' de Antonio Ruiz de Montoya* (Asunción: CEPAG, 2013).

35 B. Melià, *La lengua Guaraní en el Paraguay*.

36 J. Pacheco de Oliveira, 'Uma etnologia dos "Índios misturados"? Situação colonial, territorialização e fluxos culturais', *Mana*, 4 (1998): 47–77.

37 G. Wilde, 'The political dimension of space-time categories in the Jesuit missions of Paraguay (17th and 18th centuries)', in G. Marcocci, W.D. Boer and A. Maldavsky (eds.), *Space and Conversion in Global Perspective* (Leiden: Brill, 2014), pp. 175–213.

38 Printed books mention Loreto and Santa Maria de Fe as places where books were printed; for further details see G. Wilde, 'Adaptaciones y apropiaciones en una cultura textual de frontera.

bilingual books were printed *in situ* and conformed to a high written standard, a new social order was emerging.

In this process Guaraní was a territorialising tool but also a territorialised language attached to the missions. Mental and individual prayers were combined with collective and sung recitations. These oral practices were based on written support and reading. The missionaries needed Guaraní to be written in order to give lectures in a comprehensible language; and the Indians needed the religious vocabulary to be fixed on paper in order to memorise the orthodox version. In that way they could both learn by heart a proper, unified, Christian Guaraní. Constantly repeated, this Guaraní religious vocabulary ended up being indexed to objects (crosses, statues), architecture (church, streets, houses) and body practices (kneeling, joining hands). Fixed and disseminated by writing, staged and repeated in daily practice, this religious Guaraní was coextensive with the social space of the missions. The paradox is that by taking roots it also became a form of vernacular. Every missionary town seems to have developed a few linguistic particularities.[39]

The Jesuits adapted new linguistic tools in order to update their metalinguistic knowledge.[40] Pablo Restivo's grammar and vocabulary (1727–28) are currently considered to be updates of those by Montoya.[41] During this period, the Jesuits also translated Latin and Spanish books into Guaraní: a spiritual 'bestseller' of the 17th century, *De la diferencia entre lo temporal y lo eterno* (1640), was translated and printed at the mission in 1705.[42] Montoya's chronicle *Conquista espiritual del Paraguay* (1639) was translated into Guaraní in 1733, probably by Pablo Restivo.[43] A monolingual Guaraní book, whose title could be translated as *The Good Use of Time*, was printed in two volumes in Madrid in 1759 and 1760. It follows the four-week structure of St Ignatius's *Spiritual Exercises*. It is a devotional book dedicated to the edification of the Indians and addressed in

Impresos misionales del Paraguay Jesuítico', *Revista História UNISINOS*, 18 (2014): 270–86.

39 G. Chamorro, 'PHRASES SELECTAS: Un diccionario manuscrito castellano-guaraní anónimo', *Corpus*, 4 (2) (2014).

40 L. Cerno and F. Obermeier, 'Nuevos aportes de la lingüística para la investigación de documentos en guaraní de la época colonial, siglo 18', *Folia histórica del Nordeste*, 21 (2013): 33–56 (42).

41 The linguist S. Liuzzi also re-edited A. Ruiz de Montoya's work and particularly the work by P. Restivo, *Gramática Guaraní Jesuítico*, Enciclopedia de Misiones, 1996, http://www. fondazioneintorcetta.info/pdf/HISTACT2982.pdf [accessed 4 Sept. 2019].

42 The front page of the Guaraní version indicates it was 'impreso en las doctrinas'. For further details, retro-translations and analysis see T. Brignon, *Mba'e Mỹmba Pype, la traduction en Guaraní d'un bestiaire salutaire : L'édition missionnaire de la diferencia entre lo temporal y eterno de Juan Eusebio Nieremberg (Loreto, 1705)* (Paris: Mémoire de Master 2 Sorbonne Nouvelle - IHEAL, 2016).

43 M. Ringmacher, '"La conquista espiritual del Paraguay" en Guaraní clásico como objeto de conquista filológica', in W. Dietrich and H. Symeonidis (eds.), *Guaraní y Mawetí-Tupí-Guaraní. Estudios históricos y descriptivos sobre una familia lingüística de América del Sur* (Berlin: LIT, 2006), pp. 223–39.

turn to 'my little brother', 'my sons', 'my sons and daughters'.[44] This suggests that the *Spiritual Exercises* of St Ignatius of Loyola were given to the Indians. Furthermore, as many pages are dedicated to the way one should read – little by little, every day, night and day – we think that individual reading was encouraged, or at least proposed as an ideal to the Indians. This observation is congruent with the fact, as noted, that the majority of the printed books and manuscripts circulated in monolingual Amerindian versions. For what? Only for loud, collective reading? Or also for individual, possibly silent, reading as recommended by Father Insaurralde at the beginning of his book?

At this time some indigenous elites were writing Christian Guaraní with much more proficiency then the Jesuits themselves, if we give credit to Jesuit comments about Nicolas Yapuguay. This Guarauní musician and *cacique* is known for his two printed, monolingual Guaraní books written under Jesuit control: *Explicacion del catecismo* (1724) and *Sermones y exemplos* (1727). As recently demonstrated, these books are evidence of the scholastic training he received as a literate indigenous. For instance, depending on the genre (catechism or sermon), he practised the *reductio* and *dilatio* of the same *exempla* (Christian moral histories repeated since at least the 13th century).[45]

A twofold process was underway. Jesuits were becoming familiar with colloquial Guaraní and native peoples with the literacy practices of the Jesuits. It seems that they collaborated in the emergence of a secular corpus, one composed of a war diary, *Diario de guerra* (1704–05);[46] a set of dialogues from everyday life (that is to say, labour) known as the Gülich manuscript or *Dialogos Guaraní* (undated, *c.* 1720);[47] and a pharmacopoeia manual called *Pohã ñana* (*c.* 1725).[48] In the Church, the yerba mate plantations, the cattle stations and the carpentry workshop, at the infirmary and during municipal assemblies, directions were given and obeyed in Guaraní. Sermons, technical instructions and political decisions are said to have been executed and often written in Guaraní; and this specific register of the Guaraní language was taught to children intended to govern their missions.

44 Insaurralde, *Ara poru aguyjei háva*, pp. a3–a4. See C. Boidin, L. Cerno and F. Vega, '"This is your book": Jesuits edition's policy and native individual reading (Paraguay, 18th century)', *Ethnohistory*, forthcoming.

45 T. Brignon, *Un traducteur exemplaire. Le cacique Nicolás Yapuguay et ses exempla en langue Guarani (Missions Jésuites du Paraguay, 1724–1727)* (Toulouse: Mémoire de Master Université Toulouse 2, 2017).

46 See a complete translation in H. Thun, L. Cerno and F. Obermeier (eds.), *Guarinihape Tecocue – Lo que pasó en la guerra (1704–1705). Memoria anónima en Guaraní .... Edición Crítica*, Fontes Americanae (Kiel: Westensee, 2015).

47 See M. Orantin, *La cloche, le rabot et la houe: Fragments d'un quotidien de travail dans les missions Jésuites du Paraguay (1714?)* (Paris: Mémoire de master 2 Sorbonne Nouvelle - IHEAL, 2017).

48 See A. Otazú Melgarejo, 'Contribución a la medicina natural: Pohã Ñana, un manuscrito inédito en Guaraní (Paraguay, S. XVIII)', *Corpus*, 4 (2) (2014).

Within the missions, many indigenous authorities (*caciques* and *cabildantes*) became literate in Guaraní. Not only were they able to 'sing', 'imitate' and 'copy', but also think, express and defend their interests in this language, which could be a 'second' indigenous language for them. As a medium of their historical interactions, conflicts, discussions and negotiations, a common political vocabulary in Guaraní, embedded in religious and kinship vocabulary, was constantly produced and manipulated. By mastering alphabetic writing and colonial conventions of written correspondence, native elites managed to negotiate a space of power and of cultural reproduction within colonial society.[49]

Guaraní: a language to defend and administrate a territory

The first document written, signed and dated by native hands was discovered by Eduardo Neumann in the Archivo General de Simancas in Spain.[50] On 20 February 1753 the deputy mayor Alexandro Mbaruari, probably of the estancia San Miguel, sent a folded paper to the mayor Pasqual Tirapare at San Antonio. Its mastery of epistolary rules (addressee, Catholic salutations, signature, etc.) suggests that natives had long been used to reading and writing. Nonetheless, it is the first letter found in the archives. It was probably kept because of its wartime context, the War of the Seven Reductions (1756).

In 1750 the Treaty of Madrid redefined the borders between the Iberian empires in South America. It established that in exchange for Colonia de Sacramento, the Spanish crown ceded to Portugal the territory on which seven Jesuit missions of Guaraní had been established along with numerous *estancias* and *yerbales*. The order was given to move 30,000 people and millions of head of cattle in one year. After some unsuccessful attempts by the Jesuits and the Indian authorities to influence the decree and then to respect it, armed resistance was organised. In February 1753 a Guaraní expedition prevented the boundary commission from entering mission territory. The Spanish governor José de Andonaegui then declared war on the missions. In a series of letters *caciques* and town councils denounced the injustice of the displacement (*jakaho*) and the war (*guarini*), which was inflicted on them: 'They who are "poor Christian Indians"'. Their letters exhibit a refined Amerindian verbal art as well as use of the neo-scholastic political vocabulary of the time.

The Guarani leaders express their demands in the language of man's natural rights: God (*Tupã*) gave them 'this land that is their place of life' (*ko yvy ore rekoha*); the king, who is the tenant of God (*-ekovia*), has to be a justice-

---

49 W.F. Hanks, 'Intertextualité de l'espace au Yucatan', *L'Homme*, 32 (122) (1992): 53–74.

50 'Corregidor Pasqual Tirapare upe guarãma Coquatia miri S. Ant.', AGS Secretaria de Estado, Legajo 7433 doc. 278 and AGS Secretaria de Estado, Legajo 7378, doc. 91 for a partial translation. See the analysis in E. Santos Neumann and C. Boidin, 'A escrita política e o pensamento dos Guarani em tempos de autogoverno (c.1753)', *Revista Brasileira de História*, 37 (2017): 97–118.

keeper (*teko joja rerekua*) and its protector against his enemies (*amotare'y*), the Portuguese. They refer to the pact, established with the Spanish monarchs several generations previously: vassals (*voja*) of the king of their own will, they have always respected (*mboaje*) and trusted (*mbojerovia*) his orders, never failed (*javy*) and never boasted (*ñemboete*) against their sovereign, from whom they have so far received only love (*mborayhu*) and consolation (*angapyhy*), protection (*porerekua*) and conservation (*ñangareko*), help (*pytyvõ*) and salvation (*pyhyrõ*). It is as subjects of the king that they justify their resistance, a king who broke the pact which bound him to God as much as to men. If the king let himself be deceived by the Portuguese, who only know how to lie (*japu*), they do not let themselves be deceived (*ñembotavy*) and are ready to live at war against those who only want to impoverish them (*momboriahu*), reduce them to ashes (*motanimbu*) and make them disappear (*mokañy*).

All this Catholic and monarchical vocabulary and Amerindian rhetorical style are to be found in the rest of the corpus, even in documents exchanged between natives.[51] Letters sent from indigenous *caciques* and town councils to governors or military commandants of Buenos Aires articulate what we could call a Euro-Amerindian political space. It is neither simply European, nor simply Amerindian. It is a Catholic, monarchical, Guaraní rhetoric which was not necessarily understood by the Creoles – also Guaraní-speakers – living in the neighbouring city of Asunción or Villarica.[52] Some elements suggest that the Spanish authorities also communicated in Guaraní with the native authorities. Usually they sent Spanish letters or decrees which were translated orally into Guaraní, probably by a Jesuit. However, there are also two letters in Guaraní.[53] Furthermore, we have discovered that by 1791 every sub-delegate of the missions had Guaraní scribes at his service.[54]

51 We have a continuous corpus of documents from 1752 until 1813 and a scattered one until 1832. We have collected 252 references to documents written in Guaraní and effectively gathered the digital copy of 180. Fewer than half appear with a translation into Spanish. The palaeography, transliteration, translation and retranslation of this corpus are still in progress. A first semantic analysis of this political vocabulary can be found in C. Boidin and A. Otazú Melgarejo, 'Toward Guaraní semantic history (XVI–XIX)', in A. Durston and B. Mannheim (eds.), *Indigenous Languages, Politics, and Authority in Latin America: Historical and Ethnographic Perspectives* (Notre Dame, IN: University of Notre Dame Press, 2018), pp. 125–60.

52 Carta de una autoridad española desde San Juan a Don Miguel Parapy, cacique, San Juan, 6 Jun. 1757 AGN, sala IX 6-5-8. This letter argues that even a Spaniard versed in their language could not translate the Guaraní letter and that Antonio Parapy should come himself. My thanks to C. Pereira for sending us the document, now online at: http://www.langas.cnrs.fr/#/consulter_document/extraits/128 [accessed 15 Sept. 2019].

53 In 1757 (see n. 52) and Carta de Juan Francisco de la Riba a los oficiales de la guardia (n.p., n.d. [*c.* 1769]), AGN, sala IX 18-5-1. This document was also identified by C. Pereira in 2016.

54 *Intendencia del Paraguay, correspondiencia* [*sic*], *y despacho de los Treinta Pueblos* (Memorial de Don Olegario Papa, Don Manuel Ayruca y Francisco Romualdo Avambi, los escribientes de Francisco Bruno de Zavala al Virrey Nicolas Arredondo), Candelaria, 1 Dec. 1791, AGN, room IX, Interior, leg. 31, exp. 21, fols. 801–9.

The majority of the documents we have found (70 per cent) were written after the expulsion of the Jesuits in 1767 to 1768. Why? Did the Indian authorities take greater control over the relationship with the governors after the Jesuits' departure? If the current state of our archives is proportional to what was really written, we could say yes. Guaraní leaders might have experienced more liberty and need to communicate with imperial state authorities themselves. However, for the moment we cannot be sure. To our surprise, the prohibition of any language but Spanish, pronounced in 1770 by the Spanish administration, had little effect in the Rio de la Plata, as compared to Mexico, for instance.[55] After 1767 Guaraní missions were administered by the clergy in spiritual matters and by an administrator in the case of secular issues. A significant number of letters are testimonies which make demands for retribution or punishment of a native *corregidor*, *mayordomo*, or Spanish administrator, priest, commander, etc. Some letters reveal concern about poverty; demands for support and protection against Spanish tenants whose cattle were invading the community's property; commercial or military questions. They are more often written by individuals and on more diverse topics than before. Syntax and lexicon show evidence of some changes: Spanish borrowings are more frequent and some Guaraní morphemes are abandoned or modified.

Conclusion

Besides being texts which record knowledge and make foreign-policy arguments, grammars, dictionaries and doctrines also served to extend the domain of a specific Guaraní language, able to produce Christian subjects and to govern the missions. Jesuits were not enculturated in a unique, holistic, genuinely precolonial 'Guaraní world': they operated in multilinguistic spaces. The *lingua brasilica* on the one hand and Guaraní on the other were media constructed to reduce this multilingualism. The evangelisation, westernisation and Guaranisation of those margins of the Spanish empire went hand in hand. To evangelise and westernise Indians implies to Guaranise them and vice versa. The Jesuits missions of Paraguay were modern, colonial spaces where Guaraní literacy flourished. Native elites read and wrote a Catholic, monarchical Guaraní language in order to defend and administer their lives and territories. As with Nahuatl in the *altepetl* of central Mexico and Yucatec Maya within Franciscan missions, the Guaraní language in the Jesuit missions of Paraguay articulated a Euro-Amerindian legal and political space. Native elites negotiated – resisting and collaborating at the same time – in Spanish and

---

55 Real Cédula, Carlos III, 10 de mayo de 1770, 'para que en los Reinos de Indias, Filipinas y adyacentes, se observen los medios para conseguir que se destierren los diferentes idiomas que se usan en aquellos dominios y solo se hable el castellano' (AGI, Indiferente General, Leg. 540, online).

Latin but also in 'their' languages, native languages previously territorialised by missionaries and clergy.[56]

Bibliography

Anchieta, J. de (1595) *Arte de grammatica da lingoa mais vsada na costa do Brasil* (Coimbra: Antonio de Mariz).

Andresen, J. and D. Baggioni (2000) *Histoire des idées linguistiques*, vol. 3, *L'hégémonie du comparatisme*, ed. by S. Auroux (Brussels: Mardaga).

Auroux, S. (ed). (1989) *Histoire des idées linguistiques*, vol. 1, *La naissance des métalangages en Orient et en Occident* (Liège: Mardaga).

— (ed.) (1992) *Histoire des idées linguistiques*, vol. 2, *Le développement de la grammaire occidentale* (Liège: Mardaga).

— (1994) *La révolution technologique de la grammatisation: introduction à l'histoire des sciences du langage* (Paris: Mardaga).

Avellaneda, M. (2014) *Guaraníes, criollos y Jesuitas. Luchas de poder en las revoluciones comuneras del Paraguay, siglos XVII y XVIII* (Asunción: Tiempo de Historia).

Barros Drumond Mendes, M.C. (1994) 'O Intérprete Jesuita na constituição de um Tupi supraétnico', *Papia*, 3 (2): 18–25.

— (2003) 'A relaçao entre manuscritos e impressos em tupi como forma de estudo da política lingüística jesuítica do século XVIII na Amazonia', *Revista letras*, 61: 125–52.

— (2015) 'Em razão das conquistas, religião, commercio. Notas sobre o conceito de língua geral na colonização portuguesa da Amazônia nos séculos XVII–XVIII', *Mélanges de la Casa de Velázquez*, 45 (1): 99–112.

Boidin, C. (2017) 'Mots guarani du pouvoir, pouvoir des mots guarani. Essai d'anthropologie historique et linguistique (XIX–XVI et XVI–XIX siècles)' (habilitation à diriger des recherches, Université Sorbonne Nouvelle Paris 3).

Boidin, C. and A. Otazú Melgarejo (2018) 'Toward Guaraní semantic history (XVI–XIX)', in A. Durston and B. Mannheim (eds.), *Indigenous Languages, Politics, and Authority in Latin America: Historical and Ethnographic Perspectives* (Notre Dame, IN: University of Notre Dame Press), pp. 125–60.

Brignon, T. (2016) *Mba'e Mỹmba Pype, la Traduction en Guarani d'un bestiaire salutaire: L'édition missionnaire de la diferencia entre lo temporal y eterno*

---

56 C. Cunill, 'La negociación indígena en el imperio ibérico: aportes a su discusión metodológica', *Colonial Latin American Review*, 21 (2012): 391–412; B. Owensby, 'Pacto entre rey lejano y súbditos indígenas. Justicia, legalidad y policía en Nueva España, siglo XVII', *Historia Mexicana*, 61 (2011): 59–106.

de Juan Eusebio Nieremberg (Loreto, 1705) (Paris: Mémoire de Master 2 Sorbonne Nouvelle – IHEAL).

— (2017) *Un traducteur exemplaire. Le cacique Nicolás Yapuguay et ses exempla en langue Guarani (Missions Jésuites du Paraguay, 1724–1727)* (Toulouse: Mémoire de Master Université Toulouse 2).

Burke, P. (2008) *Languages and Communities in Early Modern Europe* (Cambridge: Cambridge University Press).

Caballos, A. (2013) *Etnografía Guaraní según el 'Tesoro de la lengua Guaraní' de Antonio Ruiz de Montoya* (Asunción: CEPAG).

Cerno, L. and F. Obermeier (2013) 'Nuevos aportes de la lingüística para la investigación de documentos en guaraní de la época colonial, siglo 18', *Folia histórica del Nordeste*, 21: 33–56.

Chamorro, G. (2009) *Decir el cuerpo historia y etnografía del cuerpo en los pueblos Guaraní diccionario etnográfico histórico de la lengua Guaraní*, vol. 1 (Asunción: Fondec Tiempo de Historia).

— (2014) 'PHRASES SELECTAS: Un diccionario manuscrito castellano-guaraní anónimo', *Corpus* 4 (2).

Cunill, C. (2012) 'La negociación indígena en el imperio Ibérico: Aportes a su discusión metodológica', *Colonial Latin American Review*, 21: 391–412.

De Castelnau L'Estoile, C. (2015) 'En raison des conquêtes, de la religion et du commerce. L'invention de la langue générale dans le Brésil du XVIe siècle', *Mélanges de la Casa de Velázquez*, 45: 77–98

Dietrich, W. (1995) 'La Importancia de los diccionarios Guaraníes de Montoya para el estudio comparativo de las lenguas Tupí-Guaraníes de hoy', *Amerindia*, 19–20: 287–99.

Estenssoro, J.C. (2015) 'Las vías indígenas de la occidentalización', *Mélanges de la Casa de Velázquez*, 45: 15–36.

Estenssoro, J.C. and C. Itier (2015) 'Présentation', *Mélanges de la Casa de Velázquez*, 45: 9–14.

Fabian, J. (1986) *Language and Colonial Power: The Appropriation of Swahili in the Former Belgian Congo: 1880–1938* (Cambridge: Cambridge University Press).

Freire, J. Ribamar Bessa (2004) *Rio babel: a história das línguas na Amazônia* (Rio de Janeiro: EdUERJ: Atlântica Editora).

Freire, J. Ribamar Bessa and M.C. Rosa (eds.) (2003) *Linguas gerais: politica linguistica e catequese na América do Sul no periodo colonial* (Rio de Janeiro: Universidade do Estado do Rio de Janeiro).

Hanks, W.F. (1992) 'Intertextualité de l'espace au Yucatan', *L'Homme*, 32 (122): 53–74.

— (2009) *Pour qui parle la croix: la colonisation du langage chez les Mayas du Mexique* (Nanterre, France: Société d'ethnologie).

— (2010) *Converting Words: Maya in the Age of the Cross* (Berkeley, CA: University of California Press).

Lockhart, J. (1999) 'Double mistaken identity: some Nahua concepts in postconquest guise', in J. Lockhart (ed.), *Of Things of the Indies: Essays Old and New in Early Latin American History* (Stanford, CA: Stanford University Press), pp. 98–119.

Melià, B. (2003) *La lengua Guaraní en el Paraguay colonial que contiene la creación de un lenguaje cristiano en las reducciones de los Guaraníes en el Paraguay* (Asunción: CEPAG).

Mignolo, W. (1995) *The Darker Side of the Renaissance: Literacy, Territoriality, and Colonization* (Ann Arbor, MI: University of Michigan Press).

Neumann, E. Santos (2005) 'Práticas letradas Guaranis: Produção e usos da escrita indígena – séculos XVII e XVIII' (unpublished doctoral thesis, Universidade Federal do Rio de Janeiro), http://objdig.ufrj.br/34/teses/EduardoSantosNeumann.pdf [accessed 4 Sept. 2019].

Neumann, E. Santos and C. Boidin (2017) 'A escrita política e o pensamento dos Guarani em tempos de autogoverno (c.1753)', *Revista Brasileira de História*, 37 (75): 97–118.

Oliveira, J. Pacheco de (1998) 'Uma etnologia dos "Índios misturados"? situação colonial, territorialização e fluxos culturais', *Mana*, 4: 47–77.

Orantin, M. (2017) *La cloche, le rabot et la houe: fragments d'un quotidien de travail dans les missions Jésuites du Paraguay (1714?)* (Paris: Mémoire de master 2 Sorbonne Nouvelle – IHEAL).

Otazú Melgarejo, A. (2006) *Práctica y semántica en la evangelización de los Guaraníes del Paraguay (S. XVI–XVIII)* (Asunción: Centro de Estudios Paraguayos 'Antonio Guasch').

— (2014) 'Contribución a la medicina natural: Pohã Ñana, un manuscrito inédito en Guaraní (Paraguay, S. XVIII)', *Corpus* 4 (2).

Owensby, B. (2011) 'Pacto entre rey lejano y súbditos indígenas. Justicia, legalidad y policía en Nueva España, siglo XVII', *Historia mexicana*, 61: 59–106.

Page, C.A. (2016) 'Los primeros misioneros Jesuitas entre Guaraníes y la experiencia de las aldeias de Brasil', *Historia Unisinos*, 20: 26–38.

Pottier, B. (1998) 'La gramática del padre Ioseph de Anchieta', *Suplemento Antropológico*, 32: 155–76.

Restivo, P., (1996) *Gramática Guaraní Jesuítico*, edited by S.M. Liuzzi (Enciclopedia de Misiones), http://www.fondazioneintorcetta.info/pdf/HISTACT2982.pdf [accessed 4 Sept. 2019].

Ringmacher, M. (2006) '"La conquista espiritual del Paraguay" en Guaraní clásico como objeto de conquista filológica', in W. Dietrich and H. Symeonidis (eds.), *Guaraní y Mawetí-Tupí-Guaraní. Estudios históricos y descriptivos sobre una familia lingüística de América del Sur* (Berlin: LIT), pp. 223–39.

Rodriguez-Alcala, C. (2007) 'L'exemple dans les grammaires jésuitiques du guarani', *Langages*, 166: 112–26.

Thun, H., L. Cerno, and F. Obermeier (2015) 'El proyecto Kuatia Ymaguare (PEKY) – "Libros del Pasado"', *Estudios Históricos* 7 (14).

— (eds.) (2015) *Guarinihape Tecocue – Lo que pasó en la guerra (1704–1705). Memoria anónima en Guaraní ... Edición Crítica*, Fontes Americanae (Kiel: Westensee).

White, R. (2010) *The Middle Ground: Indians, Empires, and Republics in the Great Lakes Region, 1650–1815* (Cambridge: Cambridge University Press).

Wilde, G. (2011) 'Relocalisations autochtones et ethnogenèse missionnaire à la frontière sud des empires Ibériques (Paracuaria, 1609–1768)', *Recherches Amérindiennes au Quebec*, 41: 13–28.

— (2014) 'Adaptaciones y apropiaciones en una cultura textual de frontera. Impresos misionales del Paraguay Jesuítico', *Revista História UNISINOS* 18: 270–86.

— (2014) 'The political dimensions of space-time categories in the Jesuit missions of Paraguay (17th and 18th centuries)', in G. Marcocci, W.D. Boer and A. Maldavsky (eds.), *Space and Conversion in Global Perspective* (Leiden: Brill), pp. 175–213.

III. Jesuit approaches to evangelisation

7. Administration and native perceptions of baptism at the Jesuit peripheries of Spanish America (16th–18th centuries)

Oriol Ambrogio

By the end of the 16th century the Jesuits had already started a worldwide missionary enterprise which spanned India, Japan, China, the Congo, Mozambique and Angola to Brazil, Peru, Paraguay and central Mexico. The apparently relentless expansion of Jesuit overseas missions was severely tested by the encounter with the semi-sedentary and non-sedentary populations of southern Chile, the Chaco and north-western Mexico, where groups scattered across rugged valleys, mighty rivers and arid deserts strongly resisted Spanish conquest. The difficulties raised by the conversion of decentralised natives had been dramatically anticipated by the failure of the Florida mission, where seven Jesuit missionaries were killed in 1572.[1] If in north-western Mexico missions managed, with difficulty, to pacify the Sinaloa and Sierra Madre regions and extend by the end of the 17th century to Baja California, the results in the southern borderlands of Spanish America were different. After the 1598 Araucanian revolt succeeded in expelling the Spaniards from southern Chile, the missionary presence in the area remained partial and unstable throughout the entire colonial period. Similarly, late 16th- and 17th-century Jesuit attempts among the non-sedentary Guaycuruas of the Chaco failed due to the warlike conditions in the region and the paucity of missionary personnel. Missions operated on a permanent basis only between 1743 and 1767.[2]

The present chapter focuses mainly on the Jesuit missions of northern Mexico, southern Chile and the Gran Chaco, all remote regions only partially controlled by the Spaniards and sites of persistent native military and cultural resilience.

---

1   See F. Marotti, 'Juan Baptista de Segura and the failure of the Florida Jesuit mission, 1566–1572', *The Florida Historical Quarterly*, 63 (1985): 267–79.

2   For the Jesuit efforts in southern Chile and the Chaco, see R. Foerster, *Jesuitas y Mapuches, 1593–1767* (Santiago de Chile: Editorial Universitaria, 1996); B. Vitar Mukdsi, *Guerra y misiones en la frontera chaqueña del Tucumán, 1700–1767* (Madrid: Consejo Superior de Investigaciones Científicas, 1997); and J.S. Saeger, *The Chaco Mission Frontier: The Guaycuruan Experience* (Tucson, AZ: University of Arizona Press, 2000).

O. Ambrogio, 'Administration and native perceptions of baptism at the Jesuit peripheries of Spanish America (16th–18th centuries)', in L.A. Newson (ed.), *Cultural Worlds of the Jesuits in Colonial Latin America* (London: Institute of Latin American Studies, 2020), pp. 149–69. License: CC-BY-NC-ND 2.0.

Such difficulties limited missionary control over these regions and hampered the diffusion of Christianity and its rituals. In particular, this chapter dwells on native perceptions and local acceptance of baptism, considered a privileged point of view for the understanding of native-missionary interactions and the formation of the post-conquest societies. How did native populations perceive baptism; and how did reception of the sacrament affect local understanding of the missionary role? What were the reasons for accepting Christianity and missionary life at the fringes of the Spanish American empire?

The study demonstrates how baptism shaped local perceptions of the role of the missionary as a foreign *curandero-hechicero* [healer-sorcerer] able both to heal the dying and to cause death.[3] The integration of Christian elements into the traditional cultural system caused struggles between baptised and non-baptised natives, leading some members of local communities to perceive baptism as an instrument of cultural novelty which could be used to shift socio-political and economic intertribal balances. Although the analysis of illnesses and the impact of mortality is crucial for the understanding of the reception of baptism, this chapter mainly focuses on the array of cultural and political reasons which led natives to accept baptism.

Jesuit baptismal administration at the fringes of Spanish America

Although the Jesuits produced a large number of rules, precepts and orders regulating spiritual and temporal missionary life, they made relatively few references to the administration of baptism to the natives. This was in part due to the well-known Jesuit flexibility and adaptability to local customs and beliefs, which limited the validity of general rules but was mainly caused by the sense of urgency associated with baptism. Since the administration of baptism was perceived as a critical issue when dealing with *gentiles*, this reduced the attention the Jesuits paid to the matter in the first moments of the establishment of a mission.[4] As soon as the new communities evolved in their doctrinal knowledge and were integrated into the colonial system, references to the administration of the sacrament and native response tended to disappear. The Chilean case represents a significant exception due to the repeated rebellions and subsequent

---

3   The term *curandero-hechicero* will be used throughout the text to emphasise the duality of native perceptions and to represent the everyday activities of the healer-sorcerers at the fringes of Spanish America. These two terms were both used in Jesuit sources, while native populations had various ways of describing this concept in their own languages.

4   J.W. O'Malley, S.J., *I primi Gesuiti* (Milan: Vita e Pensiero, 1999), pp. 29–59; M. Catto, 'Missioni e globalizzazioni: l'adattamento come identità della Compagnia di Gesù', in M. Catto (ed.), *Evangelizzazione e globalizzazione: le missioni gesuitiche nell'età moderna tra storia e storiografia* (Rome: Società editrice Dante Alighieri, 2010), pp. 1–16.

threat of apostasy which increased missionary concerns about local conversions for the entire colonial period.[5]

Jesuit efforts to baptise local populations on the fringes of America shared common practices. The scepticism about adult doctrinal ability and the fear of apostasy and abandonment of the missions led to an extremely cautious administration of the sacrament, especially in the first moments of missionary efforts, such that baptism was generally conferred only to the dying, with the exception of candidates with a good disposition. The rules given by the Paraguayan provincial Diego de Torres Bollo to Orazio Vecchi and Martín de Aranda for the establishment of the Arauco mission in 1608 illustrate this:

> Never baptise Indians *nisi in casu mortis*, first: if they have refused to reject their women those who have more than one. Second: if there is no certainty concerning their peaceful condition. Third: if they have not asked for baptism in a while. Fourth: if they do not perfectly understand the statements of our holy faith and recite doctrine by heart. … In case of imminent death, it is enough the understanding of the principal mysteries of our holy faith. In the same way, do not baptise infidel infants *extra periculum mortis*, without their parent's permission and presence, if they live in a warlike condition with a high probability of returning to their traditional customs.[6]

The unstable political circumstances of the southern fringes forced missionaries to face the challenge of apostasy, a common native response to the evangelisation process. For these reasons, the new Jesuit rules strictly limited the administration of baptism to the dying and those natives able to understand the Christian doctrine. Although these rules were directed to the specific Araucanian context, they outlined common missionary concerns. Doctrinal knowledge, abandonment of traditional practices, voluntary acceptance of the sacrament and peaceful political conditions were considered crucial requirements for native access to baptism in the borderlands. Moreover, continuous pastoral care of the neophytes and a stable community were important prerequisites for baptism, since daily Christian education was considered the first essential barrier against local idolatries and apostasy. Nevertheless, the missionary quest for souls and the widespread illnesses led to some exceptions, such as those among the non-sedentary Abipones of Chaco in 1591, where Juan Fonte and

---

5   See, e.g., the debate inside the Chilean province concerning the suspension of the missions in Arauco and Valdivia in 1675 due to the limited results of evangelization (ARSI Provincia Chilensis 5, fols. 170–73, P. de Sotomayor, 'Preguntase si sera conveniente el que la Compañía de Jesús prosiga o no con las misiones que tiene en el estado de Arauco? Ponense las razones por una y otra parte, 31 Jan. 1675'; ARSI Provincia Chilensis 5, fols. 177–7v, G.B. Camargo, 'Propuesta de las razones que militan en favor de la asistencia de la missión de Valdivia y de las que ay en contra de ella', 22 April 1675).

6   F. Enrich, *Historia de la compañía de Jesús en Chile* (Barcelona: Rosal, 1891), p. 143.

Francisco de Angulo decided to baptise local infants even though a permanent priest could not be provided due to the warlike conditions and local mobility.[7]

Among the north-western Mexican missions, after the baptism of infants a programme of catechesis, usually lasting eight days, was offered to the adults.[8] However, this period could vary according to every candidate's disposition and preparation. In 1597 a Tepehuan man surprised local missionaries by learning the main prayers and commandments of the Church in only three hours, being immediately baptised.[9] On the other hand, in the mission of Santa María de las Parras, among the Laguneros of the state of Coahuila, an old man traditionally adverse to Christianity was finally baptised after two months.[10] Scepticism towards potentially recalcitrant adults generally resulted in a longer preparation, while younger catechumens, who demonstrated particular ability and sacramental predisposition, were usually baptised more quickly.

The particular political situation of Chile forced the Jesuits to organise their baptismal efforts differently from north-western Mexico. The rebellion of 1598, which led to the destruction of the seven Spanish towns founded to the south of the Bío-Bío River, opened a period of Mapuche independence and substantial political autonomy. There the dispersion of native villages and the paucity of missionary personnel both hampered the evangelisation process and impeded the formation of stable communities. For this reason, Jesuit sacramental administration did not result in the general baptisms common in north-western Mexico, but rather in baptisms administered in *articulo mortis*. This policy could change according to particular political conditions. There was, in fact, a clear relationship between wider native access to baptism and the peace treaties signed during the *hispano*-Mapuche parleys.[11] The temporary pacification of the borderlands, which occurred especially during the *Guerra Defensiva* policy introduced by Luis de Valdivia in 1612, led to the administration of the sacrament no longer being limited to the dying, clearly contrasting with renewed missionary restrictions in the aftermath of the rebellions. Luis de Valdivia started to accept adults *extra periculum mortis*,

---

7 P. Lozano, *Descripción corográfica del gran Chaco gualamba* (Tucumán: Instituto de antropología, 1941), p. 114.

8 A. Pérez de Ribas, *Historia de los triunfos de n.s. fé entre gentes las más barbaras y fieras del nuevo orbe* (México: Layac, 1944), vol. I, pp. 288 and 344.

9 ARSI, Provincia Mexicana 14, fol. 24v, 'Carta anua de la provincia de México de 1597, 30 March 1598'. See also ARSI, Provincia Mexicana 14, fol. 578, 'Carta anua de la provincia de la Nueva España del año de 1610, 18 May 1611'.

10 ARSI, Provincia Mexicana 14, fol. 472v, 'Carta anua de la provincia de la Nueva España de la Compañía de Jesús del año de 1606, 14 May 1607'.

11 For the *Guerra Defensiva* policy and the *parlamentos de indios*, see J.M. Díaz Blanco, *Razón de estado y buen gobierno. La guerra defensiva y el imperialismo español en tiempos de Felipe III* (Sevilla: Universidad de Sevilla, 2010); A. Levaggi, *Diplomacia hispano-indígena en las fronteras de América* (Madrid: Centro de Estudios Políticos y Constitucionales, 2002).

beginning in 1613 in Lebu, where 900 baptisms were administered.[12] This trend reached its peak in 1619, when in the area of Arauco Valdivia baptised 300 natives a day, these receiving only a brief instruction in the catechism sufficient only for the acceptance of baptism.[13] The favourable peaceful conditions were a strong inducement for the acceleration of the baptismal process, at the expense of doctrinal preparation.[14] The impact of the changing political conditions on Jesuit baptismal policy is further demonstrated by the attitude of Lorenzo Chacón in the district of La Imperial in 1655, who refused to confer baptism on the applicants due to the ongoing rebellion, baptising only three or four adults *extra periculum mortis*.[15] The Jesuit policy of administering baptism in Chile was, therefore, greatly influenced by the unstable military conditions in the borderlands, which periodically resulted in a wider or more restricted native access to baptism. As a result, the Mapuche baptismal conquest proved to be a discontinuous process, characterised by provisional expansions followed by violent setbacks, rather than a linear progression towards a widespread conferment of baptism on the natives.[16]

The information available on the administration of baptism by the Jesuits in the Chaco missions is extremely scarce. Paradoxically, the most significant data refer to the 17th-century, short-lived attempts, while the chronicles written during the actual missionary period between 1743 and 1767 are quite reticent on the issue. In 1641, among the Abipones under the local *cacique* Caliguila, Juan Pastor and Gaspar Cerqueira refused to administer baptism *extra periculum mortis*, 'fearing that tired by the rigidity of Christian faith they could regret the missionary entrance and remain after baptism without pastoral care'.[17] Due to the absence of stable pastoral care, the distance of the Guaycuruas from the Spanish towns and their mobility, the Jesuits administered baptism only in *articulo mortis* until the foundation of permanent missions in 1743, following the general precepts used in Chile.

12   Foerster, *Jesuitas y Mapuches*, p. 273; Enrich, *Historia*, vol. 1, p. 285.

13   Carta Anua de 1618–1619, 17 Febrero 1620, in C. Leonhardt, *Iglesia. Cartas Anuas de la provincia del Paraguay, Chile y Tucumán, de la compañía de Jesús, 1609–1614* (Buenos Aires: Instituto de Investigaciones Históricas, 1927), p. 189; and A. de Ovalle, *Historica relación del reyno de Chile y de las misiones y ministerios que ejércita en él la Compañia de Jesús* (Santiago de Chile, 1888), vol. 2, p. 291.

14   For a Franciscan late colonial critique of the Jesuit administration of the sacrament in southern Chile, see M. de Ascasubi, 'Informe cronológico de las misiones del reino de Chile hasta 1789', in C. Gay (ed.), *Historia física y política de Chile segun documentos adquiridos en esta república durante doze años de residencia en ella. Documentos* (Paris, 1846), vol. I, pp. 300–400 (p. 321).

15   Enrich, *Historia*, vol. 1, p. 598.

16   For the acceptance of baptism as a linear process, see Foerster, *Jesuitas y Mapuches*.

17   Lozano, *Descripción Corográfica*, p. 186. See also 'Carta Anua de 1641–1643', in E. Maeder, *Cartas anuas de la provincia jesuitica del paraguay, 1641 a 1643* (Resistencia: Instituto de Investigaciones Geohistóricas-Conicet, 1996), pp. 47–51.

Deadly ritual or healing act? The dual perception of missionaries

The native encounter with Christianity needs to be understood in the framework of the tremendous demographic and cultural impact of illnesses on indigenous populations. Epidemics sharply affected local economic and cultural life, forcing communities to reorganise their political structures in a changing world while coping with powerful foreign beings such as the missionaries. Illnesses also influenced Jesuit baptismal policy, limiting its access to the dying, and were thus crucial in the first perceptions of baptism. The Jesuit chronicler of the Chilean province, Francisco Enrich, states: 'They [the Mapuche] developed the wicked idea that the holy baptism was a deadly poison killing them in few moments. They believed that after everyday life experience; since in those times missionaries were administering baptism only *in articulo mortis*, they used to see people die after its imposition'.[18]

Natives misunderstood the missionaries' quest for the salvation of the souls of the sick, seeing baptism as a deadly act which worsened the health of the dying. Cases of mortal perception of baptism were common on the fringes of Spanish America, where, especially in Mexico, illnesses circulated through mining and missionary routes, spreading havoc in local communities.[19] The association of mortality with baptism expanded all over Sinaloa, the Sierra Madre and the deserts of Mapimí, usually fostered by local religious leaders in a first attempt to challenge the missionaries' authority and regain their own political and cultural power.[20] The same fear pervaded Chaco communities in their first encounters with Christianity. In 1672, in the mission of San Javier among the Tobas and Mocobies, a mother hid her sick children under a blanket, terrified by the effects of baptism, while 40 years later, in 1711, a Lule woman warned her community against the activities of Antonio Macioni, who 'kills people by pouring on their head a kind of poisoned water he uses in these occasions'.[21]

The sources analysed show that a deadly perception of baptism developed almost simultaneously with the opposite idea of the sacrament as a healing ritual. Jesuit documentation and current historiography have described native responses to baptism as a gradual process moving from an initial rejection to

18 Enrich, *Historia*, vol. 1, p. 164.

19 See especially D.T. Reff, *Disease, Depopulation, and Culture Change in Northwestern New Spain, 1518–1764* (Salt Lake City, UT: University of Utah Press, 1991).

20 Pérez de Ribas, *Libro septimo de algunos puntos dignos de notar en la historia de las missiones de la Compañía de Jesús en la Nueva España, en particular de la de Cinaloa. Travajos que en ellas han pasado sus operarios y frutos que de ellas an cogido. Y de los medios de que se han ayudado para coger tan abundantes frutos* (undated, ARSI Provincia Mexicana 19, fol. 152v); F.J. Alegre, *Historia de la Provincia de la Compañía de Jesús de Nueva España* (Rome: Institutum Historicum S. I, 1958), vol. 2, pp. 20 and 152.

21 Lozano, *Descripción corográfica*, pp. 221 and 395.

a later acceptance, often confusing the increased number of baptisms and the diffusion of Spanish names with an imposition of the ritual at the expense of local, traditional concepts of culture and healing.[22] However, this interpretation suggests a clear separation between the ideas of baptism as a rite at the point of death and as a cure, seeing the two concepts as mutually exclusive. This does not completely reflect the response of the population in the borderlands to the sacrament, since the two concepts tended to co-exist. Occasional healings were decisive for the emergence of the idea of the curative powers of baptism. In Arauco six wounded local warriors recovered after being baptised at the same time as a woman died after refusing it, while the Nebomes of Sinaloa resorted to the priest to intervene as soon as they fell ill. These episodes proved crucial in the acceptance of baptism as a cure.[23] In the same way, among the Guanas of the mission of San Juan Nepomuceno in Chaco, founded in 1764, an unconverted woman informed of a previous healing of a baby, offered her children to the missionary, seeking protection against illnesses.[24]

The supposed healing effectiveness of the sacrament guaranteed the success of the baptismal ritual, which came to be conceived of as a viable cure.[25] However, baptism did not totally replace traditional cures, but rather became one of the possible healing rituals to which natives resorted in order to find a solution to sickness. An anonymous account of 1750 about the San Javiér mission of Mocobies highlights this fact: 'There are some *agoreras*. One of those women seriously ill asked the father for baptism. He told her he was not sure she sincerely desired it, and it was like this; because later she was accompanied to the house of a *hechicera*. The father came and asked her why she accepted the traditional cure. She answered; I came here because you did not heal me, and here I was unwittingly sucked by the *hechicera* [*me ha chupado*]'.[26] The episode underlines the clear identification of baptism with a healing ritual and its equivalence with local medical practices. It shows how the traditional system

22   See Foerster, *Jesuitas y Mapuches*; and Saeger, *The Chaco Mission Frontier*.

23   M. De Olivares, *Historia de la compañía de Jesús en Chile, 1593–1736* (Santiago de Chile: Bello, 1874), p. 291; Pérez de Ribas, *Historia*, vol. 1, p. 255.

24   J. Sánchez Labrador and S.A. Lafone y Quevedo, *El Paraguay católico. Homenaje de la universidad nacional de La Plata al XVII. congreso internacional de los americanistas en su reunión de Buenos Aires, en Mayo 16 á 21 de 1910* (Buenos Aires: Coni ermanos, 1910), vol. 2, p. 293.

25   RAH, Colección Juan Bautista Muñoz, tomo 15, fol. 178, 'Carta del Padre Andrés Pérez, dirigida al Padre Provincial, año de 1617'. Documentary evidence shows the diffusion of the perception of baptism as a cure also in the Balkans and China (G. Pizzorusso, 'I dubbi sui sacramenti dalle missioni *ad infideles*. Percorsi nelle burocrazie di curia', in P. Broggio, C. de Castelnau-L'estoile and G. Pizzorusso (eds.), *Administrer les sacrements en Europe et au Nouveau Monde: la curie romaine et les dubia circa sacramenta* (= *Mélanges de l'École française de Rome, Italie et Méditerranée*, 121 (2009)), pp. 39–61 (p. 53).

26   'Noticia sobre a reduçao en San Xavier de indios Mocobi, na jurisdiçao de Santa Fe (1750)', in J. Cortesão (ed.), *Do Tratado De Madrid à Conquista Dos Sete Povos (1750–1802)* (Rio de Janeiro: Biblioteca Nacional, 1969), pp. 15–23 (p. 19).

survived and acted as a complementary cure, especially in the first decades after the establishment of a mission. Natives perceived baptism as an *extrema ratio* solution in case of the failure of all other traditional healings.[27] This explains why requests for baptism increased dramatically during periods of acute epidemics and why local *curanderos-hechiceros* [healer-sorcerers] and native leaders accepted the new ritual when they fell seriously ill.[28] Therefore, the curative powers of baptism did not eradicate local scepticism about the ritual. Especially in the southern borderlands, adults tended to reject baptism if in good health.[29] Therefore, the acceptance of the sacrament during the colonial period was often limited to specific circumstances such as imminent death and could be related to a previous consultation with traditional healers. The situation differed in north-western Mexican missions, where a large number of natives requested baptism even *extra periculum mortis*.[30]

In order to understand the complexity of natives' approach to baptism it is necessary to understand local perceptions of missionary activity in the framework of extant cultural traditions and healing practices. In a manuscript account of the missions of Sinaloa written between 1620 and 1625, Andrés Péres Ribas refers to the administration of the baptismal rite and the subsequent local response: 'In the ceremonies made with the children, the father used to go around the circle made up of the mothers and their children and impose salt, saliva and oil, and it sometimes happened due to their ignorance of these ceremonies ... that while the father was proceeding in the ceremony on one side of the circle, some mothers on the other side escaped from the circle taking their babies and washing them in the near river'.[31] In a similar way, among the Yaquis in 1617: 'At the time of the holy ceremony of the imposition of the holy salt in the mouth of the catechumen, certain mothers cleaned their children's mouth and tongue, showing that they still believed we bewitched them with the salt, in the same way their *hechiceros* kill them with other things'.[32] Natives accepted baptism and asked for the sacrament for their children, searching for protection against illnesses. Nevertheless, a great scepticism towards the priests' actions persisted. Some adults removed oil, salt and saliva as soon as possible, indicating a clear fear of their possible fatal effects. These episodes reinforce the

---

27 For similar cases in southern Chile, see Carta Anua de la Provincia del Peru, 29 Abril 1599, in E. Fernández Dávila and A. de Egaña (eds.), *Monumenta Peruana*, Apud *Monumenta Historica Soc. Iesu* (Rome: Institutum Historicum Societatis Iesu, 1954), pp. 660–733 (p. 703).

28 Enrich, *Historia*, vol. 1, pp. 209 and 578; Pérez de Ribas, *Historia*, vol. 1, p. 346.

29 See ARSI Provincia Chilensis 6, fol. 56v, 'Letras Anuas desta Provincia de Chile de los años 1629 y 30, 2 April 1630'; and M. Dobrizhoffer and E. Wernicke, *Historia de los Abipones. Traducción de Edmundo Wernicke* (Resistencia: Universidad Nacional del Nordeste, 1967–70), vol. 3, p. 301.

30 Pérez de Ribas, *Historia*, vol. 1, pp. 224, 260, 285.

31 Pérez de Ribas, *Libro septimo*, fol. 140.

32 Pérez de Ribas, *Historia*, vol. 2, p. 92.

idea of the perceived dual identity of the missionary, who could cure the dying but at the same time cause death.[33] How can we explain the simultaneity of these opposed ideas?

A common indigenous response to the missionaries was their cultural identification with local shamans, the *curanderos-hechiceros*. Missionaries were, in fact, dealing with the treatment of illnesses, the management of the community, soil fertility and the afterworld, the same activities carried out by *curanderos-hechiceros*.[34] Native people did not see Christian rituals and local beliefs as mutually antagonistic; rather, they looked for a syncretic inclusion of useful practices in the indigenous cultural systems. The case of holy water is significant. In the first encounters with Christianity, natives perceived it as an instrument of death, a mortal poison.[35] However, its apparent effectiveness in curing sore throats, fever and various illnesses soon changed local perspective.[36] In the 1660s in the mission of Buena Esperanza in southern Chile, a local Mapuche eliminated the infestation of the crops by a pest by spreading holy water on the plants, while José Tardá and Tomás de Guadalajara used the same remedy among the Tarahumaras of Santa Ana mission in 1676.[37] Holy water assumed curative powers not only for humans but also for the natural world, a practice fostered by the same Jesuits, as demonstrated by the case among the Tarahumaras of the healing of a dog with holy water and a relic of St Ignatius.[38] Missionary practices also influenced the activities of local *curanderos-hechiceros*. In 1649 a Mapuche healer from the district of La Imperial treated the sick, 'spraying the body of the dying with some kind of water'.[39] An alien ritual was therefore incorporated into the cultural and religious system. *Padres* and *curanderos-hechiceros* became two comparable identities, sharing common practices and dealing with similar issues.

33   The German philosopher Ernst Cassirer clearly stated in his *Philosophy of Symbolic Forms* that all symbols are reversible. Therefore, who can cure the dying man can also cause his death (E. Cassirer, *The Philosophy of Symbolic Forms* (New Haven: Yale University Press, 1965)).

34   R. Folsom, *The Yaquis and the Empire: Violence, Spanish Imperial Power, and Native Resilience in Colonial Mexico* (New Haven, CT: Yale University Press, 2010), p. 106.

35   Lozano, *Descripción corográfica*, p. 395.

36   Ribas, *Historia*, vol. 3, p. 276.

37   Olivares, *Historia*, p. 125; ARSI Provincia Mexicana 17, fol. 378, 'Copia de una carta que los Padres José Tardá y Tomás de Guadalajara escribieron al P Francisco Ximenez Provincial sobre su entrada a los Tarahumares despues de haber estos abandonado la fe matando a los Padres Cornelio Godinez y Santiago Basilio, 1676'.

38   ARSI Provincia Mexicana 15, fol. 248v, 'Letras Anuas de la provincia de la Compañía de Jesús de Mexico por los años 1646 y 1647'. For an analysis of human-animal relationship among the Amerindians, see M. Norton, 'The chicken or the *Iegue*: human-animal relationships and the Columbian exchange', *American Historical Review*, 120 (2015): 28–60.

39   ARSI Provincia Chilensis 6, fol. 265, 'Letras Anuas de la Viceprovincia de Chile del año de 1649, 17 Dec. 1650'. For similar native versions of the baptismal ritual in late colonial Nayarit, see J.A. Bugarín, *Visita de las misiones del Nayarit 1768–1769* (México D.F: Centro de Estudios Mexicanos y Centroamericanos, 1993), p. 100.

In the Chaco the rivalry between missionaries and local shamans paradoxically contributed to their assimilation as *curanderos-hechiceros*. In a period of drought the Abipones of the San Jerónimo mission looked for the intervention of the priest to make it rain. When rain started to fall, it did not irrigate the crops of the leader of local shamans, Pariekaikin, who therefore accused the priest José Brigniel of being a *curandero-hechicero*.[40] The episode clearly underlines the double nature of the *curandero-hechicero*. If Pariekaikin's accusations were directed at discrediting the role of the Jesuits inside the new communities, at the same time they contributed to the formation of the idea of the fathers as shamans with similar features. Therefore, native leaders' ritual struggle against the missionaries reinforced local perceptions of the equivalences of the two parties.[41]

Among Amerindian communities *curanderos* were both respected and feared. Both the Abipones and Mocobies were convinced that man was immortal and illnesses and death were caused by the deadly spells of the *curanderos-hechiceros*.[42] The Abipones called the *curandero-hechicero* 'Queveet', which was the 'bad spirit', since they thought that this evil entity was the origin of the *curandero-hechiceros*' power.[43] The *curanderos-hechiceros* were at the same time both a terrifying and an indispensable presence in the everyday life of local communities. According to this cultural explanation, death was caused not by illnesses or physical diseases, but instead by a deadly external intervention.[44]

The populations of southern Chile shared similar beliefs. According to Miguel de Olivares, '[t]hey never believe that someone can die for an infirmity or an illness, but for the *Huecubu*, a sorcery inserted into the body, and they confer to the holy baptism and confession this kind of sorcery if someone dies after its reception'.[45] The *Huecubu* was generally considered the ultimate cause of every evil and death, sometimes interpreted as the soul of a foe who introduced thorns or small sticks into someone's heart, or identified with a

---

40 Dobrizhoffer, *Historia de los Abipones*, vol. 2, p. 86.

41 On the struggle between *curanderos-hechiceros* and missionaries in southern Chile, see also Olivares, *Historia*, p. 289.

42 F. Paucke and E. Wernicke, *Hacia allá y para acá. Una estadía entre los indios Mocobíes, 1749–1767. Traducción castellana por Edmundo Wernicke* (Tucumán: Universidad Nacional de Tucumán, 1942), vol. 3, p. 252. The same perception of the immortality of the self was present among the Mapuches and Tepehuanes (Enrich, *Historia*, vol. p. 87; Alegre, *Historia*, vol. 1, p. 471).

43 Dobrizhoffer, *Historia de los Abipones*, vol. 2, p. 78. According to Saeger, Queveet was a mythical ancestor who distributed courage to the Abipones in war against the neighbouring groups and gold and silver to the Spaniards (Saeger, *The Chaco Mission Frontier*, pp. 57 and 136).

44 An exception is Mbaya belief that maladies were caused by the exit of the soul from the body, establishing a strong relationship between spiritual and corporal health (D. Muriel and G. Fúrlong Cárdiff, *Breve noticia de las missiones vivas de la compañía de Jesús en la provincia del Paraguay* (Buenos Aires: Escritores Coloniales Rioplatenses, 1955), p. 135).

45 Olivares, *Historia*, p. 278.

deadly poison introduced in drinks or food.[46] Since corporeal diseases were caused by the introduction of deadly elements into the body of the infirm, native medicine developed the practice of sucking on the painful part. *Curanderos* used to introduce thorns and worms into the mouth while treating the sick by sucking the wound and then spitting them out, showing the cause of pain and the effectiveness of the cure.[47] What is crucial is the fact that the *curandero* was considered to be responsible for the introduction of the *Huecubu* into a body, but at the same time the parents of the deceased resorted to his help in order to find those responsible for the death, which occasionally led to their being killed.[48] In a clear affinity to the beliefs about illnesses held by the Wendat in 17th-century Ontario, indigenous populations on the fringes of empire believed that the agent which ritually precipitated an illness was also considered the only one able to undo it.[49] *Curanderos-hechiceros* caused maladies and death but could also find a solution to the problem.

Since Jesuits were perceived as traditional healers, missionaries possessed a double identity too. If death was caused by ritual acts, then missionary rituals, in particular baptism and confession, could be held responsible for the high mortality.[50] However, they could also save lives and protect the crops with holy water in continuity with the role played in the pre-contact era by local *curanderos*. Therefore, local perception of baptism was not only influenced by the unprecedentedly high mortality rate, but rather had its origins in the traditional system of beliefs. The initial perception of baptism as a deadly ritual was caused not by the novelty of the administration of the sacrament or the use of holy water, but rather by the assimilation of similar Christian features into their traditional system of beliefs. In the same way, the birth of the perception of baptism as a cure can be traced not only to the occasional successes achieved by the Jesuits, but also to the secular medical activity developed in pre-contact times by local *curanderos-hechiceros*, both for the human and animal world.

46   ARSI, Provincia Chilensis 6, fol. 264v, 'Anua de la Viceprovincia de Chile de 1649'; Ovalle, *Historica Relación Del Reyno De Chile*, vol. 2, p. 196. An anonymous late 18th-century Jesuit chronicle refers to the *Huecubu* as a dreadful demi-god causing epidemics and plagues (BNC, FG 1407, fol. 37v, 'Breve relación de los indios de Chile').

47   On the medical practice of sucking and Jesuit reflections on traditional healing systems, see, e.g., Sánchez Labrador and Lafone y Quevedo, *El Paraguay Católico*, vol. 3, p. 37; Paucke, *Hacia allá y para acá*, vol. 3, p. 252; Dobrizhoffer, *Historia de los Abipones*, vol. 2, p. 246; ARSI, Provincia Chilensis 6, fol. 265, 'Anua de la Viceprovincia de Chile de 1649'.

48   ARSI Provincia Chilensis 6, fol. 24, 'Adjunta a Letras Annuas de la Viceprovincia del Reino de Chile desde el año de mil y seiscientos y cuarenta y siete hasta el presente de 1648'. 7. A similar fate awaited *curanderos-hechiceros* in Northern Mexico (Reff, *Disease*, p. 268).

49   E. Anderson, 'Blood, fire and baptism. three perspectives on the death of Jean de Brébeuf, seventeenth-century Jesuit martyr', in J. Martin (ed.), *Native Americans, Christianity, and the Reshaping of the American Religious Landscape* (Chapel Hill, NC: University of North Carolina Press, 2010), pp. 125–58 (pp. 145–6).

50   See, e.g., the accusations made against Diego de Rosales during a plague epidemic in Arauco in 1631, in Enrich, *Historia*, vol. I, p. 412; and Olivares, *Historia*, p. 278.

Baptism and the reconfiguration of socio-political and economic intertribal relations

Since missionaries were perceived as powerful *curanderos-hechiceros*, natives accepted baptism as an act to be added to their extant practices in order to enlarge the array of ritual responses to the changing conditions of the post-conquest societies.[51] Nevertheless, native acceptance of the sacrament was not only related to its impact on illnesses and healing practices. There were also social and economic reasons which led indigenous populations to accommodate a missionary presence.[52]

In 1636, in the district of Arauco in Chile, a Mapuche was captured and imprisoned by the *indios amigos*, the local allies of the Spaniards.[53] Before his ritual execution, Diego de Rosales tried to convince the prisoner to accept baptism: 'When he was conducted to the sacrifice, he decided to let me bury his body, because when he was still obstinate in rejecting baptism, what most convinced him, with the help of the divine grace, was telling him that if he refused Christianity his body would have been thrown in a dunghill, consumed by dogs and birds, but if he decided to receive our holy faith, he would have been buried in the church'.[54] The missionary strategy proved successful. The prisoner eagerly accepted baptism, not for religious reasons but only as an instrument for obtaining a traditional and honourable burial. The achievement of a specific, traditional goal led to the acceptance of baptism, while the Jesuits were recognising the two driving forces of Mapuche social structure: war and honour.[55] Internal rivalry and warrior competition acted as central institutions in the material and symbolical reproduction of the basic social unit, the *lebo*.[56] Gift exchange and reciprocity fostered intertribal competition, since the circulation of a Spaniard's head or a horse started a dynamic process

---

51 For the Chilean context and the concept of cumulative magic see G. Boccara, *Los vencedores. Historia del pueblo mapuche en la época colonial* (San Pedro de Atacama: Línea Editorial IIAM, 2007), p. 366. On the inclusiveness of Mesoamerican communities, especially in the formation of a vast and composite pantheon of deities, see N.M. Farriss, *Maya Society under Colonial Rule: The Collective Enterprise of Survival* (Princeton, NJ: Princeton University Press, 1984).

52 On native acceptance of the missions as an opportunistic endeavor, see for the northern Mexican missions Reff, *Disease*, p. 16.

53 See A. Ruiz-Esquide Figueroa, *Los indios amigos en la frontera araucana* (Santiago de Chile: Universidad Nacional del Litoral, 1993).

54 ARSI Provincia Chilensis 6, fol. 24, 'Letras Anuas de la Viceprovincia de Chile de los años de 1635 y 1636', 1 March 1637.

55 Boccara, *Los Vencedores*, p. 373.

56 G. Boccara, 'Etnogénesis Mapuche: resistencia y restructuración entre los indígenas del centro-sur de Chile (Siglos XVI–XVIII)', *The Hispanic American Historical Review*, 79 (1999): 431 and 434.

of reciprocity in which every group was forced to obtain new trophies through war and return the gift obtained.[57]

Reciprocity and intertribal rivalry played a pivotal role in the development of baptism. When a *cacique* of Arauco fell seriously ill, the only reason which convinced him to embrace Christianity was the desire to imitate the great Catumalo, a native leader who had died and who had been baptised and accepted a Christian burial.[58] The dynamic of local society was based on imitation and hence baptism became part of the symbolic indigenous system, a sign of social prestige in the continuous quest for military and political power. The perception of baptism and Christian values as opportunities for the reinforcement of wealth and social prestige is confirmed by the phenomenon of chapel construction which developed in southern Chile in the 1630s and 1640s.[59] The building of a church by a specific *lebo* immediately activated the system of reciprocity, leading to a constant search for a bigger shrine and a more solemn celebration of inauguration, as happened in 1636 between the *cacique* of Carampangui Juan Igaipil and the leader of Lavapié, Catumalo.[60] The introduction of Christianity represented a new sphere of intertribal competition, causing internal divisions between the baptised and non-baptised.[61]

Economic interest did not constitute the crucial inducement for the acceptance of Christianity among north-western Mexican communities. D. Reff has, in fact, refuted the idea that Jesuit innovations such as the plough, wheat, chicken and cattle represented a major incentive to accept missionisation and the revolution in native life during the 17th century.[62] Although cattle had an unquestionable impact on the food supply, especially during epidemics, natives mainly accepted missions since the Jesuits took charge of the economic activities, regional commerce and distribution of surpluses, which had been managed in pre-contact times by local leaders.[63] Pedro Méndez reported an interesting episode among the Mayos in 1614 which stresses the relationship between the economic and organisational sides of the missionary experience. The accidental damage to the crop of a non-baptised man by a group of mission natives caused serious strife, only solved by the missionary with the gift of a piece of iron as compensation to the aggrieved party. In response to

---

57   Boccara, 'Etnogénesis Mapuche', 436.

58   Olivares, *Historia*, p. 299.

59   See Boccara, *Los Vencedores*, pp. 368–70.

60   ARSI, Provincia Chilensis 6, fols.129–31v, 'Letras anuas de 1635 y 1636'.

61   ARSI Provincia Chilensis 6, fol. 32, 'Letras annuas de las missiones de la tierra de guerra en el Reyno de Chile por los Padres de la Compañía de Jesús desde el año de 1616 hasta el mes de Diciembre de Seiscientos y diez y siete'. For similar cases in the Mexican context, see RAH, Colección Juan Bautista Muñoz, vol. 19, fol. 36, 'Carta Anua de 1598'.

62   Reff, *Disease*, p. 13.

63   Reff, *Disease*, pp. 259 and 278.

this, the man gathered his 16 relatives in front of the father, asking for baptism, 'because this is commanded by your law ... and my relatives and I want to baptise in order to live under such good law'.[64] What motivated the request for baptism was not the distribution of goods, but instead the missionary's ability to re-establish a social equilibrium. Baptism was, therefore, perceived as an instrument for social and political reorganisation around the figure of a new leader, the missionary.[65]

The organisational and managerial function of the missionary as seen in the north-western Mexican context was overshadowed by his economic and gift-giving role among the Guaycuruas of Chaco. During the 17th century, non-sedentary groups constantly attacked Spanish neighbouring towns in search of meat, cotton, tobacco, iron and yerba mate.[66] The development of protective policies in the middle decades of the following century consistently restricted native access to European goods, accelerating the process of acceptance of the missions.[67] Unlike north-western Mexican populations, the Guaycuruas did not conceive of missions as new organisational communities, but rather as a place of refuge, trade exchange and food supply.[68] This was due to their non-sedentary nature and the difficulties of acquiring an everyday supply of food, which transformed the missions into an indispensable instrument of survival, especially during periods of famine or epidemics. The case of the distribution of yerba mate among the members of the San Javier mission of Mocobies, founded in 1743 in the jurisdiction of Santa Fe, epitomises local approaches towards missions and shows the emergence of a peculiar perception of baptism.

In order to extinguish the common practices of drunkenness and alcoholic feasts known as *borracheras*, Jesuits fostered the consumption of mate, a cold

---

64 Ribas, *Historia*, vol. 2, p. 16.

65 According to H. Dobyns, acceptance of missionary life in north-western Mexico was a direct consequence of the similarity between the missionary structure itself and the town-life model in pre-contact times, now rebuilt by the priests (H.F. Dobyns, *Their Number Become Thinned: Native American Population Dynamics in Eastern North America* (Knoxville, TN: University of Tennessee Press, 1983), pp. 303–4).

66 C. Lucaioli, 'Los espacios de frontera en el Chaco desde la conquista hasta mediados del siglo XVIII', in C. Lucaioli (ed.), *Fronteras: espacios de interacción en las tierras bajas del sur de América* (Buenos Aires: Sociedad Argentina de Antropología, 2010), pp. 21–68 (pp. 38 and 58).

67 A.J. Gullón Abao, *La frontera del Chaco en la gobernación del Tucumán: 1750–1810* (Cádiz: Universidad De Cádiz, 1993), p. 107; and Saeger, *The Chaco Mission Frontier*, pp. 64–5.

68 The demographical study of Guaycuruan mission population, especially the case of the Abipon communities, underlines the great freedom of mobility of local groups, which redefined their non-sedentary features around the integration of the mission as a dwelling for women, children and the elders and a temporary space for food supply, gift exchange and political meetings. See R.H. Jackson, *Demographic Change and Ethnic Survival among the Sedentary Populations on the Jesuit Mission Frontiers of Spanish South America, 1609–1803: The Formation and Persistence of Mission Communities in a Comparative Context* (Leiden: Brill, 2015), pp. 128–43; C. Lucaioli, *Abipones en las fronteras del Chaco: una etnografía histórica sobre el siglo XVIII* (Buenos Aires: Sociedad Argentina de Antropología, 2011), pp. 159–65.

drink highly appreciated by local Mocobies and produced in the Guaraní missions.[69] Mate not only succeeded in reducing alcohol consumption, but also proved to be a powerful instrument of coercion, as shown by the following case. In the San Javier mission, there were two principal *caciques*, Cithaalin and Aletin. Their traditional rivalry was amplified because only the latter accepted Christianity and, unlike in the Mapuche context, this did not result in imitation, but rather in even stronger opposition and obstruction of Cithaalin to missionary activities. Therefore, baptism caused a major internal fracture between Aletin's group, composed of Christians who were helping the father in missionary works, and the rival Cithaalin, who spent most of his days organising *borracheras* and hindering missionary life. The situation changed with the distribution of mate. The access to food supplies was, in fact, controlled by the missionaries and granted as a reward to the most righteous. A lack of participation in mass and Christian doctrine, or the failure to provide sufficient labour force for the everyday mission life, resulted in a reduced distribution of goods and a loss of political power. Since Cithaalin could not access the same quantities of mate due to his non-baptised status, his group members started to join Aletin, who had superior economic and distributive power.[70] Differential access to missionary products was, therefore, rebuilding intertribal relations and solidarities, putting aside non-baptised elements which failed to contribute to the prosperity of the community. Baptised local leaders could rapidly weaken rival groups thanks to the redistribution to their members of local products in exchange for the acceptance of baptism and participation in the everyday working activities of the mission. Local rivalries and the quest for material goods influenced native perception of baptism. Baptism was, therefore, seen as the only way to enter the community as a full member and benefit from missionary products, while non-baptised *caciques* considered the sacrament an instrument for regaining lost power and political consensus.

Conclusion

The spreading of illnesses and an unprecedented mortality rate shocked local populations into calling into question the power and social status of local healers. The emergency created by epidemics led to an immediate perception of the missionaries as responsible for the development of the maladies. Branded as deadly beings, Jesuits started to be perceived also as healers. As shown by the study of traditional beliefs about the origin of the illnesses, local healers

---

69   Paucke, *Hacia allá y para acá*, vol. 2, p. 93. Mate was widely known and consumed in pre-conquest Paraguay. It was a bitter drink obtained from the yerba mate, which Jesuits started to produce in the Guaraní seven missions during the first half of the 17th century. Sometimes used as a medicine, it was also involved in regional commerce and exchange due to its wide appreciation by the natives (A.M. Frankel, *La yerba mate: producción, industrialización, comercio* (Buenos Aires: Albatros, 1983).

70   Paucke, *Hacia allá y para acá*, vol. 2, p. 106.

possessed a dual identity which made them able to both cause death and save the dying. Therefore, the assimilation of the missionaries as *curanderos-hechiceros* paved the way for the development of similar beliefs about the Jesuits' dual abilities. They could kill and save, fostering an initial scepticism towards baptism.

Indigenous populations on the fringes of Spanish America developed various perceptions of baptism according to the different socio-political conditions. The crucial role carried out by the Jesuits in the reorganisation of native communities after the havoc of the conquest years, especially in north-western Mexican communities, led to new approaches towards the sacrament. Local populations reconfigured baptism as a viable way to rebuild social, economic and political structures around a new leader who proved able to replace traditional pre-contact rulers. Assimilation of foreign practices and continuity with local beliefs were two common features of natives' approaches to missionary life. Access to baptism and church construction became important parts of the Mapuche social system based on reciprocity and imitation. Acceptance of the sacrament and the preparation of solemn Christian ceremonies resulted in the perpetuation of intertribal rivalry and the quest for political power, with a limited religious meaning. Although it would be simplistic to reduce native approaches to missionary life to an opportunistic endeavour, certainly material interests proved decisive for Guaycuruan acceptance of the missions.[71] The economic organisation of the Chaco missions based on cattle-raising, hunting and gathering and the cultivation and distribution of salt, maize and mate, perfectly matched the non-sedentary peoples' constant search for food supply.[72]

The Mapuche cultural system of reciprocity was reinforced by the introduction of the sacrament, perceived as a new way of showing political power and authority. Due to the continued resistance which hampered the evangelisation process, the abandonment of traditional practices in favour of foreign beliefs caused shame and internal strife among local communities. On the other hand, the attainment of economic stability and regular food supply led north-western Mexican communities and non-sedentary Guaycuruas to conceive of the missions as a way to obtain a new socio-economic and political balance. For this reason, the abandonment of traditional customs represented the way to obtain an improvement of economic conditions by accepting missionary rules. Those who resisted colonial rule usually suffered pressure within the tribe and witnessed a decrease in their political influence amid a clear reshaping of the tribal framework of power around the new leading figure of the missionary. The Jesuits generally perceived native distortions of baptism, but fostered the healing aspect of the sacrament, understanding its positive impact on local communities. At the same time, the natives transformed a foreign

71 Saeger, *The Chaco Mission Frontier*, p. 53.

72 On Chaco Jesuit missions as an economic success, see Gullón Abao, *La frontera del Chaco*, p. 160.

practice into a ritual which could be inserted into the extant cultural systems. The acts of the missionaries did not differ substantially from the activities of the *curanderos-hechiceros*; and baptism could be completely accepted only through its assimilation of local practices.

Archival abbreviations

ARSI Archivum Romanum Societatis Iesu, Rome

BNC Biblioteca Nazionale Centrale, Rome

RAH Real Academia de la Historia, Madrid

Bibliography

Manuscript sources

ARSI Provincia Chilensis 5, P. de Sotomayor, 'Preguntase si sera conveniente el que la Compañía de Jesús prosiga o no con las misiones que tiene en el estado de Arauco? Ponense las razones por una y otra parte, 31 Jan. 1675'.

ARSI Provincia Chilensis 5, G.B. Camargo, 'Propuesta de las razones que militan en favor de la asistencia de la missión de Valdivia y de las que ay en contra de ella, 22 April 1675'.

ARSI Provincia Chilensis 6, 'Letras annuas de las missiones de la tierra de guerra en el Reyno de Chile por los Padres de la Compañía de Jesús desde el año de 1616 hasta el mes de Diciembre de Seiscientos y diez y siete'.

ARSI Provincia Chilensis 6, 'Letras Anuas desta Provincia de Chile de los años 1629 y 30, 2 April 1630'.

ARSI Provincia Chilensis 6, 'Letras Anuas de la Viceprovincia de Chile de los años de 1635 y 1636, 1 March 1637'.

ARSI Provincia Chilensis 6, 'Adjunta a Letras Annuas de la Viceprovincia del Reino de Chile desde el año de mil y seiscientos y cuarenta y siete hasta el presente de 1648'.

ARSI Provincia Chilensis 6, 'Letras Anuas de la Viceprovincia de Chile del año de 1649, 17 December 1650'.

ARSI Provincia Mexicana 14, 'Carta anua de la provincia de México de 1597, 30 March 1598'.

ARSI, Provincia Mexicana 14, 'Carta anua de la provincia de la Nueva España de la Compañía de Jesús del año de 1606, 14 May 1607'.

ARSI, Provincia Mexicana 14, 'Carta anua de la provincia de la Nueva España del año de 1610, 18 May 1611'.

ARSI Provincia Mexicana 15, 'Letras Anuas de la provincia de la Compañía de Jesús de Mexico por los años 1646 y 1647'.

ARSI Provincia Mexicana 17, 'Copia de una carta que los Padres José Tardá y Tomás de Guadalajara escribieron al P Francisco Ximenez Provincial sobre su entrada a los Tarahumares despues de haber estos abandonado la fe matando a los Padres Cornelio Godinez y Santiago Basilio, 1676'.

ARSI Provincia Mexicana 19, A. Pérez de Ribas, 'Libro septimo de algunos puntos dignos de notar en la historia de las missiones de la Compañía de Jesús en la Nueva España, en particular de la de Cinaloa. Travajos que en ellas han pasado sus operarios y frutos que de ellas an cogido. Y de los medios de que se han ayudado para coger tan abundantes frutos'.

BNC, FG 1407, 'Breve relación de los indios de Chile'.

RAH, Colección Juan Bautista Muñoz, tomo 15, 'Carta del Padre Andrés Pérez, dirigida al Padre Provincial, año de 1617'.

RAH, Colección Juan Bautista Muñoz, vol. 19, 'Carta Anua de 1598'.

Printed sources

Anderson, E. (2010) 'Blood, fire and baptism. Three perspectives on the death of Jean de Brébeuf, seventeenth-century Jesuit martyr', in J. Martin (ed.), *Native Americans, Christianity, and the Reshaping of the American Religious Landscape* (Chapel Hill, NC: University of North Carolina Press), pp. 125–58.

Ascasubi, M. de. (1846) 'Informe cronológico de las misiones del reino de Chile hasta 1789', in C. Gay (ed.), *Historia física y política de Chile segun documentos adquiridos en esta república durante doce años de residencia en ella. Documentos* (Paris: at the house of the author; Chile: el Museo de Historia Natural de Santiago,1846), pp. 300–400.

Boccara, G. (1999) 'Etnogénesis Mapuche: resistencia y restructuración entre los indígenas del centro-sur de Chile (Siglos XVI–XVIII)', *The Hispanic American Historical Review*, 79: 425–61.

— *Los vencedores. Historia del pueblo mapuche en la época colonial* (San Pedro de Atacama: Línea Editorial IIAM, 2007).

Bugarín, J.A. (1993) *Visita de las misiones del Nayarit 1768–1769* (México D.F: Centro de Estudios Mexicanos y Centroamericanos).

'Carta Anua de la Provincia del Peru, 29 Abril 1599', in E. Fernández Dávila and A. de Egaña (eds.), *Monumenta Peruana*, Apud *Monumenta Historica Soc. Iesu* (Rome: Institutum Historicum Societatis Iesu, 1954), pp. 660–733.

Cassirer, E. (1965) *The Philosophy of Symbolic Forms* (New Haven, CT: Yale University Press).

Catto, M. (2010) 'Missioni e globalizzazioni: l'adattamento come identità della Compagnia di Gesù', in *Evangelizzazione e globalizzazione: le missioni gesuitiche nell'età moderna tra storia e storiografia,* edited by M. Catto, 1–16 (Rome: Società editrice Dante Alighieri).

Dobrizhoffer, M. and E. Wernicke (ed. and trans.) (1967–70) *Historia de los Abipones,* 3 vols. (Resistencia: Universidad Nacional del Nordeste).

Enrich, F. (1891) *Historia de la compañia de Jesús en Chile,* 2 vols. (Barcelona: Rosal).

Díaz Blanco, J.M. (2010) *Razón de estado y buen gobierno. La guerra defensiva y el imperialismo español en tiempos de Felipe III* (Sevilla: Universidad de Sevilla).

Dobyns, H.F. (1983) *Their Number Become Thinned: Native American Population Dynamics in Eastern North America* (Knoxville, TN: University of Tennessee Press).

Farriss, N.M. (1984) *Maya Society under Colonial Rule: The Collective Enterprise of Survival* (Princeton, NJ: Princeton University Press).

Foerster, R. (1996) *Jesuitas y Mapuches, 1593–1767* (Santiago de Chile: Editorial Universitaria).

Folsom, R. (2010) *The Yaquis and the Empire: Violence, Spanish Imperial Power, and Native Resilience in Colonial Mexico* (New Haven, CT: Yale University Press).

Frankel, A.M. (1983) *La yerba mate: producción, industrialización, comercio* (Buenos Aires: Albatros).

Gullón Abao, A.J. (1993) *La frontera del Chaco en la gobernación del Tucumán: 1750–1810* (Cádiz: Universidad de Cádiz).

Jackson, R.H. (2015) *Demographic Change and Ethnic Survival among the Sedentary Populations on the Jesuit Mission Frontiers of Spanish South America, 1609–1803: The Formation and Persistence of Mission Communities in a Comparative Context* (Leiden: Brill).

Leonhardt, C. (1927) *Iglesia. Cartas Anuas de la provincia del Paraguay, Chile y Tucumán, de la compañía de Jesús, 1609–1614* (Buenos Aires: Instituto de Investigaciones Históricas).

Levaggi, A. (2002) *Diplomacia hispano-indígena en las fronteras de América* (Madrid: Centro de Estudios Políticos y Constitucionales).

Lozano, P. (1941) *Descripción corográfica del gran Chaco gualamba* (Tucumán: Instituto de Antropología).

Lucaioli, C. (2010) 'Los espacios de frontera en el Chaco desde la conquista hasta mediados del siglo XVIII', in C. Lucaioli (ed.), *Fronteras: espacios de interacción en las tierras bajas del sur de América* (Buenos Aires: Sociedad Argentina de Antropología), pp. 21–68.

— *Abipones en las fronteras del Chaco: una etnografía histórica sobre el siglo XVIII* (2011) (Buenos Aires: Sociedad Argentina de Antropología).

Maeder, E. (1996) *Cartas anuas de la provincia jesuítica del Paraguay, 1641 a 1643* (Resistencia: Instituto de Investigaciones Geohistóricas-Conicet).

Marotti, F. (1985) 'Juan Baptista de Segura and the Failure of the Florida Jesuit Mission, 1566–1572', *The Florida Historical Quarterly*, 63: 267–79.

Muriel, D. and G. Fúrlong Cárdiff (1955) *Breve noticia de las missiones vivas de la compañía de Jesús en la provincia del Paraguay* (Buenos Aires: Escritores Coloniales Rioplatenses).

Norton, M. (2015) 'The chicken or the *Iegue*: human-animal relationships and the Columbian exchange', *American Historical Review*, 120: 28–60.

'Noticia sobre a reduçao en San Xavier de indios Mocobi, na jurisdiçao de Santa Fe (1750)', in J. Cortesão (ed.), *Do Tratado De Madri à Conquista Dos Sete Povos (1750–1802)* (Rio de Janeiro: Biblioteca Nacional, 1969), pp. 15–23.

Olivares, M. de (1874) *Historia de la compañia de Jesús en Chile, 1593–1736* (Santiago de Chile: Bello).

O'Malley, J.W., S.J. (1999) *I Primi Gesuiti* (Milano: Vita e Pensiero).

Ovalle, A. de (1888) *Historica relación del reyno de Chile y de las misiones y ministerios que ejércita en él la compañia de Jesús* (Santiago de Chile).

Paucke, F. and E. Wernicke (ed. and trans.) (1942) *Hacia allá y para acá. Una estadía entre los indios Mocobíes, 1749–1767* (Tucumán: Universidad Nacional de Tucumán).

Pérez de Ribas, A. (1944) *Historia de los triunfos de n.s. fe entre gentes las más barbaras y fieras del nuevo orbe* (México: Layac).

Pizzorusso, G. (2009) 'I dubbi sui sacramenti dalle missioni *ad infideles*. Percorsi nelle burocrazie di curia', in P. Broggio, C. de Castelnau-L'estoile and G. Pizzorusso (eds.), *Administrer les sacrements en Europe et au Nouveau Monde: la curie romaine et les dubia circa sacramenta* (= *Mélanges de l'École Française de Rome, Italie et Méditerranée*, 121), pp. 39–61.

Reff, D.T. (1991) *Disease, Depopulation, and Culture Change in Northwestern New Spain, 1518–1764* (Salt Lake City, UT: University of Utah Press).

Ruiz-Esquide Figueroa, A. (1993) *Los indios amigos en la frontera araucana* (Santiago de Chile: Universidad Nacional del Litoral).

Saeger, J.S. (2000) *The Chaco Mission Frontier: The Guaycuruan Experience* (Tucson, AZ: University of Arizona Press).

Sánchez Labrador, J. and S.A. Lafone y Quevedo (1910) *El Paraguay católico. Homenaje de la universidad nacional de La Plata al XVII. congreso internacional de los americanistas en su reunión de Buenos Aires, en Mayo 16 á 21 de 1910* (Buenos Aires: Imprenta de Coni Hermanos).

Vitar Mukdsi, B. (1997) *Guerra y misiones en la frontera chaqueña del Tucumán, 1700–1767* (Madrid: Consejo Superior de Investigaciones

8. 'Con intención de haçerlos Christianos y con voluntad de instruirlos': spiritual education among American Indians in Anello Oliva's Historia del Reino y Provincias del Perú

Virginia Ghelarducci

The presence of the Jesuits in Latin America dates back to 1549, when the first missionaries arrived in Brazil along with the governor Tomé de Souza.[1] As J. Klaiber remarks, '[b]y the eighteenth century the Society of Jesus was the most important educational and missionary order in Brazil'.[2] Through the centuries Jesuits reached not only South and Central America but also Africa, Asia, North America and Canada, building churches, schools and hospitals, running farms and estates, but also, most importantly, proselytising among native populations. Education and spiritual guidance have always been central to the Jesuit approach to evangelism.[3]

This chapter explores the role of the spiritual education carried out by a Jesuit mission in 17th-century colonial Peru through an analysis of the work of the Jesuit father Giovanni Anello Oliva. Some chapters in his *Historia del Reino y Provincias del Perú* address the evangelisation of indigenous people and the eradication of practices which were deeply rooted in pre-Hispanic Peru

---

1 On the influence of Jesuits in Brazil see S. Leite, *Cartas dos Primeiros Jesuitas do Brasil*, 3 vols., Comissão do IV Centenário da Cidade de São Paulo (São Paulo: Editora São Paulo, 1956); D. Alden, *The Making of an Enterprise: The Society of Jesus in Portugal, Its Empire, and Beyond 1540–1750* (Stanford, CA: Stanford University Press, 1996); T. Cohen, *The Fire of Tongues: Antonio Vieira and the Missionary Church in Brazil and Portugal* (Stanford, CA: Stanford University Press, 1998); S. Knauß, 'Jesuit engagement in Brazil between 1549 and 1609 – a legitimate support of Indians' emancipation or eurocentric movement of conversion?', *Astrolabio*, 11 (2010): 227–38; J.M. Dos Santos, 'Writing and its functions in sixteenth century Jesuit missions in Brazil', *História*, 34 (2015): 109–27.

2 J. Klaiber, 'The Jesuits in Latin America: legacy and current emphases', *International Bulletin of Missionary Research*, 28 (2) (2004): 63–66.

3 The bond between Jesuits and education reinforces the personal and spiritual progress of the missionaries: 'However the Jesuit is always learning; so formation remains a lifelong process of continual conversion and growth in the Spirit' ('Tertianship and final vows', in Zimbabwe-Mozambique Province of the Society of Jesus, http://www.jesuitszimbabwe.co.zw/index.php/what-we-do/forms/tertianship-final-vows [accessed 1 Oct. 2017].

V. Ghelarducci, '"Con intención de haçerlos Christianos y con voluntad de instruirlos": spiritual education among American Indians in Anello Oliva's *Historia del Reino y Provincias del Perú*', in L.A. Newson (ed.), *Cultural Worlds of the Jesuits in Colonial Latin America* (London: Institute of Latin American Studies, 2020), pp. 171–88. License: CC-BY-NC-ND 2.0.

but viewed as idolatrous, pernicious and morally unacceptable according to Christian precepts. Converting Amerindian societies to Christian values and principles was deemed to require the establishment of a well-organised education system which relied on a combination of good teaching and persuasive argumentation imbued with religious indoctrination. In order decisively to change 'inappropriate' behaviour, acquiring a deep knowledge of indigenous cultures, including mastery of local languages, was essential and was a particular strength of the Jesuit mission of Juli, where Father Anello Oliva spent part of his missionary life. The chapter examines the historical importance of missionary efforts in the Andean region, with a particular focus on Anello Oliva's detailed descriptions of indigenous rituals, his arguments for the necessity of their reformation and the wider implications of Jesuit characterisation of traditional Andean practitioners as being 'under the devil's influence'.

Nearly twenty years after the Jesuits' first arrival in the New World, in 1568 missions were successfully established in Peru.[4] The first Peruvian missionary settlement was Huarochirí on the western part of the Cordillera Occidental. The community was formed of 77 small villages, with poor communication. With only a few missionaries in each pueblos, the programme of evangelisation was extremely difficult and the results unsatisfactory. Few Indians were constant in their devotion and, due to the distance between villages, the fathers could not dedicate sufficient time to their indoctrination. Gradually some of the missionaries fell ill and died and the mission was finally abandoned at the beginning of the 1570s.[5]

After the failure of the Huarochirí mission, the Jesuits began to serve the community of Santiago de Cercado, a *reducción de indígenas* founded in 1571 with the purpose of gathering together the dispersed native migrant population which lived in the north east of Lima. Under the Jesuits' guidance, El Cercado flourished.[6] Surrounded by a three-metre-high wall, the town kept the indigenous population under control and separate from the Spanish population, who were

---

4   For the history of the Society of Jesus in Peru and their relationship with Andean culture, see also R. Vargas Ugarte, *Historia de la Compañía de Jesús en el Perú*, 4 vols. (Burgos: 1963–65); L. Martín, *The Intellectual Conquest of Peru: The Jesuit College of San Pablo, 1568–1767* (New York: Fordham University Press, 1968); J.W. O'Malley, S.J., *The First Jesuits* (Cambridge, MA: Harvard University Press, 1993); S. Hyland, *The Jesuit and the Incas: The Extraordinary Life of Padre Blas Valera, S.J.* (Ann Arbor, MI: University of Michigan Press, 2003); J.W. O'Malley et al., *The Jesuits II: Cultures, Sciences, and the Arts, 1540–1773* (Toronto: University of Toronto Press, 2006); A.C. Hosne, *The Jesuit Missions to China and Peru, 1570–1610: Expectations and Appraisals of Expansionism* (London and New York: Routledge, 2013). For a more global insight see A. Coello De La Rosa, J. Burrieza Sánchez and D. Moreno (eds.), *Jesuitas e imperios de ultra-mar, Siglos XVI–XX* (Madrid: Siélex, 2012).

5   See C. Carcelén Reluz, 'Los jesuitas en su primera misión: Huarochirí, siglo XVI', *Anuario, Archivo y Biblioteca Nacional de Bolivia* (2003): 111–33.

6   See D. Rodríguez, 'Los jesuitas y su labor evangelizadora en la doctrina de Santiago del Cercado', *Investigaciones Sociales*, 9 (2005): 133–52.

not allowed to live there. The missionaries successfully ran a school, a hospital and a *casa de reclusión para hechiceros* [prison for sorcerers]. In the school in Santa Cruz indigenous children were taught to read and write, participated in music classes and learnt the catechism and Catholic doctrine. The hospital provided the local population with medical care and assistance, while the *casa de reclusión* prevented Indian priests or sorcerers from disseminating traditional beliefs which could have undermined the process of evangelisation. Enjoying considerable independence from the Church hierarchy, the Jesuit community in El Cercado created a perfectly structured society which efficiently inculcated Christian values and ideas.[7] It became a particularly successful socio-religious laboratory and, as N. Cushner remarks, gradually, El Cercado became a centre for the formation of Jesuits, with a novitiate and a house dedicated to the final training of priests.[8]

Another example of similar success was the mission of Juli, an Andean village close to Lake Titicaca in the province of Chucuito.[9] Far from Lima and characterised by climatic extremes, Juli was densely populated with 15,000 indigenous inhabitants.[10] As in Santiago de Cercado, the missionaries built a church, a school and a hospital, but Juli became famous due to its language school, a place where missionaries could improve their knowledge of Quechua and Aymara before starting their missions. Command of the indigenous languages was essential to the Jesuit method of evangelisation and viewed as a valuable tool with which the better to understand the culture of the local communities.

Preaching in a *lengua de indios* was central to the listeners' achieving total apprehension of the biblical message, particularly among Andean people, since, according to the missionaries, they were extremely reluctant to abandon their rituals and idolatrous practices. The question of a correct understanding of Christian doctrine was a real concern for the missionaries due to their observation that too many natives simply repeated what they had learned by

7   See A. Coello de la Rosa, 'La reducción de Santiago de El Cercado y la. Compañía de Jesús', in G. Dalla Corte (ed.), *Conflicto y violencia en América: VIII Encuentro-Debate América Latina ayer y hoy* (Barcelona: Universitat de Barcelona, 2002), pp. 53–68.

8   See N.P. Cushner, *Soldiers of God: The Jesuits in Colonial America, 1565–1767* (Buffalo, NY: Language Communications, 2002), p. 76.

9   Part of the seven districts of the province of Chucuito, Juli was, and still is, a strategic location, along the ancient trade route to Bolivia (Cuzco-Puno-La Paz). The climate of the district is dry and cool. There is a wet season, which runs from September to March/April, and temperatures oscillate between 0° C and 15° C. Although precipitation in the region does not normally exceed 800 mm per year, Juli features a humid, subtropical montane forest climate which supports agriculture and cattle raising. See M. Arteta et al., 'Plantas vasculares de la Bahía de Juli, Lago Titicaca, Puno-Perú', *Ecología Aplicada*, 5 (2006): 29–36; R.D. Díaz Aguilar, 'Estudio de caracterización climática de la precipitación pluvial y temperatura del aire para las cuencas de los ríos Coata e Ilave', in *Servicio Nacional de Meteorología e Hidrología del Perú* (2013), pp. 1–45, www.senamhi.gob.pe/load/file/01401SENA-4.pdf [accessed 2 Oct. 2018].

10   Ibid.

heart without knowing the meaning of the words. This is reported clearly in the 1600 *Crónica Anónima*: '[W]e see some very old *indios* and *indias* saying the prayers and the doctrine in Latin and Castilian like parrots without knowing what they are saying'.[11] At the beginning, the school was intended to cover three main languages, Quechua, Aymara and Pukina, but gradually came to focus only on Aymara.[12] To facilitate the process of indoctrination, the confessional manuals and catechism booklets which were used during apostolic work were translated into vernaculars. Ludovico Bertonio's *Vocabulario de la lengua aymara*, approved by Father Francisco de Contreras in 1610 and printed two years later, and Alonso de Barzana's *Arte y vocabulario de la lengua general del Perú llamada quichua, y en la lengua española*, published in Lima in 1586, came to be regarded as essential reference texts for the study of the two main languages of the region.[13]

The Juli mission was particularly renowned for 'the high cultural and moral level of the missionaries, their community life, their authoritative missiology, the methodical study of vernacular languages and also for the original institution of a fund for the poor'.[14] Daily life in the mission was strictly regulated and marked by a rigid routine: mass; catechesis for adults and children; pastoral care; food preparation and distribution to elderly and poor people; procession;

11 '[P]ues vemos que algunos indios e indias muy viejos y viejas rezan las oraciones y dizen la doctrina en lengua latina y castellana, sin saber lo que dicen como papagayos' (F. Mateos, *Historia general de la Compañía de Jesús en la provincia del Perú. Crónica anónima del 1600 que trata del establecimiento y misiones de la Compañía de Jesús en los paises de habla española en la América meridional*, vol. 1, part 2 (Madrid: Consejo Superior de Investigaciones Científicas, 1944), p. 17.

12 X. Albó, 'Notas sobre jesuitas y lengua aymara', in S. Negro Tua and M.M. Marzal (eds.), *Un reino en la frontera: las misiones jesuitas en la América colonial* (Quito: Abya Yala, 2000), pp. 277–88 (p. 278). Commitment to education has always been at the core of Jesuit philosophy. The first Jesuit school dated back to 1548, when the fathers founded an educational institute in Messina, Italy. Three years later the prestigious Collegio Romano was established in Rome and destined to become one of the most important Catholic universities in the world, the Pontifical Gregorian University. Through the centuries schools were also built in East Asia, Africa and Latin America. '[A] special care for the instruction of children' is one of the promises in the Jesuits' final vows. On the importance of children's education see J.W. O'Malley, S.J., 'How the first Jesuits became involved in education', in V.J. Duminuco (ed.), *The Jesuit Ratio Studiorum: 400th Anniversary Perspectives* (New York: Fordham University Press, 2000), pp. 56–74; P.-H. Kolvenbach, *Go Forth and Teach: The Characteristics of Jesuit Education*, Jesuit Secondary Education Association Foundations (2005), pp. 1–32, https://www.fairfieldprep.org/uploaded/Documents/15-16_School_Year/GoForthAndTeach.pdf [accessed 1 Oct. 2017].

13 Both the Jesuit fathers were talented linguists and served the mission in Juli. On the editions of Bertonio's *Vocabulario* see H. Van den Berg, 'Las ediciones del *Vocabulario de la lengua aymara*', *Revista Ciencia y Cultura*, 28 (2012): 9–39.

14 M. Helmer, 'Juli, un experimento misionero de los jesuitas en el altiplano andino (siglo xvi)', *Boletín del Instituto Riva-Agüero*, 12 (1982–83): 191–216. Author translation from the Spanish.

and choir practice.[15] What the Jesuits had found in Juli was worrying. The Dominican friars who had preceded them and run the mission for nearly thirty years left a legacy of profound hostility and animosity against Christian missionaries, due to their abusive treatment and exploitation of the local people.[16] Despite the ambiguous feelings of some of the fathers, who advocated abandoning the mission due to the attitude of the native people and difficulties in the process of indoctrination, which often involved recourse to violence and coercion, the perseverance of the Jesuits was rewarded by success. The mission in Juli lasted for almost two centuries and became the destination of the ablest and most experienced missionaries. As X. Albó has observed: 'Almost all the famous Jesuits in this cultural and linguistic Andean area passed through Juli: Barzana, Bertonio, Torres Bollo, Valera, Gonzalez Holguín, Cobo, among others'.[17] José de Acosta, provincial of the Society of Jesus for the province of Peru from 1576, was particularly pleased with the mission at Juli and the work of its superior, Diego de Torres. In a letter to Claudio Acquaviva, the Jesuit father also stressed the importance of preserving this mission, prized for its language school and the local evangelisation project.[18] Although probably far from being a prototypically ideal mission, Juli was regarded as a landmark and an inspiration for further apostolic work in Latin America.[19]

Serving the mission in Juli was, therefore, a matter of prestige. Among all the aforementioned names we should include Father Anello Oliva, who arrived in Peru in 1597 as part of an expedition originally comprising twelve brethren under the direction of Felipe Claver.[20] At that time Anello Oliva was still a

15 T. Bouysse-Cassagne, 'Endoctriner, normaliser, discriminer: l'utopie jésuite de Juli (xve-xviie siècle)', in J.C. Garavaglia, J. Poloni-Simard and G. Rivière (eds.), *Au miroir de l'anthropologie historique. Mélanges offerts à Nathan Wachtel* (Rennes: Presses universitaires de Rennes, 2014), pp. 401–14.

16 See S. Hyland, *The Jesuit and the Incas: The Extraordinary Life of Padre Blas Valera, S.J.* (Ann Arbor, MI: The University of Michigan Press, 2003), p. 56 ff.

17 Albó, 'Notas sobre jesuitas', p. 278.

18 J. de Acosta, 'El Padre José de Acosta al Padre Claudio Acquaviva, Lima, 14 de abril de 1585', in A. de Egaña (ed.), *Monumenta Peruana*, vol. 3, *1581–1585* (Rome: Monumenta Historica Societatis Iesu, 1961), p. 632 ff. On Juli see also J. de Acosta, 'El Padre José de Acosta al Padre Everardo Mercuriano, Lima, 15 de febrero de 1577', in A. de Egaña (ed.), *Monumenta Peruana*, 2, *1576–1580* (Rome: Monumenta Historica Societatis Iesu, 1958), pp. 210–86, particularly pp. 226–7.

19 As V. Battisti Delia remarks, 'Juli is a mission constantly used as an example. It is cited as a key mission which plays vital roles in the development of Jesuit evangelisation and which inspired all other Jesuit missions and Indian *reducciones* in Southern Peru, Bolivia, Argentina and Paraguay' (V. Battisti Delia, 'The Doctrine of Juli: Foundation, Development and a New Identity in a Shared Space', in S. Botta (ed.), *Manufacturing Otherness: Missions and Indigenous Cultures in Latin America* (Newcastle upon Tyne: Cambridge Scholars Publishing, 2014), pp. 37–62 (p. 40).

20 Sent by superior general Claudio Acquaviva to Peru, Felipe Claver was highly praised as a spiritual guide and, like Anello Oliva, had a profound desire to serve his mission among indigenous people. Once in Peru, Father Claver started learning one of the local languages

student and would have to complete his training before he applied for his final vows at the Colegio Máximo de San Pablo in Lima, probably in 1602. We do not have much information on Anello Oliva's background but we know he was born in Naples in 1572 or 1574. Anello Oliva entered the order in his home town in 1593, where he studied under the guidance of Mutio Vitelleschi, who years later would be appointed superior general of the Society. His greatest desire as a young Jesuit was to be sent to work among indigenous people; he would go on to spend about thirty years in the Andes. One of his missions was in the same remote village of Juli. During his apostolic work he had the opportunity to observe, collect and record the customs and traditions of the people among whom he worked. Anello Oliva's project was quite ambitious: to write a comprehensive, four-volume history of Peru and of its famous missionaries. As the complete title suggests, his *Historia del reino y provincias del Perú y vidas de los varones insignes* was inspired by his commitment to his order and, more precisely, to the celebration of the exemplary life of some of its members. However, in his writings he also devoted ample space to a discussion of Peru's history and traditions.

Unfortunately, the only volume still extant is the first book, the *Historia del Reino y Provincias del Perú*, completed in Lima in 1631. The book did not ever receive the approval of General Mutio Vitelleschi, who had requested a revision in 1634, and was not published in Lima until 1895. Despite the difficulties he encountered in publishing his work, Anello Oliva achieved a high position within the Jesuit hierarchy, being appointed rector of three *colegios*: the Colegio de Oruro in 1625, Colegio del Callao (1630–36) and Colegio de San Martín de Lima. He was also rector of the Colegio de San Pablo for six years, from 1636 until his death in 1642.[21]

Like many other fathers, Anello Oliva was a very well read man, with a solid grounding in the scriptures and the classics, but also a solid knowledge of historians and *cronistas* who wrote on Peru, such as Antonio de Herrera, Francisco López de Gómara, Inca Garcilaso de la Vega, Pedro Cieza de León, or Blas Valera. Familiar with local sources and informants, Anello Oliva did

---

before taking up a post in Lima to teach theology. Despite his vocation and effort to do apostolic work, Felipe Claver was among those Jesuits who asked to come back to Europe and saw their request denied by Acquaviva. On this see E. Fernández (ed.), *Monumenta peruana*, vol. 8, *1603–1604* (Rome: Institutum Historicum Societatis Iesu, 1986), p. 7. On Father Claver and his Peru mission see Mateos, *Historia general*, pp. 430–31.

21 The Colegio de San Pablo was the first Jesuit college in Latin America and one of the most prestigious. Established in Lima in 1568, the Colegio was supposed to become a university and already offered courses in Latin, philosophy and theology along with a language course aimed at training the future missionaries in native languages. Due to a dispute with viceroy Toledo, who favoured the University of San Marcos, the Colegio never reached the status of university but continued to play a central role in colonial Peru, providing high-quality education. For a more detailed account of the history of the Colegio see Martín, *The Intellectual Conquest of Peru*; A.I. Prieto, *Missionary Scientists: Jesuit Science in Spanish South America, 1570–1810* (Nashville, TN: Vanderbilt University Press, 2011).

not confine himself to a history of the Andean region using previous materials, but also carried out ethnographic fieldwork, collecting stories on Peru's past and traditions directly from the native people with whom he lived. It took him some time to organise all his data; the manuscript was probably composed between 1600 and 1630.[22]

Evangelisation was the focus of Oliva's mission and the main purpose of King Philip II of Spain and the general of the Society, due to their perception of the great need of the Indians: 'por ser gente incomparablemente neçessitada'.[23] The most difficult task the missionaries had to face was the eradication of idolatry, which was regarded as particularly deep-rooted in the Andean region. In the eyes of the Jesuits, 'Andean gods were simply manifestations of the devil, native priests were Satan's ministers, and Huarochirí, the first Jesuit mission in the Andes, was labelled the 'Cathedral of Idolatry'.'[24] Anello Oliva dedicates an entire chapter to this subject, describing superstitions, rituals and beliefs which were interpreted as a direct consequence of the devil's influence.[25] Nevertheless,

22   The edition consulted here is based on the original manuscript held by the Biblioteca Nacional de Lima and probably lost after the fire of 1943; it was published by J.F. Varela and L. Varela y Obregoso (Lima: Libreria de San Pedro, 1895). C. Gálvez Peña has edited a critical edition, published by the Pontificia Universidad Católica del Perú in 1998, which is based on the manuscript once held by the British Museum (MS. Add. 25327) and now in the British Library. Another manuscript of the *Historia* has been found in the Biblioteca Cassanatense in Rome (MS. 1815) and examined by Gálvez Peña. For a detailed analysis of this manuscript see C. Gálvez Peña, 'La censura al interior de la Compañía de Jesús: notas sobre un manuscrito desconocido del P. Giovanni Anello Oliva S.J. (1639)', *Histórica*, 25 (2001): 215–27.

23   Anello Oliva, *Historia*, p. 198.

24   Cushner, *Soldiers of God*, p. 74.

25   Ten years after the publication in Lima of Pablo José de Arriaga's *La Extirpación de la Idolatría en el Pirú* in 1621, which was meant to provide a guide for preachers, priests, confessors and inspectors, the problem of idolatry in Peru was still worthy of Anello Oliva's deep concerns. For a more comprehensive understanding of the topic see P.J. de Arriaga, *La extirpación de la idolatría en el Pirú*, Biblioteca de Autores Españoles, 209 (Madrid: Atlas, 1968 [1621]). The theme of the extirpation of idolatry in colonial Peru has been thoroughly explored by contemporary scholars. See also F. Pease G.Y., 'El Príncipe de Esquilache y una relación sobre la extirpación de la idolatría', *Cuadernos del seminario de historia, Instituto Riva-Agüero*, 9 (1968): 81–92; I.M. Silverblatt, *Moon, Sun, and Witches: Gender Ideologies and Class in Inca and Colonial Peru* (Princeton, NJ: Princeton University Press, 1987); K. Mills, *Idolatry and Its Enemies: Colonial Andean Religion and Extirpation, 1640–1750* (Princeton, NJ: Princeton University Press, 1997); I. Gareis, 'Extirpación de idolatrías e identidad cultural en las sociedades andinas del Perú virreinal (siglo XVII)', *Boletín de Antropología*, 18 (2004): 262–82; H. Urbano, 'Pablo Joseph de Arriaga, S.J. Retórica y extirpación de idolatrías en el arzobispado de Lima, siglos XVI–XVII', in R. Izquierdo Benito and F. Martínez Gil (eds.), *Religión y heterodoxias en el mundo hispánico: siglos XIV–XVIII* (Madrid: Sílex Ediciones, 2011), pp. 153–69; L. León Llerena, 'Narrating conversion: idolatry, the sacred, and the ambiguities of Christian evangelization in colonial Peru', in S. Arias and R. Marrero-Fente (eds.), *Coloniality, Religion, and the Law in the Early Iberian World* (Nashville, TN: Vanderbilt University Press, 2013), pp. 117–36; P. Shah, 'Language, discipline, and power: the extirpation of idolatry in colonial Peru and indigenous resistance', *Voces Novae*, 5 (2013), https://digitalcommons.chapman.edu/cgi/viewcontent.cgi?article=1074&context=vocesnovae [accessed 9 Sept. 2019].

he did not seem surprised by the phenomenon of idolatry, which was common even among the Greeks and Romans, who were considered to be the highest expression of Western civilisation: 'When I recall the large number of idols and idolatries, superstitions and gentile ceremonies that were held among the two most wise and cultured people in the world, the Greeks and Romans, I am not at all surprised that the Peruvians, who are not that cultured and [remain] buried in the darkness of ignorance, have had such a multitude of idols and superstitions like no other peoples'.[26]

However, like other missionaries Anello Oliva was convinced that, even before the arrival of the Europeans, the Incas had at least had a notion of a supreme god, which he identified with Pachacamac, the Almighty (el Todopoderoso): 'I believe that it is a fact that the *indios* of Peru, before the preaching of the Holy Gospel, had some notions [that there is] only one God and that [the fact that] He is the Maker of the Universe is as true and undoubted as it is among them and in their language, the name and word Pachacamac'.[27] In the Andean pantheon, Pachacamac was the maker of heaven and earth and all the creatures which inhabit them (and could be easily associated with the Christian God). According to Anello Oliva, if the indigenous people worshipped other gods in addition to Pachacamac, it was because the devil had confused them with lies and deceptions: '[A]nd if, after that, they worshipped the Sun, this was because the Devil, combining many lies with some truths or apparent truths, convinced them that this planet has a great power in war and generated the main source of survival on Earth'.[28] Again, a few pages later, Anello Oliva persists with the theory of the devil's influence:

> [T]he little or nothing the *indios* of Peru knew about the true God was
> so clouded or, better, drowned and destroyed by the multitude of their
> idolatries and superstitions, such that for many centuries they had no idea
> of God, because the Devil not only was preserving their [idolatries and
> superstitions] but also increased them over time in such a way that I doubt
> there is a number in [our] numeral system [large enough to allow us] to
> count them.[29]

26 'Quando me acuerdo de la gran muchedumbre de Ydolos y Ydolatrias, supersticiones y çeremonias gentílicas que tuuieron las dos naciones mas sabias y entendidas del mundo, quales fueron la Griega y la Romana, nada me admiro que la peruana no tan entendida, sepultada en las tinieblas de la ignorançia, aya tenido tanta infinidad de ydolos y supersticiones, quanto ninguna otra mas' (Anello Oliva, *Historia*, p. 124).

27 'El auer tenido los Yndios del Perú antes de la predicaçion del Sancto Euangelio alguna notiçia de un Solo Dios Y como este es el criador del Uniuerso lo tengo por tan çierto y indutable quanto lo es entre ellos y en su lengua el nombre y palabra Pachacamac' (Anello Oliva, *Historia*, p. 126).

28 'y si después adoraron al Sol, esto fue por que les hiço creer el Demonio que era este planeta poderoso en las guerras y que criaba los mantenimientos en la tierra mesclando muchas mentiras con algunas verdades o aparençia dellas' (Anello Oliva, *Historia*, p. 126).

29 'La poca y muy corta notigia que tuuieron los yndios del Perú del verdadero Dios, quedo tan anublada, o por mejor degir ahogada y acabada con la muchedumbre de sus Ydolatrias y

...

> All these superstitions and rituals were established by the Devil in order to stop them worshipping *Pachacamac*, which they did to the extent that they forsook the sumptuous and magnificent temple and it has been many years since they have abandoned it. [30]

There was no doubt about the causes of this blindness. Unaware of true wisdom, he argued, the Incas basically seemed to worship every single natural element which could have caused them harm or done them any good: '*What I suppose is that* the *indios* from Peru were so blind in their gentile condition that they worshipped as gods and idolised anything from which they could hope to receive any good or [could] fear any harm and they even worshipped animals no matter how brutal and cruel they were'.[31]

Mountains, animals, coloured stones, the sun, the stars and, most importantly, the earth or *Pachamama* were objects of worship, often worthy of offerings or sacrifices. A variety of 'idols' and spirits, which were part of the traditional religion, were seen by the missionaries as images of Satan which should be destroyed. In addition to the pantheon of Andean deities, the local people worshipped *huacas*, sacred things or places which were represented by small statues in the shape of human beings or animals. In the world view of local populations, *huacas* 'had been the organisers of the known world. And thus the world could be explained and managed'.[32]

What was particularly problematic for the missionaries was that *huacas* were not only abstract holy entities or objects which should rightfully be replaced by Christian concepts: they also embodied a strong sense of continuity between people, nature and the local people's ancestors. This profound sense of belonging and continuity was nurtured by ritual practices and frequent visits to sacred

---

supertigiones, quanto en muchos siglos no tuuieron rostro della, por que el Demonio no solo fue conseruando las suias, pero las fue acregentando con el tiempo, de tal suerte que dudo aya numero en el guarismo que las pueda contar' (Anello Oliva, *Historia*, p. 128).

30   'Todas estas supertiçiones y ritos fueronse entablando por orden del Demonio para que dexassen de adorar al Pachacamac, como lo hiçieron hasta desampararle su sumptuoso y grandioso templo, pues a muchissimos años que le dexaron' (Anello Oliva, *Historia*, p. 131).

31   '*Y lo que supongo es que* fueron tan giegos los yndios del Perú en su gentilidad que qualquiera cossa de que pudiessen esperar algún bien, o temer algún mal, la adoraban por Dios y idolatraban en ella y assi adoraban hasta los animales por brutos y crueles que fuessen' (Anello Oliva, *Historia*, p. 130). Italics in original.

32   K. Mills, *Idolatry and Its Enemies*. On the concept of *huaca* in the Andean world see S. MacCormack, *Religion in the Andes: Vision and Imagination in Early Colonial Peru* (Princeton, NJ: Princeton University Press, 1991); K.J. Andrien, *Andean Worlds: Indigenous History, Culture, and Consciousness Under Spanish Rule, 1532–1825* (Albuquerque, NM: University of New Mexico Press, 2001); A.B. Scott, 'Sacred politics: an examination of Inca Huacas and their use for political and social organization', *Totem*, 17 (2009): 23–36; S. Hyland, *Gods of the Andes: An Early Jesuit Account of Inca Religion and Andean Christianity* (University Park, PA: Pennsylvania State University Press, 2011); C. Brosseder, *The Power of Huacas: Change and Resistance in the Andean World of Colonial Peru* (Austin, TX: University of Texas Press, 2014).

places which Andean people were reluctant to abandon: 'Huacas became places of religious pilgrimage and congregation, shrines where the people who believed themselves descended from these divine progenitors would bring offerings, give regular worship, and look for continuing support and guidance'.[33] *Conopas* or *chancas*, as they were called in Cuzco, which contained the spirits of plants and things, were also sacred as protection for the household. In her monograph *Huarochirí*, K. Spalding helps us to understand the nature of these 'idols': 'At the household level, the oldest member held the guardians of the welfare of the household – small idols, stones, or odd-shaped objects called *conopas*. The *conopas* were the material representation of the family's resources, passed down from father to son and wife to daughter'.[34] To Anello Oliva, *conopas* were for the Indians what *lares* and *Penates* were for the Romans: tutelary deities, originally the souls of the ancestors, then guardians of the household: 'They also worship and revere the *Conopas* that in Cuzco people call *Chancas* and they are their gods *lares* and *Penates*; they call them *Huacicamayoc* which is the majordomo or landlord. These idols usually come in different materials and shapes but, normally, they are made by some particular small stones that have something special or remarkable in their colour of shape'.[35] 'Idols' were, for Anello Oliva, 'infernales semillas'[36] or fiendish seeds which needed to be eradicated as soon as possible.[37]

Nevertheless, these 'idols' were not the only target. To secure power over the Amerindians, the devil worked even more directly through the numerous *hechiceros* or sorcerers, who were considered to be ministers of the devil (*ministros del Diablo*).[38] *Hechiceros* were highly respected by the Andean populations and regularly consulted for guidance and advice. They were accused by the missionaries of continuing to practise old traditional rituals and, in so doing, were viewed as obstacles to the process of evangelisation: 'It

33 Mills, *Idolatry and Its Enemies*, p. 47.

34 K. Spalding, *Huarochirí: An Andean Society Under Inca and Spanish Rule* (Stanford, CA: Stanford University Press, 1984).

35 'También adoran y reverençian las Conopas que en el Cuzco llaman Chancas y son sus Dioses lares y Penates y assi los llaman Huacicamayoc que es el mayordomo o dueño déla casa. Estos ydolos suelen ser de diversas materias y figuras, pero de ordinario son de algunas Pjiedras particulares y pequeñas que tengan algo de singular, o notable en la color o figura' (Anello Oliva, *Historia*, p. 134).

36 Anello Oliva, *Historia*, pp. 133–4.

37 'y es también infinito el numero deltas que los padres de la compañía que estos años an continuado con tanta gloria del Señor y bien de las al mas las missiones de los llanos, an quitado, quemado y consumido de estas infernales semillas' (Anello Oliva, *Historia*, pp. 133–4).

38 'Descubrióse gran número de hechizeros que con sus supersticiones teman engañados a los miserables yndios que con la penitençia que higieron dieron muestras de su contriçion y conuersion que confirmaron con la enmienda que se via en ellos. Fue muy grande la muchedumbre de ydolos que se quemaron y boluieron en geniza' (Anello Oliva, *Historia*, p. 201). On the presence of the devil in the Andes see A. Redden, *Diabolism in Colonial Peru, 1560–1750* (London and New York: Routledge, 2008).

has already happened many times that an indio or an india has found a small stone of this kind and, taking it into great consideration, they bring it to the sorcerer with great interest, asking him to tell them what will be. The Devil's instrument answers them with great admiration: "This is the *Conopa*, worship it and cut it very carefully because, thanks to its favour and protection you will have lots of food and rest"'.[39]

Rituals which ensured prosperity or guaranteed a good harvest also required eradication as examples of pagan devotion. There was a specific ritual which Anello Oliva considered particularly 'infernal' but was popular among caciques and curacas. It involved a special drink called *achuma*, nocturnal birds and soothsayers:

> in order to know the good or bad that they have for each other, they take a drink, that they call *Achuma*, which is a kind of water that they make with the juice of one of these thick and smooth cacti that grow in these hot valleys, drink it with many ceremonies and dances and, because it is very strong, afterwards, those who drink it are left unconscious and have visions that the Devil gives them. On the basis of these [visions], they make judgements about their suspicions and other people's intentions. For this cult, they take some nocturnal birds that they call *chucic* and *tucu* – which are the owl and the eagle owl – guinea pigs, toads, snakes and other wild animals and, opening their interiors, they observe their intestine, reading in them their desires and other things that people ask them.[40]

As Cushner points out, in order to stop these pernicious practices and counteract the influence of sorcerers and fortune-tellers, 'the Bishop of La Plata ... recommended to Fr. Diego de Torres in 1582 that hechiceros and their followers be executed, preferably by burning at the stake'.[41] However, the Jesuits in Juli decided to follow the orders of the Council of Lima, which in 1553 had stated that the rightful punishment for *hechiceros* was imprisonment. For this purpose, a prison called the Casa Blanca [White House] was built in Juli to isolate sorcerers and prevent them from influencing the rest of the

---

39 'Ya a acontegido no pocas veçes hallar un yndio o yndia bien acaso alguna piedreçita desta suerte y reparando en ella llenársela al hechiçero y con gran affecto preguntalle le diga que sera? y el instrumento del Demonio respondelle con mucha admiragion. Esta es Conopa; reuerençiala y móchala con gran cuidado, por que mediante su fauor y amparo tendrás mucha comida y descanso' (Anello Oliva, *Historia*, p. 134).

40 'para saber la voluntad mala o buena que se tienen unos a otros toman un breuage que llaman Achuma que es una agua que hacen del çumo de unos cardones gruessos y lisos que se crian en valles calientes, bebenla con grandes ceremonias y cantares, y como ella sea muy fuerte luego los que la beben quedan sin juicio y priuados de su sentido, y ven vissiones que el Demonio les repressenta y conforme a ellas juzgan sus sospechas y de los otros las intenciones. Para este ministerio cogen algunas aues nocturnas que llaman chucic y Tucu que son lechusa y buho, cuyes, sapos y culebras y otros animales siluestres; y abrieadoles las entrañas miranle los intestinos adiuinando en ellos sus desseos y otros lo que le preguntan' (Anello Oliva, *Historia*, p. 135).

41 Cushner, *Soldiers of God*, p. 88.

population. There the *hechiceros* could be converted and re-educated by the missionaries.

In the view of the Jesuit fathers, the presence of the devil was everywhere in the Andes. Not only was it found in complex systems of ritual practices and beliefs related to different objects, often associated with ancient traditions, but also in many details of everyday life which could be regarded as diabolical. To Anello Oliva, even the way the Indians wore their hair was a symbol of satanic influence: 'In the end, as the First Council of Lima warns … the *indios* offered themselves and were devoted to the cult of demons, sometimes letting their hair grow down to their waist, some other times cutting them in many different ways'.[42] The Jesuit father insisted on the necessity of reforming native customs, mainly because of the condition of the indigenous people, who were blind and lost without the true light of the Gospel.[43] Saving souls and educating minds were core principles for the missionaries, who worked endlessly towards this purpose, waging war against superstitions and evil influences.[44]

Baptism was the first step towards joining the Christian community and abandoning a nomadic life, considered more appropriate to a beast than to a man: 'There was a great number of adults who were baptised and many of them were as old as 80, 90 and almost 100. They used to wander through *páramos* and forests more like beasts and animals of the countryside than rational men'.[45] Fundamental was the frequency of public preaching, of sermons and lectures to attract new people to the Church, alongside everyday support for the poor. Medicines, food and clothes were dispensed by the missionaries, who visited those in need, providing them with pastoral care and practical help. Anello Oliva highlights how important it was to eradicate vanity and frivolity, particularly in Lima, and for this purpose exemplarity was essential. He praises the moral qualities of the missionaries in Peru, who were able not only to convert the natives and eliminate undesirable habits, such as *fiestas* and *danzas*,

---

42 'Finalmente como aduierte el conçilio primero Limense … de diuersas maneras se ofreçian y dedicaban los yndios a los Demonios, algunas vezes dexando creçer los cabellos bástala çintura, otras vezes cortándolos, no de una manera, sino de muchas' (Anello Oliva, *Historia*, pp. 135–6).

43 'La primera el miserable estado que tenia la christiandad en el Perú después que se conquisto por la corona de Castilla y León … por mayor podre también aqui añadir algo por menor del gran desorden y relaxagion de vida y costumbres de aquella gente en aquel tiempo y los grandes abusos y multitudes de peccados que de diario se cometían' (Anello Oliva, *Historia*, pp. 135–6).

44 See also L. Clossey, *Salvation and Globalization in the Early Jesuit Missions* (Cambridge: Cambridge University Press, 2008); G. Wilde (ed.), *Saberes de la conversión: jesuítas, indígénas e imperios coloniales enlas fronteras de la cristiandad* (Buenos Aires: SB, 2011).

45 'Fue grande el numero de los adultos que se baptizaron y muchos dellos tan viejos que eran de ochenta, nouenta y casi çien años de edad, estos andaban por aquellos paramos y lugares siluestres mas como bestias y animales del campo que como hombre raçionales' (Anello Oliva, *Historia*, p. 201).

but also to introduce monogamy and a regular routine in the administration of the sacraments among the newly converted.

As Cushner remarks, the mission of Juli was a success and a model for future missions, particularly those in Paraguay. Jesuits missionaries exercised great influence in shaping the life and society of the Andean region and remained in Juli for over a century.[46] Despite the difficulties, many factors contributed to ensuring the success of this particular mission: deep knowledge of the local languages, culture and customs of native people; conversion through perseverance and good example; establishment of a regular religious routine along with education and health care; but also the attention given to fostering positive relations using astute political negotiation.[47]

Nevertheless, the evangelisation and pastoral care of Amerindians were centrally crucial for Anello Oliva, who was among those Jesuits who preferred to focus their attention on the indoctrination of native people rather than serving the needs of the local Spanish community. During his mission Anello Oliva was probably close to Nicola Mastrilli, who had arrived in Peru five years before him in 1592 and who had been appointed rector of the Colegio de Arequipa in 1598 and superior of Juli in 1600. Mastrilli considered pastoral work among Amerindians a priority to which many other missionaries gave insufficient attention. He openly complained about the lack of interest in native people which some missionaries demonstrated, along with their inattention to local languages ('pocos a mostrado mucha virtud y affecto a los indios').[48] In his role as superior, Anello Oliva viewed the material and spiritual

46 Although well tested in Europe, the idea of 'misiones volantes' [itinerant missions] did not seem appropriate for the indoctrination of native populations in Peru. The Jesuit fathers needed to spend more time with the Amerindians, due to their tendency to fall back into idolatry; but to serve their missions according to the statutes of the Society of Jesus they could not stay permanently in one place. In his *De procuranda Indorum salute* (1588), José de Acosta tried to find a compromise, suggesting that the missionaries remained in the so-called 'doctrinas de asiento' as long as it was required to convert local people and eradicate idolatry. On Acosta and his accommodating attitude towards Francisco de Toledo see Hosne, *Jesuit Missions to China and Peru*, p. 18 ff.; M. Cordero Fernández, 'Rol de la Compañía de Jesús en las visitas de idolatrías. Lima. Siglo XVII', *Anuario de historia de la Iglesia*, 21 (2012): 361–86 (366–7).

47 The ability to negotiate with local authorities became essential to securing the permanence of the Jesuits in colonial Peru. Apart from personal disagreements, one of the main difficulties lay in the principles of the order, which were often in opposition to government requests. In the *Historia general de la Compañía de Jesús en la provincia del Perú*, the tensions between the Jesuit fathers and the viceroy Francisco de Toledo were not denied. After a period of collaboration and support, the viceroy not only ordered the classes held in the Colegio de Lima to be ended but also closed the *colegios* in Arequipa and Potosí, directing the Inquisition against the Jesuits. See Mateos, *Historia general*, pp. 20–21.

48 N. Mastrilli Durán, 'El P. Nicolás Mastrilo Durán a P. Claudio Aquaviva, Juli 15 de Marzo 1601', in A. de Egaña and E. Fernández (eds.), *Monumenta Peruana*, vol. 7, *1600–1602* (Rome: Institutum Historicum Societatis Iesu, 1981), p. 277. In 1578 King Philip II made the knowledge of indigenous languages compulsory for those who wanted to be ordained as priests. See 'Real Cédula de Felipe II, El Pardo, 2 de diciembre de 1578', Archivo General

conditions of native people as matters of great concern. It is not preposterous, therefore, to suppose that a highly influential figure such as Father Mastrilli was an inspiration to Anello Oliva in the way he came to conceive of the duties of Jesuit missionaries. Even at an early stage of his training, Anello Oliva had already shown a particular vocation for working with indigenous people and this was probably encouraged by his exposure to his highly regarded superior. However, Mastrilli was not the only model to look up to.

As C. Gálvez Peña suggests, Anello Oliva was inspired by the works of Las Casas and this probably cost him the publication of his *Historia*. In his work the Italian Jesuit emphasised the hardships and abuses endured by the native population in Peru after the conquest, drawing attention to the destructive consequences of the greed (*codicia*) which characterised the excessive Spanish ambitions. At the same time, Anello Oliva praised the numerous conversions and baptisms as well as the relentless efforts of some of the fathers, who devoted themselves to eradicating idolatry and sorcery among the Amerindians.

Although little is known about Anello Oliva's life and connections with other missionaries, he must have gained the trust and respect of his Jesuit superiors as he became rector of three *colegios* in Peru. Nevertheless, the Lascasian tone of his chronicle is likely to have been regarded with some suspicion and interpreted as contrary to the interests of the Spanish monarchy. His views on missionary life and emphasis on evangelical strategies, as represented in his writings, may well have clashed with the more orthodox approach of some members of the order in Rome. This could explain why general Mutio Vitelleschi did not authorise the publication of the *Historia*. In this respect, it is important to notice that Anello Oliva died in 1642, three years before Vitelleschi, who remained in charge as superior general of the Society until his own death.

Leaving aside the possible reasons for the Jesuit father being denied the right to publish his work, Anello Oliva's *Historia* remains a precious ethnographic source on colonial Peru, providing information about indigenous traditional practices and the Jesuit contribution to the formation of Christian communities in Latin America. The work of Father Anello Oliva shows us not only his personal commitment to the mission, but also his curiosity and desire to leave a testimony of his deep knowledge of Andean culture and to keep a record of 'things worthy of eternal memory' ('cosas dignas de eternal memoria').[49]

---

de Indias, Lima, 300; F. Zubillaga and J. Baptista, 'Lenguas', in C.E. O'Neill and J.M. Domínguez (eds.), *Diccionario histórico de la Compañía de Jesús*, vol. 1, *AA–Costa Rica* (Rome: Institutum Historicum S.J.; Madrid: Universidad Pontificia Comillas, 2001), p. 110.

49   G. Anello Oliva, 'Al lector', in *Historia del Reino y Provincias del Perú*, edited by C. Gálvez Peña (Lima: Pontificia Universidad Católica del Perú, Fondo Editorial, 1998), p. 16. As C. Gálvez Peña points out, this foreword is not part of the edition published by Varela and Varela y Obregoso in 1895.

Bibliography

Acosta, de J. (1958) 'El Padre José de Acosta al Padre Everardo Mercuriano, Lima, 15 de febrero de 1577', in A. de Egaña (ed.), *Monumenta Peruana*, vol. 2, *1576–1580* (Rome: Monumenta Historica Societatis Iesu), pp. 210–86.

— (1961) 'El Padre José de Acosta al Padre Claudio Acquaviva, Lima, 14 de abril de 1585', in A. de Egaña (ed.), *Monumenta Peruana*, vol. 3, *1581–1585* (Rome: Monumenta Historica Societatis Iesu), pp. 631–3.

Albó, X. (2000) 'Notas sobre jesuitas y lengua aymara', in S. Negro Tua and M.M. Marzal (eds.), *Un reino en la frontera*: *las misiones jesuitas en la América colonial* (Quito: Abya Yala), pp. 277–88.

Alden, D., (1996) *The Making of an Enterprise: The Society of Jesus in Portugal, Its Empire, and Beyond 1540–1750* (Stanford, CA: Stanford University Press).

Andrien, K.J. (2001) *Andean Worlds*: *Indigenous History, Culture, and Consciousness Under Spanish Rule, 1532–1825* (Albuquerque, NM: University of New Mexico Press).

Anello Oliva, G. (1895) *Historia del Reino y Provincias del Perú*, ed. by J.F. Varela and L. Varela y Obregoso (Lima: Libreria de San Pedro).

Arteta, M., M. Corrales, C. Dávalos, A. Delgado, F. Sinca, L. Hernani and J. Bojórquez (2006) 'Plantas vasculares de la Bahía de Juli, Lago Titicaca, Puno-Perú', *Ecología aplicada*, 5: 29–36.

Battisti Delia, V. (2014) 'The doctrine of Juli: foundation, development and a new identity in a shared space', in S. Botta (ed.), *Manufacturing Otherness*: *Missions and Indigenous Cultures in Latin America* (Newcastle Upon Tyne: Cambridge Scholars Publishing), pp. 37–62.

Bouysse-Cassagne, T. (2014) 'Endoctriner, normaliser, discriminer: l'utopie jésuite de Juli (xve–xviie siècle)', in J.C. Garavaglia, J. Poloni-Simard and G. Rivière (eds.), *Au miroir de l'anthropologie historique. Mélanges offerts à Nathan Wachtel* (Rennes: Presses universitaires de Rennes), pp. 401–14.

Brosseder, C. (2014) *The Power of Huacas*: *Change and Resistance in the Andean World of Colonial Peru* (Austin, TX: University of Texas Press).

Carcelén Reluz, C. (2003) 'Los jesuitas en su primera misión: Huarochirí, siglo XVI', *Anuario, Archivo y biblioteca nacional de Bolivia*: 111–33.

Clossey, L. (2008) *Salvation and Globalization in the Early Jesuit Missions* (Cambridge: Cambridge University Press).

Coello de la Rosa, A. (2002) 'La reducción de Santiago de El Cercado y la Compañía de Jesús', in G. Dalla Corte (ed.), *Conflicto y violencia en América*: *VIII Encuentro-Debate América Latina ayer y hoy* (Barcelona: Universitat de Barcelona), pp. 53–68.

Coello de la Rosa A., J. Burrieza Sánchez and D. Moreno (eds.) (2012) *Jesuitas e imperios de ultra-mar, Siglos XVI–XX* (Madrid: Sílex ediciones).

Cohen, T. (1998) *The Fire of Tongues: Antonio Vieira and the Missionary Church in Brazil and Portugal* (Stanford, CA: Stanford University Press).

Cordero Fernández, M. (2012) 'Rol de la Compañía de Jesús en las visitas de idolatrías. Lima. Siglo XVII', *Anuario de historia de la Iglesia*, 21: 361–86.

Cushner, N.P. (2002) *Soldiers of God: The Jesuits in Colonial America, 1565–1767* (Buffalo, NY: Language Communications).

De Arriaga, P.J. (1968 [1621]) *La extirpación de la Idolatría en el Pirú*, Biblioteca de Autores Españoles, 209 (Madrid: Atlas).

Díaz Aguilar, R.D. (2013) 'Estudio de caracterización climática de la precipitación pluvial y temperatura del aire para las cuencas de los ríos Coata e Ilave', in *Servicio Nacional de Meteorología e Hidrología del Perú*, pp. 1–45, http://www.senamhi.gob.pe/load/file/01401SENA-4.pdf [accessed 2 Oct. 2018].

Dos Santos, J.M. (2015) 'Writing and its functions in sixteenth century Jesuit missions in Brazil', *História*, 34: 109–27.

Fernández, E. (ed.) (1986) *Monumenta peruana*, vol. 8, *1603–1604* (Rome: Institutum Historicum Societatis Iesu).

Gálvez Peña, C. (ed.) (1998) *Historia del reino y provincias del Perú* (Lima: Pontificia Universidad Católica del Perú).

— (2001) 'La censura al interior de la Compañía de Jesús: notas sobre un manuscrito desconocido del P. Giovanni Anello Oliva S.J. (1639)', *Histórica*, 25: 215–27.

Gareis, I. (2004) 'Extirpación de idolatrías e identidad cultural en las sociedades andinas del Perú virreinal (siglo XVII)', *Boletín de Antropología*, 18: 262–82.

Helmer, M. (1982–3) 'Juli, un experimento misionero de los jesuitas en el altiplano andino (siglo xvi)', *Boletín del Instituto Riva-Agüero*, 12: 191–216.

Hosne, A.C. (2013) *The Jesuit Missions to China and Peru, 1570–1610: Expectations and Appraisals of Expansionism* (London and New York: Routledge).

Hyland, S. (2011) *Gods of the Andes: An Early Jesuit Account of Inca Religion and Andean Christianity* (University Park, PA: Pennsylvania State University Press).

Izquierdo Benito, R. and F. Martínez Gil (eds.) (2011) *Religión y heterodoxias en el mundo hispánico: siglos XIV–XVIII* (Madrid: Sílex).

Klaiber, J. (2004) 'The Jesuits in Latin America: legacy and current emphases', *International Bulletin of Missionary Research*, 28: 63–6.

Knauß, S. (2010) 'Jesuit engagement in Brazil between 1549 and 1609 – A legitimate support of Indians' emancipation or eurocentric movement of conversion?', *Astrolabio*, 11: 227–38.

Kolvenbach, P.-H. (2005) *Go Forth and Teach: The Characteristics of Jesuit Education*, Jesuit Secondary Education Association Foundations, pp. 1–32, https://www.fairfieldprep.org/uploaded/Documents/15-16_School_Year/GoForthAndTeach.pdf [accessed 1 Jan. 2017].

Leite, S. (1956) *Cartas dos primeiros Jesuitas do Brasil*, Comissão do IV Centenário da Cidade de São Paulo (3 vols., São Paulo: Editora São Paulo).

León Llerena, L. (2013) 'Narrating conversion: idolatry, the sacred, and the ambiguities of Christian evangelization in colonial Peru', in S. Arias and R. Marrero-Fente (eds.), *Coloniality, Religion, and the Law in the Early Iberian World* (Nashville, TN: Vanderbilt University Press), pp. 117–36.

MacCormack, S. (1991) *Religion in the Andes: Vision and Imagination in Early Colonial Peru* (Princeton, NJ: Princeton University Press).

Martín, L. (1968) *The Intellectual Conquest of Peru: The Jesuit College of San Pablo, 1568–1767* (New York: Fordham University Press).

Mastrilli Durán, N. (1981) 'El P. Nicolás Mastrilo Durán a P. Claudio Aquaviva, Juli 15 de Marzo 1601', in A. de Egaña and E. Fernández (eds.), *Monumenta Peruana*, vol. 7, *1600–1602* (Rome: Institutum Historicum Societatis Iesu).

Mateos, F. (1944) *Historia general de la Compañía de Jesús en la provincia del Perú. Crónica anónima del 1600 que trata del establecimiento y misiones de la Compañía de Jesús en los paises de habla española en la América meridional*, vol. 1, part 2 (Madrid: Consejo Superior de Investigaciones Científicas).

Mills, K. (1997) *Idolatry and Its Enemies: Colonial Andean Religion and Extirpation, 1640–1750* (Princeton, NJ: Princeton University Press).

O'Malley, J.W., S.J., (1993) *The First Jesuits* (Cambridge, MA: Harvard University Press).

— (2000) 'How the first Jesuits became involved in education', in V.J. Duminuco (ed.), *The Jesuit Ratio Studiorum: 400th Anniversary Perspectives* (New York: Fordham University Press), pp. 56–74.

O'Malley, J.W., G.A. Bailey, S.J. Harris and T.F. Kennedy (eds.) (2006) *The Jesuits II: Cultures, Sciences, and the Arts, 1540–1773* (Toronto: University of Toronto Press).

Pease García Yrigoyen, F. (1968) 'El Príncipe de Esquilache y una relación sobre la extirpación de la de la idolatría', *Cuadernos del seminario de historia, Instituto Riva-Agüero*, 9: 81–92.

Prieto, A.I. (2011) *Missionary Scientists: Jesuit Science in Spanish South America, 1570–1810* (Nashville, TN: Vanderbilt University Press).

Real Cédula de Felipe II, El Pardo, 2 de diciembre de 1578 (Archivo General de Indias, Lima, 300).

Redden, A. (2008) *Diabolism in Colonial Peru, 1560–1750* (London and New York: Routledge).

Rodríguez, D. (2005) 'Los jesuitas y su labor evangelizadora en la doctrina de Santiago del Cercado', *Investigaciones sociales*, 9 (15): 133–52.

Scott, A.B. (2009) 'Sacred politics: an examination of Inca huacas and their use for political and social organization', *Totem*, 17: 23–36.

Shah, P. (2013) 'Language, discipline, and power: the extirpation of idolatry in colonial Peru and indigenous resistance', *Voces Novae*, 5, https://digitalcommons.chapman.edu/cgi/viewcontent.cgi?article=1074&context=vocesnovae [accessed 9 Sept. 2019].

Silverblatt, I.M. (1987) *Moon, Sun, and Witches: Gender Ideologies and Class in Inca and Colonial Peru* (Princeton, NJ: Princeton University Press).

Spalding, K. (1984) *Huarochirí: An Andean Society Under Inca and Spanish Rule* (Stanford, CA: Stanford University Press).

Urbano, H. (2011) 'Pablo Joseph de Arriaga, S.J. Retórica y extirpación de idolatrías en el arzobispado de Lima, siglos XVI–XVII', in R. Izquierdo Benito and F. Martínez Gil (eds.), *Religión y heterodoxias en el mundo hispánico: siglos XIV–XVIII* (Sílex ediciones), pp. 153–69.

Van den Berg, H. (2012) 'Las ediciones del *Vocabulario de la lengua aymara*', *Revista ciencia y cultura* 28: 9–39.

Vargas Ugarte, R. (1963–5) *Historia de la Compañía de Jesús en el Perú* (4 vols., Burgos: Aldecoa).

Wilde, G. (ed.) (2011) *Saberes de la conversión: jesuítas, indígenas e imperios coloniales enlas fronteras de la cristiandad* (Buenos Aires: SB).

Zimbabwe-Mozambique Province of the Society of Jesus (n.d.) 'Tertianship and final vows', http://www.jesuitszimbabwe.co.zw/index.php/what-we-do/forms/tertianship-final-vows [accessed 1 Oct. 2017].

Zubillaga, F. and J. Baptista (2001) 'Lenguas', in C.E. O'Neill and J.M. Domínguez (eds.), *Diccionario histórico de la Compañía de Jesús*, vol. 1, *AA–Costa Rica* (Rome: Institutum Historicum S.J.; Madrid: Universidad Pontificia Comillas).

9. Translation and prolepsis: the Jesuit origins of a Tupi[1] Christian doctrine

Vivien Kogut Lessa de Sá and Caroline Egan

When the Portuguese first arrived in Brazil, in April 1500, the prospect of taking possession of the newly found land was, from its very inception, directly bound up with the project of conversion. The fleet's scribe, Pero Vaz de Caminha, in his famous letter to King Manuel describing the indigenous Brazilians and their land for the first time, would conclude: '[T]he best fruit that could be gathered hence would be, it seems to me, the salvation of these people'.[2] The Jesuits, who began arriving in Brazil in 1549, eagerly took up the call to proselytise. In comparative terms the arrival of the Jesuits in Brazil in 1549 is both early and late. Within the history of the Society of Jesus, Brazil constitutes the first New World Jesuit province; and it rises to prominence within the order's organisation more quickly than comparable Spanish provinces.[3] Due to their relatively recent founding, however, the Jesuits arrived in Brazil nearly fifty years after Caminha penned his letter to the king and decades after other regular orders such as the Franciscans and Dominicans had made inroads elsewhere in the New World.[4] For the Jesuits in Brazil, the project of 'saving the heathen' (*gentio*) also involved an ambitious linguistic endeavour: that of mastering local tongues. This resulted in some of the most remarkable texts in the Jesuits' cultural legacy: linguistic and doctrinal works written in indigenous Brazilian languages. Although their earliest printed text dates from the late 16th century, with José de Anchieta's *Arte de grammatica da*

---

1   In order to retain consistency between the manuscript and text, Tupi does not have a diacritical mark in this chapter.

2   'o melhor fruto, que dela [a terra] se pode tirar me parece que será salvar esta gente' (J. Cortesão (ed.), *A Carta de Pêro Vaz de Caminha* (Lisbon: Imprensa Nacional-Casa da Moeda, 2000), p. 174); English translation in S.B. Schwartz (ed. and trans.) and C. Willis (trans.), *Early Brazil: A Documentary Collection to 1700* (Cambridge: Cambridge University Press, 2010), p. 9.

3   J.G. Martínez Serna, 'Procurators and the making of the Jesuits' Atlantic network', in B. Bailyn and P.L. Denault (eds.), *Soundings in Atlantic History: Latent Structures and Intellectual Currents, 1500–1830* (Cambridge, MA: Harvard University Press, 2009), pp. 181–209, at p. 190.

4   D. Alden, *The Making of an Enterprise: The Society of Jesus in Portugal, Its Empire, and Beyond, 1540–1750* (Stanford, CA: Stanford University Press, 1996), p. 75.

V. Kogut Lessa de Sá and C. Egan, 'Translation and prolepsis: the Jesuit origins of a Tupi Christian doctrine', in L.A. Newson (ed.), *Cultural Worlds of the Jesuits in Colonial Latin America* (London: Institute of Latin American Studies, 2020), pp. 189–206. License: CC-BY-NC-ND 2.0.

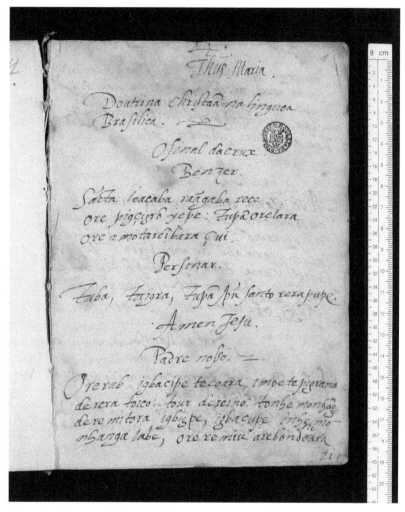

Figure 9.1. First page of 'Doutrina Christã na Linguoa Brasilica'. (Courtesy of the Bodleian Libraries, University of Oxford, MS. Bodl. 617, fol. 1r).

lingoa mais usada na costa do Brasil [*Grammar of the Most Used Language on the Coast of Brazil*] (Coimbra, 1595), doctrines and prayers tentatively translated into Tupi had circulated in manuscript form since the early 1550s. However, extant manuscripts of these early translations are few in number.

A significant exception to this documentary scarcity is a manuscript (fig. 9.1) held by the Bodleian Library at the University of Oxford which bears the title 'Doutrina Christã na Linguoa Brasilica' [Christian Doctrine in the Brazilian Tongue], hereafter referred to as 'Doutrina' or by its current shelfmark, MS.

Bodl. 617. The story of how it moved from Portuguese into English hands and ended up in the Bodleian is a fascinating and little-explored episode in the history of the Jesuits in colonial Brazil. In the course of its itinerary – from the southern coast of Brazil across the Atlantic to England – the manuscript charts the encounters of indigenous Brazilians, Iberian Jesuits and English privateers in the late 16th century.

The present chapter examines this text in two parts. First, we analyse the historical context in which MS. Bodl. 617 was produced during the early decades of Jesuit missionary work in Brazil. We reconstruct the history of its relocation and the various actors involved in its appropriation by the English. We then discuss the ways in which the manuscript responds to early modern preoccupations about translation and orthodoxy through an analysis of its use of Portuguese loan words and a close reading of a peculiar passage in Portuguese which instructs the reader how to perform the sacrament of baptism *in extremis*.

Brazil in the late 16th century

The first Jesuit mission to arrive in Brazil in 1549 accompanied the recently appointed governor general Tomé de Sousa, who was charged with building a new central government. The Portuguese crown had decided in 1548 to establish a 'Governo Geral' as an attempt to counter the failing captaincy system and regain control of its new territory through a centralised administration.[5] Sousa was tasked with building a new capital (Salvador, in Bahia), enforcing the law and appointing local officials. All this was to be done in the service of God and king, as set out in the *regimento* (charter) he carried. In that charter King João III emphasised that promoting indigenous conversion was 'the principal reason I gave orders for the settling of land in Brazil'.[6] It is unsurprising, then, that the first Jesuits in Brazil arrived with a governor who was charged with advancing the conversion of indigenous peoples.

Subsequent years saw more Jesuits arrive and by the late 1550s those in Bahia, Porto Seguro, Espírito Santo and São Vicente were working to convert Amerindian populations.[7] Still, the number of missionaries was quite low: up until 1598 there were only 128 Jesuits in the Province of Brazil.[8] One of the main objectives of these Jesuit missions was the conversion of local indigenous populations. An important aspect of their efforts was the creation of villages

5   H.B. Johnson, 'Portuguese settlement, 1550–1580', in L. Bethell (ed.), *Colonial Brazil* (Cambridge: Cambridge University Press, 1991), pp. 1–38, at pp. 13–20.

6   'a principal coisa que me moveu a mandar povoar as ditas terras do Brasil' (S. Leite (ed.), *Monumenta Brasiliae*, vol. 1 (Rome: Monumenta Historica Societatis Iesu, 1956), p. 6); translation in Schwartz (ed.), *Early Brazil*, p. 45. Unless otherwise noted, translations are the authors' own.

7   S. Leite (ed.), *Monumenta Brasiliae*, vol. 2 (Rome: Monumenta Historica Societatis Iesu, 1957), p. 49.

8   Johnson, 'Portuguese settlement', p. 22.

(*aldeias*). Proposed by the first provincial, Manuel da Nóbrega, soon after the arrival of the Jesuits in Brazil, these *aldeias* served as centres for catechesis.[9] Most peoples with whom the Portuguese settlers and missionaries initially had contact belonged to the Tupi-Guarani language family.[10] Far from homogeneous, this large language family comprised numerous independent groups which were sometimes allies and at other times in conflict. Local and far-flung indigenous groups alike were subjected to 'forced acculturation' in the *aldeias*, regardless of individual cultural or linguistic traits: as S. B. Schwartz notes, the inhabitants of *aldeias* 'received an education in how to live a Christian life, a concept that included not only European morality but work habits as well'.[11]

After their arrival with Sousa in Brazil, the first Jesuits fanned out in order to visit other regions and create new missions, like that at São Vicente – the site of the first Portuguese colony in Brazil (1532) – founded by Leonardo Nunes in 1551.[12] The Jesuits there knew that nearby, on the plateau beyond the Serra do Mar (a mountain ridge roughly following the coastline in south-eastern Brazil), a Portuguese outcast called João Ramalho had been living for decades among the indigenous people and had become a local leader. While Ramalho had for some time acted as what A. Metcalf calls a 'go-between' for Portuguese settlers and indigenous groups in the region, his relationship with the Jesuits at São Vicente was distinctly more tense.[13] Still, by the time the Jesuits founded the mission in São Paulo de Piratininga (later the city of São Paulo) in 1553, Nóbrega mentions one of Ramalho's sons as a potential aid in the work of conversion: 'I am now traveling with the oldest one to the *sertão* in order to carry out our ministry with greater authority, for he is very well known and respected among the pagans'.[14] The mission at São Paulo de Piratininga, along with the nearby São Vicente and Santos, would become a hub for efforts at converting the Tupi in the southern region. The 'Doutrina' is one example of manuscript doctrines that would have been kept by the Jesuits to assist them in this work.

9   Johnson, 'Portuguese settlement', p. 23.

10 M.K. Lee, 'Language and conquest: Tupi-Guarani expansion in the European colonization of Brazil and Amazonia', in S.S. Mufwene (ed.), *Iberian Imperialism and Language Evolution in Latin America* (Chicago, IL: University of Chicago Press, 2014), pp. 143–67 (p. 155).

11 S.B. Schwartz, *Sugar Plantations in the Formation of Brazilian Society: Bahia, 1550–1835* (Cambridge: Cambridge University Press, 1986), pp. 39–40.

12 A.C. Metcalf, *Go-Betweens and the Colonization of Brazil: 1500–1600* (Austin, TX: University of Texas Press, 2005), p. 91.

13 Metcalf, *Go-Betweens*, pp. 106–8.

14 'el mayor de ellos llevo yo ahora conmigo al *sertão* por más autorizar nuestro ministerio, porque es muy conocido y venerado entre los gentiles' (Leite (ed.), *Monumenta Brasiliae*, vol. 1, p. 524; we have occasionally modernised the spelling of citations for ease of reading).

Early Jesuit work with Tupi

MS. Bodl. 617 is a Christian doctrine written almost entirely in what it calls the 'Brazilian tongue', which, as M. K. Lee points out, was used broadly by colonial writers 'to refer to the Brazilian lingua franca they learned to speak or heard spoken between linguistically dissimilar peoples'.[15] While a number of studies have examined the Tupi-Guarani language family, the varieties encountered and studied by Europeans in colonial Brazil and the evolution of those languages over time,[16] our aim in the present chapter is not to undertake a linguistic analysis of the 'Brazilian tongue' used in the manuscript, but rather to provide a study of the origins and relocation of the manuscript and an analysis of its use of Portuguese. We therefore use the terms 'Brazilian tongue' and the broad 'Tupi' to refer to the main language of the text. Although it is difficult to date the manuscript, we can say that it must have been composed between 1549 and 1591, the forty-odd year period between the arrival of the Jesuits in Brazil and the raid on the Jesuit library at Santos during which the manuscript was removed and later taken to England.

Like dating the manuscript, assigning authorship to the 'Doutrina' is a complicated matter. Even if the hand could be identified, this particular text belongs to a tradition of translation, circulation and practical use which in Brazil dates back to the arrival of the Jesuits. In 1550 João de Azpilcueta Navarro wrote from Bahia that he had translated articles of faith on creation and the incarnation, as well as the commandments and other prayers, 'so that they might learn and enjoy [them] more quickly'.[17] In 1553 Pero Correia wrote from São Vicente to Simão Rodrigues in Lisbon, stressing the importance of preparing catechistic materials in the indigenous language and requesting resources for this purpose: 'I always speak to them [indigenous children] and to all the others who come together in the church in their own tongue and I teach them matters of faith; but I lack books in a tongue I can study, because I do not know Latin and cannot use the books written in Latin'.[18] He goes on to list five relevant works by 'Doctor Constantino' (Constantino Ponce de la Fuente) and asks that they be sent to him.

In the same year that Correia made this request, Luís da Grã and José de Anchieta arrived in Brazil. These two would be instrumental in the twinned

---

15 Lee, 'Language and conquest', p. 145.

16 See, e.g., O. Zwartjes, *Portuguese Missionary Grammars in Asia, Africa and Brazil, 1550–1800* (Amsterdam: Benjamins, 2011), pp. 143–203; Lee, 'Language and Conquest', pp. 144–6.

17 'para que más presto aprendiesen y gustasen' (Leite (ed.), *Monumenta Brasiliae*, vol. 1, p. 180).

18 'Yo siempre les hablo así a ellos como a la más gente que se ayunta en la iglesia en su lengua y les predico las cosas de la fe; mas fáltanme libros en lenguaje que puedo estudiar, porque non soy latino y no me puedo ayudar de los de latín' (Leite (ed.), *Monumenta Brasiliae*, vol. 1, p. 440).

linguistic and catechistic efforts of the Jesuit missions.[19] In 1555, for instance, Grã oversaw the revision of certain existing doctrinal texts and would have been assisted in this endeavour by a number of translators, Anchieta outstanding among them.[20] Anchieta would also compose the 'Diálogos da Fé' (or 'das Coisas da Fé'), as well as a confessionary and instructions for catechumens and those *in extremis*.[21] In 1566 the new Portuguese-language doctrine by Marcos Jorge seems to have arrived in Brazil, where it was translated by Leonardo do Vale.[22] While catechistic texts like these flourished in the Jesuit missions, they remained unpublished in the 16th century. In 1592 the Jesuits in Brazil requested (and later received) permission to print a doctrinal work in Portugal, along with Anchieta's *Arte de grammatica da lingoa mais usada na costa do Brasil*. However, in the end, probably due to financial constraints, only the latter of these two texts was printed, in 1595.[23]

Despite the fact that the doctrinal text proposed for publication in 1592 was never printed, surviving manuscript doctrines like those prepared by Anchieta or the anonymous 'Doutrina' held in the Bodleian give a sense of the practical processes through which such texts were composed and revised. For instance, in the manuscript later titled *Catecismo Brasílico* (a copy of a copy of an autograph manuscript of Anchieta), the first item to appear is the 'Instrução para "In Extremis"'. This protocol, according to A. Cardoso, was the first translation prepared by Anchieta, a fact that may reflect its practical use in urgent situations.[24] The 1592 printing request alludes to the regular use and revision of indigenous-language doctrinal texts: 'As for the Doctrine, it was composed forty years ago and since then it has been continually taught, improved and corrected, in terms of both theology and language'.[25] Finally, in 1618 Antonio Araújo published a catechism in the 'Brazilian tongue'. The title page of that doctrine, printed in Lisbon by Pedro Crasbeeck, declares that the work is a *Catecismo na lingoa Brasilica* and clarifies that it was '[c]omposed in the form of dialogues by learned fathers and good interpreters of the Company of Jesus', which has been 'newly arranged, ordered, and augmented by Father

19 A. Agnolin, *Jesuítas e selvagens: a negociação da fé no encontro catequético-ritual americano-tupi (séculos XVI–XVII)* (São Paulo: Humanitas, 2007), pp. 64–6; M.F. Medeiros Barbosa, *As letras e a cruz: pedagogia da fé e estética religiosa na experiência missionária de José de Anchieta, S.I. (1534–1597)* (Rome: Pontificia Università Gregoriana, 2006), pp. 124–8.

20 J. Anchieta, *Doutrina cristã*, edited and translated by A. Cardoso, vol. 1 (São Paulo: Loyola, 1992), p. 27.

21 Anchieta, *Doutrina cristã*, vol. 1, p. 27.

22 Anchieta, *Doutrina cristã*, vol. 1, p. 35.

23 Agnolin, *Jesuítas e selvagens*, p. 62.

24 Anchieta, *Doutrina cristã*, vol. 1, p. 20.

25 'Quanto à Doutrina, quarenta anos há que se compôs e até agora sempre se ensinou, apurando-se e emendando-se, assim no tocante à teologia, como na língua' (Anchieta, *Doutrina cristã*, vol. 1, p. 36).

Antonio d'Araújo'.[26] The manuscript held in the Bodleian closely resembles portions of the text printed in 1618. The prayers and dialogues in Tupi which appear verbatim in both works demonstrate that these two texts derive from the same process of use, revision and emendation.

The transatlantic itinerary of the 'Doutrina'

Although we have not established the exact date MS. Bodl. 617 was produced, its fair state of conservation suggests it was probably composed not long before it was taken from the Jesuit library in Santos, between December 1591 and February 1592. We know who was responsible for this removal due to the revealing ex-libris: 'Ex-dono Thomas Lodge D. M. Oxoniensis. qui sua manu a Brasilia deduxit' [Previously owned by Thomas Lodge, M.D., from Oxford University, who with his own hand removed it from Brazil]. Lodge was a playwright and poet, usually credited with having inspired Shakespeare's *As You Like It* with his 1590 prose romance *Rosalynd*. Not long after this, in 1591, Lodge embarked on a voyage to the South Seas, possibly to escape from his creditors.

The captain of the voyage was Thomas Cavendish, who had made his name as the second Englishman to circumnavigate the world.[27] This period saw the climax of English maritime ventures, with several expeditions sailing the Atlantic in the hope of seizing Spanish cargo on its return from the New World. These voyages, often termed 'privateering' and bearing the royal seal of approval, were typically little more than corsair expeditions seeking to challenge Iberian power in the Americas. In Brazil, English incursions were mainly commercial before the 1580s. In the period following the 1580 union of the Spanish and Portuguese crowns, however, these incursions degenerated into hostile encounters, more often than not resulting in lengthy sieges and pillaging. The arrival of Cavendish in Brazil followed the traumatic English siege of Salvador in 1587, which, together with rumours of raids by Francis Drake on Spanish American ports, had worked to spread panic along the coastal settlements.

Cavendish's 1591 expedition was no different. On the way to the Pacific via the Straits of Magellan the fleet of five vessels stopped at the small harbour village of Santos, which was believed to be unfortified. Cavendish's plan was to replenish food and water supplies and, he hoped, to make some gains through plunder. The English arrived on Christmas Day and stayed for

---

26 'Composto a modo de Diálogos por Padres Doutos, & bons línguas da Companhia de IESU'; 'novamente concertado, ordenado, & acrescentado pelo Padre Antonio d'Araujo' (A. Araújo (ed.), *Catecismo na lingoa brasílica, no qual se contêm a summa da doctrina christã* (Lisbon: Pedro Crasbeeck, 1618)).

27 D.B Quinn, *The Last Voyage of Thomas Cavendish 1591–1592* (Chicago, IL: University of Chicago Press, 1975); P. Edwards (ed.), *Last Voyages – Cavendish, Hudson, Raleigh: The Original Narratives* (Oxford: Clarendon Press, 1988).

five weeks, during which time they looted the village, burned a number of neighbouring sugar mills and razed the nearby settlement of São Vicente. In the meantime, the English officers – Lodge among them – made their lodgings in the Jesuit residence, left empty by the missionaries. One of the company, Anthony Knivet, described going 'up and downe from Cell to Cell' looking for valuables until chancing upon a chest filled with silver coins.[28] For Lodge the target seems to have been the Jesuit library. There is reason to believe that, in addition to the 'Doutrina', he may have taken other items from the library, for in the preliminaries to his 1596 *A Margarite of America* he claims to have taken inspiration from a 'historie in the Spanish tongue' found 'in the library of the Jesuits in Sanctum'.[29]

It is no small feat that the Jesuit manuscript found safe passage to England, since Cavendish's enterprise ended in disaster and only a handful of men, including Lodge, managed to return. Lodge seems to have kept the manuscript until the 1610s, when he donated it to the burgeoning collection being assembled in Oxford by Thomas Bodley. R.W. Hunt includes the donation from Lodge in *A Summary Catalogue of Western Manuscripts in the Bodleian Library at Oxford*. Hunt provides 'Tupi' as the short title of the work and lists Lodge as its donor, dating the acquisition of the manuscript to between 1613 and 1620.[30] Lodge's life had changed considerably by that time. In 1597 he had left England for France and trained as a medical doctor, but since the College of Physicians repeatedly rejected his application for a medical licence, he travelled constantly between England and the Continent from 1598 until 1610. The rejection may have been due to Lodge's Catholicism, which his biographers suggest had been a constant source of trouble since the 1580s.[31] Interestingly, Oxford recognised his medical degree in 1602. Might it have been as a sign of gratitude that Lodge donated to the University a manuscript he had kept throughout those turbulent years? We shall never know. It was not until 1610 that Lodge was finally granted a medical licence and in the following year, after swearing an oath of allegiance, was issued an order by the Privy Council protecting him from prosecution. Despite practising as 'Doctor of Physike' for the Catholic community in London, Lodge did not interrupt his literary career, though in later life he published mostly translations. His choice of texts

---

28 A. Knivet, *The Admirable Adventures and Strange Fortunes of Master Anthony Knivet: An English Pirate in Sixteenth-Century Brazil*, edited by V. Kogut Lessa de Sá (Cambridge: Cambridge University Press, 2015), p. 48.

29 T. Lodge, *A Margarite of America*, edited by D. Beecher and H.D. Janzen (Toronto: Centre for Reformation and Renaissance Studies, 2005), p. 75.

30 R.W. Hunt, *A Summary Catalogue of Western Manuscripts in the Bodleian Library at Oxford*, vol. 1 (Oxford: Clarendon Press, 1953), p. 102.

31 A. Halasz, 'Lodge, Thomas (1558–1625)', in *Oxford Dictionary of National Biography* (2008), https://doi.org/10.1093/ref:odnb/16923 [accessed 31 May 2018].

and authors may suggest what critics have seen as 'an increasing preoccupation with problems of spirituality inflected by Lodge's Catholicism'.[32]

The story of the genesis of the manuscript and its trajectory from Brazil to England is a mixture of the routine and the exceptional. Its creation, as described above, reflects common Jesuit concerns about the catechisation of the indigenous population and the intensive linguistic study needed in this process. It is not surprising that this manuscript was produced. In contrast, the intervention of Lodge, a literary man who removed the manuscript from Santos and preserved it – despite being unable to read it – for so many years, has something of the serendipitous about it. This particular manuscript travelled from Brazil to England because, for some reason, it happened to catch his eye.

Just as the history of the manuscript reflects both common practices and contingency, so too do some of its features. As the next section details, the decision to render certain doctrinally significant words into the 'Brazilian tongue' and leave others in Portuguese reflects ongoing concerns about the practice of translation in catechesis. This varying use of indigenous words and loan words connects MS. Bodl. 617 to the wider body of Jesuit catechisms in Tupi, as well as other missionary texts produced throughout colonial Latin America. At the same time, the 'Doutrina' importantly includes a brief passage which sets it apart from this wider tradition: an explanation, in Portuguese, of the protocol for baptism *in extremis*. These instructions are not only unique in the manuscript, where they constitute the only sustained use of Portuguese, but also in comparison with the contemporary tradition of Amerindian catechisms.

Translation in the 'Doutrina'

In his 1576 *História da província de Santa Cruz que vulgarmente chamamos Brasil* [*History of the Province of Santa Cruz, which we commonly call Brazil*], Pero de Magalhães Gândavo remarks on a notable feature of the coastal language: it 'lacks three letters, namely, *f*, *l* and *r*'.[33] Gândavo then elaborates on the idea that the 'lack' of these three consonants corresponds to a lack of 'fé', 'lei' and 'rei' ('faith', 'law' and 'king'). Regarding faith, Gabriel Soares de Sousa would contend in his 1587 *Tratado descriptivo do Brasil* (Descriptive Treatise on Brazil): 'The fact that they have no F is due to their lack of faith in anything that they might worship. Not even those born among Christians and catechised by the Jesuit Fathers have any faith in Our Lord God, nor

32   Halasz, 'Lodge, Thomas'.

33   'carece de três letras, convém a saber, não se acha nela F, nem L, nem R' (P. Magalhães Gândavo, *A Primeira História do Brasil: História da província de Santa Cruz a que vulgarmente chamamos Brasil*, edited by S. Moura Hue and R. Menegaz (Rio de Janeiro: Zahar, 2004), p. 135); translation in J.B. Stetson, Jr. (ed. and trans.), *The Histories of Brazil*, vol. 2 (New York: The Cortes Society, 1922), p. 166.

have any regard for truth or any loyalty to anyone who does them a favour'.[34] The notion that having faith goes hand in hand with having a *word* for faith (indeed, only its first letter) reflects, according to J.A. Hansen, the notion that the relationship of sign, sound and signifier is material rather than arbitrary.[35] In other words, the Tupi language has no word for 'faith' because its speakers lack faith itself. This notion, in turn, makes it theoretically possible for missionaries to engender faith by providing the right vocabulary.[36]

This perceived lack of faith, law and king, moreover, was linked to a far more pervasive trait which the missionaries identified in the indigenous culture and which would shape their evangelising strategies: that the indigenous Brazilians were irreversibly 'inconstant' or changeable.[37] Such inconstancy was, of course, mainly shown in their incapacity for lasting conversion – just as easily as they embraced Catholicism, they would fall back on the 'vomit of old habits' (vômito dos antigos costumes), as Anchieta so eloquently put it in a 1554 letter.[38] However, to the Jesuit observers impermanence seemed to permeate the indigenous Brazilian way of life: nomadism, polygamy, nakedness and orality were taken as signs of an existence built on ever-changing foundations in which boundaries were notably lacking. The Jesuits, therefore, were concerned first and foremost with imposing a stable, permanent framework onto everyday indigenous life, a framework which would create the conditions for lasting conversion. This included, for instance, the creation of villages (*aldeias*) and the imposition of monogamous marriages. The domestication of space and relationships was compounded by the regulation of time: the priests would enforce a strict daily routine punctuated by prayer and work at pre-determined intervals. A major feature of this attempt to impose stability on an otherwise 'inconstant' way of life consisted in subsuming Tupi orality into European grammatical structures, thus appropriating, domesticating and organising the language by giving it a written, apparently stable form (see also chapter 6). In other words, in the early days of their mission in Brazil the Jesuits were invested with the task of converting not only the Tupi peoples but also the Tupi

---

34 'se não têm F, é porque não têm fé em nenhuma coisa que adorem; nem os nascidos entre os cristãos e doutrinados pelos padres da Companhia têm fé em Deus Nosso Senhor, nem têm verdade, nem lealdade a nenhuma pessoa que lhes faça bem' (G. Soares de Sousa, *Tratado descriptivo do Brasil em 1587*, edited by F.A. Varnhagen (Rio de Janeiro: João Ignacio da Silva, 1879), pp. 280–81); translation in Schwartz (ed.), *Early Brazil*, p. 120.

35 J.A. Hansen, 'Sem F, sem L, sem R: cronistas, jesuítas e índios no século XVI', in E.A. Kossovitch (ed.), *A conquista da América* (Campinas: Cedes, 1993), pp. 45–55, at p. 53).

36 A. Daher, 'A conversão dos Tupinambá entre oralidade e escrita nos relatos franceses dos séculos XVI e XVII', *Horizontes Antropológicos* 10 (22) (2004): 67–92, at p. 81.

37 E. Viveiros de Castro, *A inconstância da alma selvagem e outros ensaios de antropologia* (São Paulo: Cosac & Naify, 2002).

38 Leite (ed.), *Monumenta Brasiliae*, vol. 2, p. 107.

language or, as Hansen puts it, 'supplementing the lack of language in the Tupi tongue' by infusing it with the 'missing' concepts.[39]

Supplementing the tongue with language, however, would not prove a simple task. As the first provincial, Manuel da Nóbrega, would claim as early as 1549: 'They have very few words with which to profess our faith well, but still we explain it to them as best we can, demonstrating certain points in a roundabout way'.[40] Not only in Brazil, but also in Iberian missions in the Americas more generally, clerics needed to seek out terms which would be understandable to both converts and potential converts and to ensure that these terms conveyed meaning in orthodox ways. The complexity of this balancing act generated diverse and changing views on the best way to translate particular concepts into indigenous languages. In some instances missionaries sought equivalences or created neologisms in indigenous languages; and in others they employed loanwords. Both these strategies appear in the Bodleian manuscript. Throughout the text, a number of doctrinally significant words appear in Tupi. In addition to the word 'Tupã', originally associated with thunder and lightning and selected by missionaries in Brazil early on as an equivalency for the Christian 'God',[41] the first two figures of the Catholic Trinity, the 'Father' and 'Son', are rendered 'Tuba' (father) and 'Taigra' (son in relation to the father).[42] At the same time, a number of important concepts are rendered in Portuguese or in a combination of Portuguese and Tupi. Terms for concepts like grace ('graça'), saint ('Sam', 'Santa' and 'Santos'), earthly paradise ('paraiso terreál'), sin ('pecado') and Christians ('Christãos') all appear in Portuguese. The figure of the Holy Spirit, the third person of the Catholic Trinity, is rendered 'Tupã Spu Santo' (where 'Spu' is a contracted form of 'Espíritu'); and the holy cross is 'santa ioaçaba', combining the Portuguese word for 'holy' with the Tupi term used for cross. That term, 'ioasaba', is rooted in the act of crossing one thing with another ('o atravessar um com o outro').[43]

Both kinds of translation described above impose meaning on the Tupi language. Designating Tupi terms like 'Tupã' as equivalencies for 'God' entails the appropriation of the word and its forced accommodation of an imposed idea. Likewise, the blunt introduction of words like 'pecado',

39 J.A. Hansen, 'A escrita da conversão', in L.H. Costigan (ed.), *Diálogos da conversão* (Campinas: Unicamp, 2005), pp. 15–43 (p. 20).

40 'Tienen muy pocos vocablos para le poder bien declarar nuestra fe, mas con todo dámossela a entender lo mejor que podemos y algunas cosas le declaramos por rodeos' (Leite (ed.), *Monumenta Brasiliae*, vol. 1, p. 153).

41 H.H. do Couto, 'Amerindian Language Islands in Brazil', in S.S. Mufwene (ed.), *Iberian Imperialism and Language Evolution in Latin America* (Chicago, IL: University of Chicago Press, 2014), pp. 86–107 (p. 86).

42 E. Almeida Navarro, *Dicionário tupi antigo: a língua indígena clássica do Brasil* (São Paulo: Global, 2013), pp. 493, 75.

43 'Doutrina Christã na Linguoa Brasilica', MS. Bodl. 617, fols. 1r, 41v; Almeida Navarro, *Dicionário tupi antigo*, p. 188.

deemed incommensurable with any term which might already have existed in the Brazilian tongue, imposes the idea and the word itself, or, rather, the idea *through* the word itself. A number of scholars have analysed this process and other kinds of catechistic translation which flourished in the early Jesuit missions in Brazil, with a particular focus on the works attributed to Anchieta: A. Bosi, for instance, characterises the linguistic project of Anchieta as the creation of a 'third symbolic sphere', a new realm of meaning which does not fully reflect either the language of the missionary or the language of the Tupi; J.-C. Laborie goes further in describing Anchieta's use of Tupi as the creation of a completely artificial or expendable object, mutually unrecognisable for its interlocutors.[44] In his taxonomy and analysis of the different types of translation undertaken by Anchieta, C. Braga-Pinto points out the temporal implications of the form of translation he designates 'conversion', exemplified, for instance, in the use of the term 'Tupã' to mean 'God': 'Conversion would hardly take place if it were purely the erasure of an old system of signification and the imposition of another, completely foreign meaning. When a new concept is added to a word, it does not destroy the memory of the word's previous lives . . . In its newness, conversion presents itself as that which was already there'.[45] What Braga-Pinto identifies as a recasting of the past may also be understood in terms of prolepsis, that is, the present realisation of an anticipated future. In this proleptic gesture, the act of alphabetic writing is key. If, from the Jesuit perspective, the Tupi language 'lacked' any understanding of faith, if it 'lacked' any notion of 'God', 'sin' and so on, much as it 'lacked' alphabetic writing and other forms of cultural fixity, then inventing or imposing terms for those ideas and recording them in writing were a way of guaranteeing their present and future existence.

Baptism *in extremis*

What we are describing as the 'proleptic' impulse of the 'Doutrina' is evident not only in its use of loanwords, but also in a specific and unusual passage on the protocol for baptising those *in extremis,* that is, those on the point of death (fig. 9.2):

> Instrução necessária, e bastante para se batizarem os que estão in extremis:
> E não sabem nada das coisas de Deus.
>
> Primeiramente que creia que há Deus. E que é remunerador de bons e maus.

44 A. Bosi, *Dialética da colonização* (São Paulo: Companhia das Letras, 1994), p. 20; J.-C. Laborie, 'From orality to writing: the reality of a conversion through the work of the Jesuit Father José de Anchieta (1534–1597)', translated by J. Vale, *Diogenes*, 48 (191) (2000): 56–71, at pp. 65–6.

45 C. Braga-Pinto, 'Translating, meaning and the community of languages', *Studies in the Humanities*, 22 (1996): 33–49, at p. 38.

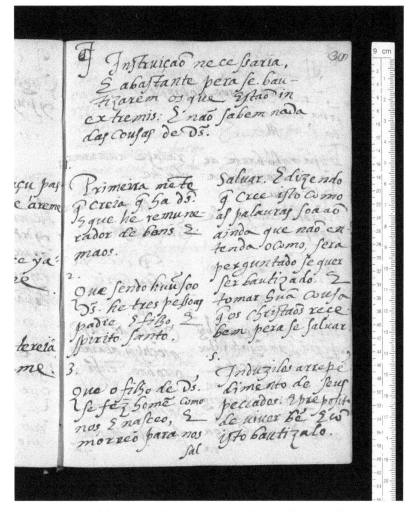

Figure 9.2. Protocol for baptising those on the point of death in 'Doutrina Christã na Linguoa Brasilica'. (Courtesy of the Bodleian Libraries, University of Oxford, MS. Bodl. 617, fol. 38r).

Que sendo um só Deus é três pessoas padre, e filho, e Espirito Santo.

Que o filho de Deus se fez homem como nós e nasceu, e morreu para nos salvar. E dizendo que crê isto como as palavras soam ainda que não entenda o como, será perguntado se quer ser batizado. E tomar uma coisa que os cristãos recebem para se salvar.

Induzi-los arrependimento de seus pecados. E propósito de viver bem. E com isto batizá-lo.[46]

[Necessary and sufficient instruction for baptising those *in extremis* who know nothing of God.

First, that they believe that there is a God, who rewards the good and punishes the wicked.

That in one sole God there are three persons, Father, and Son, and Holy Spirit.

That the Son of God became a man like us, and was born, and died, to save us. And in saying that they believe this, as the words sound, even if they do not understand, they will be asked if they want to be baptised. And to take something that Christians receive in order to save themselves.

Make them repent their sins and determine to live well. And with this baptise them.]

This section is notable for several reasons. It is the only substantive use of Portuguese in the entire manuscript, beyond features such as loanwords and titles. It is also unique in comparison with other known Tupi catechisms which would have circulated or were published at the time: copies of doctrinal manuscripts attributed to Anchieta do not include instructions of this kind, nor does the catechism compiled by Araújo and printed in 1618 in Lisbon. Indeed, even the fact that these clarifications were made in Portuguese is unusual in comparison to other indigenous American catechisms more generally. Instructions for administering the sacrament do appear, for instance, in the Nahuatl *Confessionario mayor* by Alonso de Molina (1569), but these are relatively detailed and written in Nahuatl, clearly meant to explain the process to indigenous lay assistants who might have been called on in emergencies to perform the baptism in the absence of a priest.[47] In MS. Bodl. 617, in contrast, the 'Instrução' assures its reader in Portuguese, indicating that this passage was probably intended for a missionary reader, or perhaps for an indigenous convert who had already been educated in Portuguese.

In addition to the rather unusual fact of this Portuguese protocol being included in the manuscript, it is also important to remark on one of its key

---

46 'Doutrina', fol. 38r; we have modernised the orthography of this passage. The original may be seen in fig. 9.2.

47 M.Z. Christensen, *Translated Christianities: Nahuatl and Maya Religious Texts* (University Park, PA: Pennsylvania State University Press, 2014), pp. 64–7.

phrases: 'E dizendo que crê isto como as palavras soam ainda que não entenda o como, será perguntado se quer ser batizado' [And in saying that they believe this, as the words sound, even if they do not understand, they will be asked if they want to be baptised]. This clarification reminds us of the formulaic and urgent nature of baptism *in extremis*. The protocol outlines only those matters of faith which are deemed indispensable for the baptism of someone on the point of death. Indeed, following this Portuguese instruction we find a few pages dedicated to the 'Same instruction in the language of Brazil'. In dialogic fashion, a 'Master' asks questions and a 'Disciple' simply responds 'I believe' ('Arobia'). It seems, moreover, that the 'Doutrina' anticipates a reader who may need to be reminded of the legitimacy of this simplified procedure, of its authenticity regardless of its rudimentary nature and the possibility that the recipient of the sacrament may not even understand it ('ainda que não entenda'). The instruction reassures its reader that baptism may be performed on the basis of enunciation rather than understanding. While presented as an exception in the text ('ainda que'), this remark appears to draw, once again, on the conviction that enunciation and faith are inseparable. However, faith need not precede utterance; instead, utterance creates faith. *In extremis*, words are not only the vehicle for conversion, they constitute it proleptically, anticipating and laying early claim to a hypothetical future in which the dying person really does believe the words uttered.

Conclusion

To conclude, we would like to suggest that the 'proleptic' quality of MS. Bodl. 617 offers a conceptual bridge connecting the Amerindian, Jesuit and English worlds which occasioned the creation and transatlantic itinerary of this text. Although the manuscript made its way to England, it was not this work that Lodge would later highlight as a spoil from the New World. Instead, in 1596 he published what he claimed to be the translation of a 'history in the Spanish tongue' found in the Jesuit library in Santos. That book, his romance titled *A Margarite of America*, tells a tale of bloodthirstiness, violence and treachery. Its alleged Spanish source has never been found and scholars tend to agree that this reference to a Spanish precursor is probably a contrivance.[48] The title could be suggestive, as D. Vitkus has pointed out, of an attempt by Lodge to offset losses from Cavendish's disastrous journey by offering readers in England a precious commodity fresh from the New World, a 'margarite', or pearl.[49] Still, it is interesting to note that at the same time that Lodge claimed the existence of a

---

48 D. Beecher, 'A life of Thomas Lodge', in T. Lodge, *A Margarite of America*, ed. by D. Beecher and H.D. Janzen (Toronto: Centre for Reformation and Renaissance Studies, 2005), pp. 51–70, at pp. 56–8.

49 D. Vitkus, 'Ridding the world of a monster: Lodge's *A Margarite of America* and Cavendish's last voyage', *The Yearbook of English Studies*, 41 (2011): 99–112, at p. 101.

fictional text as the source for his *Margarite*, an actual manuscript he brought home and kept for several years remained unknown until he donated it to the Bodleian. In this way, perhaps, *A Margarite of America* – which has nothing to do with Brazil or indigenous conversion there – is the unlikely, yet perfect, complement to MS. Bodl. 617. Whereas the 'Doutrina' exemplifies the Jesuit invention of an alphabetic Tupi tradition and proleptically saves souls through the enunciation – rather than the understanding – of a formula, *A Margarite of America* retrospectively invents a 'Spanish history' in order to create a work of fiction which, in all likelihood, had not existed before. Although these two texts have been drawn together only through the contingencies of history, it is tempting to see the proleptic features of the 'Doutrina' as fertile ground for the spurious use of the 'found manuscript' trope in *A Margarite of America*.

Bibliography

Manuscript source

'Doutrina Christã na Linguoa Brasilica', MS. Bodl. 617, Bodleian Libraries.

Printed sources

Agnolin, A. (2007) *Jesuítas e selvagens: a negociação da fé no encontro catequético-ritual americano-tupi (séculos XVI–XVII)* (São Paulo: Humanitas).

Alden, D. (1996) *The Making of an Enterprise: The Society of Jesus in Portugal, Its Empire, and Beyond, 1540–1750* (Stanford, CA: Stanford University Press).

Almeida Navarro, E. (2013) *Dicionário tupi antigo: a língua indígena clássica do Brasil* (São Paulo: Global).

Anchieta, J. (1992) *Doutrina cristã*, ed. and trans. by A. Cardoso, vol. 1 (São Paulo: Loyola).

Araújo, A. (ed.) (1618) *Catecismo na lingoa brasílica, no qual se contêm a summa da doctrina christã* (Lisbon: Pedro Crasbeeck).

Beecher, D. (2005) 'A life of Thomas Lodge', in T. Lodge, *A Margarite of America*, ed. by D. Beecher and H.D. Janzen (Toronto: Centre for Reformation and Renaissance Studies), pp. 51–70.

Bosi, A. (1994) *Dialética da colonização* (São Paulo: Companhia das Letras).

Braga-Pinto, C. (1996) 'Translating, meaning and the community of languages', *Studies in the Humanities*, 22: 33–49.

Christensen, M.Z. (2014) *Translated Christianities: Nahuatl and Maya Religious Texts* (University Park, PA: Pennsylvania State University Press).

Daher, A. (2004) 'A conversão dos Tupinambá entre oralidade e escrita nos relatos franceses dos séculos XVI e XVII', *Horizontes Antropológicos*, 10 (22): 67–92.

Do Couto, H.H. (2014) 'Amerindian language islands in Brazil', in S.S. Mufwene (ed.), *Iberian Imperialism and Language Evolution in Latin America* (Chicago, IL: University of Chicago Press), pp. 76–107.

Edwards, P. (ed.) (1988) *Last Voyages – Cavendish, Hudson, Raleigh: The Original Narratives* (Oxford: Clarendon Press).

Halasz, A. (2008) 'Lodge, Thomas (1558–1625)', in *Oxford Dictionary of National Biography*, https://doi.org/10.1093/ref:odnb/16923 [accessed 31 May 2018].

Hansen, J.A. (1993) 'Sem F, sem L, sem R: cronistas, jesuítas e índios no século XVI', in E.A. Kossovitch (ed.), *A conquista da América* (Campinas: Cedes, 1993), pp. 45–55.

— (2005) 'A escrita da conversão', in L.H. Costigan (ed.), *Diálogos da conversão* (Campinas: Unicamp), pp. 15–43.

Hunt, R.W. (1953) *A Summary Catalogue of Western Manuscripts in the Bodleian Library at Oxford*, vol. 1 (Oxford: Clarendon Press).

Johnson, H.B. (1991) 'Portuguese settlement, 1550–1580', in L. Bethell (ed.), *Colonial Brazil* (Cambridge: Cambridge University Press, 1991), pp. 1–38.

Knivet, A. (2015) *The Admirable Adventures and Strange Fortunes of Master Anthony Knivet: An English Pirate in Sixteenth-Century Brazil*, ed. by V. Kogut Lessa de Sá (Cambridge: Cambridge University Press).

Laborie, J.-C. (2000) 'From orality to writing: the reality of a conversion through the work of the Jesuit Father José de Anchieta (1534–1597)', trans. by J. Vale, *Diogenes*, 48 (191): 56–71.

Lee, M.K. (2014) 'Language and conquest: Tupi-Guarani expansion in the European colonization of Brazil and Amazonia', in S.S. Mufwene (ed.), *Iberian Imperialism and Language Evolution in Latin America* (Chicago, IL: University of Chicago Press), pp. 143–67.

Leite, S. (ed.) (1956) *Monumenta Brasiliae*, vol. 1 (Rome: Monumenta Historica Societatis Iesu).

— (ed.) (1957) *Monumenta Brasiliae*, vol. 2 (Rome: Monumenta Historica Societatis Iesu).

Lodge, T. (2005) *A Margarite of America*, ed. by D. Beecher and H.D. Janzen (Toronto: Centre for Reformation and Renaissance Studies).

Magalhães Gândavo, P. (2004) *A Primeira história do Brasil: história da província de Santa Cruz a que vulgarmente chamamos Brasil*, ed. by S. Moura Hue and R. Menegaz (Rio de Janeiro: Zahar).

— (1922) *The Histories of Brazil*, ed. and trans. by J.B. Stetson, Jr., vol. 2 (New York: The Cortes Society).

Martínez Serna, J.G. (2009) 'Procurators and the making of the Jesuits' Atlantic network', in B. Bailyn and P.L. Denault (eds.), *Soundings in Atlantic History: Latent Structures and Intellectual Currents, 1500–1830* (Cambridge, MA: Harvard University Press), pp. 181–209.

Medeiros Barbosa, M.F. (2006) *As letras e a cruz: pedagogia da fé e estética religiosa na experiência missionária de José de Anchieta, S.I. (1534–1597)* (Rome: Pontificia Università Gregoriana).

Metcalf, A.C. (2005) *Go-Betweens and the Colonization of Brazil: 1500–1600* (Austin, TX: University of Texas Press).

Quinn, D.B. (1975) *The Last Voyage of Thomas Cavendish 1591–1592* (Chicago, IL: University of Chicago Press).

Schwartz, S.B. (1986) *Sugar Plantations in the Formation of Brazilian Society: Bahia, 1550–1835* (Cambridge: Cambridge University Press).

— (ed.) (2010) *Early Brazil: A Documentary Collection to 1700*, trans. by S.B. Schwartz and C. Willis (Cambridge: Cambridge University Press).

Soares de Sousa, G. (1879) *Tratado descriptivo do Brasil em 1587*, ed. by F.A. Varnhagen (Rio de Janeiro: João Ignacio da Silva).

Vaz de Caminha, P. (2000) *A Carta de Pêro Vaz de Caminha*, ed. by J. Cortesão (Lisbon: Imprensa Nacional-Casa da Moeda).

Vitkus, D. (2011) 'Ridding the world of a monster: Lodge's *A Margarite of America* and Cavendish's last voyage', *The Yearbook of English Studies*, 41: 99–112.

Viveiros de Castro, E. (2002) *A inconstância da alma selvagem e outros ensaios de antropologia* (São Paulo: Cosac & Naify).

Zwartjes, O. (2011) *Portuguese Missionary Grammars in Asia, Africa and Brazil, 1550–1800* (Amsterdam: Benjamins).

IV. Jesuit agriculture, medicine and science

10. Jesuits and mules in colonial Latin America: innovators or managers?

William G. Clarence-Smith[1]

H istorians generally agree that the Jesuits in colonial Latin America were effective managers of their extensive rural properties, which by the 18th century generated substantial streams of income. Initially, many fathers opposed money-making activities, but the order urgently needed funds to finance its urban colleges, for which tuition was free. Money was also required for other charitable activities, mission stations and general administration. Moreover, the order gradually accumulated large estates, either through direct donations of land, or through gifts of cash and valuables which could be invested in property. Rural enterprises were generally judged to be preferable to urban real estate, mining or banking, since they would avoid possible breaches of canon law in regard to clerics handling money. Furthermore, the Jesuits benefited from significant fiscal advantages in terms of tithes and sales taxes and did not pay members of the order acting as estate managers.[2]

As no general overview of the question has yet been published, this chapter is intended as a 'state of the art' contribution to the debate, drawing on a wide variety of regional case studies. The literature is uneven. It is best for what are today Mexico and the lands of the 'Southern Cone' of South America and passable for modern Peru, Bolivia, Colombia and Venezuela. The main gaps are for Central America, the Caribbean islands and Portuguese Brazil, for which published evidence is scanty. Where scholarly opinion diverges is over

---

1 This chapter is dedicated to the memory of Juliana Bosselet, whose young life was tragically cut short in late 2017.

2 F. Chevalier, 'The formation of the Jesuit wealth', in M. Mörner (ed.), *The Expulsion of the Jesuits from Latin America* (New York: Knopf, 1965), pp. 94–103 (pp. 99–101); U. Ewald, *Estudios sobre la hacienda colonial en México: las propiedades rurales del Colegio Espíritu Santo de Puebla* (Wiesbaden: Steiner, 1976), pp. 11–17; D. Alden, *The Making of an Enterprise: The Society of Jesus in Portugal, its Empire, and Beyond, 1540–1750* (Stanford, CA: Stanford University Press, 1996), pp. 15–19; E.M. Segurado, *Expulsión e exilio de la provincia jesuita Mexicana, 1767–1820* (San Vicente del Raspeig: Universidad de Alicante, 2005), pp. 32–41; J.F. Schwaller, *The History of the Catholic Church in Latin America: From Conquest to Revolution and Beyond* (New York: New York University Press, 2011), pp. 83–4, 104–6, 113.

W.G. Clarence-Smith, 'Jesuits and mules in colonial Latin America: innovators or managers?', in L.A. Newson (ed.), *Cultural Worlds of the Jesuits in Colonial Latin America* (London: Institute of Latin American Studies, 2020), pp. 209–28. License: CC-BY-NC-ND 2.0.

the question of whether Jesuits were simply efficient managers, or were actually rural innovators. For business historians, 'novel entrepreneurs' introduce new methods and may even revolutionise whole branches of production. In contrast, 'routine entrepreneurs' just plod along established furrows, at most seeking to adopt best practice.[3]

F. Chevalier launched a tradition of lauding Jesuit agricultural methods in his pioneering research on New Spain.[4] L. Byrd Simpson, in a foreword to the English translation of his book on haciendas, goes so far as to call the Jesuits 'scientific farmers'.[5] H. Konrad describes their Santa Lucía estate in New Spain as 'one of the largest and most successful haciendas of its time'.[6] W. Hanisch Espindola echoes a positive view of Jesuit agricultural practices in the case of Chile.[7] G. Colmenares singles out for praise the growing of alfalfa (lucerne; *Medicago sativa L.*) on Peruvian coastal estates, as a forage crop and an improver of soils. That said, he notes that an ecclesiastical visitor opined that the land might better have been devoted to grapes or sugar cane.[8]

On the opposing side of the debate, U. Ewald denies that Jesuits were innovators in New Spain, despite acknowledging their pioneering role in the cultivation of alfalfa. Guidelines for New Spain dating from the second quarter of the 18th century specifically stated that the order should adopt the agricultural customs of the region in which they were situated and should not engage in dangerous novelties. According to Ewald, the Jesuits clung to existing crops and did little to improve pasture. Although some of the fathers came from northern Europe, they did not transfer advanced agricultural techniques from their homelands.[9] J. Riley writes along much the same lines in the context of New Spain, adding that their crop yields were no greater than average.[10] Edda Samudio similarly considers that the Jesuits were not innovators in New Granada. To be sure, they were wedded to economic rationality, had a relatively clear hierarchy of management, lived austerely and kept excellent accounts. Moreover, each estate tended to specialize in one product. However,

3   Z. Acs et al., 'Public policy to promote entrepreneurship: a call to arms', *Small Business Economics*, 47 (2016): 35–51 (37–8).

4   Chevalier, 'Formation of the Jesuit Wealth', pp. 99–101.

5   F. Chevalier, *Land and Society in Colonial Mexico: The Great Hacienda* (Berkeley, CA: University of California Press, 1963), p. ix.

6   H.W. Konrad, *A Jesuit Hacienda in Colonial Mexico: Santa Lucía, 1576–1767* (Stanford, CA: Stanford University Press, 1980), p. 348.

7   W. Hanisch Espindola, *Historia de la Compañia de Jesús en Chile* (Buenos Aires: Francisco de Aguirre, 1974), pp. 142–7.

8   G. Colmenares, *Haciendas de los Jesuítas en el Nuevo Reino de Granada, siglo XVIII* (Bogotá: Universidad Nacional de Colombia, 1969), pp. 99–100, 108.

9   Ewald, *Estudios sobre la hacienda colonial en México*, pp. 136–55.

10   J.D. Riley, *Hacendados jesuitas en México: la administración de los bienes inmuebles del Colegio Máximo de San Pedro y San Pablo* (Mexico City: SEP-Setentas, 1976), pp. 214–18.

they employed the same tools, techniques and systems of labour as other landowners.[11] In brief, 'they did not introduce a single innovation'.[12]

The question is addressed here through the prism of the mule economy. Many Jesuit urban colleges owned and managed large, commercially run ranches, especially in the 'Southern Cone', the Llanos and the northern expanses of New Spain. As animals could transport themselves to market, pastoral latifundia tended to be situated further away from towns than plantations and farms. As for missions, they usually focused on self-sufficient minifundia for their Amerindian wards, but sometimes participated more vigorously in the mule economy.

Mules and hinnies in colonial Latin America

The term 'mules' is often employed loosely, to encompass both mules proper (*mulas*) and hinnies (*burdéganos, bardotos, machos*). A mule results from mating a male donkey (jack) with a female horse (mare) and this is the usual cross. A hinny, or jennet, comes from mating a female donkey (jenny) with a male horse (stallion). Although genetically identical to mules, hinnies tend to be smaller, due to the smaller womb of a jenny. Both mules and hinnies benefit from 'hybrid vigour', being stronger, tougher, cheaper to feed, surer-footed, more resistant to disease and longer-lived than horses. However, both are sterile, though sexually active, so that mule breeding has to start anew with each generation. Animals do not naturally interbreed across species and particular techniques are needed to get them to do so. Moreover, conception rates are lower and miscarriage rates higher than when breeding within a species. Producing mules and hinnies thus requires a certain level of attention and skill.[13]

There was keen demand for these robust hybrids in colonial Latin America, mainly for transport and mining, but also for agriculture and industry.[14] In truth, these sturdy beasts largely powered the colonial economy, reflecting demographic collapse in most Amerindian societies after conquest, the restriction of indigenous beasts of burden to llamas in the Andes and the stupendous multiplication of newly imported species of European animals.

11 E.O. Samudio A., *Las haciendas del Colegio San Francisco Javier de la Compañía de Jesús en Mérida, 1628–1767* (Mérida: Universidad de los Andes, 1985), pp. 86–9; E.O. Samudio A., *El Colegio San Francisco Javier en el contexto de la Mérida colonial* (Mérida: Universidad de los Andes, 2003), pp. 200–01, 207–8.

12 E.O. Samudio A. and J. del Rey Fajardo, *Jesuitas, haciendas y promoción social en la Orinoquia* (Mérida: Universidad de los Andes, 2006), pp. 75, 111–12.

13 W.B. Tegetmeier and C.L. Sutherland, *Horses, Asses, Zebras, Mules, and Mule Breeding* (London: Cox, 1895); L.W. Knight, *The Breeding and Rearing of Jacks, Jennets and Mules* (Nashville, TN: Cumberland, 1902); T.H. Savory, *The Mule: A Historic Hybrid* (Shildon: Meadowfield, 1979); L. Travis, *The Mule* (London: Allen, 1990).

14 I. Mijares Ramírez, 'La mula en la vida cotidiana del siglo XVI', in J. Long Towell and A. Attolini Lecón (eds.), *Caminos y mercados de México* (Mexico City: Universidad Nacional Autónoma de México, 2010), pp. 291–310 (pp. 294–7).

There may have been two million mules in Latin America by the end of the colonial period, equivalent to one for every five-to-ten inhabitants, the highest ratio in the world.[15] Their social prestige varied, as they served as mounts only for lowly *castas* and yet pulled the carriages of the elite.[16] Surprisingly, a recent edited collection on the history of animals in Latin America ignores these beasts.[17]

For a few decades from 1531 the Spanish authorities stimulated imports of donkeys, both jacks and jennies, belonging to special types employed to produce mules.[18] Analyses of DNA reveal that Andalusian beasts were most numerous in constituting the modern Mexican donkey, followed by those from Zamora-León and Majorca.[19] Little is known about later efforts to maintain and improve populations of donkeys destined for breeding mules.[20] In the early 17th century a Jesuit noted that donkeys were most valued for siring mules in the New World, but that they had not multiplied as much as horses and that there were too few large ones.[21] Quality was more important than quantity, as a single stud jack might be put to a herd of 25 to 55 mares in New Spain, with 40 as the average.[22] These valuable jacks were known by a variety of names in Spanish (*burros sementales, burros hechores, burros garañones, burros padres, burros oficiales*) and in Portuguese (*burros pais, burros de lançamento, pegas*).

Fine donkeys and hybrid equids fetched high prices. A good stud jack was especially costly, sometimes worth more than the best horse.[23] This may explain the saying that in the 16th century an ass was the most expensive thing in Quito.[24] In contrast, a brood jenny might be worth only a quarter of a stud

---

15   F. Braudel, *Civilization and Capitalism, 15th to 18th Century*, vol. 1, *The Structures of Everyday Life* (London: Collins; New York: Harper & Row, 1981), pp. 341–2.

16   R.M. Serrera Contreras, *Guadalajara ganadera: estudio regional novohispano, 1760–1805* (Seville: Escuela de Estudios Hispanoamericanos, 1977), pp.176–8, 189, 277–80.

17   M. Few and Z. Tortorici (eds.), *Centering Animals in Latin American History* (Durham, NC: Duke University Press, 2013).

18   M. Beteta Ortiz, 'Apuntes históricos de la expansión de los asnos y mulas españoles en América', unpublished paper (Segundo Congreso Nacional de Zootecnia, Universidad de Santiago de Compostela, 2010).

19   C. López López, R. Alonso and A.S. de Aluja, 'Study of the origins of the Mexican Creole donkey (*Equus asinus*) by means of the analysis of the D-loop region of mitochondrial DNA', *Tropical Animal Health and Production*, 37 (supplement 1) (2005): 173–88.

20   Mijares Ramírez, 'La mula', p. 295.

21   B. Cobo, *Obras del Padre Bernabé Cobo de la Compañía de Jesús*, vol. 1 (Madrid: Atlas, 1964), p. 384.

22   Konrad, *A Jesuit Hacienda*, p. 387, n. 20.

23   R.W. Patch, *Maya and Spaniard in Yucatan, 1648–1812* (Stanford, CA: Stanford University Press, 1993), pp. 117, 144, 285, n. 29.

24   P.T. Bradley and D. Cahill, *Habsburg Peru: Images, Imagination and Memory* (Liverpool: Liverpool University Press, 2000), p. 56.

jack.[25] As for mules, a fine specimen was priced at about three times an ordinary horse in 18th-century New Spain and twice as much as an ox.[26] Hinnies were said to fetch less than mules.[27] However, discounts for hinnies, while widely asserted, are not always reflected in documents of the period.[28]

As there was a marked imbalance between regions suitable for breeding mules and those which required them, a large trade soon sprang up. The best studied of these commercial flows stretched over about 4,000 kilometres, from the Pampas to Peru. Some 25,000 mules a year took this route by the middle of the 18th century, wintering first in the Córdoba area, and then again in the region of Salta. High death rates in the mining zones, coupled with the sterility of mules, fuelled the need for continuing imports.[29] Almost as significant for the prosperity of the Spanish empire, albeit hardly studied, were the mules sent from the Gulf of Fonseca in Central America to the Isthmus of Panama, wintering in modern Costa Rica. Mortality was high on the short but vital transport artery linking the Pacific and Atlantic oceans, again stoking demand.[30]

Officials generally classed other substantial branches of the trade as smuggling, despite much tolerance and occasional periods of legality. From the early 17th century increasing numbers of mules left the Spanish-controlled mainland, especially present-day Venezuela, destined for the Caribbean islands of northern European powers.[31] From around 1730, and probably earlier, mules from the Río de la Plata headed for central Brazil, wintering in Paraná.[32] To avoid the taint of contraband, mules arriving in the mining region of Minas

25 Konrad, *A Jesuit Hacienda*, p. 190 (table).

26 Konrad, *A Jesuit Hacienda*, p. 188. See also D.A. Brading, *Haciendas and Ranchos in the Mexican Bajío, León 1700–1860* (Cambridge: Cambridge University Press, 1978), pp. 78, 85–8; Serrera Contreras, *Guadalajara ganadera*, pp. 194–5; Ewald, *Estudios sobre la hacienda colonial en México*, pp. 50, 163, n. 5.

27 Serrera Contreras, *Guadalajara ganadera*, p. 195.

28 Mijares Ramírez, 'La mula', p. 300.

29 N. Sánchez-Albornoz, 'La saca de mulas de Salta al Perú, 1778–1808', *Anuario del Instituto de Investigaciones Históricas*, 8 (1965): 261–312; N. Sánchez-Albornoz, 'La extracción de mulas de Jujuy al Perú: fuentes, volumen, y negociantes', *Estudios de Historia Social*, 1 (1965): 107–20; G. Paz, 'A la sombra del Perú: mulas, repartos y negocios en el norte argentino a fines de la colonia', *Boletín del Instituto de Historia Argentina y Americana 'Dr. Emilio Ravignani'*, 3 (20) (1999): 45–68.

30 M.J. MacLeod, *Spanish Central America: A Socioeconomic History, 1520–1720* (Austin, TX: University of Texas Press, 2008 [1973]), pp. 218, 274.

31 R. Aizpurúa A., 'Las mulas venezolanas y el Caribe oriental del siglo XVIII: datos para una historia olvidada', *Boletín Americanista*, 38 (1988): 5–15; L.M. Rupert, *Creolization and Contraband: Curaçao in the Early Modern Atlantic* (Athens, GA: University of Georgia Press, 2012), *passim*.

32 J.A. Goulart, *Tropas e tropeiros na formação do Brasil* (Rio de Janeiro: Conquista, 1961), pp. 36–7; A. Barrios Pintos, *Historia de la ganadería en el Uruguay, 1574–1971* (Montevideo: Biblioteca Nacional, 1973), pp. 66–7.

Gerais were said to come from Colonia do Sacramento, the Portuguese outpost in what is today Uruguay.[33]

The economic mainstay of Jesuits in the Río de la Plata

From about the 1640s mules came to be the Jesuits' chief source of income in their Paraquaria (Paraguay) province, centred on Córdoba, in what became the viceroyalty of the Río de la Plata in 1776.[34] According to N. Cushner's estimates, Jesuits accounted for about a fifth of all mules bred in the area before 1767. Moreover, the order exported 12 to 15 per cent of the mules which were sent overland every year to the mining zones of Peru in the mid 18th century.[35] A dozen or more Jesuit colleges owned and managed ranches in the province. Most prominent were the colleges of Córdoba (La Candelaria and Alta Gracia estancias), Santa Fe (Santo Tomé estancia), Buenos Aires (Areco estancia) and Asunción (Paraquari estancia). In addition, the Jesuit provincial administration, situated in Córdoba, exploited the Santa Catalina estancia.[36] As well as mules proper, the Jesuit college in Tucumán bred many hinnies, *machos* in Latin American parlance.[37] Tucumán lay in a dry, rain-shadow area, where horses were scarce but donkeys thrived.[38]

Jesuit mission 'reductions' (*reducciones*) also bred hybrid equids, but relatively few. These were lands peopled by Amerindians whom the Jesuits ruled, treating them as their wards, with the aim of turning them into model peasantries. Equids on reductions were usually for local use by missionaries and Amerindians rather than for sale to the wider world.[39] Small numbers of donkeys and mules thus characterised the Chiquitos and Moxos missions in present-day Bolivia.[40] Statistics for 1768 for the Guaraní missions reveal

---

33 F.A. Pereira da Costa and A. Fernandes, *Cronologia histórica do estado de Piauí* (Rio de Janeiro: Artenova, 1974), pp. 156–7.

34 N.P. Cushner, *Lords of the Land: Sugar, Wine and Jesuit Estates of Coastal Perú, 1600–1767* (Albany, NY: State University of New York Press, 1980), p. 170.

35 N.P. Cushner, *Jesuit Ranches and the Agrarian Development of Colonial Argentina, 1650–1767* (Albany, NY: State University of New York Press, 1983), p. 67.

36 Cushner, *Jesuit Ranches*, frontispiece map, pp. 2, 15, 56–9, 64; Cushner, *Lords of the Land*, p. 165.

37 Cushner, *Jesuit Ranches*, pp. 49–50.

38 M. Dobrizhoffer, *An Account of the Abipones, an Equestrian People of Paraguay* (London: Murray, 1822), vol. 1, p. 245.

39 P. Caraman, *The Lost Paradise: An Account of the Jesuits in Paraguay, 1607–1768* (London: Sidgwick and Jackson, 1975), pp. 120–1.

40 A. Parejos Moreno and V. Suárez Salas, *Chiquitos: historia de una utopía* (Santa Cruz: Universidad Privada de Santa Cruz de la Sierra, 1992), p. 89; D. Block, *Mission Culture on the Upper Amazon: Native Tradition, Jesuit Enterprise and Secular Policy in Moxos, 1660–1880* (Lincoln, NE: University of Nebraska Press, 1994), pp. 57–8; R.H. Jackson, *Demographic Change and Ethnic Survival among the Sedentary Populations on the Jesuit Mission Frontiers of*

somewhat more substantial herds, with over 15,000 mules, though this compared to just over 700,000 cattle and nearly 250,000 sheep.[41]

The mule numbers in the Guaraní missions reflected an unusual arrangement, whereby some Jesuit commercial ranches were administratively attached to missions rather than to colleges.[42] A cluster of 11 estancias stretched across what is today north-western Uruguay, concentrating on raising livestock. The two largest were Yapeyú and San Miguel. The most southerly Guaraní mission station, Santos Reyes de Yapeyú, was located on the Corrientes side of the River Uruguay, but its large estancia lay on the eastern side of the river.[43] According to an inventory drawn up in 1768, following the expulsion of the Jesuits, these estancias were breeding mules on a fair scale, even if the emphasis was on cattle and sheep.[44]

A pillar of the Jesuit economy in New Spain

By 1767 the Jesuits enjoyed great opportunities for breeding animals in the viceroyalty of New Spain, where they owned some 1.5 million hectares of land, which were scattered over more than 140 estates, excluding mission stations.[45] Mules were raised especially to the north of the city of Mexico. As agriculture recovered from the post-conquest demographic collapse and as new silver mines came into production, the livestock frontier gradually drifted northwards into the 'Tierra Adentro'.[46] This trend was reflected in Jesuit estates owned by urban colleges, of which the best-studied are the Santa Lucía lands of the Colegio Máximo de San Pedro y San Pablo in Mexico City.[47] There has also been research on the Toluquilla estates of the Jesuit college of Santo Tomás in Guadalajara.[48] More evidence comes from the Cieneguilla and Tetillas ranches of the college of San Luis Gonzaga in Zacatecas.[49]

Spanish South America, 1609–1803: The Formation and Persistence of Mission Communities in a Comparative Context (Leiden: Brill, 2015), pp. 32–4.

41 Caraman, *The Lost Paradise*, p. 121, n.

42 Caraman, *The Lost Paradise*, p. 122.

43 B. Ganson, *The Guaraní under Spanish Rule in the Río de la Plata* (Stanford, CA: Stanford University Press, 2003), pp. 61–6.

44 Barrios Pintos, *Historia de la ganadería*, pp. 36, 98–9.

45 L. Arnal Simón, 'Formación de las haciendas jesuíticas en el norte de México: el caso del Colegio de Zacatecas', in S. Negro and M.M. Marzal (eds.), *Esclavitud, economía y evangelización: las haciendas jesuitas en la América virreinal* (Lima: Pontificia Universidad Católica del Perú, 2005), pp. 125–39 (p. 125).

46 J. Tutino, *Making a New World: Founding Capitalism in the Bajío and Spanish North America* (Durham, NC: Duke University Press, 2011), pp. 291–2.

47 Konrad, *A Jesuit Hacienda*.

48 E.J. Palomera, *La obra educativa de los Jesuitas en Guadalajara, 1586–1986: visión histórica de cuatro siglos de labor cultural* (Guadalajara: Instituto de Ciencias, 1997); E. Van Young, *Hacienda and Market in Eighteenth-Century Mexico: The Rural Economy of the Guadalajara Region, 1675–1820*, 2nd edn (Lanham, MD: Rowman and Littlefield, 2006 [1981]).

49 Arnal Simón, 'Formación de las haciendas jesuíticas'.

Jesuit rural enterprises in New Spain were more diversified than in the Río de la Plata and mules were initially bred for the order's own needs. When the Jesuits acquired the Santa Lucía estate in 1576, situated just to the north of the city of Mexico, there were a modest 131 equids and agricultural activities were significant. The orientation towards the production of mules rather than horses was already clear, however, as there were two donkey jacks, compared to only one stallion, to service 125 mares. There were also two donkey jennies, probably to achieve self-sufficiency in jacks, although hinnies were later listed in the estate's inventories. Santa Lucía initially produced mules for the hacienda itself and for the college in Mexico City, as well as to transport produce from the one to the other.[50] The Cieneguilla hacienda of the Zacatecas college, established in 1616, disposed of a similar mix of equids. In this dry area, well suited to donkeys, the Jesuits bred quite a few hinnies.[51] In contrast, the Guadalajara estates rarely produced hinnies, which were judged to be smaller and weaker than mules.[52]

Mules became steadily more significant sources of cash income for some Jesuit properties from the middle of the 17th century. Santa Lucía obtained the new estate of Altica in the late 1660s, mainly for mule breeding. At this time the fathers of the Colegio Máximo in Mexico City considered this to be 'one of the most profitable business ventures in New Spain'. Indeed, Santa Lucía's sales increased to the point that the estate sometimes ran short of animals for its own requirements. Another ranch was acquired in 1687 and three more in 1723.[53]

Markets for Jesuit mules were varied. Many of Santa Lucía's animals were sold to operators of rural and urban transport businesses. The estate also supplied the sugar *trapiches* of present-day Morelos, just to the south of the city of Mexico, as the milling of sugar cane came to be powered increasingly by mules rather than by water. Silver mines were another significant market, notably the Pachuca mine, close to the Santa Lucía estate.[54] As for the colleges of Zacatecas and Durango, they specialised in supplying mules to the dynamic silver mines in their regions.[55] The Toluquilla estates of the college in Guadalajara evolved in a contrary direction. Initially they also prospered through sales of mules, but later they reduced their emphasis on livestock. Wheat became the dominant source of cash earnings from the 1680s, together with the milling of flour. This gradually relegated animal rearing to servicing the college's own agricultural and transport needs.[56]

---

50   Konrad, *A Jesuit Hacienda*, pp. 34, 48–9, 187–90.

51   Arnal Simón, 'Formación de las haciendas jesuíticas', p. 128.

52   Serrera Contreras, *Guadalajara ganadera*, p. 212, n. 106.

53   Konrad, *A Jesuit Hacienda*, pp. 81–4, 90–5, 187–9.

54   Konrad, *A Jesuit Hacienda*, pp. 82, 188.

55   Arnal Simón, 'Formación de las haciendas jesuíticas', pp. 126–8.

56   Van Young, *Hacienda and Market*, pp. 207–20.

Southern areas were less pastoral and the Jesuits did not sell mules on any scale. The Colegio Espíritu Santo of Puebla gradually accumulated land to the east and south of the city, with ranches located further away than farms. Mules were for the order's own transport needs, though it is probable that a few were sold locally. While horses initially cultivated lands sown with wheat and maize, mules tended to take over farm work in the 18th century. Donkeys served exclusively to make mules on Jesuit properties, as only Amerindian smallholders employed donkeys as work animals.[57]

Mission stations bred mules locally for their own use, notably in the far north-west, but they also received funds from specialised estates in the heartlands. Thus, in 1718 the city of Mexico ceded ten rural properties to the Fondo Piadoso de las Californias. Located in the north-western vicinity of the city, these estates mainly raised cattle and sheep, but at that time also contained 271 mares and colts and 12 donkeys. By 1767 these numbers had swollen to 3,728 mares, 653 colts and fillies and 40 donkeys.[58] The Jesuit college in Zacatecas also remitted money earned from its pastoral activities to remote north-western missions.[59]

The Jesuits of Andean America: supplementary funds

From around the 1660s mules provided significant revenues for the Jesuit province of New Granada, situated in what are today Colombia and Venezuela. That said, cocoa earned more for the order and possibly also cattle and sugar.[60] Colleges in highland cities benefited most from ranching, though some funds were allocated to mission stations in the Orinoco Basin.[61] The Colegio Máximo San Bartolomé, in Santa Fe de Bogotá, was the largest owner of lowland ranches, followed by Jesuit colleges in Tunja, Pamplona and Mérida, the latter of which is today in western Venezuela.[62]

Jesuit mule-breeding was concentrated in tracts of the seasonally inundated Llanos plains, which are today partitioned between Colombia and Venezuela. The aptly named hacienda of La Yegüera, now Hato Corozal, was their first

---

57 Ewald, *Estudios sobre la hacienda colonial en México*, pp. 17–24, 73, 119–25, 133–4, 165.

58 I. del Río, 'Las haciendas del Fondo Piadoso de las Californias', in S. Negro and M.M. Marzal (eds.), *Esclavitud, economía y evangelización: las haciendas jesuitas en la América virreinal* (Lima: Pontificia Universidad Católica del Perú, 2005), p. 143.

59 Arnal Simón, 'Formación de las haciendas jesuíticas', p. 136.

60 Samudio A., *El Colegio San Francisco Javier*, pp. 145–51, 157, 168–73, 188–9.

61 J. del Rey Fajardo, *Los Jesuitas en Venezuela*, vol. 5, *Las misiones germen de la nacionalidad* (Caracas: Universidad Católica Andrés Bello, 2007), pp. 673–4, 680.

62 Colmenares, *Haciendas de los Jesuítas*, pp. 18–22, 108–11; Rey Fajardo, *Los Jesuitas en Venezuela*, pp. 674–5, 683, 702, 710; E.O. Samudio A., 'Las haciendas jesuíticas en la Orinoquia en su contexto económico', in S. Negro and M.M. Marzal (eds.), *Esclavitud, economía y evangelización: las haciendas jesuitas en la América virreinal* (Lima: Pontificia Universidad Católica del Perú, 2005), pp. 183–214 (p. 200).

main centre of mule breeding. That of Pagüey, in the Venezuelan zone of Barinas, was only donated to the order in 1748. There were numerous mares on these estates, together with a few *burros hechores*, the local name for precious stud donkeys.[63] From the lowlands, mules and cattle were driven up the steep flanks of the Cordillera on arduous trails. The exhausted animals were then rested and fattened in specialised Jesuit ranches, notably at La Chamicera, close to Bogotá. There they joined smaller numbers of mules which had been raised in Jesuit properties in the Neiva region, modern Huila, in the upper reaches of the Magdalena Valley. Finally, the animals were sold in highland cities, with Bogotá as the main market.[64] Some mules were also dispatched to the Venezuelan coastal zone, mainly to labour in the booming cocoa plantations.[65] However, there is almost no trace of Jesuit participation in the vast contraband trade in mules exported to foreign Caribbean islands from this coast. A solitary denunciation of 1745 from Cumaná, to the effect that Jesuits of the Orinoco missions had engaged in this traffic, was never proven.[66]

Mules for the Jesuits' own needs in the rest of Latin America

Jesuits bred mules in many other parts of colonial Latin America, but essentially to service their own operations. Sales of these animals thus contributed little directly to the order's finances. This may have reflected local ecological conditions, market opportunities, or choices made by local Jesuit leaders.

The order was not well represented in Central America, though there were two colleges, in the Nicaraguan towns of El Realejo and Granada, which were attached to the Jesuit province of Quito.[67] Men of the cloth obtained licences to send mules from Nicaragua to Panama, for example in the 1730s, but these seem to have been secular rather than regular clergymen.[68]

The intermontane Andean basin was the heartland of the Jesuit province of Quito and is today mainly in Ecuador. A dense cluster of urban colleges, together with the provincial administration, owned estancias there, which raised mules

---

63 Colmenares, *Haciendas de los Jesuítas*, pp. 108–11; Samudio A., *Las haciendas del Colegio San Francisco Javier*, pp. 29–30, 89–95, 99; Samudio A., *El Colegio San Francisco Javier*, pp.176, 190, 209–11; Samudio A., 'Las haciendas jesuíticas en la Orinoquia', pp. 193, 200; Samudio A. and Rey Fajardo, *Jesuitas, haciendas*, pp. 52, 63–5, 73–5, 132–3; Rey Fajardo, *Los Jesuitas en Venezuela*, pp. 673–83, 699, 710–13.

64 Colmenares, *Haciendas de los Jesuítas*, pp. 105–7; Samudio A. and Rey Fajardo, *Jesuitas, haciendas*, p. 102; Rey Fajardo, *Los Jesuitas en Venezuela*, pp. 461–2, 676, 722–3.

65 A. McFarlane, *Colombia before Independence: Economy, Society and Politics under Bourbon Rule* (Cambridge: Cambridge University Press, 1993), p. 21, n. 34.

66 Rey Fajardo, *Los Jesuitas en Venezuela*, p. 213, n. 1306.

67 J.M. Sariego Rodríguez, 'Tradición jesuita en Guatemala: una aproximación histórica' (Universidad Rafael Landívar, 2010), http://www.url.edu.gt/portalurl/archivos/246/archivos/sariego.pdf [accessed 10 Sept. 2019], p. 4.

68 G.J. Romero Vargas, 'Les structures sociales du Nicaragua au XVIIIème siècle' (unpublished doctoral thesis, Université de Paris-IV, 1977), p. 474.

among many other animals.[69] Around 1700 the college of Quito alone owned ten estates, on which there were about 1,200 mules.[70] However, these beasts apparently did not give rise to substantial sales.[71] A possible exception was the Jesuit college of Popayán, today in Colombia, which sourced many mules from its Llanogrande estate.[72] These animals were widely employed in the gold-mining concerns of the region, which were supplied by such haciendas in the 18th century.[73] It remains to be demonstrated whether Jesuits took part in this process.

Jesuit properties in the coastal oases of Peru apparently bred both hinnies and mules, probably because donkeys were unusually plentiful in this arid environment.[74] At the very end of the 16th century, the fattening of mules and horses for sale occurred on one vineyard, donated to the Colegio Máximo San Pablo of Lima.[75] However, as mules from the Pampas flooded into Peru from the middle of the 17th century, breeding came to be restricted to the fathers' own requirements. In some cases, it did not even suffice for this purpose.[76] Further south, Jesuit colleges and missions in Chile were again involved in the mule economy, but on a small scale.[77] The hacienda of San Francisco de Borja Guanquehua, which financed both the Jesuit college in Concepción and the Arauco missions, bred some mules.[78] That said, Chile remained a net importer of these animals from the eastern side of the Andes.[79]

69 N.P. Cushner, *Farm and Factory: The Jesuits and the Development of Agrarian Capitalism in Colonial Quito, 1600–1767* (Albany, NY: State University of New York Press, 1982), pp. 76–8; Colmenares, *Haciendas de los Jesuítas*, pp. 18–22, 108–11.

70 Schwaller, *History of the Catholic Church*, p. 105.

71 Cushner, *Farm and Factory*, pp. 79, 158.

72 McFarlane, *Colombia before Independence*, pp. 63–4; Colmenares, *Haciendas de los Jesuítas*, p. 124.

73 K. Lane, *Quito 1599: City and Colony in Transition* (Albuquerque, NM: University of New Mexico Press, 2002), pp. 79, 127, 178, 243, n. 16; J. Rappaport, *The Politics of Memory: Native Historical Interpretation in the Colombian Andes* (Durham, NC: Duke University Press, 1998), pp. 43–4.

74 Cushner, *Lords of the Land*, pp. 37, 71–2

75 D. Rodríguez, 'Juan Martínez Rengifo y los Jesuitas: formación de la Hacienda Santa Marta del Puquio (La Huaca), 1560–1594', in S. Negro and M.M. Marzal (eds.), *Esclavitud, economía y evangelización: las haciendas jesuitas en la América virreinal* (Lima: Pontificia Universidad Católica del Perú, 2005), pp. 263–98 (p. 288, n. 60).

76 S. Negro, 'Arquitectura, poder, y esclavitud en las haciendas jesuitas de la Nasca en el Perú', in S. Negro and M.M. Marzal (eds.), *Esclavitud, economía y evangelización: las haciendas jesuitas en la América virreinal* (Lima: Pontificia Universidad Católica del Perú, 2005), pp. 449–92 (pp. 456, 464); Cushner, *Lords of the Land*, pp. 72, 197, n. 22.

77 R. Moreno Jeria, *Misiones en Chile austral: los Jesuitas en Chiloé* (Seville: CSIC, 2007) p. 347.

78 A.G. Bravo, 'La administración económica de la hacienda jesuita San Francisco de Borja Guanquehua', in S. Negro and M.M. Marzal (eds.), *Esclavitud, economía y evangelización: las haciendas jesuitas en la América virreinal* (Lima: Pontificia Universidad Católica del Perú, 2005), pp. 377–94 (pp. 385–6).

79 Dobrizhoffer, *An Account of the Abipones*, vol. 1, p. 4.

The most striking case of limited Jesuit involvement in the mule economy occurred in Brazil, reflecting peculiarities in Portuguese policy. The crown either prohibited or limited mule breeding from the mid 17th century, especially in the north, to protect supplies of horses for military purposes.[80] Not until after the expulsion of the Jesuits in 1759 was mule breeding encouraged in the far south, while remaining technically prohibited elsewhere.[81] Even though restrictions were hard to enforce, and were periodically lifted or modified, northern Brazil still contained remarkably few mules as late as the 1830s.[82]

The law-abiding Jesuits thus seem to have abstained from breeding mules in Brazil and there is only limited evidence of this abstinence being breached. A census of 1742 for the Fazenda de Santa Cruz, dependent on the Jesuit college of Rio de Janeiro, lists 1,140 head of *gado eqüino*, possibly indicating the presence of mules and donkeys together with horses.[83] In the north, Domingos Afonso 'Mafrense' or 'Sertão' bequeathed some thirty ranches in Piauí to the Jesuits of Salvador da Bahia on his death in 1711. It was repeatedly asserted that there were 1,860 *bestas*, almost certainly meaning mules, on these properties at that time, compared to 1,010 horses. However, this was not stated in Domingo Afonso's will, which merely referred to unspecified *gado cavallar*. The figure probably dated from an inventory compiled in 1782, after the expulsion of the Jesuits, though it was also cited in 1811. Only in 1854 was there solid evidence of donkeys on what had become publicly-owned estates.[84]

Innovation or routine management?

The Jesuits were undoubtedly important players in the mule economy. In some cases, notably in the Río de la Plata and northern New Spain, they derived significant income from participating in this activity. However, this leaves open the question as to the nature of their entrepreneurship. In terms of labour, the Jesuits adapted to local conditions, while priding themselves on treating their slaves better than the norm.[85] They were less likely to employ slaves on ranches than on plantations in New Granada, as slaves were hard to supervise

---

80 R. Southey, *History of Brazil, Part the Second* (London: Longman, Hurst, Rees, Orme, and Brown, 1817), pp. 469, 633–4; C.A. Marques, *Dicionário histórico-geográfico da Província do Maranhão*, 3rd edn (Rio de Janeiro: Fon-Fon e Seleta, 1970 [1870]), p. 185.

81 M.T. Schorer Petrone, *O Barão de Iguape: um empresário da época da independência* (São Paulo: Editora Nacional, 1976) pp. 18–20.

82 G. Gardner, *Travels in the Interior of Brazil, Principally through the Northern Provinces and the Gold and Diamond District, during the Years 1836 to 1841* (London: Reeve Brothers, 1846), pp. 83, 174–5, 474.

83 E.B. Barcelos Fernandes, *Futuros e outros; homens e espaços: os aldeamentos jesuíticos e a colonização na América portugueza* (Rio de Janeiro: Contra Capa, 2015), p. 62.

84 Costa and Fernandes, *Cronologia histórica*, pp. 45, 74–5, 136–8.

85 Hanisch Espindola, *Historia de la Compañía de Jesús en Chile*, p. 147.

on distant properties raising livestock.[86] There were African slaves on their Córdoba estates, perhaps 700 to 1,000 of them by the 18th century, who laboured with different kinds of free workers.[87] On one of the Santa Lucía ranches in New Spain in the 1740s, all workers in the livestock sector were free, although they were largely paid in kind rather than in cash.[88]

Innovation can occur in marketing as well as production. In the 1680s the Jesuits set up a procurator's office in Salta, where mules from the Pampas were wintered and fattened prior to the last stretch of their journey to the mining zones. By the 18th century another office functioned in Potosí, at the centre of the mining economy. Procurators in both places researched prices and market conditions, advised the headquarters in Córdoba on numbers to send and suggested whether to sell in Salta or take mules on to Upper or Lower Peru. The order often preferred to sell in Salta, rather than facing the risks and delays of escorting mules any further. However, this system of market intelligence can be seen as a benefit arising from the extensive networks of a large 'firm' rather than as an innovation.[89]

In terms of breeding, Cushner does not overtly praise the Jesuits in the Río de la Plata, but his research suggests they were at least at the cutting edge of best practice. In the Córdoba area they divided their operations between two estates. Altagracia, closest to town, maintained a special breeding herd of donkeys, with 500–600 jennies and some two hundred jacks, presumably sending surplus donkeys to other Jesuit properties. The actual breeding of mules was carried out in Altagracia. The young animals were then transferred to the more distant Candelaria ranch, for raising and fattening up to three years of age.[90]

For New Granada, J. del Rey Fajardo cautions that information on Jesuit techniques of animal-raising is scarce. However, he points out that travellers in the area after the expulsion of the Jesuits, for example Alexander von Humboldt, noted that the efficacy of ranching had declined steeply.[91] This suggests that Jesuit methods were above average. H. Konrad states of Santa Lucía that 'production of horses and mules was carefully regulated'. Herds of donkeys were maintained on various properties and much more attention was paid to jacks than to stallions. Careful records were kept and animals were branded and segregated by species and sex. Both mules and hinnies were broken in prior to

---

86 Samudio A., *El Colegio San Francisco Javier*, pp. 209, 211, 260; Samudio A. and Rey Fajardo, *Jesuitas, haciendas*, p. 112.

87 Cushner, *Jesuit Ranches*, p. 56.

88 Konrad, *A Jesuit Hacienda*, p. 289.

89 Cushner, *Lords of the Land*, pp. 165–6; Cushner, *Jesuit Ranches*, pp. 51, 57, 59–61, 64, 163–4.

90 Cushner, *Jesuit Ranches*, pp. 52–5.

91 Rey Fajardo, *Los Jesuitas en Venezuela*, pp. 712–13; A. von Humboldt and A. Bonpland, *Personal Narrative of Travels to the Equinoctial Regions of America, during the Years 1799–1804*, vol. 2 (London: Routledge, 1890), p. 287.

sale and males were castrated to make them docile. Barley was grown to feed mules and oxen, rather than the usual maize.[92]

Ewald is much less laudatory, while recognizing that specific Jesuit instructions on mule breeding in New Spain have unfortunately been lost. She characterises their livestock activities as extensive and requiring few workers; and considers that they made little effort to improve pasture. She further states that there is no indication they attempted to import superior animals, although she admits that they did upgrade local stock through careful attention to breeding.[93]

An unresolved and vital question is whether Jesuits did anything about jacks, which were seen as the key to successful mule breeding at a time when it was believed that common mares were all that was required. Martin Dobrizhoffer, a Jesuit originating from the Austro-Czech borderlands who was in the Río de la Plata from 1749 to 1767, reported that large estates kept special donkeys. 'Distinguished from the common sort', they served to breed mules. He further noted that they enjoyed 'a perpetual exemption from labour', as they were employed only to propagate mules. While some of the mules were as tall as horses, they were generally smaller than the best which were bred in Spain and Italy, which may imply that breeding jacks were somewhat smaller overall.[94] Unfortunately, Dobrizhoffer does not say whether the recourse to special types of donkeys was particular to Jesuit estates, although his own experience would have been mainly on the order's ranches.

In short, it would be hard to deny that the Jesuits became skilled and successful breeders of mules in colonial Latin America. They gave great thought and attention to the process at a time when animal husbandry was generally extremely rough and ready. Whether they were truly innovators in the matter remains to be determined by further research. Moreover, while business historians distinguish between novel and routine entrepreneurship for heuristic purposes, historical reality tends to be much less clear-cut.

Conclusion

Mules certainly mattered to Jesuits in colonial Latin America, as many Jesuit legacies were built on the backs of these humble and often forgotten beasts. Profits from sales, and from activities serviced by mules, formed the material basis for much of the educational progress achieved on the continent, notably through financing the famous free colleges in the main cities. These institutions often became the first universities of newly independent countries. The architectural and artistic achievements of the order further depended on the funds they were able to accumulate. To a lesser degree, profits were ploughed

92 Konrad, *A Jesuit Hacienda*, pp. 91, 189–91, 197.

93 Ewald, *Estudios sobre la hacienda colonial en México*, pp. 133–55.

94 Dobrizhoffer, *An Account of the Abipones*, vol. 1, pp. 240–1, 244–5.

back into healthcare and other social services, notably in cities. It is harder to assess to what extent income streams from breeding and selling mules, and from rural economic activities more generally, contributed to the controversial process of converting Amerindians to Catholic Christianity. The Jesuits, in their mission stations and reductions, aimed mainly at creating a self-sufficient peasantry, rather than a cash-earning one. Mules played a role in this, but not an especially prominent one.

Bibliography

Acs, Z., T. Åstero, D. Audretsch and D.T. Robinson (2016) 'Public policy to promote entrepreneurship: a call to arms', *Small Business Economics*, 47: 35–51.

Aizpurúa A., R. (1988) 'Las mulas venezolanas y el Caribe oriental del siglo XVIII: datos para una historia olvidada', *Boletín Americanista*, 38: 5–15.

Alden, D. (1996) *The Making of an Enterprise: The Society of Jesus in Portugal, Its Empire, and Beyond, 1540–1750* (Stanford, CA: Stanford University Press).

Arnal Simón, L. (2005) 'Formación de las haciendas jesuíticas en el norte de México: el caso del Colegio de Zacatecas', in S. Negro and M.M. Marzal (eds.), *Esclavitud, economía y evangelización: las haciendas jesuitas en la América virreinal* (Lima: Pontificia Universidad Católica del Perú), pp. 125–39.

Barrios Pintos, A. (1973) *Historia de la ganadería en el Uruguay, 1574–1971* (Montevideo: Biblioteca Nacional).

Beteta Ortiz, M. (2010) 'Apuntes históricos de la expansión de los asnos y mulas españoles en América', unpublished paper (Segundo Congreso Nacional de Zootecnia, Universidad de Santiago de Compostela).

Block, D. (1994) *Mission Culture on the Upper Amazon: Native Tradition, Jesuit Enterprise and Secular Policy in Moxos, 1660–1880* (Lincoln, NE: University of Nebraska Press).

Brading, D.A. (1978) *Haciendas and Ranchos in the Mexican Bajío, León 1700–1860* (Cambridge: Cambridge University Press).

Bradley, P.T. and D. Cahill (2000) *Habsburg Peru: Images, Imagination and Memory* (Liverpool: Liverpool University Press).

Braudel, F. (1981) *Civilization and Capitalism, 15th to 18th Century*, vol. 1, *The Structures of Everyday Life* (London: Collins; New York: Harper & Row).

Bravo, A.G. (2005) 'La administración económica de la hacienda jesuita San Francisco de Borja Guanquehua', in S. Negro and M.M. Marzal (eds.),

Esclavitud, economía y evangelización: las haciendas jesuitas en la América virreinal (Lima: Pontificia Universidad Católica del Perú), pp. 377–94.

Caraman, P. (1975) *The Lost Paradise: An Account of the Jesuits in Paraguay, 1607–1768* (London: Sidgwick and Jackson).

Chevalier, F. (1963) *Land and Society in Colonial Mexico: The Great Hacienda* (Berkeley, CA: University of California Press).

— (1965) 'The formation of the Jesuit wealth', in M. Mörner (ed.), *The Expulsion of the Jesuits from Latin America* (New York: Knopf, 1965), pp. 94–103.

Cobo, B. (1964) *Obras del Padre Bernabé Cobo de la Compañía de Jesus* (2 vols., Madrid: Atlas).

Colmenares, G. (1969) *Haciendas de los Jesuítas en el Nuevo Reino de Granada, siglo XVIII* (Bogotá: Universidad Nacional de Colombia).

Costa, F.A. Pereira da and A. Fernandes (1974) *Cronologia histórica do estado de Piauí* (Rio de Janeiro: Artenova).

Cushner, N.P. (1980) *Lords of the Land: Sugar, Wine and Jesuit Estates of Coastal Perú, 1600–1767* (Albany, NY: State University of New York Press).

— (1982) *Farm and Factory: The Jesuits and the Development of Agrarian Capitalism in Colonial Quito, 1600–1767* (Albany, NY: State University of New York Press).

— (1983) *Jesuit Ranches and the Agrarian Development of Colonial Argentina, 1650–1767* (Albany, NY: State University of New York Press).

Dobrizhoffer, M. (1822) *An Account of the Abipones, an Equestrian People of Paraguay* (3 vols., London: Murray).

Ewald, U. (1976) *Estudios sobre la hacienda colonial en México: las propiedades rurales del Colegio Espíritu Santo de Puebla* (Wiesbaden: Steiner).

Fernandes, E.B. Barcelos (2015) *Futuros e outros; homens e espaços: os aldeamentos jesuíticos e a colonização na América portugueza* (Rio de Janeiro: Contra Capa).

Few, M. and Z. Tortorici (eds.) (2013) *Centering Animals in Latin American History* (Durham, NC: Duke University Press).

Ganson, B. (2003) *The Guaraní under Spanish Rule in the Río de la Plata* (Stanford, CA: Stanford University Press).

Gardner, G. (1846) *Travels in the Interior of Brazil, Principally through the Northern Provinces and the Gold and Diamond District, during the Years 1836 to 1841* (London: Reeve Brothers).

Goulart, J.A. (1961) *Tropas e tropeiros na formação do Brasil* (Rio de Janeiro: Conquista).

Hanisch Espindola, W. (1974) *Historia de la Compañía de Jesús en Chile* (Buenos Aires: Francisco de Aguirre).

Humboldt, A. von and A. Bonpland (1890) *Personal Narrative of Travels to the Equinoctial Regions of America, during the Years 1799–1804* (London: Routledge).

Jackson, R.H. (2015) *Demographic Change and Ethnic Survival among the Sedentary Populations on the Jesuit Mission Frontiers of Spanish South America, 1609–1803: The Formation and Persistence of Mission Communities in a Comparative Context* (Leiden: Brill).

Knight, L.W. (1902) *The Breeding and Rearing of Jacks, Jennets and Mules* (Nashville, TN: The Cumberland).

Konrad, H.W. (1980) *A Jesuit Hacienda in Colonial Mexico: Santa Lucía, 1576–1767* (Stanford, CA: Stanford University Press).

Lane, K. (2002) *Quito 1599: City and Colony in Transition* (Albuquerque, NM: University of New Mexico Press).

López López, C., R. Alonso and A.S. de Aluja (2005) 'Study of the origins of the Mexican Creole donkey (*Equus asinus*) by means of the analysis of the D-loop region of mitochondrial DNA', *Tropical Animal Health and Production*, 37 (Supplement 1): 173–88.

McFarlane, A. (1993) *Colombia before Independence: Economy, Society and Politics under Bourbon Rule* (Cambridge: Cambridge University Press).

MacLeod, M.J. (2008 [1973]) *Spanish Central America: A Socioeconomic History, 1520–1720*, 3rd edn (Austin, TX: University of Texas Press).

Marques, C.A. (1970 [1870]) *Dicionário histórico-geográfico da Província do Maranhão*, 3rd edn (Rio de Janeiro: Fon-Fon e Seleta).

Mijares Ramírez, I. (2010) 'La mula en la vida cotidiana del siglo XVI', in J. Long Towell and A. Attolini Lecón (eds.), *Caminos y mercados de México* (Mexico City: Universidad Nacional Autónoma de México), pp. 291–310.

Moreno Jeria, R. (2007) *Misiones en Chile austral: los Jesuitas en Chiloé* (Seville: CSIC).

Negro, S. (2005) 'Arquitectura, poder, y esclavitud en las haciendas jesuitas de la Nasca en el Perú', in S. Negro and M.M. Marzal (eds.), *Esclavitud, economía y evangelización: las haciendas jesuitas en la América virreinal* (Lima: Pontificia Universidad Católica del Perú), pp. 449–92.

Palomera, E.J. (1997) *La obra educativa de los Jesuitas en Guadalajara, 1586–1986: visión histórica de cuatro siglos de labor cultural* (Guadalajara: Instituto de Ciencias).

Parejos Moreno, A. and V. Suárez Salas (1992) *Chiquitos: historia de una utopía* (Santa Cruz: Universidad Privada de Santa Cruz de la Sierra).

Patch, R.W. (1993) *Maya and Spaniard in Yucatan, 1648–1812* (Stanford, CA: Stanford University Press).

Paz, G. (1999) 'A la sombra del Perú: mulas, repartos y negocios en el norte argentino a fines de la colonia', *Boletín del Instituto de Historia Argentina y Americana 'Dr. Emilio Ravignani'*, 3 (20): 45–68.

Petrone, M.T. Schorer (1976) *O Barão de Iguape: um empresário da época da independência* (São Paulo: Editora Nacional).

Rappaport, J. (1998) *The Politics of Memory: Native Historical Interpretation in the Colombian Andes* (Durham, NC: Duke University Press).

Rey Fajardo, J. del (2007) *Los Jesuitas en Venezuela*, vol. 5, *Las misiones germen de la nacionalidad* (Caracas: Universidad Católica Andrés Bello).

Riley, J.D. (1976) *Hacendados jesuitas en México: la administración de los bienes inmuebles del Colegio Máximo de San Pedro y San Pablo* (Mexico City: SEP-Setentas).

Río, I. del (2005) 'Las haciendas del Fondo Piadoso de las Californias', in S. Negro and M.M. Marzal (eds.), *Esclavitud, economía y evangelización: las haciendas jesuitas en la América virreinal* (Lima: Pontificia Universidad Católica del Perú), pp. 141–54.

Rodríguez, D. (2005) 'Juan Martínez Rengifo y los Jesuitas: formación de la Hacienda Santa Marta del Puquio (La Huaca), 1560–1594', in S. Negro and M.M. Marzal (eds.), *Esclavitud, economía y evangelización: las haciendas jesuitas en la América virreinal* (Lima: Pontificia Universidad Católica del Perú), pp. 263–98.

Romero Vargas, G.J. (1977) 'Les structures sociales du Nicaragua au XVIIIème siècle' (unpublished doctoral thesis, Université de Paris-IV).

Rupert, L.M. (2012) *Creolization and Contraband: Curaçao in the Early Modern Atlantic* (Athens, GA: University of Georgia Press).

Samudio A., E.O. (1985) *Las haciendas del Colegio San Francisco Javier de la Compañía de Jesús en Mérida, 1628–1767* (Mérida: Universidad de los Andes).

— (2003) *El Colegio San Francisco Javier en el contexto de la Mérida colonial* (Mérida: Universidad de los Andes).

— (2005) 'Las haciendas jesuíticas en la Orinoquia en su contexto económico', in S. Negro and M.M. Marzal (eds.), *Esclavitud, economía y evangelización: las haciendas jesuitas en la América virreinal* (Lima: Pontificia Universidad Católica del Perú), pp. 183–214.

Samudio A., E.O. and J. del Rey Fajardo (2006) *Jesuitas, haciendas y promoción social en la Orinoquia* (Mérida: Universidad de los Andes).

Sánchez-Albornoz, N. (1965) 'La extracción de mulas de Jujuy al Perú: fuentes, volumen, y negociantes', *Estudios de Historia Social*, 1: 107–20.

— (1965) 'La saca de mulas de Salta al Perú, 1778–1808', *Anuario del Instituto de Investigaciones Históricas*, 8: 261–312.

Sariego Rodríguez, J.M. (2010) 'Tradición jesuita en Guatemala: una aproximación histórica' (Universidad Rafael Landívar), http://www.url.edu.gt/portalurl/archivos/246/archivos/sariego.pdf [accessed 10 Sept. 2019].

Savory, T.H. (1979) *The Mule: A Historic Hybrid* (Shildon: Meadowfield).

Schwaller, J.F. (2011) *The History of the Catholic Church in Latin America: From Conquest to Revolution and Beyond* (New York: New York University Press).

Segurado, E.M. (2005) *Expulsión e exilio de la provincia jesuita Mexicana, 1767–1820* (San Vicente del Raspeig: Universidad de Alicante).

Serrera Contreras, R.M. (1977) *Guadalajara ganadera: estudio regional novohispano, 1760–1805* (Seville: Escuela de Estudios Hispanoamericanos).

Southey, R. (1817) *History of Brazil, Part the Second* (London: Longman, Hurst, Rees, Orme, and Brown).

Tegetmeier, W.B. and C.L. Sutherland (1895) *Horses, Asses, Zebras, Mules, and Mule Breeding* (London: Cox).

Travis, L. (1990) *The Mule* (London: Allen).

Tutino, J. (2011) *Making a New World: Founding Capitalism in the Bajío and Spanish North America* (Durham, NC: Duke University Press).

Van Young, E. (2006 [1981]) *Hacienda and Market in Eighteenth-Century Mexico: The Rural Economy of the Guadalajara Region, 1675–1820*, 2nd edn (Lanham, MD: Rowman and Littlefield).

11. Jesuit recipes, Jesuit receipts: the Society of Jesus and the introduction of exotic *materia medica* into Europe

Samir Boumediene

They have Papal bulls allowing them to practise this art and they have, in several places, like Rome or Lyon or elsewhere, apothecary shops they supply from their stores in the Indies and, therefore having drugs, they make medicines at a low cost and they sell them for a high price, which results in a very big traffic.[1]

One of the best descriptions of the role played by the Jesuits in the early modern drug trade is to be found in a text written in 1669 by the Jansenist logician Antoine Arnauld, under the name of Sébastien-Joseph du Cambout de Pontchâteau. In his book entitled *La morale pratique des jésuites* Arnauld identified three factors to explain the involvement of the Jesuits in the pharmaceutical marketplace: their influence on the papacy; their 'corruption', i.e., their taste for money; and their presence in the Indies. In spite of the anti-Jesuit propaganda expressed in his text, and independently of any discussion about the 'corruption' of the Jesuits, this chapter would like to demonstrate that in some way Arnauld was right.

For several years the Jesuit drug trade has attracted the interest of many scholars who do not necessarily share the same agenda. Some are specialists in Jesuit studies; others come from the history of science and medicine or from commercial history. A few studies have been specifically devoted to Jesuit pharmacy,[2] but the topic also appears in works which have a different focus: the intellectual life of the colleges, the biographies of Jesuits, the material culture

1   A. Arnauld, *La morale pratique des Jésuites présentée en plusieurs histoires arrivées dans toutes les parties du Monde* (Cologne: Gervinus Quentel, 1669), p. 61.

2   J.L. Valverde, *Presencia de la Compañía de Jesús en el desarrollo de la farmacia* (Granada: Universidad de Granada, 1978); M.E. del Río Huas and M. Revuelta González, 'Enfermerías y boticas en las casas de La Compañía en Madrid siglos XVI–XIX', *Archivum Historicum Societatis Iesu*, 64 (1995): 46–8; S. Anagnostou, 'Jesuit missionaries in Spanish America and the transfer of medical-pharmaceutical knowledge', *Archives internationales d'histoire des sciences*, 52 (2002): 176–97; and 'Jesuits in Spanish America: contributions to the exploration of the American materia medica', *Pharmacy in History*, 47 (2005): 3–17.

S. Boumediene, 'Jesuit recipes, Jesuit receipts: the Society of Jesus and the introduction of exotic *materia medica* into Europe', in L.A. Newson (ed.), *Cultural Worlds of the Jesuits in Colonial Latin America* (London: Institute of Latin American Studies, 2020), pp. 229–54. License: CC-BY-NC-ND 2.0.

of the missions, etc.[3] Despite this diversity all these works agree on three points also covered by the current chapter: first, the Society of Jesus was a truly worldwide organisation; second, the involvement of the Jesuits in the trade in drugs was an important aspect of their temporal activities; third, any of these temporal activities, and notably those dealing with knowledge, were, at least theoretically, subordinate to the apostolic goal of the Society.

In accordance with this scholarship, this chapter tries to understand the involvement of the Society in the medical marketplace, situating it within all the processes which defined the 'Jesuit presence' in their urban colleges and the most remote missions, as well as in the mobility of its members. Nevertheless, this chapter is not an overview of Jesuit pharmaceutical activities since this has already been done, for instance by S. Anagnostou for their American provinces.[4] Neither is it a study of the business the Jesuits developed in respect of medicines. Its goal is, rather, to analyse the way the Jesuits converted things into commercialised items, that is, the process of commodification itself. What does it mean to introduce a new product onto the market and why did the Jesuits play a significant role in this process with respect to medicine?

In order to answer this question, this chapter focuses on remedies imported into Europe from Spanish America. This does not mean that the introduction of a new product onto the market was necessarily similar to the introduction of other overseas products into Europe: early modern pharmacy was also transformed, for instance, by the arrival of chemical products. Nevertheless, exotic products are of particular interest since their novelty and their distant origin raised, in a significant manner, the issues of accreditation and supply. Their case allows one to venture the hypothesis that, between the 16th and the 18th centuries, the Jesuits were perhaps the only organisation able to handle every aspect of drug importation, from the extraction of materials and knowledge overseas to the design of recipes and the sale of products in Europe. Hence, the first section of the chapter presents the different sources documenting the Jesuit practice of pharmacy in order to locate it within the broader activities of the Society: education and mission. The second section shows how the Jesuits introduced into Europe new remedies from the Indies, demonstrating how this process of commodification was linked to the practice

---

3   L. Martín, *The Intellectual Conquest of Peru: The Jesuit College of San Pablo, 1568–1767* (New York: Fordham University Press, 1968); M. Feingold (ed.), *Jesuit Science and the Republic of Letters* (Cambridge, MA: Harvard University Press, 2003) and *The New Science and Jesuit Science: Seventeenth Century Perspectives* (Dordrecht: Kluwer, 2003); J.W. O'Malley et al. (eds.), *The Jesuits II: Cultures, Sciences and the Arts, 1540–1773* (Toronto: University of Toronto Press, 2006); A. Prieto, *Missionary Scientists: Jesuit Science in Spanish South America, 1570–1810* (Nashville, TN: Vanderbilt University Press, 2011); F.C. Hsia, *Sojourners in a Strange Land: Jesuits and Their Scientific Missions in Late Imperial China* (Chicago, IL: University of Chicago Press, 2011); M. de Asúa, *Science in the Vanished Arcadia: Knowledge of Nature in the Jesuit Missions of Paraguay and Río de La Plata* (Leiden: Brill, 2014).

4   Anagnostou, 'Jesuit missionaries in Spanish America'.

of gift-giving[5] and to the existence of a network through which remedies moved along with texts, images and curiosities. Finally, the last section is devoted to the most important novelty introduced by the Jesuits into European medicine: Peruvian, or Jesuit, bark.

The textual legacy of Jesuit pharmacopoeia: a brief overview

The intervention of the Jesuits in the history of remedies can be observed, at a first glance, in the texts they wrote and sometimes published about them. However, even focusing on the Jesuits' American provinces it is impossible to provide an exhaustive account of their writings on the subject. On the one hand, this is because the discontinuous presence of the Jesuits implies the dispersion of their texts, which was intensified with the expulsions and the dissolution of the order which occurred in the 18th century. On the other hand, it is because their studies concerned with remedies could appear in different kinds of works – missionary reports; letters; natural histories; pharmacopoeia treatises or recipes – written by men who could themselves have different profiles. Rather than providing a complete overview, the following section examines this geographical, thematic and sociological complexity, distinguishing three configurations – natural history in urban colleges; natural history in the missions; and recipes in the Jesuit pharmacies – before showing how they were articulated.

Natural history in the colleges

A decisive aspect of the apostolic project of the Jesuits, one on which Ignatius of Loyola strongly insisted, was the education of Catholic elites. From 1548 onward, in Europe and in some urban centres of America, the Jesuits founded a growing number of colleges, for which they tried to recruit the best-trained professors. The Constitutions of the order, however, explicitly excluded them from teaching medicine,[6] so their inquiries in the field were, in the majority of cases, undertaken by people who had studied it previously or on their own. As a consequence, their intellectual activities associated with remedies were linked above all to natural history.

Although it did not properly belong to the *Ratio studiorum*, natural history was an attractive field for the most learned members of the Society.[7] The Humanist study of Greek and Latin was indeed linked to the translation of ancient texts, in which Pliny occupied a prominent place. Furthermore, especially in relation to non-European worlds, the study of nature was a way to celebrate the glory of God. This dimension was particularly effective, for

5   Z. Biedermann, A. Gerritsen and G. Riello (eds.), *Global Gifts: The Material Culture of Diplomacy in Early Modern Eurasia* (Cambridge: Cambridge University Press, 2018).

6   This prohibition was sometimes ignored, e.g., in Bogotá.

7   L. Millones-Figueroa and D. Ledezma (eds.), *El saber de los Jesuitas. Historias naturales y el Nuevo Mundo* (Frankfurt and Madrid: Vervuert-Iberoamericana, 2005).

instance, in the works of Juan Eusebio Nieremberg. He was a professor at the Colegio Imperial in Madrid, where he devoted a part of his teachings to natural history and published countless books in which the Jesuits' Aristotelian conceptions tended to be replaced by a neo-Platonic approach to nature. In the belief that the knowledge of the secrets of animals or plants was a way to know God, Nieremberg was keenly interested in the new lands of America and consulted many manuscript sources coming from across the Atlantic when writing his *Historia Naturae, Maxima Peregrinea* (Antwerp: Plantin, 1635). He used, for instance, Francisco Hernández's works on Mexican medicinal plants, but his primary intention was less to produce a discourse on their medical virtues than to use them as a tool for edification.

The Jesuit's interest in natural history was also rooted in the passion for curiosities which many shared with their contemporaries. From that point of view, Nieremberg could be compared to another famous protagonist of what has been called 'the baroque science' of the 17th century: Athanasius Kircher. Professor of natural philosophy at the Collegio Romano, he devoted several of his books to natural history, especially *Mundus Subterraneus* (1664) and *Arca Noë* (1675). However, his celebrity was due above all to his cabinet of curiosities, for which he gathered objects from all over the world, especially from China. Following P. Findlen, several scholars have shown how important the spectacle of these curiosities was for the Society of Jesus.[8] Thanks to their relations with missionaries, who sent them letters and brought them objects, the Jesuits were able to address the appeal of the exotic among the European aristocracy and the republic of letters. The manufactured items or the 'marvellous' remedies the Jesuits exhibited in European towns allowed them to recruit to their colleges promising students who, sometimes, also wanted to become missionaries. This can be seen in the *Litterae Indipetae*, the letters sent to the general by the Jesuits who wanted to be dispatched to the Indies. Even if it seems quite far from the history of *materia medica*, this passion for curiosities was, as we shall see, closely linked to the Jesuit commerce in drugs.

Natural history in the missions

Practical writings

Nevertheless, the attitude of the Jesuits towards curiosity was more complex than the case of Nieremberg or Kircher suggested. The missionary activities

8   P. Findlen, *Possessing Nature: Museums, Collecting, and Scientific Culture in Early Modern Italy* (Berkeley, CA: University of California Press, 1994); P. Findlen (ed.), *Athanasius Kircher: The Last Man Who Knew Everything* (New York and Abingdon: Routledge, 2004); M.J. Gorman, 'From "The Eyes of All" to "Useful Quarries in Philosophy and Good Literature": consuming Jesuit science, 1600–1665', in J.W. O'Malley et al. (eds), *The Jesuits II: Cultures, Sciences and the Arts, 1540–1773* (Toronto: University of Toronto Press, 2006), pp. 170–89; M.A. Waddell, *Jesuit Science and the End of Nature's Secrets* (Farnham: Ashgate, 2016).

of the Society also led its members to face more practical aspects of natural and moral history. Observation, collection, description and classification of plants, animals or minerals were crucial for the beginning and subsequent development of every mission. This was true for the Jesuits as well as for other religious orders, such as the Franciscans in 16th-century New Spain. With regard to the Jesuits, the most important work in the field was without doubt José de Acosta's *Historia natural y moral de las Indias* (1590). Mainly, but not exclusively, devoted to Spanish America, this book expresses an interest in curiosities. It was grounded in Acosta's experience in Peru, but also in the information he gathered on his way back to Europe, especially in Mexico, where he consulted manuscript chronicles devoted to the history of indigenous people and contacted Alonso Sánchez, a missionary in the Philippines, and other Jesuits coming back from Macau. The fourth book of the *Historia natural y moral* contains several chapters devoted to plants and remedies – such as cacao, coca, liquidambar or the bezoar stone – in which Acosta probably combined his experience with the descriptions written, for example, by the Sevillian physician Nicolás Monardes.

Acosta's book influenced many writings, both inside and outside the Society of Jesus, and led several missionaries to inquire further about the medical traditions they observed in the field. One of the best examples of such inquiries is Michal Piotr Boym's *Flora Sinensis* (1656), devoted to China, but other books with a broader scope, like Alonso de Ovalle's *Historica relación del Reino de Chile* (Rome, 1648), contained a study of local pharmacopoeias. The *Historia del Nuevo Mundo*, written around 1653 by Bernabé Cobo, for example, was originally intended to be a comprehensive history of the New World, covering both Peru and New Spain. The remaining parts of this work illustrate Cobo's interest in medicinal plants. The Jesuit described no fewer than 350 vegetables and was amongst the first to describe the Peruvian bark tree or the San Pedro cactus (*huachuma*). Many of the descriptions contain information about the properties of the plants and, sometimes, succinct indications about dosage. His inquiry not only required detailed observation or classification, but also the acquisition of knowledge from the Indians.

Converting medicines

Like Acosta or Ovalle and later works such as José Sánchez Labrador's *El Paraguay natural* (c.1771), Cobo's history is primarily grounded in his work as a missionary. In the most remote regions the ability to appropriate local pharmacopoeia was essential for the survival of the missionaries, who could not rely on any stable supply of medicines. That is why, as early as the last decades of the 16th century, missionaries, and especially the Jesuits, were the first to learn the properties of remedies still unknown in Europe. In Brazil, for instance, father José de Anchieta (1534–97), a missionary who wrote the first Guaraní grammar, learnt the properties of ipecacuanha, a root used to treat diarrhoea, and informed the general of the Jesuits in a letter on the 'natural things' of the Brazil. A few years later, the missionary Pedro Cardim mentioned the same plant in his *Tratados*.[9]

Besides the necessity of survival, the quest for local remedies was also part of the other great apostolic goal pursued by the Jesuits: evangelisation. If, for both Catholics and Protestants, conversion was itself considered a medicine for healing the souls of pagans, the cure of souls was always narrowly linked to the cure of bodies.[10] However, the role played by medicine in evangelisation varied, depending on the local context and strategies. Meanwhile, in the early modern Asiatic world the medical action of missionaries was used mainly as a diplomatic tool for making alliances with elites at courts. The situation differed radically in Spanish America, where Catholic missionaries aimed to convert everybody, so healing was required for everybody. This strategy of conversion-through-medicine had two sides. First, as expressed by the German Jesuit Juan de Esteyneffer in 18th-century New Spain, healing sick people 'opens the doors of their souls'.[11] This principle, directly derived from Christ's experience, implied improving the life of the Indians in order to demonstrate the goodness of Christianity. In his *carta anua* of New Granada province (1622–23),[12] for example, Florián de Ayerbe insisted on medical assistance being given by missionaries in order to relieve the 'pagans' from diverse diseases, especially the pox.[13] This led the religious orders to introduce European remedies, but because of difficulties of supply and the necessity to adapt to local habits they were forced to use local remedies. In Cáceres or San Jerónimo del Monte, for instance, the Jesuits learned from local populations to use balsams, Campeche, dragon blood or *anime*.[14]

The other benefit expected from medical assistance to 'pagans' was the possibility of challenging the power of indigenous 'priests'. Missionaries knew the latter were also 'healers': if they wanted to replace the indigenous priests as mediators with the spiritual world, they had to replace them as therapists and to know how to use local plants. Health, therefore, was an important field in the fight against 'idolatry'. As a matter of fact, the missionaries leading the extirpation of indigenous practices could incidentally learn the properties of useful plants. This confession by a woman healer in 17th-century Peru illustrates the process quite well:

9   F. Cardim, *Tratados da terra e gente do Brasil* (Rio de Janeiro: Leite, 1925), pp. 73–4.

10   I.G. Županov, 'Conversion, illness and possession: Catholic missionary healing in early modern south Asia', in C. Guenzi and I.G. Županov (eds.), *Divins remèdes. Médecine et religion en Asie du Sud* (Paris: EHESS, 2008), pp. 263–300.

11   'A los muy RR. PP. missioneros', Juan de Esteyneffer, *Florilegio medicinal de todas las enfermedades* (Madrid: Alonso Balvas, 1729).

12   Real Academia de la Historia, Madrid (hereafter RAH), 9/3702, no. 21.

13   RAH, 9/3702, fol. 258r.

14   RAH, 9/3702, fol. 271r–v.

With which herbs does she heal?

She said that coca is good for acequias ...

Asking her with which remedy she cures scrofula, diarrhoea.[15]

As A. Prieto has shown, much of the medicinal information contained in the writings of Alonso de Ovalle probably derived from such rites of confession; and the same could be said about the works of Acosta or Cobo.[16]

The information gathered in the missions could thus have different fates: some might appear in treatises on natural history; some in treatises on 'idolatry'; some were simply lost. The various ways in which local knowledge was processed included trials aimed not only at checking the properties of the remedies, but also at defining efficient and safe dosages, which were recorded in more practical texts like recipes, collections of recipes or pharmacopoeia.

Jesuit recipes and pharmacies

The writing of such texts, however, was not limited to missionary contexts. In Europe as well as America and other continents many Jesuits wrote about the practical use of remedies. The majority of them were brothers working as an 'apothecary' or 'nurse' in the pharmacies of the Society. Encouraged by the Constitutions of the Jesuit order, assistance to the sick was indeed an important aspect of everyday life in Jesuit settlements. Baldassare Torres, a former physician, founded the first pharmacy of the order in Rome in the middle of the 1550s. Subsequently, countless colleges equipped themselves with an apothecary shop, the original purpose of which was to take care of the Jesuits, with the distribution of remedies outside a college being limited to charitable donations. Quite rapidly, however, the Jesuits began to take part in the medical marketplace. If, in the colleges established close to missionary fringes, the main role of the pharmacy remained to supply the priests, elsewhere the Jesuit apothecaries rapidly took part in the medical marketplace of several cities, in Europe as well as in America.

The Jesuit in charge of the pharmacy had to master the basics of Galenic pharmacopoeia and to know how to use texts such as recipe books or medical treatises. The medicinal products described in such texts might be grown in the garden of the college, if there was one, or be bought by the *mayordomo*. According to library catalogues and account books, Jesuit apothecaries were open to new medical ideas and used the most recent pharmacopoeias

---

15 Archivo Arzobispal de Lima, Idolatrías, V/8, fols. 10v, 21r, 27v; reproduced in A. Sánchez, *Amancebados, hechiceros y rebeldes (Chancay, siglo XVII)* (Cuzco: Centro de Estudios Regionales Andinos Bartolomé de Las Casas, 1991), esp. p. XXXV.

16 Prieto, *Missionary Scientists*, p. 58; S. Boumediene, *La colonisation du savoir. Une histoire des plantes médicinales du 'Nouveau Monde' (1492–1750)* (Vaulx-en-Velin: Les éditions des mondes à faire, 2016), pp. 365–6.

written in Europe.[17] More generally, in Spanish America the Jesuit practice of pharmacy changed notably when the king granted the right to participate in the New World to non-Spanish Jesuits. Several brothers and fathers from the Germanic lands and Central Europe compiled important texts on what they called 'missionary medicine'. In 1712 Juan de Esteyneffer published his *Materia medica misionera* in Mexico; meanwhile Pablo Clain was publishing his *Remedios fáciles para diferentes enfermedades* in Manila. At the end of the 18th century, father Sigismund Aperger engaged himself in a very similar enterprise, though his work is still known only indirectly.

This remark requires further comment. First, many practical texts written by the Jesuits on pharmacopoeia were never printed. This is the case for at least two *Materia médica missionera* written in Paraguay at the beginning of the 18th century, one in Spanish by Pedro Montenegro and one in Guarani and Spanish by Marcos Villodas. However, it was also the case with countless recipes used inside the pharmacies. If some of these recipes were actually printed as instruction leaflet accompanying the remedies sold by the Jesuits, the majority of them circulated in manuscript form. The Real Academia de la Historia, for example, holds several recipes written or received by the Jesuits of the Colegio Imperial in Madrid and containing Choch bark; San Ignatius bean; a *contrahierba* from New Spain; Peruvian balsam; and a bean of the Darzel.[18] In the Portuguese world, Jesuit recipes were compiled in a work entitled *Coleção de várias receitas e segredos particulares das principais boticas da nossa companhia de Portugal, da Índia, de Macau e do Brasil* which has yet to be published.[19]

This leads to another comment, this time on circulation. Until the end of the 17th century it was almost essential for missionaries who wanted to be published to send their texts to Europe and even to take them there in person. Acosta published his work in Spain; Ovalle in Rome; but Cobo, who remained in Peru, was unable to do so. Later, Esteyneffer and Clain managed to publish their work, but first in Mexico and Manila, whereas the pharmacopoeias written in Paraguay did not cross the threshold of any printing house before the 19th century.

The example of pharmacy perfectly shows the complex interplay between the circulation of texts, the circulation of people and the circulation of things. Nieremberg and Kircher's work relied on the arrival in Europe of texts, plants and objects; and their texts contributed to persuading young people to become missionaries: circulation was both a means and a goal of the apostolic project of the Society and of the personal ambitions of its members. Conversely, the natural history written by Acosta contributed to raising the interest in

17   L. Martín, 'La biblioteca del Colegio de San Pablo (1568–1767), antecedente de la Biblioteca Nacional', *Fenix*, 21 (1971): 29–30.

18   RAH, 9/3426, no. 2; RAH, 9/3631; RAH, 9/3671, no. 65; RAH, 9/3823.

19   Archivum Romanum Societatis Iesu, Rome (hereafter ARSI), Opera Nostrorum 17.

American plants and the diffusion in Europe of recipes developed in the New World, thereby contributing to the creation of new supply chains. This explains the role the Jesuits played in the introduction of new remedies into Europe.

A Jesuit network expanding across the world

The strength of the Jesuits, compared with other religious orders, was not only their ability to gather information in their missions: behind all the texts mentioned above there was, indeed, a true art of circulation. S. Harris, amongst others, has shown how the Jesuits' mobility furthered the development of their 'scientific' activities.[20] In fact, this mobility also fostered their participation in commercial activities. In order to create what Arnauld calls 'a very big traffic' the Jesuits used the regular trade routes, but also organised a system of exchange quite similar to that existing in other religious orders. This network happened to be useful for communication both inside and outside the order.

An order of communication

Since the foundation of the company, the Jesuits had developed a network of communication in order to inform the upper echelons of the order about the progress of Christianisation and to ease coordination between its different houses. The official correspondence, held by the superiors of the missions, the rectors of the colleges, the provincials and the general, included several documents: missionary reports (*cartas annuas*); catalogues; accounts; and necrologies. The Jesuits also exchanged more informal letters, such as Rafael Pereyra's correspondence, now held by the Real Academia de la Historia in Madrid. In touch with Jesuits from all over Europe, this Sevillian father informed himself about diplomatic and military events, sent letters to America[21] and sent novelties from the Indies to his correspondents.[22] In a letter addressed to Gaspard Barzée on 12 February 1554, Ignatius Loyola already insisted on the importance of such communication:

> [S]ome important people who, in this city [Rome], read with great
> edification the letters from the Indies, ordinarily desire or ask quite often
> that we write something on the cosmography of the countries where ours
> go, for instance, on the length of the day during winter and summer,
> if a shadow moves from the right or from the left, if there were other

20 S. Harris, 'Long-distance corporations, big sciences, and the geography of knowledge', *Configurations*, 6 (1998): 269–304; 'Jesuit scientific activity in the overseas missions, 1540–1773', *Isis*, 96 (2005): 71–79; 'Mapping Jesuit science: the role of travel in the geography of knowledge', in J.W. O'Malley et al. (eds.), *The Jesuits II: Cultures, Sciences and the Arts, 1540–1773* (Toronto: University of Toronto Press, 2006), pp. 212–40.

21 See, e.g., RAH, 9/3687, fol. 158r–v; RAH, 9/3788, fol. 381r.

22 See, e.g., the letters written by Juan de Lugo to Rafael Pereyra on 13 Jan. 1635, 19 Feb. 1635 and 26 May 1636 (RAH, 9/3686, fols. 225r–v, 263r–v; RAH, 9/3684, fols. 353r–v).

extraordinary appearances, animals or unknown or rare plants, and give information about them. [23]

Within the Spanish territories, two Jesuits played key roles in these transmissions: the *procuradores* or procurators of the Indies.[24] Established at the end of the 1560s and at the beginning of the 1570s by General Borja, they were supposed to represent the company vis-à-vis the institutions responsible for the administration of the Indies. One *procurador* operated in Seville before the Casa de la Contratación, where he organised the reception, registration and departure of missionaries and where he sought to secure finance for the missions. Another *procurador* of the Indies worked in Madrid before the Council of the Indies, where he negotiated the foundation of new missions, visas for missionaries and fiscal exemptions from the crown. Everything coming from the Indies theoretically came through the hands of these two procurators.

Besides them, the circulation of objects among the Jesuits relied on the journeys of another kind of procurators, the ones representing their province during the general congregations of the order. Organised every six years in Rome, or after the death of the general in order to replace him, these meetings gathered together Jesuits from all over the world. These procurators took advantage of their trip to hire new missionaries but also to bring letters and objects to Europe. Thanks to their position, they could check the transactions at every stage of the process. By doing so, they could limit the costs and risks linked to commercial transactions: nobody could open their letters; nobody could steal part of the cargo. The Jesuits in Europe, even the most prominent, appreciated the security this provided. In 1636, for instance, General Vitelleschi suggested to the provincial Toledo that he might send him Nieremberg's work through a *procurador*: 'I cannot determine who has to send here the history of Father Juan Eusebio [Nieremberg]; it is easy to avoid the two inconveniences of cost and insecurity, remitting it to the procurador if nobody else from the company can bring it before'.[25] Outside the company, this benefit of security was also appreciated by institutions such as the Inquisition or the Council of the Indies,[26] or by powerful families needing to transfer letters or money.[27] In other words, this system of exchange contributed to defining the Jesuits as

23 Ignatius de Loyola, *Écrits* (Paris: Desclée de Brouwer, 1991), p. 873.

24 F. Zubillaga, 'El procurador de las Indias Occidentales', *Archivum Historicum Societatis Iesu*, 22 (1953): 367–417; A. Galán García, *El 'oficio de Indias' de Sevilla y la organización económica y misional de la compañía de Jesús: 1566–1767* (Seville: Fundación Fondo de Cultura de Sevilla, 1995); J.G. Martínez-Serna, 'Procurators and the making of Jesuits' Atlantic network', in B. Baylin and P. Denault (eds.), *Soundings in Atlantic History: Latent Structures and Intellectual Currents, 1500–1830* (Cambridge, MA: Harvard University Press, 2009), pp. 181–209.

25 RAH, 9/7259, no fol.

26 Archivo Histórico Nacional de España, Madrid (hereafter AHNE), Inquisición, leg. 5345 exp. 2, doc. 1.

27 Archivo General de la Nación de Perú, Lima (hereafter AGNP), Jesuitas, PR 1/14, doc. 710, fols. 41r, 70r; Caja 16, 734, fol. 6; Caja fols. 8, 492, 502.

particularly reliable suppliers. In some cases they were the only people able to make available certain objects, from *naturalia* to *artificialia* and texts. This gave European Jesuits a privileged access to the things from the Indies, but the members of the company also knew how to earn profits, sharing this privilege with non-Jesuits.

Internal affairs

Situated at the core of both the apparatus of the Spanish monarchy and the apparatus of the papacy, the Jesuit network was able to link the appropriation of things and knowledge in the Indies with their distribution in Europe and vice-versa.[28] The *procuradores* were the key to such a system since they directly created the link between the worlds. Their journey enabled European Jesuits to admire unseen artistic production;[29] to consult rare, if not forbidden, books and manuscripts, such as descriptions of Amerindian rites;[30] and to receive new drugs and curiosities. In 1578, for example, in the wings of the first general congregation involving the province of New Spain, its *procurador* Pedro Diaz brought 'balsams, bezoar stones, singular roots and other medicinal things'[31] to his co-religionists in Europe. During the following decades the procurators coming from Peru continually brought with them bezoar stones.[32] A letter written on 29 January 1636 by Juan de Lugo, then professor at the Collegio Romano, sheds light on the kind of economy in which such gifts were given. Coming from Spain, Lugo was asked by the apothecary of the Collegio Romano to find him *tacamahaca*, an American resin. In order to do so, Lugo suggested to his correspondent that the procurator might undertake this task:

> A lay brother in this Collegio, whose pharmacy is, according to the
> pope, the best in the world ... asked me insistently to make somebody
> bring him some tacamahaca. If a procurador came to the congregation,
> Your Reverence will do me the favour of asking him to endeavour to
> undertake this task, because this brother will pay him the whole cost, or
> any commodity from Rome of any kind because he will know better than
> anyone how to find it.[33]

Juan de Lugo repeated the request several times,[34] which indicates that the apothecary of the Collegio Romano desperately wanted the resin. He was ready

28 On the distribution of European – often manufactured – items in America by the *procuradores* on their way back, see L.E. Alcalá, '"De compras por Europa": procuradores jesuitas y cultura material en Nueva España', *Goya*, 318 (2007): 141–58.

29 Boumediene, *La colonisation du savoir*, p. 205.

30 RAH, 9/3692, fol. 670r.

31 F.J. Alegre, *Historia de la Compañia de Jesús en Nueva España* (México: J. M. de Lara, 1841), p. 125.

32 AGNP, Jesuitas, PR 1/14, doc. 710, fol. 70r; Caja 16, 734, fol. 1v.

33 RAH, 9/3686, fol. 224r.

34 RAH, 9/3684, fols. 353r–v, 367r.

to pay its price, with money or in exchange for commodities in Rome. In short, the *procuradores* were at the heart of a gift-exchange economy. Bezoar stones from Peru, for instance, could be swopped for news from Europe.[35] Even without reciprocity, gift-giving was an important concern for missionaries in America because it allowed them to pay their respects to important Jesuits in Europe, such as the procurators of the Indies or Juan de Lugo, who would later become a cardinal.

If, across the Atlantic, the procurators' gifts were often related to patronage, in Europe more horizontal, even friendly, exchanges could link the members of the company. From Seville, for instance, Rafael Pereyra sent tobacco and chocolate to many of his correspondents.[36] From Cadiz or Granada other Jesuits supplied the colleges of Madrid and Rome, especially Diego de Carrión, Juan del Marmol, Martín de Fonseca and Joan de Pina.[37] They invented recipes which mixed cocoa with *achiote*, cinnamon, chili, vanilla, amber or musk.[38] Such recipes reached the whole of Europe. At the beginning of the 1630s, for example, Father Benito de Sojo exchanged curiosities and remedies with the 'apothecary of the Collegio Romano' and Jesuits from Warsaw or Vienna. Soto also wanted to send them chocolate but, not knowing how to prepare it, he asked Juan de Camacho, procurator of the Indies, to specify the amount for him.[39]

The gift, the commodity and the sample

Outside the Jesuit network this 'traffic' played an important role in the wealth and political destiny of the company. In order to understand this point, it is necessary to say a few words about the canonical legislation relating to 'commerce'. In a narrow sense, commerce consists of selling at a higher price what has been previously bought at a lower price; and the clergy were not meant to be involved in it. However, they could bypass this prohibition by obtaining exceptional exemptions or by adapting their mercantile practices: reselling a previously purchased commodity at the same price, or selling what had not been bought but produced were ways to practise commerce in a broader sense without practising it in a narrow sense. In 1635, for example, the Jesuit Francisco Vilches received from Juan Viera in Jaén some chocolate which he promised to 'convert into money' in order to pay legal expenses.[40]

35 AHNE, Jesuitas, leg. 121, doc. 16.

36 See, e.g., RAH, 9/3672, fol. 144; RAH, 9/3687, fols 53r, 56v, 76r–v, 725r–v; RAH, 9/3788, fol. 460v; RAH, 9/7274.

37 RAH, 9/7333.

38 Juan del Marmol to Martín de Fonseca, Seville, 18 Feb. 1641: RAH, 9/7260.

39 RAH, 9/3687, fol. 38r–v.

40 RAH, 9/3800, fols 110r, 306r, 307r–v.

However, the interest of exotic remedies did not reside only in their commercial value. In Seville the *procurador* of the Indies continuously received boxes of curiosities, chocolate or drugs which could be offered to influential people.[41] This generosity allowed the Jesuits to secure the friendship of a prince, bishop or counsellor of the Indies or a member of the Curia Romana, who, when the time came, could pay them back, granting them a fiscal exemption or a visa for missionaries.[42] In 1602 to 1603, for instance, the founder and provincial of the Paraguay mission, Diego de Torres Bollo, went to Europe in order to assist as *procurador* of Peru at the general congregation. Between Madrid, Milan and Rome, he distributed numerous American curiosities and was able to recruit 40 missionaries. In Milan, where he hired Agostino Salumbrino,[43] Torres Bollo gave some of the most precious items he had collected in America to the powerful Cardinal Carlo Borromeo, as has been shown by A. Maldavsky.[44] Later, in 1646, it was also in Milan that Alonso de Ovalle, as procurator of Chile, gave precious American objects to another prominent member of the urban elite, Manfredo Settala, who included them in his famous collection.[45] Several of these objects were painted in an illustrated catalogue,[46] which showed, for example, a 'priest mantle from the Indie',[47] several balsams, especially the one from Tolú,[48] bezoar stones[49] and various curiosities from Peru, Chile, Paraguay or the Philippines.

In this system whereby the Jesuit influence in Europe reinforced the Jesuit influence outside Europe and vice versa, the commerce of drugs – in a broad sense – played a significant role. Nevertheless, this does not mean that all the religious orders were important protagonists of the medical marketplace; and even the power of the Jesuits was quite limited if we take into account the quantities in which they were dealing. However, their activity should not be judged in terms of quantity for it was above all a qualitative one. The system of exchange they developed allowed them to access and spread not only manuscripts and books, but also products like drugs, curiosities, tobacco or chocolate. The boundary between these kinds of object is less clear than

41 M. Norton, *Sacred Gifts, Profane Pleasures: A History of Tobacco and Chocolate in the Atlantic World* (Ithaca, NY: Cornell University Press, 2008), p. 146.

42 RAH, 9/3788, fol. 160r.

43 G. Piras, *Martin de Funes S.I. (1560–1611) e gli inizi delle riduzioni dei gesuiti nel Paraguay* (Rome: Edizioni di Storia e letteratura, 1998), pp. 41–102.

44 A. Maldavsky, 'Société urbaine et désir de mission: les ressorts de la mobilité missionnaire jésuite à Milan au début du XVIIe siècle', *Revue d'histoire moderne et contemporaine*, 56 (2009): 28.

45 Biblioteca Estense di Modena (hereafter BEM), MS. gamma.h.1.21 = cam.0338, fol. 73.

46 BEM, MS. gamma.h.1.21 = cam.0338; BEM, MS. gamma.h.1.22 = cam.0339.

47 BEM, MS. gamma.h.1.21 = cam.0338, fol. 5.

48 BEM, MS. gamma.h.1.21 = cam.0338, fol. 47.

49 BEM, MS. gamma.h.1.21 = cam.0338, fol. 72.

one might assume. Important products for consumption such as tobacco or chocolate, as well as many remedies sold on the market, originally came to Europe as curiosities.

The link the Jesuits created between the Indies and Europe enabled the circulation of highly esteemed products, together with unknown items whose value depended primarily on their novelty rather than on a corroborated process of accreditation. At this stage, the item was an image, an object of spectacle which could be accredited – or not – as a medicine, as a food, as a curiosity. An item took the form of a sample and was simultaneously a gift and a means of experimentation. The sample could be useful for demonstrating the properties of a remedy which it was still impossible to supply, or for testing.

Between curiosity and drug, gift and merchandise, the sample was at the very core of the process of commodification and illustrates how the Jesuits took part in it. The distribution of gifts and curiosities was followed by the development of recipes and the selling of drugs. This pattern can be identified, with many variations, in the introduction of several drugs by the Jesuits: from the Philippines they brought a bean used against fever which they called the San Ignatius bean.[50] From the Americas they brought other febrifuges,[51] especially Peruvian balsam[52] and a remedy to be studied more closely below: Peruvian or Jesuit bark.

A Jesuit bark floating between the worlds

Extracted from a tree originally growing in the Andes, now called the cinchona tree, Peruvian bark came to Europe around 1640 as a remedy against what was then called 'intermittent fevers'. Several studies have been devoted to the history of this reddish, bitter bark, stressing its importance in the fight against malaria and the way it simultaneously transformed medical thought, the government of health, the colonisation of Spanish America and, later, of Africa or Asia.[53] A major feature of its early history is the involvement of the Jesuits

---

50 'Memoria ò Receta de la virtud y modo de applicarse que tiene la Pepita llamada Catbalogan ò de S. Ignacio', in RAH, 9/3631, n° 45. See also 'Virtudes medicinales de una frutilla, ó pepita, que se cría mui comun en las Islas Philipinas, que llaman los Naturales en su idioma Ygasul, y los Españoles les pepitas de Sn. Ignacio', in RAH, 9/3823, no fol.

51 'Methodo de usar los polvos de la corteza del Arbol llamado Choch', in RAH, 9/3426, n°2. See also RAH, 9/3671, n°65.

52 RAH, 9/3693, fols 527r–28r.

53 A. Steele, *Flores para el rey. La expedición de Ruiz y Pavón y la Flora del Perú, 1777–1788* (Barcelona: Ediciones del Serbal, 1982); A. Moya, *El árbol de la vida. esplendor y muerte en los Andes ecuatorianos. El auge de la cascarilla en el siglo XVIII* (Quito: FLACSO, 1990); S. Jarcho, *Quinine's Predecessor: Francesco Torti and the Early History of Cinchona* (Baltimore, MD: Johns Hopkins University Press, 1993); M. Crawford, *The Andean Wonder Drug: Cinchona Bark and Imperial Science in the Spanish Atlantic, 1630–1800* (Pittsburgh, PA: University of Pittsburgh Press, 2016); Boumediene, *La colonisation du savoir.*

in its introduction into Europe. If they were not the only ones to bring it in, their involvement was so important that the remedy was rapidly called 'Jesuit bark' or 'Jesuit powder'.

Two accounts of a mysterious 'discovery'

Soon after its first use in Europe around 1640, two accounts spread about the discovery of the remedy. In spite of their differences they both attribute a decisive role to the Jesuits. The first one, by far the more famous, appeared in a treatise on Peruvian bark entitled *Anastasis Corticis peruvianae*. Its author, the Genoese physician Sebastiano Bado, claimed that in Lima the countess of Chinchón, the wife of the viceroy of Peru, was suffering intermittent fever: 'The rumour of her illness was rapidly known by the whole city, [and] spread over the region into Loja'. This small town, located in the heart of Andean valleys, was surrounded by mountains bearing the Peruvian bark tree. According to Bado, the Indians of this region for centuries used the bark for curing their fevers but hid its properties from the Spaniards. Finally, the latter were able to learn how to use it; and when Loja's *corregidor* heard about the countess's disease he quickly informed the viceroy that he was in possession of a 'secret remedy'. He brought the bark to the court, where he performed a public cure: '[S]urprising everybody, she was cured like by a miracle'. Then, according to Bado, the Jesuits transported the bark from Lima to Europe, especially to Rome. Their devotion to the healthcare of the citizens of Rome was recorded on the walls of Santo Spirito hospital in a painting which depicts Juan de Lugo, who became a cardinal, dispensing the bark in powder form to the poor.

Several scholars have expressed frank doubts about this account, which they consider a 'myth'. There is, indeed, no evidence for the 'miraculous' recovery in any contemporary sources. Moreover, the anti-malarial use of the bark would have implied that the Indians in the surroundings of Loja had precise knowledge about intermittent fevers, whereas this disease probably appeared on the continent after the Spanish conquest. The best answer to these difficulties can be found in the second account devoted to the early history of the bark. It is a letter written in 1663 by a Spanish physician, Gaspar Caldera de Heredia, as an answer to a query he received about the bark from a Roman physician named Girolamo Bardi. In this letter Heredia gives precise information about the way the Jesuits 'discovered' the effects of the bark:

> At the end of this land, in this province of Quito, close to the Amazon river, some Indians come spontaneously or for a salary are taken to a gold mine … In the paths the Indians are forced to cross a river … so that the majority of them, when arriving on the other bank, frozen and shaking, complain pitifully. And immediately, for their relief, they take the bark of a tree they know, powdered, ground and dissolved in hot water. At this time they remark that the cold and the shivering calm down and they can go on

> the road. Seeing this, the fathers of the Society of Jesus ... asked them from
> which tree they took the bark.[54]

By analogical reasoning, the missionaries converted bark used for calming
down shivering to a remedy against fever. This case of serendipity could explain
why the Spaniards found a remedy against intermittent fever in a region where
this disease was recent: as a matter of fact, cinchona bark does contain some
alkaloids which affect the muscles in such a way that shivering stops.[55]

The differences between the two accounts are quite clear: in the first, related
by an Italian physician, the Indians refused to give an ancestral remedy to
the Spaniards until the countess fell ill; in the second, written by a Spanish
physician, the Indians gave the remedy with pleasure. Alongside these political
divergences, the two accounts also allocate a different role to the Jesuits: in
the first, they distributed the remedy in Europe; in the second, they learnt its
properties in America. What is particularly relevant in this second account is
that this 'discovery' is linked to the exploitation of gold.

The bitter gold of Mainas

In order to understand how the Jesuits appropriated the bark and why they
set up an international trade in it, this section will discuss the Jesuit missions
of Mainas during the 1680s and1690s. A set of fascinating documents held in
Rome, Alcalá de Henares, Seville, Lima and Santiago de Chile show that the
superior of the mission at this time, the Neapolitan Francesco Viva (1656–
1702),[56] designed a project to accomplish the spiritual and military conquest of
the region.[57] In this part of Ecuador the Spaniards found important reserves of
gold during the 16th century, but they had to face the resistance of indigenous
communities they called the 'Jívaros'. The memory of the bloody assault the
latter launched against the town of Logroño was still strong in the 1680s and,
according to Viva, the province lacked well-trained missionaries and soldiers.[58]
His plan was to make a five- to six-year trip to Spain and Italy in order to set up
an expedition and to hire new missionaries. [59] Not being a Creole, Viva knew
he would find it difficult to be elected procurator, so he decided to finance the
trip himself. In 1685 he sent 30 Indians to sow no fewer than 50,000 vanilla

54 J.M. López Piñero and F. Calero (eds.), *De pulvere febrifugo Occidentalis Indiae (1663) de
    Gaspar Caldera de Heredia y la introducción de la quina en Europa* (Valencia: CSIC, 1992), pp.
    34–5.

55 F. Guerra, 'El descubrimiento de la quina', *Medicina e historia*, 69 (1977): 7–25.

56 Archivo General de Indias, Seville, Contratación 5549, n.1, R.3.

57 This project was sent several times between 1686 and 1690. See ARSI, N.R.-Q. 15, doc. 26,
    fol. 134r; Archivo de la Provincia Jesuítica de Quito (hereafter APQ), VI/540a.

58 APQ, VI/524; APQ, VI/526; APQ, VI/529; AHPTSJ, D 107.

59 APQ, VI/520; APQ, VI/523; ARSI, N.R.-Q. 15, doc. 31.

plants. [60] Four years later the plants were almost ready to be harvested, but not in sufficient quantities. Nevertheless, it was in 1689 that Francesco Viva urged his superiors to let him go to Europe. Indeed, that very year a 'commodity ended up in his hands thanks to a divine disposition'. [61] This commodity was the cinchona bark.

Francesco Viva knew the remedy very well. He had already sent the product to his brother Domenico, also a Jesuit, in Naples. In 1689 he engaged a new servant who 'grew up harvesting the bark' in the mountains around Loja and knew where to find intact forests. For several reasons trade in the bark was so high in 1688 that no merchant had a good-quality product. Thanks to finding a new forest, Viva was alone on the market and could extract 50 mule-loads of 'cascarilla'. Being in contact with Jesuits from Panama and Naples, he knew the bark would bring higher profits when it was sold in Europe. According to his calculations, the 50 mule-loads would be worth 50,000 *patacones*. Compared to that, the cost of the journey, 2,000 *pesos*, was almost derisory.

In other words, the bark was enough to fund the entire journey in Europe and to buy the gifts Viva had to offer to counsellors and members of the pontifical administration:[62]

> I sent a few Indians into the mountains gathering around 50 *mulas* of bark, which are worth 20,000 *libras* in Italy and with your permission I shall reduce it into *zurrones* well commodified in Paita … and my brother in Naples will convert it into *plata* … With all these dispositions … I shall have that necessary for recruiting 40 missionaries and negotiating two boats and *cédulas*, and I will have bark, cacao, vanilla and other things to offer to the counsellors … And for the negotiation in Madrid with His Majesty and the council I have another disposition: you have to know that close to our Missions are the Jibaros, a nation rebelling for 90 years in those mountains where there is so much gold.[63]

Ultimately, Francesco Viva failed to reach Europe: his mission was fulfilled by another Jesuit sent to Rome as the procurator of the Quito province. Nevertheless, he kept selling the bark and invested the money in buying silver, but also gunpowder and weapons. For the Jesuits in Ecuador, the political utility of the bark trade was thus to finance a war against 'Jívaros' in order to acquire the gold in the region. However, even before 1690 the Jesuits offered the bark as a gift in Madrid or Rome in order to gain support for their political plans in Ecuador.

---

60 ARSI, N.R.-Q. 15, doc. 31, fol. 230v.
61 ARSI, N.R.-Q. 15, doc. 31, fol. 231r.
62 APQ, VI/526; ARSI, N.R.-Q. 15, doc. 31, fol. 231v.
63 ARSI, N.R.-Q. 15, doc. 31.

From gifts to commodities

The first Jesuits who brought the product to Europe were the *procuradores* coming to the general congregations in Rome. The physician to viceroy Chinchón, Juan de Vega, had probably taken the bark to Seville around 1642. That very year father Bartolomé Tafur (1589–1665) was elected procurator of Peru for the congregation held in 1645; and several later sources credit him with the introduction of the remedy to Rome.[64] As a matter of fact, he seems to have been close to Cardinal de Lugo.[65] In any case, the remedy was taken to Seville by brother Pedro Salinas, who accompanied the procurator of Chile, Alonso de Ovalle, to the same congregation of 1645.[66] Two years later brother Paolo Pucciarini, then apothecary of the Collegio Romano, began to use it and saw Lugo distributing it in Rome.[67]

The *procuradores* of South American provinces were thus the first to bring back the bark, either to the procurators of the Indies in Seville or to members of the Collegio Romano. Several other examples confirm this. In 1666 father Felipe de Paz and brother Alonso Gómez took with them gold, silver, clothes, books, vanilla, cocoa, chocolate, bezoar stones and 'two boxes and one half a packet of bark against quartan fevers'.[68] Significantly, the first box was supposed to be sold and the second one was offered to Gaspar de Cugía, the former superior of the Mainas mission.[69] At the end of the 17th century this system was still in use, as is evident from the inventory of the numerous items carried by the procurators Juan de Goyochoa and Nicolás Miraval in 1699: 'About the bezoar stones, the six *zurrones* of cascarilla or quinaquina, for a weight of 900 pounds, Copacabana, *pebeteros* [incense burners], vicuña wool, he says that he gave everything in Rome, Madrid and these regions, and especially amongst us, for not being things as appreciated there as here and because they were specifically destined to be offered'.[70] The interest of such a system was to avoid the cost and insecurity of commercial mediations. As a matter of fact, in one of the rare cases of the Jesuits deciding to send the bark without entrusting it to the procurators it ended up being seized by English corsairs: 'Your Reverence

64 See, e.g., C.M. de La Condamine, 'Sur l'arbre Du Quinquina', *Histoire de l'academie royale des sciences* (1738): 226–43 (234); Real Jardín Botánico de Madrid, Mutis IV, leg. 11, 51, fol. 2v.

65 Tafur wrote the preface of Lugo's *Privilegios*. On Tafur see also E. Torres Saldamando, *Los antiguos Jesuitas del Perú. Biografías y apuntes para su historia* (Lima: Liberal, 1882), p. 294.

66 Archivo Nacional de Chile, Santiago de Chile, Jesuitas 438, fol. 244r.

67 Bado, *Anastasis Corticis Peruuiae*, pp. 240–41.

68 AGNP, Jesuitas, PR 1/1, doc. 69; AGNP, Jesuitas, PR 1/6, doc. 440; AGNP, Jesuitas, PR 1/8, doc. 508; see also AGNP, Jesuitas, PR 1/6, doc. 442, fol. 2r for the quotation.

69 AGNP, Jesuitas, PR 1/11, doc. 586, fol. 22v. See also AGNP, Jesuitas, PR 1/6, doc. 442, fol. 22v; ANC, Jesuitas 438, 324v–325v.

70 AGNP, Jesuitas, PR 1/3, doc. 334, fol. 5v. On these gifts, see also AGNP, Jesuitas, PR 1/10, fols. 526, 528–30. These different objects were declared to the Roman customs in 1699: Universidad Montoya, Lima, Colección Vargas Ugarte 39, fols 30r–30v.

would meet the father Harnando Lavayen and would know the disgrace he suffered from the English who robbed him of a box of more than 120 pounds of Loja's bark, because the brother [Francisco] Odiago told me it was the best gift to send to your reverence, the thing being so esteemed there for quartan and tercian fevers'.[71]

If the bark sent by procurators was mainly devoted to gifts, either inside or outside the Jesuit network, it was commercialised in the apothecary shops of the Company. It is impossible to know when the bark was brought from Loja or Mainas to Lima and to confirm Caldera de Heredia's statement that the apothecary Gabriel de España was the one who introduced the remedy into the Colegio San Pablo of Lima.[72] It is certain, however, that the apothecaries of this college, the Milanese Agostino Salumbrino[73] and his successor Claude Chicaut,[74] distributed the bark to other places in America between 1630 and 1660. At the same time, the bark was already commercialised in Europe. In Seville, for instance, the remedy seems to have been commercialised as soon as 1643 according to the account of Cinco Llagas hospital, but the involvement of the Jesuits here is not certain. Regarding the case of Madrid, Rafael Pereyra's letters offer an astounding illustration of the way the Jesuits commodified the new product. In Madrid in 1648 father Sebastián González discovered the effect of the 'barks for the quartans' which Pereyra had sent him.[75] A few weeks later he asked him to send him more: 'I've been asked for more bark for curing quartan fevers; the last you sent me produced such a good effect that the fever disappeared in the people who asked for it and at the same time they brought it to me they were killing me for them. I beg you to send me more, if it does not annoy you, since those who have asked for them are people to whom I am indebted'.[76] This extract perfectly demonstrates how demand creates a commodity: the Jesuit is 'in debt' to the people who have to ask him for the bark. In other words, a supply chain is created. González probably began to give the bark as a sample and, since many people wanted it, he had to make

71 Antonio Bastidas to Pedro Bermudo, procurator of the Indies in Madrid (Popayán, 16 Nov. 1690, in RAH, 9/7263, no fol.).

72 López Piñero and Calero, *De pulvere febrifugo Occidentalis Indiae*, p. 35. See also L.A. Newson, *Making Medicines in Early Colonial Lima, Peru* (Leiden: Brill, 2017), esp. p. 168.

73 Agostino Salumbrini had his name hispanised to Salumbrino. See Maldavsky, 'Société urbaine', 28. During the 1630s, he was the apothecary of San Pablo (ARSI, Peru 4, fols 99v, 151v, 199r, 270r, 330v, 358v; ARSI, Peru 15, fols. 188v–89r, 196v–98v; ARSI, Vitae 24, fol. 267v). He distributed his preparations throughout Lima and many places in Peru: (AGNP, Jesuitas, caja 119/2019, fols. 24r, 55r, 136r–38v; AGNP, Jesuitas, PR 1/16, doc. 738).

74 Martín, *Intellectual Conquest of Peru*, p. 104. On Chicaut, see ARSI, Peru 4, fols. 332r, 360r, 453r; ARSI, Peru 5, fol. 11r. In 1656 Chicaut exchanged with Bartolomé Barrera, a brother of Arequipa's college, several remedies, especially 'dos costales de corteza'. See ANC, Jesuitas 438, fol. 228r–v; AHNE, Jesuitas, leg. 121, doc. 21.

75 RAH, 9/3702, fol. 989r.

76 RAH, 9/3702, fol. 994r.

them pay. In later letters he insists on knowing in which pharmacies the bark was being sold and what its name and price were.[77]

Jesuit Charity: commodification and experimentation

Commodification was a qualitative process which occurred in several places. Besides Madrid, the same process took place in other towns, such as Lima or Rome.[78] It is, therefore, quite difficult, if not impossible, to retrace the trajectory of the bark, since it did not necessarily follow the path from Loja to Lima, Lima to Panama, Panama to Seville, Seville to Madrid, Madrid to Rome. According, for instance, to an anonymous document held by the Real Academia de la Historia in Madrid, the bark was known by the Jesuits of Spain, and especially those in Valladolid, after it was known in Rome: 'This wood or bark of the Tree of the Indies which was brought from Rome, brother Marin says that it is established that in the Indies where it grows it calms quartan [fevers] among all native peoples and from there they spread it to many regions for that purpose. And being brought to Rome by some among us, it removed fever from many people and they brought it to Spain and particularly to Valladolid'.[79] Commodification was a fragmentary, non-linear process: the accreditation granted to the effects of the bark in a place had to be replicated elsewhere. The samples sent by the Jesuits inside and outside the company were supposed to be tested. From 1647 onwards the apothecary of the Collegio Romano, Pietro Pucciarini, sent the bark to a number of hospitals in Rome, Genoa, Florence or other Tuscan cities. In order to help with the trials, he also sent a recipe which, according to him, produced the same good effects everywhere.[80] The original version of this text was known in later sources as the *Schedula Romana*. It was transcribed in several books published in Delft or Copenhagen; and a printed version, written in Italian, is available at the Bibliothèque Nationale de France.[81] According to this document a dosage of two drachms of bark had to be powdered and infused in strong wine. The patient had then to be purged and made to take the remedy before the first onset. As a matter of fact, the anonymous document held in Madrid contains a Spanish translation of this dosage and includes brief additions concerning the diet the patient had to follow: 'It would be good to have the sick man bled and purged, or at least to clean his stomach three days before the cold, with

---

77   RAH, 9/3702, fol. 996r.

78   ARSI, F.G. 1143, 'Conti e Ricevute Della Spetieria, Casa Professa', fol. 180v.

79   RAH, 9/7263, no fol.

80   S. Bado, *Anastasis corticis* Peruviae, *seu chinae chinae defensio* (Genova: Pietro Giovanni Calenzani, 1663), pp. 240–41.

81   Bibliothèque nationale de France, TE151-1220, 'Modo Di Adoprare La Corteccia Chiamata Della Febre'. See also Bibliothèque d'étude et du patrimoine de Toulouse, MS. 763, 'Recueil de recettes pharmaceutiques et culinaires', fols. 71–72.

two ounces of sugar honey and some swigs of Anise water'.[82] These comments about how to prepare not the remedy but the patient for medication are more significant than they appear. This slight addition suggests that the Jesuits truly tested both the sample and the recipe they received and found a way to improve them. They were not the only ones to do so. The printed echoes of the *Schedula romana*, reproduced in books published in Delft or Copenhagen, contain similar changes.

The utility of the sample was not only to demonstrate the virtues of a product, but also to verify them and, possibly, to increase them. This sheds an interesting light on Lugo's generous distribution of the bark in Rome: the cardinal was also testing the remedy on poor people. As a pilgrims' hospital, the Santo Spirito was the perfect site for such experiments.[83] The bark was not the only new remedy tested in hospitals: guaiacum wood in the 16th century and ipecacuanha at the end of the 17th century followed a similar pattern. Moreover, the involvement of charitable institutions, especially religious hospitals, in such experiments is an old tradition. The singularity of the Jesuits, especially when the case of Peruvian bark is considered, is that they conducted experiments at almost every stage of the process: before Lugo in Rome the Jesuits around Loja, who used analogical reasoning, did nothing other than test the bark on Indian bodies. If the Jesuits were masters of gathering and circulating things, their role in the history of pharmacy, and more generally in the history of science and commerce, shows they were also masters of experimentation.

Conclusion

The involvement of the Jesuits in the history of early modern pharmacopoeia illustrates perfectly how they applied their apostolic project to their temporal activities. The organisation of the Society and the circulation of its members around the world also illustrate the role played by the religious orders in the reconfiguration of science, commerce and politics at that time. Several scholars have underlined the importance of the 'go-betweens' in the construction of a 'global intelligence'.[84] The end of the 18th century is often seen as the climax of this 'brokered-world', possibly because states began truly to handle the techniques of intermediation. However, before them the religious orders had already mastered such techniques, especially the Jesuits, which could explain the series of expulsions they had to face from the 1750s onwards. Perhaps

---

82 RAH, 9/7263, no fol.

83 P. de Angelis, *La spezieria dell'Arcispedale di Santo Spirito in Saxia e la lotta contro la malaria, nel III centenario della nascita di Giovanni Maria Lancisi, anno 1654–1954* (Rome: Coluzza, 1954), pp. 101–3.

84 S. Schaffer et al. (eds), *The Brokered World: Go-betweens and Global Intelligence, 1770–1820* (Sagamore Beach, MA: Science History Publications, 2009).

the most important legacy of the Jesuit presence lies here: in the necessity to replace them, to appropriate their methods.[85]

Bibliography

Manuscript sources

Archivo Arzobispal de Lima, Idolatrías, V/8

Archivo General de Indias, Seville, Contratación 5549, n.1, R.3.

Archivo General de la Nación de Perú (AGNP), Lima, Jesuitas, PR 1/14, doc. 710

    AGNP, Jesuitas, PR 1/1, doc. 69

    AGNP, Jesuitas, PR 1/3, doc. 334

    AGNP, Jesuitas, PR 1/6, docs. 440, 442

    AGNP, Jesuitas, PR 1/8, doc. 508

    AGNP, Jesuitas, PR 1/10

    AGNP, Jesuitas, PR 1/11, doc. 586

Archivo Histórico Nacional de España (AHNE), Madrid, Inquisición, leg. 5345 exp. 2, doc. 1

AHNE, Jesuitas, leg. 121, doc. 16.

Archivo Histórico de la Provincia de Toledo de la Compañía de Iesus (AHPTSJ) de Alcala de Henares (AHPTSJ) D 107

Archivo Nacional de Chile, Santiago de Chile, Jesuitas 438

Archivo de la Provincia Jesuítica de Quito (APQ)

    APQ, VI/523

    APQ, VI/524

    APQ, VI/526

    APQ, VI/529

    APQ, VI/520

Archivo del Real Jardín Botánico de Madrid, Mutis IV, leg. 11, 51

---

85 On 30 April 1724, e.g., John Burnet, a physician of the South Sea Company in Cartagena de Indias, wrote to Hans Sloane that he 'should be well satisfied if the Royal Society and the South Sea Company would send [him] a Missionary (as the Jesuits do) from this to Portobello, Panama, Lima, Potosi and home by way of Buenos Aires making what observations [he was] capable of, both with respect to trade and commerce, and with respect to the Natural History of these countries' (British Library, MS. Sloane 4047, fol. 330v). Later, during the Geodic Expedition around Quito, the French geometer Charles-Marie de La Condamine expressed his interest and even his admiration for the observation made by the Jesuits of Mainas on astronomy or local pharmacopoeia (Muséum d'histoire naturelle, Paris, MS. 1671, MS. 1626, fols. 25–31 and chapter 12 in this volume).

Archivum Romanum Societatis Iesu (ARSI), Rome

ARSI, N.R.-Q. 15, doc. 26

ARSI, N.R.-Q. 15, doc. 31

Biblioteca Estense di Modena, MS. gamma.h.1.21, gamma.h.1.22

Bibliothèque d'étude et du patrimoine de Toulouse, MS. 763, 'Recueil de recettes pharmaceutiques et culinaires'

Real Academia de la Historia, Madrid (RAH)

RAH, 9/3426, no. 2

RAH, 9/3631

RAH, 9/3671, no. 65

RAH, 9/3672

RAH, 9/3684

RAH, 9/3686

RAH, 9/3687

RAH, 9/3702, no. 21

RAH, 9/3788

RAH, 9/3800

RAH, 9/3823

RAH, 9/7259

RAH, 9/7263

RAH, 9/7274

RAH, 9/7333

Universidad Montoya, Lima, Colección Vargas Ugarte 39

Printed sources

Alcalá, L.E. (2007) '"De compras por Europa": procuradores jesuitas y cultura material en Nueva España', *Goya*, 318: 141–58.

Alegre, F.J. (1841) *Historia de la Compañia de Jesus en Nueva España* (México: J. M. de Lara).

Anagnostou, S. (2002) 'Jesuit missionaries in Spanish America and the transfer of medical-pharmaceutical knowledge', *Archives internationales d'histoire des Sciences*, 52: 176–97.

— (2005) 'Jesuits in Spanish America: contributions to the exploration of the American materia medica', *Pharmacy in History*, 47: 3–17.

Angelis, P. de (1954) *La spezieria dell'Arcispedale di Santo Spirito in Saxia e la lotta contro la malaria, nel III centenario della nascita di Giovanni Maria Lancisi, anno 1654–1954* (Rome: Coluzza).

Arnauld, A. (1669) *La morale pratique des Jésuites présentée en plusieurs histoires arrivées dans toutes les parties du Monde* (Cologne: Gervinus Quentel).

Asúa, M. de (2014) *Science in the Vanished Arcadia: Knowledge of Nature in the Jesuit Missions of Paraguay and Río de La Plata* (Leiden: Brill).

Bado, S. (1663) *Anastasis corticis* Peruviae, *seu chinae chinae defensio* (Genova: Pietro Giovanni Calenzani).

Biedermann, Z, A. Gerritsen and G. Riello (eds.) (2018) *Global Gifts: The Material Culture of Diplomacy in Early Modern Eurasia* (Cambridge: Cambridge University Press).

Boumediene, S. (2016) *La colonisation du savoir. Une histoire des plantes médicinales 'Nouveau Monde' (1492–1750)* (Vaulx-en-Velin: Les éditions des mondes à faire).

Cardim, F. (1925) *Tratados da terra e gente do Brasil* (Rio de Janeiro: Leite).

Crawford, M. (2016) *The Andean Wonder Drug: Cinchona Bark and Imperial Science in the Spanish Atlantic, 1630–1800* (Pittsburgh, PA: University of Pittsburgh Press).

Esteyneffer, J. de (1729) *Florilegio medicinal de todas las enfermedades* (Madrid: Alonso Balvas).

Feingold, M. (ed.) (2003) *Jesuit Science and the Republic of Letters* (Cambridge, MA: Harvard University Press).

— (2003) *The New Science and Jesuit Science: Seventeenth Century Perspectives* (Dordrecht: Kluwer).

Findlen, P. (1994) *Possessing Nature: Museums, Collecting, and Scientific Culture in Early Modern Italy* (Berkeley, CA: University of California Press).

— (ed.) (2004) *Athanasius Kircher: The Last Man Who Knew Everything* (New York and Abingdon: Routledge).

Galán García, A. (1995) *El 'oficio de Indias' de Sevilla y la organización económica y misional de la compañia de Jesús: 1566–1767* (Seville: Fundación Fondo de cultura de Sevilla)

Gorman, M.J. (2006) 'From "The Eyes of All" to "Useful Quarries in Philosophy and Good Literature": consuming Jesuit science, 1600–1665', in J.W. O'Malley, S.J., G.A. Bailey, S.J. Harris and T.F. Kennedy (eds.), *The Jesuits II: Cultures, Sciences and the Arts, 1540–1773* (Toronto: University of Toronto Press), pp. 170–89.

Guerra, F. (1977) 'El descubrimiento de la quina', *Medicina e historia*, 69: 7–25.

Harris, S. (1998) 'Long-distance corporations, big sciences, and the geography of knowledge', *Configurations*, 6: 269–304.

— (2005) 'Jesuit scientific activity in the overseas missions, 1540–1773', *Isis*, 96: 71–9

— (2006) 'Mapping Jesuit science: the role of travel in the geography of knowledge', in J.W. O'Malley, S.J., G.A. Bailey, S.J. Harris and T.F. Kennedy (eds.), *The Jesuits II: Cultures, Sciences and the Arts, 1540–1773* (Toronto: University of Toronto Press), pp. 212–40.

Hsia, F.C. (2011) *Sojourners in a Strange Land: Jesuits and Their Scientific Missions in Late Imperial China* (Chicago, IL: University of Chicago Press).

Jarcho, S. (1993) *Quinine's Predecessor: Francesco Torti and the Early History of Cinchona* (Baltimore, MD: Johns Hopkins University Press).

La Condamine, C. M. de (1738) 'Sur l'arbre du quinquina', *Histoire de l'academie royale des sciences*: 226–43.

López Piñero, J.M. and F. Calero (eds.) (1992) *De pulvere febrifugo Occidentalis Indiae (1663) de Gaspar Caldera de Heredia y la introducción de la quina en Europa* (Valencia: CSIC).

Loyola, I. de, Letter to Gaspard Barzée, 12 February 1554, in *Écrits*, trans. and ed. by M. Giuliani (Paris: Desclée de Brouwer, 1991), p. 873.

Maldavsky, A. (2009) 'Société urbaine et désir de mission: les ressorts de la mobilité missionnaire jésuite à Milan au début du XVIIe siècle', *Revue d'histoire moderne et contemporaine*, 56 (3): 7–32.

Martín, L. (1968) *The Intellectual Conquest of Peru: The Jesuit College of San Pablo, 1568–1767* (New York: Fordham University Press).

— (1971) 'La biblioteca del Colegio de San Pablo (1568–1767), antecedente de la Biblioteca Nacional', *Fenix*, 21: 25–36.

Martínez-Serna, J.G. (2009) 'Procurators and the making of Jesuits' Atlantic network', in B. Baylin and P. Denault (eds.), *Soundings in Atlantic History: Latent Structures and Intellectual Currents, 1500–1830* (Cambridge, MA: Harvard University Press), pp. 181–209.

Millones-Figueroa, L. and D. Ledezma (eds.) (2005) *El saber de los Jesuitas. Historias naturales y el Nuevo Mundo* (Frankfurt and Madrid: Vervuert-Iberoamericana).

Moya, A. (1990) *El árbol de la vida, esplendor y muerte en los Andes ecuatorianos. El auge de la cascarilla en el siglo XVIII* (Quito: FLACSO).

Newson, L.A. (2017) *Making Medicines in Early Colonial Lima, Peru: Apothecaries, Science and Society* (Leiden: Brill).

Norton, M. (2008) *Sacred Gifts, Profane Pleasures: A History of Tobacco and Chocolate in the Atlantic World* (Ithaca, NY: Cornell University Press).

O'Malley J.W., S.J., G.A. Bailey, S.J. Harris and T.F. Kennedy (eds.) (2006) *The Jesuits II: Cultures, Sciences and the Arts, 1540–1773* (Toronto: University of Toronto Press).

Piras, G. (1998) *Martin de Funes S.I. (1560–1611) e gli inizi delle riduzioni dei gesuiti nel Paraguay* (Rome: Edizioni di Storia e letteratura).

Prieto, A. (2011) *Missionary Scientists: Jesuit Science in Spanish South America, 1570–1810* (Nashville, TN: Vanderbilt University Press).

Río Huas, M.E. del and M. Revuelta González (1995) 'Enfermerías y boticas en las casas de la Compañía en Madrid siglos XVI–XIX', *Archivum Historicum Societatis Iesu*, 64: 39–81.

Sánchez, A. (1991) *Amancebados, hechiceros y rebeldes (Chancay, siglo XVII)* (Cuzco: Centro de Estudios Regionales Andinos Bartolomé de Las Casas).

Schaffer, S., L. Roberts, K. Raj and J. Delbourgo (eds.) (2009) *The Brokered World: Go-Betweens and Global Intelligence, 1770–1820* (Sagamore Beach, MA: Science History Publications).

Steele, A. (1982) *Flores para el rey. La expedición de Ruiz y Pavón y la Flora del Perú, 1777–1788* (Barcelona: Serbal).

Torres Saldamando, E.(1882) *Los antiguos Jesuitas del Perú. Biografías y apuntes para su historia* (Lima: Liberal).

Valverde, J.L. (1978) *Presencia de la Compañía de Jesús en el desarrollo de la farmacia* (Granada: Universidad de Granada).

Waddell, M.A. (2016) *Jesuit Science and the End of Nature's Secrets* (Farnham: Ashgate).

Zubillaga, F. (1953) 'El procurador de las Indias Occidentales', *Archivum Historicum Societatis Iesu*, 22: 367–417.

Županov, I.G. (2008) 'Conversion, illness and possession. Catholic missionary healing in early modern south Asia', in C. Guenzi and I.G. Županov (eds.), *Divins remèdes. Médecine et religion en Asie du Sud* (Paris: EHESS), pp. 263–300.

12. The Jesuits and the exact sciences in Argentina*

Eduardo L. Ortiz

The Order of Jesus had a worldwide influence on the circulation of knowledge on the exact sciences and astronomy; in the late 1600s their scientific activities reached some territories in South America. This chapter discusses, more particularly, the Jesuits' early role in the transmission of some aspects of these sciences to Argentina. It first discusses the work of the Jesuit astronomer Buenaventura Suárez Garay (1679–1750), whose activities required the construction of delicate optical instruments, persistent and precise observations and complex calculations leading to the compilation of detailed astronomical tables. In the 1740s and 1750s the results of Suárez's observations and his privileged geographical location managed to attract the attention of astronomers in leading European observatories. The chapter also shows how, from the early 17th century, the influence of the Jesuits was also felt in the world of advanced education, particularly through the establishment of a Collegium Maximum in Córdoba, where the transmission of the exact sciences was enhanced by the presence of qualified teachers and by a moderate use of European textbooks.

After the expulsion of the Jesuits in 1767 a group of Spanish officers trusted with the construction of the demarcation line between the colonial territories of the Spanish and Portuguese empires in America arrived in Buenos Aires with modern instruments and books, thereby helping to bridge the gap in the exact sciences left by the Jesuits. Their extended visit helped to transmit confidence

* I wish to thank personnel at the Archivo y Biblioteca de la Universidad de Córdoba, the Archivo Provincial de Córdoba, the library of Colegio del Salvador, the Archivo Historico Nacional and the Biblioteca Nacional, Buenos Aires for their kind help when I consulted these archives. I also wish to acknowledge R. P. Dr. Luis Felipe Alberca, director of the Observatorio del Ebro at the time of my visit, for giving me permission to access fully the observatory's library and archives; the observatory's librarian, María Genescà i Sitges, for her kind support and advice; and, finally, R. P. Dr. Josep Oriol Cardús i Almeda, astronomer at the Observatorio del Ebro for over 50 years and also a former director, for his friendly reception and for interesting conversations on the history of his institution. I also wish to thank Imperial College, London, for its support and the Royal Society, London, for a grant which allowed me to work at the Observatorio del Ebro, Catalonia, and in archives in Buenos Aires and Córdoba, Argentina. Finally, I wish to express my gratitude to Professor Linda Newson and to an anonymous referee for valuable comments on an earlier draft of this contribution.

E.L. Ortiz, 'The Jesuits and the exact sciences in Argentina', in L.A. Newson (ed.), *Cultural Worlds of the Jesuits in Colonial Latin America* (London: Institute of Latin American Studies, 2020), pp. 255–83. License: CC-BY-NC-ND 2.0.

in the use of modern, delicate measuring instruments to a small group of local enthusiasts. In addition, by the end of the century the university at Córdoba, run now by the Franciscan order, acquired an extensive collection of apparatus and demonstration equipment which aided a more effective teaching of physics. In the late 1830s, after the Jesuits were allowed to return to Argentina, they concentrated their energies on education, historically a main focus of their interests. After some earlier efforts, in 1870 a Jesuit school, the Colegio del Salvador, was established in Buenos Aires; it continued the work of an earlier Jesuit school founded in that city before expulsion, the Colegio de San Ignacio.

A significant portion of this chapter is devoted to the role played by the Jesuits in cosmic physics. By the end of the 19th century, following the encyclical *Aeterni Patris*, the Colegio del Salvador made efforts to raise its standard of teaching in the fields of modern science. To achieve this goal, it imported from Spain a Jesuit teacher, José Ubach, who had been trained in science at the new cosmic-physics Observatorio del Ebro (Observatori de l'Ebre), which had recently been created by the order in Catalonia. Besides teaching at the Colegio del Salvador, Ubach recognised the importance of the public understanding of science and contributed popular lectures on contemporary topics. As early as the start of the 1920s some former students of El Salvador began to be recognised as leading young Argentine scientists.

By the mid 1930s Argentina attempted to replicate the Observatorio del Ebro in Spain in creating a national institute for astronomy near Buenos Aires, the Observatorio de Física Cósmica de San Miguel. To lead this new institution the Argentine government invited a Jesuit, Ignacio Puig, who until then had been vice-director of the Observatorio del Ebro, thereby creating a link between the two institutions through the Jesuit Order. However, in the 1940s the appeal of cosmic physics began to fade as advances in nuclear physics gradually rendered its programme outdated. The order seems to have felt that these institutions had already completed their useful life. After some twenty years of gradual decline, the San Miguel observatory was finally transferred to a wider national institution. Some years later the formidable Observatorio del Ebro was itself incorporated into a larger educational institution, the new Jesuit Universitat Ramon Llull, also in Catalonia. Clearly, having incorporated and consolidated science education in its leading schools, the order could attend to new challenges and move on to other type of tasks.

The Jesuits and the introduction of the exact sciences in Argentina

Over an extended period, and in a series of studies, the Jesuit historian Guillermo Furlong (1889–1974) has discussed the role which members of the

Jesuit Order played in the transfer of science to Argentina.[1] Despite obvious limitations, these pioneering works, informed by documents from archives in Argentina and abroad, contain valuable references and insights into the impact of Jesuit scholars on the intellectual history of Argentina, particularly in the late colonial period and on the sciences. Furlong has rightly stressed the internationalism of the contingent sent by the Jesuits to teach the exact sciences in the southern territories of America, which included Italian and German scholars as well as Spanish and Portuguese.[2] This is particularly noteworthy for these sciences: as Baldini has shown, in the 17th and 18th centuries the teaching of mathematics and its applications was not as advanced in Jesuit schools in Spain or Portugal as it was then in Italy and the German lands.[3] Therefore, the presence in America of scholars from these last two regions has considerable significance.

Soon after their arrival in America some of these priests began to collect local scientific information and to establish channels of communication with leading Jesuit and other scientists in Europe. Others used their expertise in applied mathematics to help in topographical operations, large and small, and in the design and construction of churches, other buildings, ships and large industrial plants such as sugar-cane mills. A few of them attempted to investigate the cosmos from their new, southern location. Meanwhile, on the educational front the Jesuits opened a school in Tucumán, in central Argentina, in 1604 and a university college, a Collegium Maximum, in Córdoba a decade later, around 1613.[4] Within four years a school and a college had been

1   G. Furlong, 'El primer astrónomo argentino, Buenaventura Suárez', *Estudios*, 16 (1919): 102–17 and 172–85; *Glorias Santafesinas: Buenaventura Suárez, Francisco Javier Iturri, Cristóbal Altamirano*, Estudios Bibliográficos (Buenos Aires: Surgo, 1929); *Los Jesuitas y la cultura Rioplatense* (Montevideo: Urta y Curbelo, 1933); *Historia del Colegio del Salvador y de sus irradiaciones espirituales en la ciudad de Buenos Aires, 1617–1943*, 2 vols. (Buenos Aires: Colegio del Salvador, 1943); *Matemáticos argentinos durante la dominación Hispánica* (Buenos Aires: Huarpes, 1945); *Naturalistas argentinos durante la dominación hispánica* (Buenos Aires: Huarpes, 1948).

2   Furlong, *Matemáticos argentinos*, pp. 25–6.

3   U. Baldini, '*Legem impone subactis*'. *Studii su filosofia e scienza dei Gesuiti in Italia, 1540–1632* (Rome: Bulzoni, 1992); and 'The teaching of mathematics in the Jesuit colleges of Portugal, from 1640 to Pombal', in L. Saraiva and H. Leitão (eds.), *The Practice of Mathematics in Portugal* (Coimbra: Acta Universitates Conimbrigensis, 2004), pp. 293–466; J.A. Sánchez Pérez, 'La Matemática', in *Estudios sobre la ciencia española del siglo XVII* (Madrid: Asociación Nacional de Historiadores de la Ciencia Española, 2004), pp. 597–633; D. Goodman, 'Science and the clergy in the Spanish Enlightenment', *History of Science*, 21 (1983): 111–40; and 'The scientific revolution in Spain and Portugal', in R. Porter and M. Teuch (eds.), *The Scientific Revolution in National Context* (Cambridge: Cambridge University Press), pp. 158–77; C. Ziller Camenietzki, 'A Companhia de Jesus e a ciência na America portuguesa entre 1663 e 1759', in C.M. Silva da Silva (ed.), *Segundo Seminario de História da Matemática* (Vitoria: UFES, 1999), pp. 156–65.

4   On the Jesuits' teaching system, see P.F. Grendler, 'The culture of the Jesuit teacher 1548–1773', *Journal of Jesuit Studies*, 3 (2016): 17–41.

opened in Buenos Aires.[5] All these establishments would remain under Jesuit guidance until their expulsion in 1767. Through teaching at some of these establishments, the Jesuits facilitated the emergence of local students with an interest in science. Clearly, in a new world with a great diversity of unseen animals and plants, the natural sciences were, perhaps, the main attraction for these few scholars; their efforts in these fields have been researched by several authors, including Furlong himself.[6]

Quantitative science: Suárez and a culture of instruments and calculation

In much smaller numbers, studies in the exact sciences also began to emerge, at least from the late 1600s to early 1700s. They have a special interest today because of their association with the emergence of a quantitative culture which relied heavily on the use of scientific instruments rather the exclusive use of the syllogism and reason to uncover scientific truths, as taught by Aristotle in *Physica*.[7] In addition, the period which extends beyond the Jesuit expulsion and into the first years of Argentina's independence is a particularly interesting one in this respect, as it still falls under the intellectual influence of the last generation of scholars trained by the Jesuits, or by other orders.[8]

Among the Jesuits, at the turn of the 17th century into the 18th century, Buenaventura Suárez Garay (1679–1750)[9] is a figure who has attracted considerable attention. He was a young Jesuit, born in what is today Argentina, who became interested in astronomy and the exact sciences. Later he settled in the north of the Argentine/Paraguayan Mesopotamia region and there

5   The Colegio San Ignacio (or Colegio Grande), later Real Colegio de San Carlos and, finally, from 1863 the Colegio Nacional Buenos Aires.

6   Furlong, *Naturalistas argentinos*.

7   For details on the contemporary Jesuits' understanding of the science of physics see M. Hellyer, *Catholic Physics: Jesuit Natural Philosophy in Early Modern Germany* (Notre Dame, IN: University of Notre Dame Press, 2005), chapters 4–6.

8   The publication of a valuable collection of documents by P. de Angelis, *Colección de obras y documentos relativos a la historia antigua y moderna de las Provincias del Rio de la Plata, 1836*, vols. 4–7 (Buenos Aires: Imprenta del Estado, 1836–7) (which includes Diego de Alvear's diary: 'Relación geográfica e histórica de la Provincia de Misiones'), helped to understand, more accurately and from different angles, the Jesuits' scientific heritage. It was followed by a series of interesting works, such as J.M. Gutiérrez, *Origen y desarrollo de la enseñanza pública superior en Buenos Aires* (Buenos Aires: La Cultura Argentina, 1915); and J. Probst, 'La enseñanza durante la época colonial (1771–1810)', in 'La Educación en la República Argentina durante la época colonial', *Documentos para la Historia Argentina*, vol. 18 (Buenos Aires: Universidad, 1924); and, more recently by Furlong, *Matemáticos argentinos*.

9   Several other dates have been suggested; the date quoted here is that given in the recent, well-documented work by M. de Asúa, *Science in the Vanished Arcadia: Knowledge of Nature in the Jesuit of Paraguay and Río de la Plata* (Leiden: Brill, 2014). A different set of dates is given by other authors: A. de Backer and A. de Backer suggest 1678–1756 (*Bibliothèque de la Compagnie de Jésus*, vol. 12 (Paris: Picard, 1932), p. 1660).

undertook detailed astronomical observations and calculations. Later he used his data to produce astronomical tables which still attract the attention of historians and astronomers. Suárez was born in Santa Fe, on the banks of the Paraná river, and was educated at the Jesuits' Collegium Maximum in Córdoba, Argentina. In 1695 he entered the order and in 1706 was sent to work in the Guaraní missions of San Cosme and San Damián, which had been founded by the Jesuits around 1632.

For over 33 years Suárez recorded regular astronomical observations, but a striking fact about him is that in addition he actually made the instruments he used for his observations. This last, interesting fact was first communicated by Suárez himself in the introduction to his book *Lunario*, to be discussed briefly below. Since at that time it was extremely difficult to send delicate instruments from Europe to the depths of South America, it is not surprising that a qualified, entrepreneurial scientist would decide that the only practical solution was to build them himself. The case of astronomers making their own instruments is, of course, not unique. What is perhaps more extraordinary is that Suárez succeeded in doing so in these remote latitudes.

There was, however, some experience on which Suárez could, and surely did, rely. Due to isolation the missions' leaders generally had to adapt to shortages of manufactured goods from Europe by developing their own workshops and training some of the most gifted local people to work with wood and metals. Foundries established in the missions produced bells and some agricultural tools; later they were also capable of producing larger objects such as cannons and smaller ones such as nuts. In some Jesuit missions delicate pieces, such as sundials, clocks (including chiming clocks), organ tubes, violins and several other musical instruments, were also manufactured.

In the case of telescopes, as with other scientific equipment which Suárez built in the missions, there was a need for both a sturdy mount and delicate mechanical adjustment pieces, as well as lenses. The first two were not essentially different from some pieces mentioned above. As for the lenses, it is believed that Suárez and others before him had learned to make them using a locally abundant rock crystal, traditionally used by the Guaraní to create delicate artistic objects. The quality of the lenses available to Suárez may have been far from perfect; however, it must be remembered that the lenses used by Galileo (1564–1642) in his first telescope were far from perfect either: they contained small bubbles and had some problems with their transparency.

Suárez built more than one telescope; in *Lunario* he indicates that his various instruments had focal distances of between 2.20m and 6.60m. In addition, he built astronomic clocks and a few other delicate scientific instruments. In any case, Suárez's achievements suggest that they were based on collaboration with local residents of the mission. With the instruments which Suárez and his collaborators may have built, he made careful, regular observations of solar and lunar eclipses, as well as of the occultation and emergence of Jupiter's satellites.

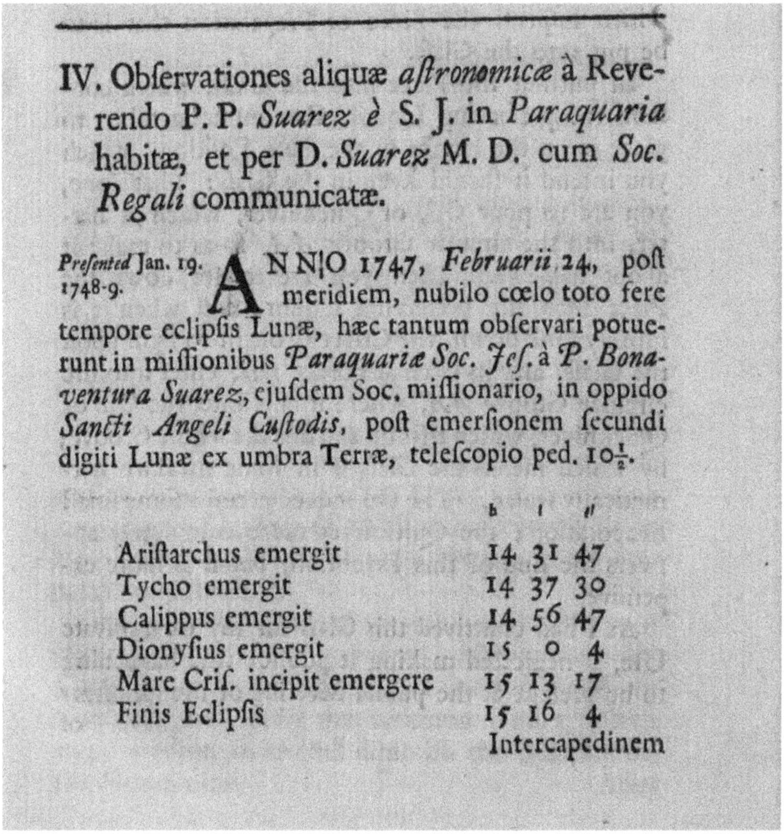

IV. Obfervationes aliquæ *aftronomicæ* à Reverendo P. P. *Suarez è* S. J. in *Paraquaria* habitæ, et per D. *Suarez* M. D. cum *Soc. Regali* communicatæ.

Prefented Jan. 19. ANNIO 1747, *Februarii* 24, poft 1748-9. meridiem, nubilo cœlo toto fere tempore eclipfis Lunæ, hæc tantum obfervari potuerunt in miffionibus *Paraquariæ Soc. Jef.* à *P. Bonaventura Suarez*, ejufdem Soc. miffionario, in oppido *Sancti Angeli Cuftodis*, poft emerfionem fecundi digiti Lunæ ex umbra Terræ, telefcopio ped. $10\frac{1}{2}$.

	h	'	''
Ariftarchus emergit	14	31	47
Tycho emergit	14	37	30
Calippus emergit	14	56	47
Dionyfius emergit	15	0	4
Mare Crif. incipit emergere	15	13	17
Finis Eclipfis	15	16	4
	Intercapedinem		

Figure 12.1. Astronomical observations by Buenaventura Suárez in Paraguay. (Source: Philosophical Transactions of the Royal Society, London, 46 (1750): 8).

The data he collected allowed him to fix the coordinates of his Jesuit mission, an achievement of some interest. In addition to his technical and observational achievements, Suárez tried to circulate the results of his regular observations among leading world experts. The latter may have been keen to acquire them, in view of the exceptional geographical position of the observations. Through a complex circuit of connections: commercial, naval and also scientific, which extended from the heart of the Jesuit missions to England, passing through intermediary scientists, some of the data Suárez collected reached London and was reported in the *Transactions of the Royal Society* in the late 1740s and early 1750s (fig. 12.1).[10]

10 P. Allen studied that international circuit, but without discussing Suárez's contacts with that Society (P. Allen, 'The Royal Society and Latin America as reflected in the *Philosophical Transactions*, 1665–1740', *Isis*, 37 (1947): 132–8). See also R. Stearns, *Science in the British Colonies of America* (Urbana, IL: University of Illinois Press, 1970).

Suárez was also the author of a *Lunario de un siglo*, which he first published some time before 1744, possibly in 1738–39;[11] it has since been reprinted several times and in different countries.[12] Essentially, a *Lunario* is a collection of *ephemerides*, or tables of astronomical data giving, at specific times, the position of one or several celestial bodies in the sky.[13] Suárez's tables were compiled on the basis of his own personal observations and on calculations he made based on this data. That information helped him to date special religious festivities, such as Easter, lunar phases and other celestial events, as well as solar and lunar eclipses visible from 'the Missions of the Company of Jesus in the Province of Paraguay adjusted to the local times and meridian passing through the town of San Cosme and San Damián'. He gave times for the beginning, maximum and end of some of these astronomical events, a task which required fairly complex calculations.

Suárez's book, of a little over two hundred pages, covers a long period of time: from January 1740 to December 1841. In addition, it had an appendix in which instructions were given on how to extend these tables up to 1903 (fig. 12.2). Furlong was one of the first historians to point to the need for a detailed scientific analysis of Suárez's work. In an attempt to give a more solid foundation to the article he published in 1919,[14] he requested the opinion of the Jesuit astronomer José Ubach, then a science teacher at the Colegio del Salvador, Buenos Aires, on the scientific value of Suárez's work. After discussing that work Ubach indicated that parts of it 'require of its author a deep, and then very unusual knowledge of Astronomy'.[15]

Suárez's work has continued to attract the attention of historians of science, such as Asúa,[16] and also of astronomers, such as Tiganelli,[17] Galindo and Rodríguez-Mesa.[18] Tiganelli discusses *Lunario* in some detail, while Galindo and Rodríguez-Mesa compared Suárez's original data with a computer database containing a large amount of observed and calculated international astronomical

11 B. Suárez, *Lunario de un siglo* (Barcelona: Pablo Nadal, *c.*1740) is one of the earliest available editions.

12 A new edition appeared in 1744, which was reprinted in 1748 and 1752; probably the last edition was published by the Universidad Nacional de Misiones, Posadas, in 2009.

13 Suárez wrote 'todos los movimientos medios de las conjunciones, oposiciones y cuartos de la Luna con el Sol, y las anomalías entrambos luminares' (Furlong, 'Buenaventura Suárez', 112).

14 Furlong, 'Buenaventura Suárez'.

15 Furlong, 'Buenaventura Suárez', 116.

16 M. de Asúa, *La ciencia de mayo. La cultura científica en el Río de la Plata, 1800–1820* (Buenos Aires: Fondo de Cultura Económica, 2010); and 'The publication of the astronomical observations of Buenaventura Suárez SJ, (1679–1750) in European Scientific Journals', *Journal of Astronomical History and Heritage*, 7 (2) (2004): 81–84; and Asúa, *Science in the Vanished Arcadia*.

17 H. Tiganelli, 'El primer lunario criollo', *Saber y Tiempo*, 17 (2004): 5–60.

18 S. Galindo and M.A. Rodríguez-Meza, 'Buenaventura Suárez, S.J. (1679–1750): telescope maker, Jovian satellites observer', *Revista Mexicana de Física*, 57 (2011): 121–33 and 144–51.

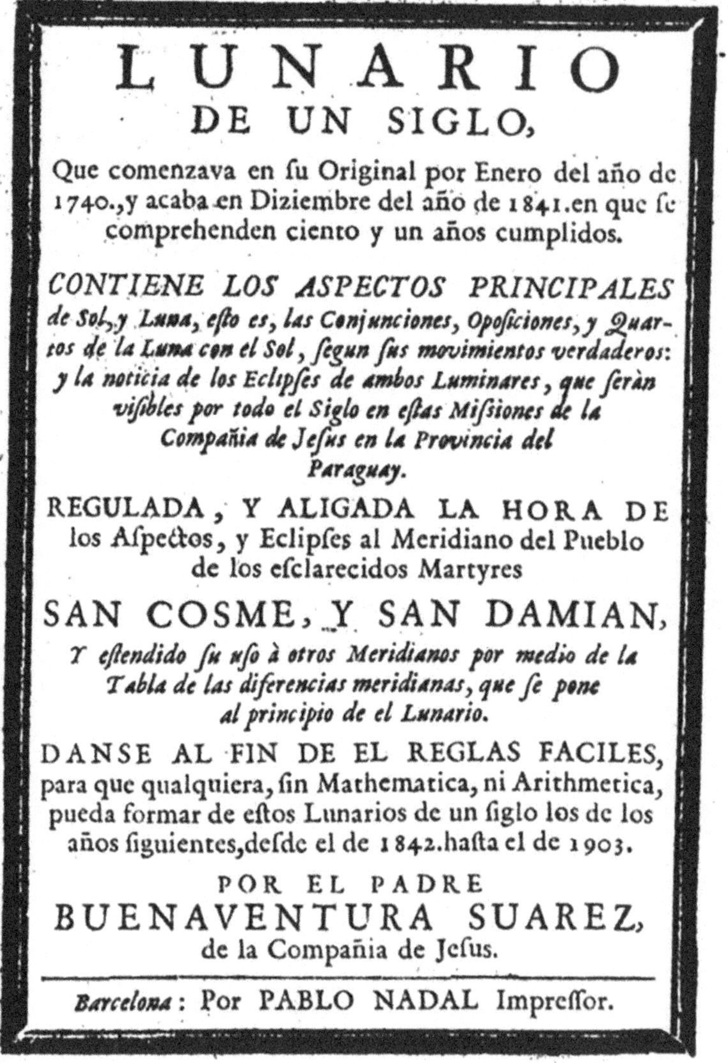

LUNARIO
DE UN SIGLO,

Que comenzava en fu Original por Enero del año de 1740., y acaba en Diziembre del año de 1841. en que fe comprehenden ciento y un años cumplidos.

CONTIENE LOS ASPECTOS PRINCIPALES de Sol, y Luna, efto es, las Conjunciones, Opoficiones, y Quartos de la Luna con el Sol, fegun fus movimientos verdaderos: y la noticia de los Eclipfes de ambos Luminares, que ferán vifibles por todo el Siglo en eftas Mifsiones de la Compañia de Jefus en la Provincia del Paraguay.

REGULADA, Y ALIGADA LA HORA DE los Afpectos, y Eclipfes al Meridiano del Pueblo de los efclarecidos Martyres

SAN COSME, Y SAN DAMIAN,

Y eftendido fu ufo à otros Meridianos por medio de la Tabla de las diferencias meridianas, que fe pone al principio de el Lunario.

DANSE AL FIN DE EL REGLAS FACILES, para que qualquiera, fin Mathematica, ni Arithmetica, pueda formar de eftos Lunarios de un figlo los de los años figuientes, defde el de 1842. hafta el de 1903.

POR EL PADRE
BUENAVENTURA SUAREZ,
de la Compañia de Jefus.

Barcelona: Por PABLO NADAL Impreffor.

Figure 12.2. Cover page of Buenaventura Suárez's Lunario, Barcelona edition of 1752 (Wikimedia Commons).

information. Through these comparisons the last two authors were able to offer, for the first time, an objective evaluation of the scientific relevance of Suárez's observations and to confirm the quality of the astronomical data he generated through his observations and calculations at the Jesuit missions.

The Jesuit expulsion and its impact on science in the territories which became known as Argentina

The expulsion of the Jesuits had an impact on the quality of the teaching offered at the University of Córdoba and, without doubt, on the status of science there, at least in the short term. Contemporary textbooks suitable for the teaching of mathematics and physics are preserved in the University of Córdoba library; however, it is not clear whether or not they were actually used by the Jesuits in their lessons. Moreover, if compared with libraries in Jesuit teaching institutions in Europe, their numbers seem to be rather slim for that purpose.[19]

Since in colonial times the cost of paper was high and there were no adequate printing facilities in Córdoba for the production of books on topics related to the exact sciences, a number of these books are manuscripts copies, possibly student lecture notes. These textbooks and manuscripts books are now found mainly in libraries and archives in Córdoba and Buenos Aires. Many of those in Buenos Aires were originally in Córdoba's library, but were moved when a national library was created in the capital in 1812; since 1999 many have been returned to Córdoba. The Jesuit books available in Córdoba are listed in the *Colección Jesuítica de la Biblioteca Mayor de la Universidad Nacional de Córdoba*.[20] In addition, there is currently a project which attempts to unify the catalogues of Argentine colonial bibliography.[21]

A few specialised texts, such as Elías del Carmen Pereira's (1760–1825) *Tractatus de Physica Generalis*, published in 1784[22] and preserved in the library of the Universidad Nacional de La Plata, were translated and reprinted over a century ago.[23] R. Loyarte has discussed this work, arguing that in it Father Elías did not accept the ideas developed by Galileo or by Newton in his 1687

---

19   For a comparison of mathematics books in Spain in the same period, see Real Academia de Ciencias Exactas, Físicas y Naturales, *Catálogo de Libros Antiguos: Siglos XV–XVIII* (Madrid: Real Academia, 1991).

20   The collection contains 1,602 titles out of an original number of about 3,200.

21   R. Casazza, *Programa nacional de catalogación, restauración y estudio histórico crítico de la bibliografía colonial actualmente existente en la República Argentina* (Buenos Aires: Biblioteca Nacional, 2001).

22   W.B. Redmond, *Bibliography of the Philosophy in the Iberian Colonies of America* (The Hague: Nijhoff, 1972), p. 24.

23   E. del Carmen Pereira, *Physica generalis*, translated and published by Juan Chiabra (La Plata: Universidad Nacional de La Plata, 1911 [1784]).

treatise *Principia*. [24] A copy of Elias del Carmen Pereira's *Physica particularis* has also recently been identified in the private library of the owner of a large country house in the province of Salta in northern Argentina.[25] Other extant contemporaneous texts are listed in the recently published dissertation by M. Sánchez Herrador.[26] References to specific leading scientists such as Newton in Jesuit (or Franciscan) texts printed in South America have been considered by a number of scholars.[27] A technical analysis of the physics and mathematics contents of surviving texts in Córdoba, comparing their ideas with those found in contemporaneous European texts on the same subjects, Jesuit or non-Jesuit, is still an open and interesting field of research.

Precise measurements: between expulsion and Independence

It is possible to detect some interesting changes in the scientific scene in Argentina in the years between the Jesuit expulsion and independence. These changes were initially connected to the work of the joint demarcation commission which, as previously mentioned, was in charge of drawing the meridian line which separated Spanish and Portuguese colonial possessions in America.[28] This complex and extensive joint geodesic operation brought to America a number of interesting Portuguese and Spanish scientists, mostly associated with the navy; they contributed to keeping alive an emergent scientific tradition there. These naval experts carried with them, to Buenos Aires and to other large towns, first-hand experience of a number of scientific topics connected with their cartographic task, as well as modern books and a valuable collection of reasonably modern scientific instruments.[29] Once their

---

24 R.G. Loyarte, *La evolución de la física* (Buenos Aires: Sociedad Científica Argentina, 1924), pp. 10, 15.

25 This recent discovery is discussed in S.G.A. Benito Moya, 'El libro manuscrito en la Córdoba del Siglo XVIII: el caso de la *Physica Particularis* de Fr. Elías del Carmen Pereyra', *Bibliographica americana*, 8 (2012): 32–63.

26 M. Sánchez Herrador, 'La biblioteca del Colegio de La Encarnación de los Jesuitas de Montilla' (unpublished doctoral thesis, Universidad Nacional de Córdoba, 2016).

27 Benito Moya, 'El libro manuscrito'; V.S. Albis and L.C. Arboleda, 'Newton's *Principia* in Latin America', *Historia mathematica*, 15 (1988): 376–9; C. Lertora Mendoza, 'Bibliografía newtoniana en el Río de la Plata, siglo XVIII', in *Newton en América. Tercer Congreso Latinoamericano de Historia de las Ciencias y la Tecnología, Mexico, 1992* (FEPAI, 1995); and 'Introducción de las teorías newtonianas en el Rio de la Plata', in A. Lafuente, A. Elena and M. Ortega (eds.), *Mundialización de la ciencia y cultura nacional* (Madrid: Universidad Autónoma-Doce Calles, 1993, pp. 307–24; Asúa, 'Astronomical observations of Buenaventura Suárez' and 'La ciencia de mayo'.

28 G. Kratz, *El tratado hispano-portugués de límites de 1750 y sus consecuencias. Estudio sobre la abolición de la Compañía de Jesús* (Rome: Bibliotheca Instituti Historici Societatis IESU, 1954).

29 J. Sala Catalá, 'La ciencia en las expediciones de límites hispano-portuguesas y sus consecuencias sobre la abolición de la Compañía de Jesús', *Dynamis*, 12 (1992): 23–33; L. Martín-Merás, 'Fondos cartográficos y documentales de la Comisión de Límites de Brasil en el siglo XVIII en el Museo Naval de Madrid', *Terra Brasilis*, 7 – 8 – 9 (2007):1–89.

work was finished, the Spanish colonial authorities in Buenos Aires requested that both the books and instruments be left in the city, which was agreed.

An extended stay by some former commission members in Buenos Aires and the availability of suitable instruments there facilitated the transfer of knowledge in the use of this apparatus to some local residents. In time this knowledge facilitated the organisation of local schools, usually called academies, where topics such as basic mathematics and topography, navigation, drawing, map-making and so forth could be learned, giving some continuity to earlier Jesuit efforts.[30] These circumstances enlarged the small circle of individuals familiar with more modern textbooks and comfortable with the use of some delicate scientific instruments. In Buenos Aires precision-measuring became a far more concrete subject than ever before.

In addition to this important stimulus there is evidence of a new social interest in scientific experimentation among some educated local people. This assumption is supported by the fact that Martín de Altolaguirre (1708–83?), a wealthy, high-ranking crown functionary, born in Spain and residing in Buenos Aires, purchased a large collection of physical instruments – a Physics Cabinet – in Spain and had it sent to his residence in Buenos Aires.[31] His son, Martín José de Altolaguirre (1736–1813?) was born in Buenos Aires and educated by the Jesuits at the San Ignacio College in his native city. Like his father, he was interested in the sciences, but not in physics. His subject was the natural sciences and he has been credited with the acclimatisation of several foreign crops in Argentina. At some stage after his father died he decided to offer the collection of instruments to the University of Córdoba.

Through the positive attitude of some of the current authorities, particularly Father Pedro José de Sullivan, a Franciscan, then dean of the college in Córdoba, the valuable Altolaguirre collection of demonstration instruments was acquired by the university, though not without the opposition of some humanities' teachers. Sullivan believed that exposing students to real experiments, using the pieces in Altolaguirre's collection rather than verbal descriptions, would enhance the teaching of physics in Córdoba.

This decision, and the cost of the collection, suggest there was, then, also in Córdoba a more favourable attitude towards teaching physics using demonstration instruments than ever before.[32] From a copy available in Córdoba, the Franciscan Monseñor Zenón Bustos y Ferreyra (1850–1925) produced a partial list of these instruments, which he published in Córdoba.

30 C. Dassen, 'La facultad de matemáticas de Buenos Aires (1874–1880) y sus antecedentes', *Anales de la Academia Nacional de Ciencias Exactas, Físicas y Naturales de Buenos Aires*, 5 (1940): 1–21.

31 On the interesting Altolaguirre family, see S.M. Socolow, *The Bureaucrats of Buenos Aires, 1769–1810: Amor Al Real Servicio* (Durham, NC: Duke University Press, 1987).

32 On contemporary education, see J.C. Chiaramonte, *La Ilustración en el Río de la Plata* (Buenos Aires: Sudamericana, 2007).

Later that list was completed by Furlong using an inventory recovered by the historian Jorge Escalada Iriondo from the Archivo General de los Tribunales.[33] It is interesting to note that one of the most expensive items in Altolaguirre's collection was a vacuum pump, a machine which had started an intense debate between the Jesuits and the German physicist Otto von Guericke (1602–1686).[34]

The slow return of Jesuit science teachers to Argentina and the emergence of the Colegio del Salvador

Let us return to the scene of science, now in independent Argentina, and to the place of the Jesuits in it. In the third decade of the 19th century, soon after being given *facultades extraordinarias* to run the government of Argentina, Juan Manuel de Rosas (1793–1877) tried to attract Spanish members of religious orders to take care of local education. He wished to replace institutions created by previous, more liberal governments, such as the defunct Colegio de Ciencias Morales of 1823, with a new college more in tune with his own views on education and politics.

On Rosas' invitation, Jesuits arrived in Buenos Aires in 1837 and established there a school that later became known as Colegio Republicano Federal, a name fit for the prevailing ideology of the government. By 1840 students began to graduate from the new school and some textbooks began to be printed locally. However, Rosas' interference with the Jesuits soon began to cause friction,[35] which resulted in deep changes in the structure of the school and the loss of teachers. Finally, in 1843 Rosas expelled the few remaining Jesuits from Argentina. Rosas was deposed in 1853, but the return of a substantial school, organised according to Jesuit structures, took some years. This finally happened in 1868 with the establishment of Colegio del Salvador (El Salvador in what follows) in Buenos Aires.[36] This school can be regarded as a distant relative of the old Jesuit school of 1617, the Colegio de Loreto. The new Jesuit school focused on the education of a small but influential section of the population. In fact, some of El Salvador's graduates would later play a significant role in the political and cultural life of the country, as well as in the law or the professions.

By the end of the 19th century the authorities of El Salvador, which then had a population of some 550 students, understood clearly the need to offer an up-to-date scientific education, which at that time was seen as an indispensable sign of modernity. Its authorities asked the Spanish Jesuits to help them to

33   Furlong, *Matemáticos argentinos*, pp. 200–15.

34   See S. Shapin and S. Schaffer, *Leviathan and the Air Pump: Hobbes, Boyle, and the Experimental Life* (Princeton, NJ: Princeton University Press, 2011).

35   For a discussion of these differences see C. Bruno, *Historia de la iglesia en Argentina*, 12 vols. (Buenos Aires: Don Bosco, 1967–1981 [1824–40]), vol. 9 (1974), chapter 10.

36   On the history of this school up to 1943, see Furlong, *Historia del Colegio*.

find a good science teacher and the name of José Ubach Medir (1871–1935) (mentioned above in connection with a 1919 evaluation of Buenaventura Suárez's work), a promising young man who had not yet been ordained a priest, was suggested.

Ubach was born in Barcelona to a religious Catalan family, but one not exclusively linked to the Jesuit Order: his younger brother, Buenaventura, reached a high rank in the Benedictine Order. He studied at the local Jesuit secondary school and at the age of 17 decided to join the order. After finishing his training, he was educated further at science centres run by the Spanish Jesuits in Oña and Tortosa, where chemistry was one of its key scientific subjects.[37] Ubach arrived in Buenos Aires in 1897 and soon started teaching sciences at El Salvador: chemistry, cosmography, mathematics and natural sciences, ostensibly with a modern approach.

Cosmic physics and the Jesuits

Cosmic physics: a new, Humboldtian, chapter in science

By the second half of the 19th century there were significant changes on the world scientific scene which did not pass unnoticed by Spanish Jesuits, who were now back from banishment. These included the emergence of a new chapter in the physical sciences: cosmic physics. In the field of astronomy the Italian Jesuit astronomer Angelo Secchi (1818–78), director of the Collegio Romano's observatory in Rome, discovered, through painstaking detailed observations, that in addition to sunspots, already observed by Galileo and by the Jesuit astronomer Christoph Scheiner (1573–1650) in the early 1600s, the sun is crossed by large jets of gas, some up to 500 kms wide, which move irregularly over its surface. In addition, during the same period and following new perspectives brought about by the formulation of new energy-conservation principles in the physical sciences, Lord Kelvin (1824–1907) showed that the energy emanating from the sun cannot be eternal, estimating its life to be between 30 and 300 million years.[38]

Scientists began to look in new directions and as some concentrated on the intense and then inexplicable activity which takes place on the sun's surface, others wondered whether those extraordinary exchanges of energy might not have a direct impact on earth. The answer came on the night of 1 to 2 September

37 F.A. Linari, 'El P. José Ubach, S.J.', *Ibérica*, 44 (1935): 276–7.

38 On this discussion see C. Smith and M. Norton Wise, *Energy and Empire: A Biographical Study of Lord Kelvin* (Cambridge: Cambridge University Press, 1989), in particular pp. 407–648: Part III: 'The economy of nature'; G. Gooday, 'Sunspots, weather, and the unseen universe: Balfour Stewart's anti-materialist representations of *Energy* in British periodicals', in G. Cantor and S. Shuttleworth (eds.), *Science Serialized: Representation of the Sciences in Nineteenth Century Periodicals* (London: MIT Press, 2004) pp. 111–47, contains a number of interesting insights on the popular understanding of the conservation principles and of solar spots.

1859, when a great flare, of the type identified by Father Secchi before, was visible as a glow near a cluster of sunspots. At the same time telegraphic communications suffered a monumental disruption all over the planet and the Aurora Borealis, the Northern Lights, became visible as far south as the equator. This showed quite definitely that changes in the sun's activity influence earth, perhaps in many more ways than we had ever imagined. Consequently, some experts suggested that if the sun's activity is capable of affecting the electrical state of the earth's atmosphere, that is, telegraphic communications and the Aurora Borealis, it may also have some effect on animals and plants and, perhaps, also on storms and other unpredictable manifestations of the sun's energy on earth, maybe even on earthquakes. If this were the case, by following the sun's activity closely it might be possible to forecast, or even prevent, some natural disasters.

Towards the end of the 19th century a worldwide programme of simultaneously registering the evolution of the sun's spots and local changes in terrestrial magnetism, atmospheric electricity, seismology, meteorology and atmospheric storms began to be considered at a high international level. These studies looked to be a promising new chapter in physics and it was internationally agreed to call this discipline, or rather inter-discipline, cosmic physics. It clearly had its roots in Alexander von Humboldt's (1769–1859) ideas, expressed in his influential book *Kosmos*.[39] Very distinguished scientists, including the future Nobel laureate Svante Arrhenius (1859–1927), were at the forefront of this new chapter in science, writing textbooks to teach cosmic physics at leading European universities.[40]

The methodology used in these large-scale, multi-country observations was, basically, the compilation of a long series of observations of one particular phenomenon, such as earth tremors, with the hope that some pattern of regularities or periodicities would emerge from them. Possibly, they could be correlated to the activity of sunspots or, perhaps, to some other, extra-terrestrial and still undiscovered cosmic phenomena. If such correlations could be established, it was thought they could bring enormous benefits to agriculture, navigation, telegraphic communications and several other areas of human activity. These correlations would not only expand the arc of science, but also save lives, property and ships at sea and help to prevent countless catastrophes. They would help the flow of life, of commerce and of communications.

The Jesuits join research into cosmic physics

However, cosmic physics could only function through worldwide simultaneous observations of a given phenomenon. This was a context in which the Jesuits

---

39 A. von Humboldt, *Kosmos. Entwurf einer physischen Weltbeschreibung* (Stuttgart and Tübingen: Cotta, 1845).

40 H. Kragh, 'The source of solar energy, ca. 1840–1910: from meteoric hypothesis to radioactive speculations', *European Physical Journal*, 41 (2016): 365–94.

had an advantage: their unique, international network of missions, covering an area far more extensive than any contemporary empire, could be put to good use for worldwide cosmic-physics observations. By the end of the 19th century the Jesuits owned 30 of the world's existing 130 astronomical observatories, almost one quarter. Quite conveniently for them, and also for science, in 1879 Pope Leo XIII's encyclical *Aeterni Patris* opened the door for Catholic institutions to embrace modern science more openly. In that encyclical the pope stated that 'many illustrious professors of the physical sciences openly testify that between certain and accepted conclusions of modern physics and the philosophic principles of the [Catholic Church] schools there is no conflict worthy of the name'.[41] Thus, Jesuits could now officially enter new areas of the contemporary science debate and do so with confidence.

Most Jesuit observatories were attached to schools and, as explained above, had reasonably well educated teachers. However, if necessary, teachers could easily be re-trained to conduct whatever measurements in cosmic physics might be required. In addition, the Jesuits circulated their teachers over the extensive area of the planet: as they moved from one country to another they helped to moderate national differences and established an international, distinctive, Jesuit approach of accuracy and reliability in their measurements. Some individual figures within the order, such as the aforementioned Father Secchi and by then also a few others, enjoyed a high international reputation and could be trusted to conduct, efficiently, high-level exchanges with scientists from any country and thereby to make such cooperation possible.

It is interesting to note that the Jesuits added some local flavour to each of their observatories engaged in cosmic physics data collection.[42] In regions affected by earthquakes, such as Granada or Malaga, their observatories gave preference to studies on the correlation between sunspots and seismic activity. In coastal areas, such as La Habana, Manila, Shanghai, Madagascar, or Cleveland, where large tides, hurricanes, heavy storms or typhoons were a frequent hazard, they concentrated on observations aimed at developing some sort of weather-forecasting scheme. In observatories operating in physically quiet areas, such as Ebro or Kalocsa, the Jesuits concentrated on the impact of solar activity on delicate electrical and magnetic phenomena, relevant, for example, to telegraphic communications. This regionalism, or local utility, found in Jesuit observatories of the time was also related to the need to attract, selectively, scientific patronage. Finding new sources of financial support was a matter of perpetual concern to officers of the order; at some stage they

---

41 See point 30 of Pope Leo XIII's encyclical '*Aeterni Patris*, Encyclical on the Restoration of Christian Philosophy', Rome, 4 Aug. 1879 (Rome: Libreria Editrice Vaticana, Roma, 1879).

42 For a detailed description of the facilities available in Jesuit observatories across the world at the beginning of the 20th century, see P. de Vregille, 'Les observatoires de la Compagnie de Jésus au début du XXe. siècle', *Revue des questions scientifiques*, 59 (1906) (3rd ser., vol. 9, 1906): 10–72 and 493–579.

even tried to absorb some of the new tactics developed in New York by the Rockefeller Foundation administrators in order to attract patronage.

At the same time, the Jesuits' engagement with scientific work encouraged the emergence, inside the order, of far better trained science teachers, some of them with first-hand experience in the complexities of experimental science. In time, these teachers contributed to giving Jesuit schools across the world as high a reputation for science teaching as they already had for classical studies. No doubt these better-trained teachers made a contribution to the emergence in the early 1900s of a new generation of top Catholic scientists with a wider, deeper knowledge than ever before and also with more open attitudes.

Cosmic physics in Spain

Spanish Jesuits possibly entered cosmic physics through the advice of the leading Spanish astronomer José Joaquín Landerer y Climent (1841–1922).[43] He was close to the order and, having received scientific training in France, was well aware of the new international scientific movement, of which he was also a distinguished member. In addition, he was a generous contributor to the order's work, possibly also to its new developments in astronomy.

At the time the Jesuits were in the process of opening a group of new observatories in Spain, so they decided to devote one of them specifically to cosmic physics. This was the Observatorio del Ebro (Observatori de l'Ebre), built near Roquetes, Tarragona, in Catalonia, some 120 miles south of Barcelona and close to the Mediterranean. The specific fields of cosmic physics to be studied at this observatory would be solar radiation, terrestrial magnetism, atmospheric and underground electrical currents and their possible connection to changes in solar spots or in protuberances.

In 1903, after teaching at El Salvador for nearly seven years, Ubach was sent back to Spain to assist in the installation of the new cosmic-physics Observatorio del Ebro. Once in Spain he finished his studies and became a Jesuit priest. Following that, Ubach was sent abroad for further training, staying at Jesuit observatories in Holland, Belgium and France. After this training he was assigned to a special group doing preparatory work for the installation of the new Observatorio del Ebro. The Observatory was officially opened in 1905, relying on the help of well-known Dutch and German Jesuit astronomers who moved there temporarily and assisted in the training of the new personnel.[44]

---

43 For a short biography of Landerer, see *Anuario de la Real Academia de Ciencias Exactas*, Físicas y Naturales (Madrid: Academia, 1923): 206-11.

44 On the scientific personality of some of these visiting astronomers see L. Pyenson, *Civilizing Mission, Exact Sciences and French Overseas Expansión, 1830–1940* (Baltimore, MD: John Hopkins University Press, 1993).

Ubach was one of these young Jesuits and later he became the leader of one of the main sections of the new observatory: the Magnetic Laboratory.[45]

The Colegio del Salvador, Buenos Aires, in the early 20th century

However, following a new request from El Salvador, Ubach returned to Buenos Aires in 1911; this began a long stay which would last until his official retirement in 1932 and death three years later. There are reasons to believe that Ricardo Cirera Salse, S.J. (1864–1932), the first director of the Observatorio del Ebro, was not happy with the idea of sending Ubach back to Argentina when so much work had to be done at his new observatory. Ubach's departure deprived that young institution of one of its few foreign-trained astronomers. However, Ubach's new destination answered the need of the Society of Jesus to strengthen the position of science teaching in one of the most prestigious schools the Society then had in Latin America.

In addition to teaching, cultural life at El Salvador was also active. In 1878, barely ten years after it opened its doors, a society of former students called the Academia Literaria del Plata was created. In addition to regular lectures and meetings, the Academia Literaria allowed El Salvador to continue to be relevant to the intellectual life of its former students and to contribute to building a new generation of Jesuit-trained Catholic intellectuals in Argentina; later, they had an impact on their country's cultural and political life. In 1911 the Academia Literaria began publishing a journal called *Estudios*. New topics of science, as well as contemporary scientific controversies such as Darwinism, were reflected in the pages of this journal. Sadly, some racist expressions found their way into its pages. Furlong's 1919 paper on the astronomical works of Buenaventura Suárez, mentioned earlier, which contained Ubach's technical remarks on Suárez's work, was originally published in the journal *Estudios*.

In the first years of his second stay in Argentina Ubach kept in close contact with the Observatorio del Ebro, which enhanced his position in South America by making him its 'Official Delegate in the River Plate'.[46] As such, Ubach's remit was to complement, from South America, the Observatorio del Ebro's studies on solar perturbations. There he would record the impact of solar-related electrical and magnetic phenomena, on which he had expertise. Later, the official designation conferred on him by the Observatorio del Ebro became useful: it allowed him to strengthen his contacts with official Argentine astronomical and cartographic centres. The army's national geographical

---

45 I. Puig, *El Observatorio del Ebro. Idea general sobre el mismo* (Tortosa: Imprenta Moderna, 1927).

46 This is reported in J. Ubach, 'Determinación de la posición geográfica del observatorio del Ebro', *Memorias del Observatorio del Ebro*, 6 (1919).

institute,[47] the main Argentine cartographic institution, shared with Ubach their own observations and results, while the naval ministry allowed him free use of its potent radio transmitters to send and receive time signals accurately.

As part of his research project he discussed the terrestrial impact of the partial solar eclipses of 1916 and 1918, for which he calculated the visibility zone. In addition to the astronomical installations at El Salvador, Ubach had access to the better astronomical instruments available at the Metropolitan Seminary in Villa Devoto, Buenos Aires. The mathematical analysis of his measurements required the solution of a fairly large ill-conditioned system of algebraic equations, which he attempted. Ubach also studied the possible effects of the solar eclipses on magnetism and for that attracted the collaboration of a group of local, as well as Chilean, observers. From his office in El Salvador he centralised all data on the specific impact of the eclipses on humidity, pressure and temperature collected by observers from outside Buenos Aires. He continued with observations of the impact of solar eclipses until the end of the 1920s. Moreover, Ubach did not neglect the importance of the public understanding of science, from time to time offering series of weekly public lectures in which he explained, in simple terms, why astrophysicists were interested in solar spots and other matters to do with cosmic physics.

The Jesuits, El Salvador and the debate on relativity theory in Argentina

In 1919, just after the end of the First World War, attempts were made to measure an astronomical consequence of Einstein's theory of relativity: the possibility that the light rays from stars might be bent by the attraction of the mass of the sun. This was an effect which could be detected during an eclipse. Once the astronomical expeditions sent to measure such hypothetical deviation published their results, astronomers from different countries made their views public. Ubach read his own conclusions at a two-day meeting held on 20 and 27 September 1920 in El Salvador's main lecture theatre. This was just a month after the celebrated poet and science enthusiast Leopoldo Lugones (1874–1938) had lectured on the same subject at the faculty of science of Buenos Aires University, which was then the local epicentre of relativism.

Ubach's views are, perhaps, the most interesting evaluation of that theory formulated in Argentina from the specific angle of the Catholic Church.[48] He discussed absolute and relative motion, invariance and the consequences of Lorentz's relativistic ideas and then considered the modifications introduced by Einstein's work on Newton's classical mechanics. He concluded his exposition with a reference to Einstein's generalised theory of relativity,

47   The Instituto Geográfico Militar.

48   E.L. Ortiz, 'A convergence of interests: Einstein's visit to Argentina in 1925', *Ibero-Amerikanisches Archiv*, 20 (1995): 67–126 (95).

its impact on the conceptions of classical mechanics and the possibility of verifying its consequences through astronomical observations. He indicated that the proof provided by the eclipse was not entirely conclusive, which was a not-uncommon point of view at the time. However, it did not escape him that Einstein's ideas had changed, deeply, our conceptions of time and space and 'contain novelties never suspected', leading to 'very reasonable and very true and acceptable conclusions'. He then reassured his audience, stating he believed that the same conclusions would, someday, be reached through the classical theories of physics and expected that 'new experiments may be able to bring new results' which might make the radical changes proposed by the new relativity theory unnecessary.[49] Two years later Ubach opened the 1922 series of popular-science lectures at El Salvador with another key scientific question: a discussion of Darwin's theory of evolution, still a contentious matter.[50]

He and his colleagues contributed to the creation of new environments of discussion at several different levels around El Salvador, initially through education, later with the help of the Academia Literaria and *Estudios* and, finally, through the Cursos de Cultura Católica,[51] a society focused on a much wider public, which Ubach helped to develop. In time, the Cursos had an impact on the development of an influential group of young Catholics who became active in culture and national politics. However, the Jesuits were not alone in their efforts to have an impact on Argentina's cultural world. They competed with other local groupings: some indifferent to religion, others with a long tradition of a liberal outlook. Nor were they alone in their efforts to promote regular visits by Spanish intellectuals to Argentina. Since soon after the centenary year of 1910, the most formidable string of celebrated Spanish intellectuals regularly visited Argentina and stayed there for extended periods; they were supported by the newly created, non-partisan but liberally oriented, Junta para Ampliación de Estudios e Investigaciones Científicas.

The latter was a new science research council set up in Madrid in 1907 through the efforts of Nobel Prize winner Santiago Ramón y Cajal (1852–1934). Within a few years of being established, the Junta launched the above-mentioned programme of intellectual and cultural rapprochement with Argentina in association with the Institución Cultural Española, which had the patronage of wealthy, and generally liberal, Spanish merchants residing in Buenos Aires.[52] These visits benefitted the University of Buenos Aires and

---

49 J. Ubach, *La teoría de la relatividad en la física moderna: Lorentz, Minkowski, Einstein* (Buenos Aires: Amorrortu, 1920).

50 J. Ubach, *El pasado y el presente del problema de la evolución* (Buenos Aires: Amorrortu, 1922).

51 J. Zanca, 'Los cursos de cultura católica en los años veinte. Intelectuales, curas y "conversos"', in P. Bruno (ed.), *Sociabilidades y vida cultural. Buenos Aires, 1860–1930* (Bernal: Editorial de la Universidad de Quilmes, 2014), pp. 281–311.

52 E.L. Ortiz, 'Las relaciones scientíficas entre Argentina y España a principios de este siglo. La JAE y la Institución Cultural Española', in J.M. Sánchez Ron (ed.), *La Junta para Ampliación*

had a serious impact on Argentine culture. Later, after the end of the Spanish Civil War, these personal contacts eased the way for the integration of Spanish immigrant intellectuals and artists in Argentina, with very considerable benefit to its cultural life.

A new generation of scientists trained at El Salvador

Ramón G. Loyarte (1888–1944) is a paradigmatic example among the students educated at El Salvador in the early years of the 20th century who later moved to the sciences. After his studies at El Salvador he joined the physics institute of the new University of La Plata; there he studied under the German physicists Emil Bose (1874–1911) and Richard Gans (1880–1954) before himself being sent to Germany for further studies. In 1925, when Gans returned to Germany, Loyarte was chosen to succeed him as director of that modern laboratory, at the time the largest in Latin America. He was also the first physicist to receive the Argentine National Science Prize in 1925; in 1928 he became president of the University of La Plata. Loyarte was also interested in the history of physics: his views on Elías del Carmen Pereira's *Tractatus de Physica Generalis* have been noted above. Loyarte combined his scientific activities with intense political activity as a member of the right-wing conservative party, which he represented in the national parliament. Later, in 1944, after a military coup d'état, he was designated *Interventor*[53] of the National Education Council. As such, he promoted the introduction of religious education, not just in Catholic establishments but also nationwide in state schools; until then the latter had been neutral on religious matters. His ideas on this matter encountered considerable opposition.

A Jesuit-supported observatory of cosmic physics for Argentina

By the mid 1930s El Salvador no longer had a sufficiently wide basis for the new science project the Jesuits were considering for Argentina, namely, the installation there of a cosmic-physics observatory in the image of the Observatorio del Ebro. At the time the new Spanish Republic was causing serious anxieties for the order, which was finally to be dissolved in early 1932. For some time astronomers at the Observatorio del Ebro evaluated the possibility of having to move personnel, and possibly also valuable instruments, to Argentina.

In parallel with the Spanish anxieties, the first half of the 1930s was also a complex period in the history of Argentine astronomy. Traditionally, since the

---

de Estudios e Investigaciones Científicas 80 años después: 1907–1987 (Madrid: CSIC, 1988), vol. 2, pp. 119–58.

53 This title was used by the authorities which emerged from the military coup d'état of September 1943 to designate a non-elected official.

national observatory had been founded by Benjamin Apthorp Gould (1824–96) in Córdoba in 1871, its director had always been a US citizen. The last in that chain of directors was the US-born astronomer Charles Dillon Perrine (1867–1951). In the early 1930s he was close to retirement and, despite clear achievements, faced some external opposition. Some locals complained, with some validity, of the absence of a training course in astronomy and a programme capable of generating local experts in that field of science. To resolve this, some suggested that the observatory should be absorbed by the University of Córdoba; others, for whatever reason, simply wished Perrine to go.

A collection of letters recovered from the Córdoba observatory's archive a few months ago have been reproduced and reviewed by S. Paolantonio.[54] They indicate that in these critical circumstances Perrine contacted local dignitaries of the Catholic Church in Córdoba in late 1932, in particular Fermín E. Lafitte (1888–1959), an influential cleric who would become bishop of Córdoba two years later. Perrine expressed concern about current events in Spain and indicated that once he retired the position of director should be given to the Spanish Jesuit astronomer Lluís Rodés i Campderá (1881–1939), the current director of the Observatorio del Ebro. Rodés was known and appreciated in Argentina; he had visited Buenos Aires and other cities in 1927. His inaugural lecture in Buenos Aires, at El Salvador, attracted the presence of distinguished persons from the local world of science, politics and the army. Among them was the minister of war General Agustín P. Justo (1876–1943), a Buenos Aires University graduate in engineering who would soon be elected president of Argentina.

However, despite the delicate situation which confronted Rodés at his own institution in early 1930s, or maybe because of it, by 1932 Rodés indicated clearly that he did not wish to be involved in these discussions. The publication of Rodés's personal diary in 2015[55] confirms, as generally believed, that he was not enthusiastic about the Spanish military uprising against the republic. It also describes how he managed to keep the Observatorio del Ebro working after the Company of Jesus was dissolved in 1932 and, after that, through the early years of the Spanish Civil War.[56]

Soon after Perrine's exchanges with Monsignor Lafitte, in mid 1933, the national government decided to create a National Council of Observatories (Consejo Nacional de Observatorios), whose duty it was to coordinate the activities of the different Argentine observatories. It designated the astronomer

54 S. Paolantonio, 'Sobre cuando se ofreció la dirección del Observatorio de Córdoba a un Catalán', in *Historia de la Astronomía*, Córdoba, https://historiadelaastronomia.wordpress.com/documentos/perrine-rodes/ [accessed 10 Aug. 2018].

55 Lluís Rodés i Campderá, *Diario en tiempo de guerra, 20 de julio de 1936–22 de octubre de 1938* (Roquetes: Observatori de l'Ebre, 2015).

56 A. Roca, 'El Diari de guerra d'un clerge demòcrata: Lluís Rodés i Camderà (1881–1939)', *Quaderns d'Història de l'Enginyeria*, 16 (2018): 279–86.

Figure 12.3. Cosmic Physics Observatory, San Miguel. Source: Ibérica, 45 (25 January 1936).

Monseñor Fortunato Devoto (1872–1941) as its director. The government had, in fact, created a new structure above the senior Córdoba National Observatory and kept it under Jesuit administration. In parallel with these developments a long arc of meridian began to be measured in Argentina in the mid 1930s. This interesting interaction between local scientists, the army and members of the Catholic Church is discussed by this author in an earlier publication.[57]

Soon after being established, the Council of Observatories created a new Cosmic Physics Observatory (Observatorio de Física Cósmica). It offered the directorship to Rodés's number two, the Jesuit astronomer Ignacio Puig (1887–1961), until then deputy director of the Observatorio del Ebro, who accepted the offer. With this choice the cosmic-physics link between Argentina and Spain was officially sealed and remained attached to the Order of Jesus. The new observatory was located in San Miguel, a town close to Buenos Aires, where the order had established, also in 1932, a top-level training college for priests, the Colegio Máximo de San Miguel; Pope Francis (1936–) is the Colegio Máximo's best known former student.

We have already referred to the Jesuits' concern with funding to support their scientific and other institutions. The order had already financed most of its scientific institutions through patronage; the new cosmic physics observatory at San Miguel was not going to be an exception. It was built and equipped using the combination of a national endowment, monies provided by a private individual (a former student at El Salvador) and the contribution of a large, local electricity-generating company in which Spanish capital was dominant.

---

57   E.L. Ortiz, 'La Comisión del Arco de Meridiano', *Saber y Tiempo*, 19 (2005):127–88.

Puig remained in charge of the San Miguel cosmic physics observatory until 1943, when he retired and returned to Spain. His main contribution was in the field of the public understanding of cosmic physics and of astronomy in general. He was the author of several publications on topics related to cosmic physics and also of a useful treatise on astronomy[58] and an introductory book on cosmic physics.[59] The latter was included in a prestigious science collection directed by mathematician and historian of science Julio Rey Pastor (1888–1962) in Buenos Aires. In addition, he regularly contributed notes on scientific subjects to Catholic newspapers, particularly to *El Pueblo*.[60]

Cosmic physics begins to lose its appeal

The fact is that by the late 1920s, even before the observatory at San Miguel was established, the original programme of cosmic physics was becoming outdated in Europe. Studies on the behaviour of matter at a more fundamental level and their implications for astronomy were replacing some of the ideas heralded by cosmic-physics enthusiasts. However, Puig should be credited with an attempt to shift the focus of his institute towards the study of cosmic rays, energy radiation coming from outside the solar system. He made attempts to use high-altitude balloons to register this radiation in the upper layers of the atmosphere, but encountered some difficulties, possibly aggravated by the restrictions on equipment imposed by the Second World War.

His successor, the Jesuit astronomer Juan Antonio Bussolini (1905–66), attempted to modernise the observatory, expanding its circle of interests. Trusted by President General Juan D. Perón (1895–1974), he acted as a member of a committee of advisors who suggested to the president that the current efforts by the Austrian physicist Roland Richter (1909–91) to generate energy through nuclear fusion, then being attempted at a specially built plant in Bariloche, lacked a solid theoretical foundation and should be discontinued.[61] In 1966 a military coup d'état, the fourth in the 20th century, deposed the elected national government of the time. The San Miguel observatory was reorganised yet again and a new Jesuit director was appointed. He acted under the tutelage of the Argentine air force, but soon, as Father Udias has indicated, 'the observatory lost its Jesuit character' and in 1970 the director was removed from his position and also from the Order of Jesus.[62] Finally, in the late 1970s the San Miguel cosmic physics observatory was absorbed by the Argentine air

58 I. Puig, *Manual de astronomía: resumen sintético de nuestros conocimientos sobre el Cosmos* (Buenos Aires: Albatros, 1942).

59 I. Puig, *Qué es la física cósmica?* (Buenos Aires: Espasa-Calpe, 1944).

60 Puig's newspaper contributions were later collected in a series of books published between 1938 and 1940: *Actualidades científicas* (Buenos Aires: Pezza, 1938–1940).

61 M. Mariscotti, *El secreto atómico de Huemul* (Buenos Aires: Sudamericana-Planeta, 1985), pp. 233–42.

62 A. Udías, *Jesuit Contribution to Science: A History* (Heidelberg: Springer, 2015), p. 151.

force, incorporated into a National Commission for Space Research and, after subsequent reorganisations, gradually lost its original identity.

This gradual decline and final abandonment of a direct Jesuit presence in cosmic physics may not have been just a matter of Argentina, or of cosmic physics either. In 1991, with a delay of some twenty years and perhaps in less traumatic circumstances than in Argentina, the far more substantial, prestigious and older Observatorio del Ebro, together with other Jesuit-supported science institutions, was also remodelled and transferred to the new Jesuit Universitat Ramon Llull, created in Barcelona in 1989, of which it became a division. A similar decision was adopted by the order with regard to other Jesuit institutes of cosmic physics and astronomical observatories established in different countries across the world. This shows the complexity, and also the elasticity, of relations between the Jesuits and their scientific establishments in the last decades of the 20th century.

Conclusion

Over a long period of time the Order of Jesus had a worldwide influence on the circulation of knowledge on the exact sciences and astronomy. In different forms, their concerns reached South America and, in particular, the territories of what is today Argentina. This happened from around the late 17th century and affected both areas of education and some early forms of research activity. In those years Jesuit expertise in the exact sciences was mainly in areas of positional astronomy. The work of Buenaventura Suárez is a remarkable example of that.

In the 19th century, after they returned from expulsion, the order began to develop an interest in new areas of the exact sciences, in particular, cosmic physics, then a novel field in astronomy related closely to astrophysics. In addition, through their research work in this and other areas of the exact sciences the Jesuits were able to generate an interesting group of skilled scientists. This helped them to improve considerably the quality of teaching they could offer in their schools: they began to match in the sciences the quality of teaching they had traditionally offered in the classics. However, by the middle of the 20th century, on a worldwide scale, the Jesuits began to make a clear change of direction and leave the field of cosmic physics, keeping only a reduced presence in astronomy. Their painstaking work has left as a legacy a highly reliable worldwide collection of data on seismology and in other areas. It is still used today as a standard for comparison with contemporary series of observations.

Bibliography

Albis, V. S. and L.C. Arboleda (1988) 'Newton's *Principia* in Latin America', *Historia mathematica*, 15: 376–9.

Allen, P. (1947) 'The Royal Society and Latin America as reflected in the Philosophical Transactions, 1665–1740', *Isis*, 37:132–8.

Angelis, P. de (1836–7) *Colección de obras y documentos relativos a la historia antigua y moderna de las Provincias del Rio de la Plata, 1836*, vols. 4–7 (Buenos Aires: Imprenta del Estado).

Anuario de la Real Academia de Ciencias Exactas, Físicas y Naturales (Madrid: Academia, 1923): 206-11 (note on 'Josep Joaquim Landerer i Climent').

Asúa, M. (2004) 'The publication of the astronomical observations of Buenaventura Suárez SJ, (1679–1750), in European scientific journals', *Journal of Astronomical History and Heritage, 7* (2): 81–4.

— (2010) *La ciencia de mayo. La cultura científica en el Río de la Plata, 1800–1820* (Buenos Aires: Fondo de Cultura Económica).

— (2014) *Science in the Vanished Arcadia: Knowledge of Nature in the Jesuit of Paraguay and Río de la Plata* (Leiden: Brill).

Backer, A. de and A. de Backer (1932) *Bibliothèque de la Compagnie de Jésus*, 12 vols. (Paris: Picard).

Baldini, U. (1992) *'Legem impone subactis'. Studii su filosofia e scienza dei Gesuiti in Italia, 1540–1632* (Roma: Bulzoni).

— (2004) 'The teaching of mathematics in the Jesuit colleges of Portugal, from 1640 to Pombal', in L. Saraiva and H. Leitão (eds.), *The Practice of Mathematics in Portugal* (Coimbra: Universitates Conimbrigensis), pp. 293–466.

Benito Moya, S.G.A. (2012) 'El libro manuscrito en la Córdoba del Siglo XVIII: el caso de la *Physica Particularis* de Fr. Elías del Carmen Pereyra, *Bibliographica Americana*, 8: 32–63.

Biblioteca, Real Academia de Ciencias Exactas, Físicas y Naturales, *Catálogo de Libros Antiguos: Siglos XV–XVIII* (Madrid: Real Academia de Ciencias, 1991).

Bruno, C. (1967–81 [1824–40]) *Historia de la iglesia en Argentina* (12 vols., Buenos Aires: Don Bosco).

Casazza, R. (2001) *Programa nacional de catalogación, restauración y estudio histórico crítico de la bibliografía colonial actualmente existente en la República Argentina* (Buenos Aires: Biblioteca Nacional).

Chiaramonte, J.C. (2007) *La ilustración en el Río de la Plata* (Buenos Aires: Sudamericana).

Dassen, C.C. (1941) 'La facultad de matemáticas de Buenos Aires (1874–1880) y sus antecedentes', *Anales de la Academia Nacional de Ciencias Exáctas, Físicas y Naturales de Buenos Aires*, 5: 1–21.

Furlong, G. (1919) 'El primer astrónomo argentino, Buenaventura Suárez', *Estudios*, 16: 102–17.

— (1929) *Glorias Santafesinas: Buenaventura Suárez, Francisco Javier Iturri, Cristóbal Altamirano. Estudios bibliográficos* (Buenos Aires: Surgo).

— (1933) *Los Jesuitas y la cultura Rioplatense* (Montevideo: Urta y Curbelo).

— (1943) *Historia del Colegio del Salvador y de sus irradiaciones espirituales en la ciudad de Buenos Aires, 1617–1943* (Buenos Aires: Colegio del Salvador).

— (1945) *Matemáticos argentinos durante la dominación hispánica* (Buenos Aires: Huarpes).

— (1948) *Naturalistas argentinos durante la dominación hispánica* (Buenos Aires: Huarpes).

Galindo, S. and M.A. Rodríguez-Meza (2011) 'Buenaventura Suárez, S.J. (1679–1750): Telescope Maker, Jovian Satellites Observer', *Revista mexicana de física*, 57: 121–33 and 144–51.

Gooday, G. (2004) 'Sunspots, weather, and the unseen universe: Balfour Stewart's anti-materialist representations of *Energy* in British scientific periodicals', in G. Cantor and S. Shuttleworth (eds.), *Science Serialized: Representation of the Sciences in Nineteenth Century Periodicals* (London: MIT Press), pp. 111–47.

Goodman, D. (1983) 'Science and the clergy in the Spanish Enlightenment', *History of Science*, 21: 111–40.

— (1992) 'The scientific revolution in Spain and Portugal', in R. Porter and M. Teuch (eds.), *The Scientific Revolution in National Context* (Cambridge: Cambridge University Press), pp. 159–77.

Grendler, P.F. (2016) 'The culture of the Jesuit teacher 1548–1773', *Journal of Jesuit Studies*, 3: 17–41.

Gutiérrez, J.M. (1915) *Origen y desarrollo de la enseñanza pública superior en Buenos Aires* (Buenos Aires: La Cultura Argentina).

Hellyer, M. (2005) *Catholic Physics: Jesuit Natural Philosophy in early modern Germany* (Notre Dame, IN: University of Notre Dame Press).

Humboldt, A. von (1845) *Kosmos. Entwurf einer physischen Weltbeschreibung* (Stuttgart and Tübingen: Cotta).

Kragh, H. (2016) 'The source of solar energy, ca. 1840–1910: from meteoric hypothesis to radioactive speculations', *European Physical Journal*, 41: 365–94.

Kratz, W. and D.B. Camacho (1954) *El Tratado Hispano-Portugués de límites de 1750 y sus consecuencias. Estudio sobre la abolición de la Compañía de Jesús* (Rome: Bibliotheca Instituti Historici Societatis IESU).

Leo XII, Pope (n.d.) *Aeterni Patris. Encyclical of Pope Leo XIII on the Restoration of Christian Philosophy, August 4, 1879*, section 30 (Roma: Libreria Editrice Vaticana), http://www.papalencyclicals.net/leo13/l13cph.htm [accessed 10 Aug. 2018].

Lertora Mendoza, C. (1995) 'Bibliografía newtoniana en el Río de la Plata, Siglo XVIII', in *Newton en América. Tercer Congreso Latinoamericano de Historia de las Ciencias y la Tecnología, Mexico, 1992* (FEPAI).

— (1993) 'Introducción de las teorías newtonianas en el Rio de la Plata', in A. Lafuente, A. Elena and M. Ortega (eds.), *Mundialización de la ciencia y cultura nacional* (Madrid: Universidad Autónoma-Doce Calles, 1993), pp. 307–24.

Linari, F.A. (1935) 'El P. José Ubach, S. J.', *Ibérica*, 44: 276–7.

Loyarte, Ramón G. (1924) *La evolución de la Física* (Buenos Aires: Sociedad Científica Argentina).

Mariscotti, M. (1985) *El secreto atómico de Huemul* (Buenos Aires: Sudamericana-Planeta).

Martín-Merás, L. (2007) 'Fondos cartográficos y documentales de la Comisión de Límites de Brasil en el siglo XVIII en el Museo Naval de Madrid', *Terra Brasilis* 7 – 8 – 9: 1–89.

Ortiz, E.L. (1988) 'Las relaciones científicas entre Argentina y España a principios de este siglo. La JAE y la Institución Cultural Española', in J.M. Sánchez Ron (eds.), *La Junta para Ampliación de Estudios e Investigaciones Científicas 80 años después: 1907–1987*, vol. 2 (Madrid: CSIC), pp. 119–58.

— (1995) 'A convergence of interests: Einstein's visit to Argentina in 1925', *Ibero-Amerikanisches Archiv*, 20: 67–126.

— (2005) 'La Comisión del Arco de Meridiano', *Saber y Tiempo*, 19: 127–88.

Paolantonio, S. (n.d.) 'Sobre cuando se ofreció la dirección del Observatorio de Córdoba a un Catalán', in *Historia de la Astronomía, Córdoba*, https://historiadelaastronomia.wordpress.com/documentos/perrine-rodes/ [accessed 10 Aug. 2018].

Pereira, E. del C. (1911 [1784]) *Physica generalis*, translated and published by Juan Chiabra (La Plata: Universidad Nacional de La Plata).

Probst, J. (1924) 'La enseñanza durante la época colonial (1771–1810)', in *La educación en la república Argentina durante la época colonial*, in *Documentos para la historia Argentina*, vol. 18 (Buenos Aires: Peuser).

Puig, I. (1927) *El Observatorio del Ebro. Idea general sobre el mismo* (Tortosa: Imprenta Moderna).

— (1942) *Manual de astronomía: resumen sintético de nuestros conocimientos sobre el Cosmos* (Buenos Aires: Albatros).

— (1944) *Qué es la física cósmica?* (Buenos Aires: Espasa-Calpe).

Pyenson, L. (1993) *Civilizing Mission, Exact Sciences and French Overseas Expansion, 1830–1940* (Baltimore, MD: John Hopkins University Press).

Redmond, W.B. (1972) *Bibliography of the Philosophy in the Iberian Colonies of America* (The Hague: Nijhoff).

Roca, A. (2018) 'El Diari de Guerra d'un clerge demòcrata: Lluís Rodés i Camderà (1881–1939)', *Quaderns d'Història de l'Enginyeria*, 16: 279–86.

Rodés i Campderá, Ll. S.J. (2015) *Diario en tiempo de guerra, 20 de julio de 1936–22 de octubre de 1938* (Roquetes: Observatori de l'Ebre).

Sala Catalá, J. (1992) 'La ciencia en las expediciones de límites hispano-portuguesas: su proyección internacional', *Dynamis*, 12: 23–33.

Sánchez Herrador, M.A. (2016) 'La biblioteca del Colegio de La Encarnación de los Jesuitas de Montilla' (unpublished doctoral thesis, Universidad de Córdoba).

Sánchez Pérez, J.A. (2004) 'La matemática', in *Estudios sobre la ciencia española del siglo XVII* (Madrid: Asociación nacional de historiadores de la ciencia española), pp. 597–633.

Shapin, S. and S. Schaffer (2011) *Leviathan and the Air Pump: Hobbes, Boyle, and the Experimental Life* (Princeton, NJ: Princeton University Press).

Smith, C. and M. Norton Wise (1989) *Energy and Empire: A Biographical Study of Lord Kelvin* (Cambridge: Cambridge University Press).

Socolow, S.M. (1987) *The Bureaucrats of Buenos Aires, 1769–1810: Amor Al Real Servicio* (Durham, NC: Duke University Press).

Stearns, R. (1970) *Science in the British Colonies of America* (Urbana, IL: University of Illinois Press).

Suárez, B. (1740) *Lunario de un siglo* (Barcelona: Pablo Nadal).

Tiganelli, H.L. (2004) 'El primer lunario criollo', *Saber y Tiempo*, 17: 5–60.

Ubach, J. (1919) 'Determinación de la posición geográfica del observatorio del Ebro', *Memorias del Observatorio del Ebro*, 6.

— (1920) *La teoría de la relatividad en la física moderna: Lorentz, Minkowski, Einstein* (Buenos Aires: Amorrortu).

— (1922) *El pasado y el presente del problema de la evolución* (Buenos Aires: Amorrortu).

Udías, A. (2015) *Jesuit Contribution to Science: A History* (Heidelberg: Springer).

Vregille, P. de (1906) 'Les observatoires de la Compagnie de Jésus au début du XXe. Siècle', *Revue des questions scientifiques* 59 (3rd ser., vol. 9): 10–72 and 493–579

Zanca, J. (2014) 'Los cursos de cultura católica en los años veinte. Intelectuales, curas y "conversos"', in P. Bruno (ed.), *Sociabilidades y vida cultural. Buenos Aires, 1860–1930* (Bernal: Editorial de la Universidad de Quilmes), pp. 281–311.

Ziller Camenietzki, C. (1999) 'A Companhia de Jesus e a Ciência na America Portuguesa entre 1663 e 1759', in C.M. Silva da Silva (ed.), *Segundo seminario de história da matemática* (Vitoria: UFES), pp. 156–65.

Index

INSTITUTE OF LATIN AMERICAN STUDIES | SCHOOL OF ADVANCED STUDY UNIVERSITY OF LONDON

Founded in 1965, the Institute of Latin American Studies (ILAS) forms part of the University of London's School of Advanced Study, based in Senate House, London.

ILAS occupies a unique position at the core of academic study of the region in the UK. Internationally recognised as a centre of excellence for research facilitation, it serves the wider community through organising academic events, providing online research resources, publishing scholarly writings and hosting visiting fellows. It possesses a world-class library dedicated to the study of Latin America and is the administrative home of the highly respected *Journal of Latin American Studies*. The Institute supports scholarship across a wide range of subject fields in the humanities and cognate social sciences and actively maintains and builds ties with cultural, diplomatic and business organisations with interests in Latin America, including the Caribbean.

As an integral part of the School of Advanced Study, ILAS has a mission to foster scholarly initiatives and develop networks of Latin Americanists and Caribbeanists at a national level, as well as to promote the participation of UK scholars in the international study of Latin America.

The Institute currently publishes in the disciplines of history, politics, economics, sociology, anthropology, geography and environment, development, culture and literature, and on the countries and regions of Latin America and the Caribbean. Since autumn 2019, the Institute's books, together with those of the other institutes of the School, have been published under the name University of London Press.

Full details about the Institute's publications, events, postgraduate courses and other activities are available online at http://ilas.sas.ac.uk.

Institute of Latin American Studies
School of Advanced Study, University of London
Senate House, Malet Street, London WC1E 7HU

Tel 020 7862 8844, Email ilas@sas.ac.uk
http://ilas.sas.ac.uk

Recent and forthcoming titles published by the Institute of Latin American Studies:

Rethinking Past and Present: Essays in memory of Alistair Hennessy (2018)
edited by Antoni Kapcia

Shaping Migration between Europe and Latin America: New Approaches and Challenges (2018)
edited by Ana Margheritis

Brazil: Essays on History and Politics (2018)
Leslie Bethell

Creative Spaces: Urban Culture and Marginality in Latin America (2019)
edited by Niall H.D. Geraghty and Adriana Laura Massidda

Cultures of Anti-Racism in Latin America and the Caribbean (2019)
edited by Peter Wade, James Scorer and Ignacio Aguiló

A Nicaraguan Exceptionalism? Debating the Legacy of the Sandinista Revolution (2020)
edited by Hilary Francis

Memory, Migration and (De)Colonisation in the Caribbean and Beyond (2020)
edited by Jack Webb, Roderick Westmaas, Maria del Pilar Kaladeen and Robert Tantam

www.ingramcontent.com/pod-product-compliance
Ingram Content Group UK Ltd.
Pitfield, Milton Keynes, MK11 3LW, UK
UKHW020049090425

1773IPUK00011BA/37